Making it comparabl

David Waddington, Peter Nentwig,
Sascha Schanze (Eds.)

Making it comparable
# Standards in science education

Waxmann 2007
Münster / New York / München / Berlin

Bibliographic information published by Die Deutsche Bibliothek
Die Deutsche Nationalbibliothek lists this publication in the
Deutsche Nationalbibliografie; detailed bibliographic data
are available in the internet at http://dnb.d-nb.de.

ISBN 978-3-8309-1901-8

© Waxmann Verlag GmbH, 2007
Postfach 8603, 48046 Münster, Germany
Waxmann Publishing Co.
P. O. Box 1318, New York, NY 10028, U. S. A.

www.waxmann.com
info@waxmann.com

Cover Design: Verena Hane, Kiel
Print: Druckerei Hubert & Co., Göttingen
Printed on age-resistant paper, acid-free as per ISO 9706
Printed in Germany

# Preface

The Leibniz-Institute for Science Education (IPN) at the University of Kiel in Germany and the University of York Science Education Group (UYSEG) in the UK are major centres of research and development in science education. Both have many years' experience of research projects on different aspects of science education practice and policy, and of the development and evaluation of innovative approaches to science teaching and learning. In recent years, one focus of the work at both centres has been the drive to improve scientific literacy at all levels of school education, in particular through the development of context-based and context-led science courses.

As a means of exploring specific issues in some depth, the two Centres recently inaugurated a series of small conferences on selected themes. The idea was that each would involve a maximum of 30 participants, selected staff drawn from the two centres and invited experts on the chosen topic from a range of countries.

This book presents some of the outcomes of the third of these conferences. The topic was standards in science education, how they might be set and monitored – and how this might stimulate improved outcomes. This is a topic which is widely discussed and debated, but where few would argue that perfect solutions have been found. The chapters of the book are based on papers presented at the conference – revised in the light of the discussions. We believe that they will be of interest to a wider audience.

Manfred Prenzel, IPN, Kiel
Robin Millar, UYSEG, York

March 2007

# Acknowledgements

We thank Professor Dr. Ilka Parchmann and Dr. Wolfgang Gräber for inspiring discussions in the process of planning and preparing this, the third IPN-UYSEG Conference in Science Education.

We are most grateful to our patient and helpful authors. They wrote their papers prior to the symposium. In order to gain coherence, and to bring out some salient points that arose during our meeting, we asked them to make some revisions. This was an iterative process as the contributions arrived and the authors were unfailingly cooperative.

We thank the German Research Foundation (DFG) for substantial funding without which it would not have been possible for the meeting to take place.

Finally, we wish our readers to note that any mistakes that they find are our responsibility.

David Waddington
Peter Nentwig
Sascha Schanze

August 2007

# Contents

# Part A

# Setting the scene

# Chapter 1

# Making it comparable – Standards in science education

*Peter Nentwig\* and Sascha Schanze*

*Leibniz-Institut für die Pädagogik der Naturwissenschaften (IPN)*
*Olshausenstraße 62, 24098 Kiel, Germany*

## The background

In 2004, the Standing Conference of the Ministers of Education and Cultural Affairs of the Länder in the Federal Republic of Germany (KMK) set out educational standards for the middle level of general education (Mittlerer Schulabschluss) at the end of grade 10 (KMK, 2003). Shortly after the standards were introduced for German language, mathematics and first foreign language, standards were also produced for biology, chemistry and physics, in December 2004 (KMK, 2004a; KMK, 2004b; KMK, 2004c; KMK, 2004d).

One reason for the introduction of standards into the school system was the disappointing results of students in large-scale studies such as TIMSS and PISA. It was believed that these international comparisons showed better results in countries with a history of setting standards for educational efforts in schools and of systematically assessing their outcomes.

## The situation in Germany

Educational experts and politicians soon agreed that it was necessary to improve the quality of education and to safeguard its sustainability. The introduction of standards was seen as a possible means (based on Heymann, 2004) to

• bring an end to the diversity of teaching aims and contents among the 16 federal states (Länder) of the republic

• focus classroom teaching on some core elements and to make it more efficient

• decrease the social injustice of unequal chances in education by describing a clear set of standards for all students.

The development of standards was based on the so-called 'Klieme Expertise' that was produced by a group of educational experts to define objectives and criteria and to give examples of educational standards (Klieme, 2003). The crucial innovation, in introducing standards, was the change from control of educational processes 'by-input' through syllabi (Lehrpläne) towards control 'by output' through performance indicators for certain stages in the learners' school career. Thus the German educational standards were not defined as either content standards or as opportunity-to-learn-standards, but as performance standards, setting the norm for all teachers and learners to follow.

For the science disciplines, biology, chemistry and physics, teams were appointed by the KMK, to produce the standards, which had to represent all the Länder. These teams mainly consisted of teachers with experience in curriculum work in consultation with university science educators. The three teams first produced a common frame with explanations concerning competences, attainment levels with subject-specific examples (Langlet, 2007; Schecker and Parchmann, 2007). The documents produced by the groups were explicitly meant as drafts for further development by the science education community and for empirical validation by the Institute for Educational Progress (IQB) (Rupp and Vock, 2007). This process is currently under way (see e.g. LISA, 2003; km-bw, 2004; Reiss, 2004; Thürmann, 2004; MBF-SH, 2005).

The introduction of standards into the German system of education has been accompanied by intense discussions. Both in the fields of general education (see e.g. Böttcher, 2003; GEW, 2003; Gröben, 2003; Saldern and Paulsen, 2003; Böttcher, 2004; Messner, 2004; Plöger, 2004; Saldern and Paulsen, 2004; GEW, 2004a; GEW, 2004b; Arnold, 2005; Demmer and Schweitzer, 2005; Lange, 2005; Regenbrecht, 2005; Spinner, 2005; Stadtfeld, 2005) and in the field of science education (see e.g. Kremer, 2004; Kullmann, 2004; MNU, 2004; Voelzke, 2004; Bayrhuber et al., 2005; Parchmann, 2005) the controversy was fought in rational as well as polemic styles.

One of the main objections to the 'standardization of education' was the worry that the traditional aim of German education – "Bildung" as the means for individual development – might be sacrificed for a pragmatic concept of testable utilitarian knowledge (see e.g. Jürgens, 2004). The fear was expressed that with the establishment of an assessment system together with the introduction of standards, teachers might anticipate the test in their teaching too narrowly. 'Teaching to the test' was the key phrase in this debate (see e.g. Altrichter, 2004; Bachmann et al., 2004; Neuweg, 2004). In this context, concern was also expressed for the future status of those school subjects for which there were no standards planned by the KMK (Huber, 2005; Heymann, 2005).

There was also concern that, in their present form, the standards, by focussing on relatively narrow cognitive learning objectives, did not consider sufficiently the quality of learning processes, the structural conditions in schools or the qualification of teachers (Brügelmann, 2003). Further, no support system was being proposed for those students, who would not be able to meet the standards – for whatever reason (Ratzki, 2005).

Last and not least, it was questioned whether the end of the middle-school level was the wisest time for the assessment of standards (GEW, 2004a). Assessment of learning progress ought to be the basis for support measures, it was argued, and, hence, it should be placed within the school career of a student rather than at the end. Moreover, some feared that standards and their assessment might be abused and used as instruments of selection for the upper secondary level of school (see e.g. Huber, 2004).

## Experience in other countries

As mentioned above, the decision to introduce standards into the German education system was based on the impression that some other countries with a history of education standards produced better results in the large international comparative studies. It was, however, obvious that formulating standards in itself was not enough to enhance the educational system.

The US, for example, had begun, towards the end of the 80s, to introduce standards and could thus look back at more than 15 years of experience. Nevertheless, the realization of the standards/assessment complex could not be considered ideal in several countries, and the PISA results were not convincing either. There were frequent complaints about superficial test-routines and the reduction of classroom practice to test-preparation (see e.g. Ravitch, 1995; Sacks, 1999; Jenkins, 2000; Kohn, 2000; Orfield and Kornhaber, 2001; Kohn, 2004; Volante, 2004; Goldberg, 2005). At the same time, Canada used the standards of the corresponding US associations for mathematics and the sciences, producing much better results. Apart from how standards are defined, it obviously matters how they are put into practice and how their attainment is assessed.

## The symposium

When the new science education standards for Germany began to be discussed widely, there existed a few reports from countries with a history of educational standards (e.g. Bonnet, 2002; BMBF, 2003; Ackeren, 2005; Baumann et al., 2005; Horstkemper, 2005; Jauhiainen, 2005). Most of them, however, were not detailed enough to answer all the questions that were being raised, and, above all, they did not specifically address the science subjects. It therefore appeared helpful to invite experts in science education from countries with experience of standards and where standards were being developed, together with science educators who are involved with the implementation of the new standards in Germany.

As there had been intensive cooperation between the Science Education Group at the University of York (UYSEG) in the UK and the Leibniz-Institute for Science Education at the University of Kiel (IPN) in Germany for some time, it was decided to make this meeting the third of the series of international symposia organised by the two institutions. The same format was used that had proven fruitful for the earlier events (Bennett et al., 2005; Nentwig and Waddington, 2005). Sixteen science educators from ten European and four other countries were invited together with nine German counterparts. All of the international experts and most of the German ones produced papers about the situation in their countries, which were made available well in advance to all participants on an internal website. These papers were not read at the meeting, but served as basis for the detailed discussions at the symposium, which were held alternately in small groups and in the plenum. Some of the participants had in advance been assigned to the roles of chairs and discussants for particular sub-sections of the discussion. Their engagement and creativity in structuring their themes led to a variety of activities and proved to be crucial for the success of the event. After the meeting, the contributors were asked to revise their papers in the light of the discussions, and these revised versions became the core of this book.

In preparation of these papers, participants had been asked to focus on five guiding questions:

## • How are standards in science education defined?

The new standards for the German school system are defined by a set of competences such as subject competence, epistemological competence, communication competence and valuation competence. This conceptual view of 'standards' differs from those in other countries, where in some cases the term 'standard' is not even used although there exists an understanding of what learners are expected to have achieved at certain steps in their learning process. In order to understand each other, it was, therefore, felt necessary to clarify the notion of 'standards' as the term is used in different countries.

## • How can the achievement of science education standards be assessed?

Instruments are necessary to assess if students have acquired the expected learning outcomes at a certain time, i.e. if they are meeting the standards. Tests of various kinds have been developed for this purpose and are being used in many countries. The character of the tests depends largely on the definition of the standards and on the intentions of the assessment.

## • What function does the assessment have?

The result of a test can lead to a variety of consequences, depending on the intended function, for example, support for the low achiever, selection of the elite, accountability of the teacher, change of educational policy. Some countries have wider experience in this field than others.

## • What side-effects of testing standards are feared or observed?

Critics fear that the assessment of standards will become the controlling principle in developing the curriculum because only that which is assessable will be taught. This implies effects on the curriculum as well as on the actual classroom activities. Different countries have developed different strategies to deal with the issue of 'teaching to the test'.

## • Can standards be implemented without centralized assessment?

In Germany, no central assessment is planned for the science subjects. Some see this as a chance for further, prudent, development of the standards. On the other hand, this might reduce the motivation for implementation. Standards that are not assessed might not be taken seriously. Other countries have experience with a non-centralized 'softer' approach.

## References

Ackeren, I. v. (2005) Vom Daten- zum Informationsreichtum? Erfahrungen mit standardisierten Vergleichgstests in ausgewählten Nachbarländern. *Pädagogik*(5), 24-28.

Altrichter, H. and Posch, P. (2005) Bildungsstandards als Teil eines Qualitätskonzepts. *forum schule* (7), 125-140.

Arnold, R. (2005) Die PISA-Lüge. *Friedrich Jahresheft* XXIII, 65-66.

Bachmann, G., Dangl, O., Mayr, J. and Sprenger, J. (2004) zukunft: schule? Stellungnahme aus der Sektion „Empirische Pädagogische Forschung" (O.E.P.F.) zum „Reformkonzept der österreichischen Zukunftskommission". *ÖFEB-Newsletter* 1, 5-14.

Baumann, R., Fessler, W. and Willimann, J. (2005) Lehrlings-, Fach- und Expertenniveau. Vom Umgang mit Standards in einem sozial belasteten Umfeld. *Friedrich Jahresheft* XXIII, 39-41.

Bayrhuber, H. *et al.* (Hrsg.) (2005) *Bildungsstandards Biologie*. Kiel: IPN.

Bennett, J., Holman, J., Millar, R. and Waddington, D. (Eds.) (2005) *Making a difference. Evaluation as a tool for improving science education*. Münster: Waxmann.

BMBF (Bundesministerium für Bildung und Forschung) (Hrsg.) (2003) *Vertiefender Vergleich der Schulsysteme ausgewählter PISA-Staaten*. Bonn: BMBF.

Bonnet, G. (2002) Schulentwicklung in Frankreich. *Pädagogik* (4), 44-48.

Böttcher, W. (2003) Besser werden durch Leistungsstandards? *Pädagogik* (4), 50-52.

Böttcher, W. (2004) Bildungsstandards und Kerncurricula – Potenzielle, intendierte und nichtintendierte Effekte eines zentralen Reformprojektes. In J. Schlömer-kemper (Hrsg.) *Bildung und Standards*. Weinheim: Juventa.

Brügelmann, H. (2003) In fünf Jahren ... Über Kerncurricula, Bildungsstandards und Leistungstests. *Neue Sammlung* 43, 235-237.

Demmer, M. and Schweitzer, J. (2005) Es fährt ein Zug nach nirgendwo. *Friedrich Jahresheft* XXIII, 68-69.

GEW (Gewerkschaft Erziehung und Wissenschaft) (2003) *Nationale Bildungsstandards – Wundermittel oder Teufelszeug*. http://www.gew.de/Binaries/Binary3666/bildungsstandards.pdf, accessed 14.02.2005.

GEW (Gewerkschaft Erziehung und Wissenschaft) (2004a) „Zweite Chance für die KMK" – Gute Bildungsstandards benötigen ein Konzept, Zeit, wissenschaftlichen Sachverstand und Akzeptanz. In J. Schlömerkemper (Hrsg.) *Bildung und Standards*. Weinheim: Juventa.

GEW (Gewerkschaft Erziehung und Wissenschaft) (2004b) *Hoffnungsträger IQB?!* http://www.le-ser.ch/_library/Fichiers_PDF/harmos/harmos_prise_de_position_gew.pdf, accessed 12.02.2005.

Goldberg, M. (2005) Test Mess 2: Are We Doing Better a Year Later? *Phi Delta Kappan* January, 389-395.

Gröben, A. v. d. (2003) Wird den Lehrern das Denken abgenommen? *Pädagogik*(3), 11-14.

Heymann, H. W. (2004) Besserer Unterricht durch Sicherung von „Standards"? *Pädagogik* 6, 6-9.

Heymann, H. W. (2005) Standards im Unterricht: Warum? Wie? Und für wen? *PÄD Forum*(1), 23-25.

Horstkemper, M. (2005) Standards. Vermessungspädagogik oder Antrieb zur Verbesserung der Bildungsqualität? *Pädagogik*(9), 6-9.

Huber, L. (2004) Nationale Standards und Gymnasiale Oberstufe. In J. Schlömer-kemper (Hrsg.) *Bildung und Standards*. Weinheim: Juventa.

Huber, L. (2005) Standards auch für die „weichen" Fächer? *Friedrich Jahresheft* XXIII, 105-107.

Jauhiainen, K. (2005) Pädagogische Standards für finnische Schulen. *Pädagogik*(9), 16-19.

Jenkins, E. (2000) The impact of the national curriculum on secondary school science teaching in England and Wales. *International Journal of Science Education* 22(3), 325-326.

Jürgens, E. (2004) Pädagogische Implikationen der KMK-Entwürfe für Bildungsstandards. In J. Schlömerkemper (Hrsg.) *Bildung und Standards*. Weinheim:
Juventa.

Klieme, E. *et al.* (Hrsg.) (2003) *Zur Entwicklung nationaler Bildungsstandards.
Eine Expertise*. Frankfurt: Deutsches Institut für Internationale Pädagogische
Forschung.

km-bw (Kultusministerium Baden-Württemberg) (2004) *Bildungsstandards*.
http://www.schule-bw.de/unterricht/bildungsstandards/, accessed 24.09.2005.

KMK (Kultusministerkonferenz) (2003) *Vereinbarung über Bildungsstandards für
den Mittleren Schulabschluss (Jahrgangsstufe 10)*.
http://www.kmk.org/schul/Bildungsstandards/
Rahmenvereinbarung_MSA_BS_04-12-2003.pdf, accessed 01.07.2005.

KMK (Kultusministerkonferenz) (2004a) *Vereinbarung über Bildungsstandards für
den Mittleren Schulabschluss (Jahrgangsstufe 10) in den Fächern Biologie, Chemie, Physik*. http://www.kmk.org/doc/beschl/RV-jg10nawi-BS308KMK.pdf,
accessed 01.07.2005.

KMK (Kultusministerkonferenz) (2004b) *Bildungsstandards im Fach Biologie für
den Mittleren Bildungsabschluss. Entwurf vom 30.8.2004.*
http://www.kmk.org/doc/beschl/Biologie_MSA_16-12-04.pdf, accessed
01.07.2005.

KMK (Kultusministerkonferenz) (2004c) *Bildungsstandards im Fach Chemie für
den Mittleren Bildungsabschluss. Entwurf vom 30.8.2004.* http://www.kmk.org/
doc/beschl/Chemie_MSA_16-12-04.pdf, accessed 01.07.2005.

KMK (Kultusministerkonferenz) (2004d) *Bildungsstandards im Fach Physik für
den Mittleren Bildungsabschluss. Entwurf vom 30.8.2004.*
http://www.kmk.org/doc/beschl/Physik_MSA16-12-04.pdf, accessed 01.07.2005.

Kohn, A. (2000) *The case against standardized testing – raising the scores, ruining
the schools*. Portsmouth, NH: Heinemann.

Kohn, A. (2004) Test Today, Privatize Tomorrow: Using Accountability to 'Reform'
Public Schools to Death. *Phi Delta Kappan* 85(8), 569-577.

Kremer, A. (2004) *Stellungnahme zum Entwurf der KMK „Bildungsstandards
Physik für den mittleren Schulabschluss (Jahrgangsstufe 10)"*.
http://www.gew.de/Binaries/Binary6015/bista-kremer-Physik.pdf, accessed
25.08.2005.

Kullmann, H. (2004) *Standardisiert die Bildungsstandards!*
http://www.gew.de/Binaries/Binary6016/bista-kullmannNaWi.pdf, accessed
01.10.2005.

Lange, B. (2005) Bildungsstandards und Unterrichtsplanung – Konsequenzen für
didaktisches Denken. *Lehren und Lernen*(5), 3-10.

Langlet, J. This book, Chapter 9.

LISA (Landesinstitut für Lehrerfortbildung, Lehrerweiterbildung und Unterrichtsforschung von Sachsen-Anhalt) (2003) Standards, niveaubestimmende Aufgaben, Vergleichsarbeiten – ein Beitrag zur Qualitätsentwicklung und Qualitätssicherung in Sachsen-Anhalt. http://www.bildung-lsa.de/db_data/442/verglarb.pdf, accessed 25.09.2005.

MBF-SH (Ministerium für Bildung und Frauen des Landes Schleswig-Holstein) (2005) *Bildungsstandards für den Mittleren Schulabschluss in den Fächern Biologie, Chemie, Physik. Handreichung für die Arbeit an Gymnasien, Realschulen, Gesamtschulen und Berufsbildenden Schulen in Schleswig Holstein.* http://bildungsqualitaet.lernnetz.de/docs/nat-standards-endfassung.pdf, accessed 25.09.2005.

Messner, R. (2004) Was Bildung von Produktion unterscheidet. In J. Schlömerkemper (Hrsg.) *Bildung und Standards.* Weinheim: Juventa.

MNU (Deutscher Verein zur Förderung des mathematischen und naturwissenschaftlichen Unterrichts) (2004) *Stellungnahme des MNU zu den Entwürfen (Stand 30. 08. 2004) der Bildungsstandards für den Mittleren Schulabschluss in Biologie, Chemie und Physik.* http://www.mnu.de/show_page.php?id=40, accessed 24.07.2005.

Nentwig, P. and Waddington, D. (Eds.) (2005) *Making it relevant. Context based learning of science.* Münster: Waxmann.

Neuweg, G. H. (2004) Bildungsstandards in Österreich. *Pädaktuell*(2), 4-13.

Orfield, G. and Kornhaber, M. (Eds.) (2001) *Raising standards or raising barriers? Inequality and high-stakes testing in public education.* New York: Century Foundation Press.

Parchmann, I. (2005) Grundlagen für ein Verständnis. Standards als Impuls für eine Veränderung von Chemieunterricht. *Friedrich Jahresheft* XXIII, 93-95.

Plöger, W. (2004) Bildungsstandards in bildungstheoretischer Sicht. In J. Schlömerkemper (Hrsg.) *Bildung und Standards.* Weinheim: Juventa.

Ratzki, A. (2005) Finnland. Erfahrungen mit Bildungsstandards und individuellen Fördermaßnahmen. *Friedrich Jahresheft* XXIII, 50-52.

Ravitch, D. (1995) *National standards in American education – A citizen's guide.* Washington, DC: The Brookings Institution.

Regenbrecht, A. (2005) Sichern Bildungsstandards die Bildungsaufgabe der Schule? *PÄD Forum*(1), 16-22.

Reiss, K. (2004) Bildungsstandards und die Rolle der Fachdidaktik am Beispiel der Mathematik. *Zeitschrift für Pädagogik* 50(5), 635-649.

Rupp, A. and Volk (2007), M. This book, Chapter 10.

Sacks, P. (1999) *Standardized minds – The high price of America's testing culture and what we can do to change it.* New York: Harper Collins.

Saldern, M. v. and Paulsen, A. (2003) *Die nationalen Bildungsstandards für den Mittleren Schulabschluss der Kultusministerkonferenz im Vergleich zu den Vorschlägen des Gutachtens „Zur Entwicklung nationaler Bildungsstandards" „Klieme-Gutachten") und den Erkenntnissen nach PISA.* http://www.gew.de/Binaries/Binary3781/Vergleich.pdf, accessed 25.08.2005.

Saldern, M. v. and Paulsen, A. (2004) Sind Bildungsstandards die richtige Antwort auf PISA? In J. Schlömerkemper (Hrsg.) *Bildung und Standards.* Weinheim: Juventa.

Schecker, H. and Parchmann, I. This book, Chapter 8.

Spinner, K. (2005) Der standardisierte Schüler. *Friedrich Jahresheft* XXIII, 88-91.

Stadtfeld, P. (2005) Nationale Bildungsstandards – Problem oder Chance für die Schulentwicklung? *Lehren und Lernen*(5), 33-37.

Thürmann, E. (2004) *Von KMK-Standards zu Kernlehrplänen in NRW: Erfahrungen aus der curricularen Praxis.* http://www.kmk.org/schul/Bildungsstandards/Fachtagung/ workshop1_thuermann.pdf, accessed 04.07.2005.

Voelzke, U. (2004) *Zusammenfassende Stellungnahme zu den Bildungsstandards in den Naturwissenschaften.* http://gew.de/Binaries/Binary6019/bista-voelzke-BiChPhNW.pdf, accessed 14.02.2005.

Volante, L. (2004) Teaching to the test: What every educator and policy-maker should know. *Canadian Journal of Educational Administration and Policy* Issue 35.

**Part B**

# Country reports

# Chapter 2

## Standards in science education in Australia

*Rosemary Hafner*

Science Teachers Association of New South Wales
PO Box 458, Strathfield NSW 2135, Australia

### Organisation of the education system within Australia

Across Australia there are approximately 2 million primary and 1.5 million secondary school students. Schooling in Australia is compulsory for children from the ages of 6 to 15, with approximately 80% of students remaining for a further two years of schooling in post compulsory education. A summary is provided in figure 1 below.

The constitution of Australia allocates primary responsibility for school education to each of the eight state and territory governments, not to the Australian government. Within each state/territory, there are government schools and non-government schools. Government schools operate under the direct responsibility of the relevant state/territory minister. Non-government schools, which have been established by various religious groups and others such as Montessori and Steiner organisations, operate under requirements determined by state/territory government registration authorities. The Australian government and state/territory ministers provide some financial support to non-government schools based on set formulas.

Within each state and territory, the Minister and/or the government's education department and/or other statutory government authorities determine the curriculum for all schools in the state/territory, course accreditation and, where applicable, mandatory state-wide student assessment. Many of the states and territories have developed standards frameworks that describe what students should know and be able to do in specified areas of learning at regular intervals throughout their schooling. These frameworks usually provide sufficient detail for schools and the community to be clear about the major elements of the curriculum and the standards expected of successful learners. At the same time schools usually have the flexibility to work out the best way to implement the curriculum and organise their own teaching and learning program, taking into account government policies and the school community's priorities, resources and expertise.

In addition to the state/territory requirements the Australian government develops national education policies, programs and, more recently, standards. They administer these for all schools through the Australian Department of Education, Science and Training (DEST). DEST allocates supplementary funding to both government and

| School year | Kindergarten/ Preparatory | 1 | 2 | 3 | 4 | 5 | 6 | 7 | 8 | 9 | 10 | 11 | 12 |
|---|---|---|---|---|---|---|---|---|---|---|---|---|---|
| Age | 5/6 | 6/7 | 7/8 | 8/9 | 9/10 | 10/11 | 11/12 | 12/13 | 13/14 | 14/15 | 15/16 | 16/17 | 17/18 |
| Level | Primary – compulsory schooling | | | | | | | Secondary – compulsory schooling | | | | Post compulsory - schooling | |
| Science | Compulsory in most states/territories | | | | | | | Compulsory | | | | Optional | |
| Scope | Typically integrated biology, chemistry, physics and earth science with the main emphasis on developing skills in working scientifically. In some states/territories, science is combined with technology. | | | | | | | Single course consisting of content drawn from biology, chemistry, physics and earth. Schools determine whether content is integrated or taught as discrete disciplines. | | | | Students may take one or more courses from a range that includes biology, chemistry, earth science (or its equivalent), physics, general science (or its equivalent) | |
| Hours of study | The number of hours allocated to teaching and learning is usually school determined. Typically schools allocate approx 1 – 2 hours per week per year. | | | | | | | Hours of study are state/territory determined and usually 100h– 120hrs per year | | | | Typically each course is approx 200–240 | |

Figure 1: Organisation of the Australian education system

non-government schools on the condition that each school supports the Australian government priorities, implement their programs or participate in reports on the standards. All state and territories, therefore, are implementing two sets of standards. One is a set of national standards in science that will be/are assessed on a national scale. The other is their own states' standards as defined in *their* compulsory science curriculum which, depending on the state, are assessed by different methods overseen by the state's accreditation authority. Some states use only school based assessment reported to the accreditation authority, others use 'external' testing designed and overseen by the state authority, others use a combination of 'external' testing and school based assessment, while other states use school based assessment with external validation and moderation overseen by the state authority.

This paper will describe a model for operationalising standards to demonstrate the links that should exist between curriculum, teaching and learning, performance and assessment and reporting. It will then address the question of standards in science education in Australia on two levels:

• on a national level by considering the national standards that are currently being introduced and the assessment of the standards for 15-year-olds and in year 6

• on a state/territory level with specific reference to assessment at the end of the compulsory and post-compulsory years of schooling in New South Wales.

## A model for operationalising standards

Standards are being increasingly introduced into education systems within Australia and internationally. The stated purpose of these standards is to:

• provide a mechanism for accountability – on a local level to parents and the school, and on a broader level to a system or government authority, and/or

• provide feedback – direct feedback on the performance of students and indirect feedback on performance of the school and the system, and/or

• identify improvement – to assist teachers in identifying areas where improvement has occurred and where remediation may be required and to assist schools and systems identify areas where improvement has occurred and where additional support may be needed.

The constructs of the standards relate to either:
• a 'continuum of learning' construct which focuses on what students can demonstrate they know and can do as they progress conceptually and is independent of the age of the student or

• a 'years of schooling' construct which focuses on what students should know and should be able to do as they progress chronologically and is dependent on the age of the student.

Standards may be defined through the curriculum and/or through descriptions of student performance:

• curriculum standards focus on guiding teaching and/or what students will learn about or learn to do

• performance standards focus on describing students' demonstration of what should know and should be able to do.

Ideally, standards should be defined through both curriculum and descriptions of performance and there should be a high correlation between the defined standards in each of these areas (figure 2). It is important, therefore, when developing or analysing the effect of standards to determine:

• the strength of the relationship between the standards and the curriculum
• the strength of the relationship between the standards and the areas of performance
• the correlation between the curriculum standards and the performance standards.

The way in which standards are defined and measured can have a significant impact on the implemented curriculum. A high correlation between the curriculum and performance standards and valid and reliable measurement of performance standards can be used to drive a stronger relationship between the intended and implemented curriculum and can even affect the pedagogy of teaching.

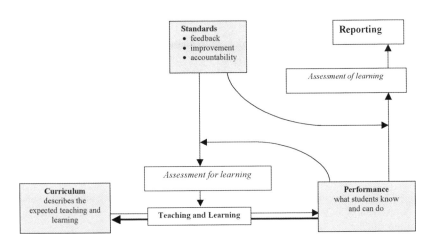

Figure 2:     How are standards defined?

Irrespective of whether standards are defined through the curriculum, through descriptions of performance or through both, assessment is the instrument through which data can be gathered on an individual level and on a systemic level about standards. Assessment is also the link between the curriculum and performance. It is used substantially to inform teaching and learning rather than for reporting purposes and can be referred to as assessment for learning. On the other hand, assessment that is used substantially to report on achievement of standards to parents or to the system is referred to as assessment of learning (Killen, 2005).

While assessment for learning and assessment of learning are not mutually exclusive, figure 3 illustrates the main focus of each of these types of assessment in relation to teaching and learning and to reporting.

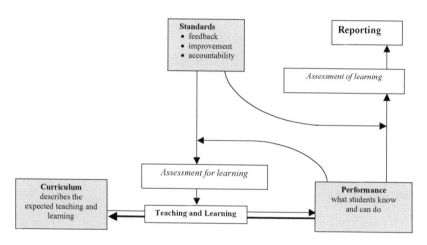

Figure 3:     How is assessment related to standards

Assessment provides teachers, schools and government authorities with information about student performance – what they know and can do. When assessment of learning is valid and reliable in relation to the performance standards, teachers, schools and government authorities are able to make judgements about the achievements of students against specified performance standards. When there is a strong relationship between curriculum standards and performance standards, assessment of learning does not force the descriptions of performance to replace curriculum standards as the implemented curriculum.

27

# National standards in science

## (i) Defining national standards in Australia

Since 1900, each state and territory has developed its own goals for schooling. Australia first adopted a set of national goals for schooling only in 1989 when education ministers from all state and territory and the Commonwealth, meeting as the Australian Education Council, adopted the *Common and Agreed National Goals for Schooling in Australia* (MCEETYA, 2002a).

The first update of the goals occurred in 1996. A major review of the goals was begun in 1998 and resulted in the *Australia's National Goals for Schooling in the Twenty-first Century* being endorsed in 1999 (Appendix 1).

The 1999 goals aimed to establish national collaboration across states and territories in order to improve the quality of schooling. The goals were also a commitment from each state and territory to collaborate with the Australian government in setting 'explicit and defensible standards to guide improvements in student achievement and to measure and evaluate the effectiveness, efficiency and equity of schooling' (MCEETYA, 2002a).

Australian state and territory Governments also affirmed a commitment to national reporting of comparable educational outcomes and agreed that the *National Goals for Schooling in the Twenty-first Century* provided an appropriate reporting framework. From the National Goals a measurement framework was developed based on Key Performance Measures (MCEETYA, 2003) (KPMs) which covered a number of areas including science.

Key Performance Measures were defined as *a set of measures limited in number and strategic in orientation, which provides nationally comparable data on aspects of performance critical to monitoring progress against the National Goals for Schooling in the 21st Century* (MCEETYA, 2005a). Key Performance Measures attempt to:

• quantify a dimension of student participation, attainment or achievement
• enable a range of student achievement to be reported
• focus on student outcomes for the reporting agenda
• enable progress to be monitored against the National Goals
• take account of State and Territory curriculum and assessment frameworks.

A national review, *The Status and Quality of Teaching and Learning of Science in Australian Schools*, by Goodrum et al (2001), argued that the broad purpose of science in the compulsory years of schooling was to develop scientific literacy for all students. The authors of the report, Hackling Goodrum and Rennie, reviewed the state of science in Australian schools in an article published in the Australian Science Teachers' Journal (Hackling et al, 2001). The Goodrum report had a major influence on the directions taken in developing the KPMs for science. At the same time, ministers in each state and territory were influenced by the international assessment agenda, particularly the OECD PISA assessments, that focus on aspects of preparedness for adult life in terms of functional knowledge and skills that allow citizens to participate actively in society.

In developing the KPMs for science the ministers adopted the OECD PISA definition[1] with the inclusion of the words 'to investigate'. This made the definition consistent with that used in the Goodrum Report (Goodrum et al, 2001). Specifically, scientific literacy is defined as:

> *the capacity to use scientific knowledge, to identify questions, to investigate and to draw evidence-based conclusions in order to understand and help make decisions about the natural world and the changes made to it through human activity* (MCEETYA, 2005a).

A scientific literacy progress map was developed based on the above definition of scientific literacy and on an analysis of state and territory curriculum and assessment frameworks (Appendix 2). The progress map was an attempt to describe the development of scientific literacy across three domains or strands of scientific literacy. The domains/strands include the five elements of scientific literacy used in PISA 2000 (OECD PISA, 1999). The domains/strands are:

Domain/Strand A. *Formulating or identifying investigable questions and hypotheses, planning investigations and collecting evidence.*

This includes: posing questions or hypotheses for investigation or recognising scientifically investigable questions; planning investigations by identifying variables and devising procedures where variables are controlled; gathering evidence through measurement and observation; and making records of data in the form of descriptions, drawings, tables and graphs using a range of information and communication technologies.

Domain/Strand B. *Interpreting evidence and drawing conclusions, critiquing the trustworthiness of evidence and claims made by others, and communicating findings.*

This includes: identifying, describing and explaining the patterns and relationships between variables in scientific data; drawing conclusions that are evidence-based and related to the questions or hypotheses posed; critiquing the trustworthiness of evidence and claims made by others; and, communicating findings using a range of scientific genres and information and communication technologies.

1 OECD, Glossary of Statistical Terms, http://stats.oecd.org/glossary/detail.asp?ID=5425

Domain/Strand C:  *Constructing science understandings by describing and explaining natural phenomena, making sense of reports, and making decisions.*

This includes demonstrating conceptual understandings by being able to: describe, explain and make sense of natural phenomena; understand and interpret reports (eg, TV documentaries, newspaper or magazine articles or conversations) related to scientific matters; and, make decisions about scientific matters in students' own lives which may involve some consideration of social, environmental and economic costs and benefits.

The Australian-modified OECD definition of scientific literacy was described in the above three domains/strands to assist the interpretation of student responses to assessment tasks. It was recognised, however, that authentic tasks should require students to apply concepts and processes together to address problems set in real-world contexts. Such tasks may involve ethical decision-making about scientific matters in students' own lives and some consideration of social, environmental and economic costs and benefits (MCEETYA, 2002b). Many of the items included in the 2003 test[2] were set in real-world contexts items but there does not appear to be any items that involve ethical decision-making about scientific matters in students' own lives and some consideration of social, environmental and economic costs and benefits.

The progress map describes progression in six levels, from 1 to 6, in terms of three aspects:

• increasing complexity, from explanations that involve one aspect, to several aspects, and then through to relationships between aspects of a phenomenon;

• progression from explanations that refer to and are limited to directly experienced phenomena (concrete) to explanations that go beyond that which can be directly observed and involve abstract scientific concepts (abstract); and

• increasing complexity in descriptions of 'what' happened in terms of the objects and events, in explanations of 'how' it happened in terms of processes, and in explanations of 'why' it happened in terms of science concepts (MCEETYA, 2002b).

Theoretically, it is expected that 50% of year 6 students should be at level 3. The performance standards described by the progress map are therefore defined through an age dependent 'years of schooling' construct. Figure 4 shows how the national standards in the form of either the OECD PISA Framework for 15-year-olds or the KPMs for Year 6 relate to curriculum and performance:

2  http://www.curriculumsupport.education.nsw.gov.au/primary/scitech/prolearn/refer/assets/PSAP_CH3.pdf

30

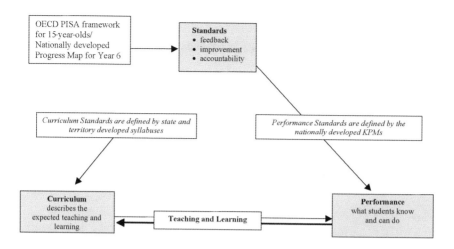

Figure 4:     Relationship between national standards to curriculum and performance

## (ii) Assessing the Australian National Standards in science

Testing against standards on a national level occurs/will occur at Year 4 using TIMSS data[3], year 6 using nationally developed standards, Year 8 using TIMSS data and for 15-year-olds using data from the OECD PISA studies[4]. The focus of this paper is the assessment of standards at year 6 and for 15-year-olds.

When considering how to assess the standards for 15-year-olds the Ministers approved the use of information from the OECD Program for International Student Assessment (PISA) for reporting students' performance in reading, mathematical and scientific literacies. The KPMs for students' performance in science were to be reported as the percentage of students achieving at or above the OECD mean score in the scientific literacy assessment of the OECD PISA, together with the range of student achievement.

Assessment of the standards at year 6 required the development of an assessment domain and accompanying items and instruments, the trialling of these items, the construction of key performance measures for measuring and reporting on the achievement of students in science, the administration of the assessments to a sample of year 6 students and marking, analysing and reporting the results.

The current agreed assessment and data collection cycle for National Key Performance Measures in Science is detailed in figure 5.

3  Trends in Mathematics and Science Study 2007, http://timss.bc.edu/
4  OECD PISA, http://www.pisa.oecd.org

31

| Year/ Level | Measure | Cycle | Data Source | 2002 | 2003 | 2004 | 2005 | 2006 | 2007 | 2008 | 2009 |
|---|---|---|---|---|---|---|---|---|---|---|---|
| Year 6 | % achieving standard in scientific literacy as per Scientific Literacy Progress Map | Trien-nial | Test of national sample of stu-dents | Trial | Aust KPM test | - | - | Aust KPM test | - | - | Aust KPM test |
| 15-year-olds | Interim measure: % achieving at or above OECD mean score | Trien-nial | Test of national sample of stu-dents | Trial | OECD PISA | - | - | OECD PISA | - | - | OECD PISA* |

\* Subject to the Ministers decision to participate in PISA post 2006

Figure 5:    The current agreed assessment and data collection cycle for National Key Performance Measures in Science

The Technical Report (MCEETYA, 2005b) on the Science Year 6, 2003 assessment describes the final assessment instrument, which consisted of two tests of 70 items worth a total of 78 marks each. Students were required to provide responses to one of two pencil-and-paper question sets. The students had then to perform one of two practical activities in small groups and answer individually pencil-and-paper items related to the activity. Each of the items and tasks included stimulus material and a series of questions relating to the material.

The progress map, developed with reference to state and territory curriculum, is not the standards for those respective curriculum. Figure 6, therefore, shows the relation-ships between the national assessment of learning and it associated standards and state and territory curriculum.

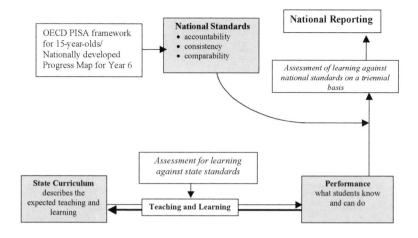

Figure 6:    The relationships between the national assessment of learning, national standards and state and territory curriculum

Since there is not a strong relationship between state and territory curriculum and the national standards it is unlikely that, at this early stage of national assessment and reporting, teachers are using the national standards for assessment for learning in their everyday teaching.

*(iii) Functions of assessment of Australian National Standards*

National and state ministers have openly stated that the aim of assessing and reporting progress against the National Goals through the assessment program is to drive school improvement and enhance outcomes for students. Following the development of KPAs, national targets are set by the government. National targets are defined as a measurable level of performance expected to be attained within a specified time.

KPMs are seen by the government as reflecting good assessment practice and supporting open transparent reporting. They are published in a manner that facilitates access by the public to information about the achievement of the targets by states and territories and sectors within those states and territories. Further, since they involve sampling on a triennial basis and not whole cohort testing on an annual basis, governments see them as a very cost effective way of providing nationally comparable data on aspects of performance that they have determined as critical to monitoring progress against the National Goals for Schooling. Public reporting against national targets may ultimately influence the state/territory curriculum to align their curriculum more closely with the assessed standards (figure 7). Until this is the case there will remain a discontinuity between the assessment for learning and the focus of teaching and learning which is drawn from state/territory curriculum standards and the national performance standards.

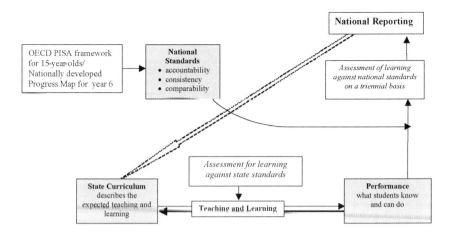

Figure 7: National reporting and the potential on states and territory curriculum

While assessment of the national standards provides data on student achievement of the goals through triennial sampling, the conclusions drawn from the analysis of these data:

• are extrapolated provide information on a national, state by state, school system (i.e. government, religious etc) by school system level on student achievement of the standards and the national goals

• are used to provide motivation for continuous state, school and systems improvement in teaching and learning

• are used to monitor achievement of the targets and improvement over time

• are used to inform planning for improved student by DEST, state jurisdictions and systems through the detailed reports that are prepared following an assessment cycle

• provide a mechanism by which the Australian government can influence the education agenda of each state. As part of schools' and systems' national funding agreement schools' and systems' receiving Australian government funding must be willing to participate in the assessment program.

In addition, the national assessment program assists educators to interpret the performances of their own schools by providing nationally comparable information about the achievements of students in other states and territories. Each of the programs, including science, is designed to provide a set of items which any Australian school can use to measure its students' performance against national standards.

*(iv) Some side-effects of testing Australian national standards*

The testing of national standards has both positive and negative side effects:

• Science literacy is now seen nationally as important in enabling citizens to question the assertions of others, establish evidence, and come to their own decisions, in relation to scientific issues.

• National standards are strongly influencing or even driving curriculum reform and revision in each state and territory. In some states, this has involved a mapping exercise that has led to minor amendments to the curriculum. In other states, it is has meant development of a new curriculum framework to more clearly incorporate content that allows the standards to be achieved at the nationally determined year level. Despite these changes, the level of comparability between the national standards and the curriculum standards across the states and territories still varies.

• There is increased accountability being felt at all levels of education.

• A significant proportion of state funding for education is redirected towards programs that assist schools to improve teaching and learning towards the national targets and the national standards.

• There is increasing assessment demands on states and systems. With a rolling triennial cycle for the assessment of Science, there will be great demands on those administering the collection of data from the fourteen (currently) national KPMs areas that require assessment. Whatever the benefits of such assessments, there will be disruption and additional workload demands at the school level. This is particularly evident in smaller states/territories where schools are approached more frequently to participate in assessment programs.

• Curriculum development and emphasis is being significantly influenced by both a state and national political agenda and the expertise of education specialists is, at times, marginalised. It is, therefore, important for education experts to develop robust and strategic relationships with governments and to have a voice in developing the agenda. Some aspects of curriculum that are not evident in the current sets of KPMs have lobby groups pushing for their inclusion. The process for establishing additional or new KPMs, other than those directly requested by ministers, is a very lengthy and not always successful process.

• Given that there are currently fourteen national KPMs areas that require assessment, the set of KPMs as a whole will be reviewed from time to time in the context of the ministers' expectation that the measures be few in number and strategic in orientation. This may mean a narrowing of the emphasis areas and a possible skewing of the overall curriculum.

• The accuracy of the validity and reliability of the data collected is very much dependent on the validity and reliability of the assessment items.

## New South Wales Standards in science

*(i) Defining standards in science education in New South Wales.*

In New South Wales (NSW) approximately 80 000 students per year complete compulsory education and approximately 65 000 go on to post compulsory education in years 11 and 12.

• For primary education (children aged 6–12), science is compulsory and teaching and learning in science is based on the *Science and Technology K – 6 Syllabus.*

• For compulsory secondary education (children aged 12–16), science is taught for a minimum of 400 hours across years 7–10 and teaching and learning in science is based on and taught in accordance with the *Science 7–10 Syllabus.*

• For post compulsory secondary education (children aged 17–18), science is not compulsory and students may elect to undertake a 240 hour course in biology and/or chemistry, and/or physics and/or Earth and environmental science or a general science course of no science at all.

Each of the science syllabuses are organized as shown in figure 8 (NSWBS, 2003a). The curriculum standards are articulated through the content and outcomes of the syllabuses. They define what students are expected to know and to be able to do as a result of effective teaching and learning at the end of the notional stages – Early Stage 1, Stage 1, Stage 2, Stage 3, Stage 4, Stage 5 and Stage 6. The content is described in terms of what students 'learn about' and what students 'learn to do' and outcomes describe the knowledge, skills and understanding expected to be gained by most students in each stage. The curriculum standards are therefore intended to be an age independent construct and related to a 'continuum of learning' e.g. students in year 6 may be working at Stage 2, Stage 3 or even at Stage 4.

The outcomes across Stages 1–6 illustrate a continuum of learning in the science expected across kindergarten to year 12. While the syllabuses from kindergarten to year 12 may use different ways to organise the content, there are clear underpinnings of knowledge and understanding, skills, values and attitudes from one stage to another. The continuum uses the course outcomes to map the transition from Stage 1 to Stage 6 in terms of the Prescribed Focus Areas, domain knowledge and understanding, domain skills and domain values and attitudes (Appendix 3).

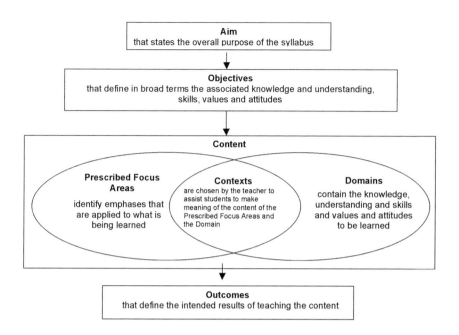

Figure 8:     NSW 7 – 10 Science syllabus organisation

The descriptions of levels of achievement of learning are derived from the curriculum outcomes which are used to develop explicit statements of student performance or performance standards. The performance standards are typically written for two years of schooling and set expectations of the quality of learning to be achieved by the end of years 2, 4, 6, 8, 10 and 12. In this way they are, therefore, an age related construct of 'years of schooling'. The performance standards for science at year 10 are provided in Appendix 4.

Performance standards are made more explicit by including performance descriptions in the standards, by providing specimen examination papers with associated sample marking guidelines (discussed in the next section of the paper), and by the increasing number of student work samples annotated against the standards that are made available to teachers. The relationship between the curriculum and the performance standards in NSW is described in figure 9:

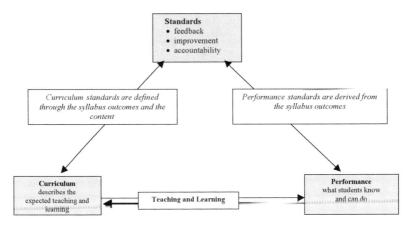

Figure 9: How are standards defined in the NSW curriculum?


*(ii) Assessing standards in science in New South Wales*

In the compulsory years of schooling teachers are encouraged to use a performance standard known as the Common Grade Scale (Appendix 5) and published work samples to match the students' achievements to the appropriate standard. The state government advocates assessment for learning as the model (see, for example, Black et al, 2003) that should be adopted for school-based assessment across Stages 1–5 in New South Wales. Assessment for learning encourages teachers to decide how and when to assess student achievement as they plan the work students will do, using a range of appropriate assessment strategies including self-assessment and peer assessment.

At Stage 5, the performance standards consist of two parts. In Stage 5 the Common Grade Scale has been used to develop subject specific Course Performance Descriptors (Appendix 4), which form part of the performance standards for this stage. In year 10, students are awarded a grade for each of the courses they have studied in years 9 and 10. The grades are allocated by each student's school based on the Course Performance Descriptors. The descriptors describe the main features of a typical student's performance measured against the outcomes for the course. They describe a number of levels of achievement and provide a detailed report of the student's overall performance.

The other part of the performance standards for Stage 5 is associated with a state-wide test. As the end of year 10 marks the end of compulsory schooling, students receive a credential called the School Certificate that records their achievement in

38

the courses studied in years 9 and 10. This credential also provides results in five state-wide tests in areas considered foundational to subsequent achievement. One of those areas is science. In New South Wales, the science performance standards at Stage 5, which are assessed at the end of year 10, are therefore defined by a combination of the Course Performance Descriptors and the year 10 test performance scale.

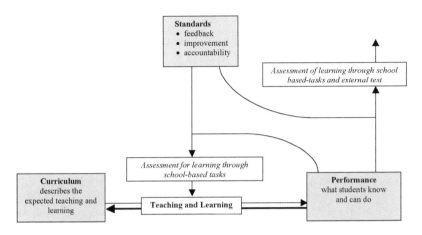

Figure 10: How is assessment related to standards in the NSW School Certificate?

The year 10 Science School Certificate test assesses the individual achievement of identified course knowledge and skills that are considered necessary to undertake further study successfully in any science subject in Years 11 and 12 and to participate effectively in the wider community. The test, therefore, does not cover the full range of content and outcomes in the science syllabus but only a subset of the course content. Students receive their own test results for these tests in the form of a test report, indicating their test mark, the performance band in which this mark placed the student for the course, and a description of typical performance in this band (Appendix 6). The performance bands are based on the performance standards taking into account the limited number of syllabus outcomes addressed by the tests.

The School Certificate Science is a two-hour test and assesses students' ability to apply their knowledge and understanding of scientific concepts and their skills of working scientifically through:

• developing investigative skills to test identified questions
• analysing data gathered from a variety of sources
• thinking critically and creatively in problem-solving processes
• evaluating data and information and drawing evidence-based conclusions.

39

The school-based assessment programs for Stage 5 courses that determine the particular Course Performance Descriptor a student receives, allows a student's achievement in relation to all the courses that a student has undertaken to be reported in terms of the respective course outcomes. In establishing a school-based assessment program to determine Course Performance Descriptors for year 10 students, schools are encouraged to ensure that the types of assessment activities or tasks used are appropriate to the full range of outcomes being assessed. Teacher judgement plays an important role in determining a student's final performance standard at the end of compulsory schooling. They make the final judgement of the most appropriate performance description grade on the basis of assessment information collected throughout the course and with reference to the course performance descriptors. There are appeal mechanisms in place for students/parents if they have concerns about the grade that has been allocated.

It is important to note then that, as the test addresses a limited number of outcomes, and the Course Performance Descriptors reflect the overall performance of the student in relation to all outcomes, the School Certificate Tests results (the performance scale position of a student) and the School Certificate grades (the Course Performance Descriptor allocated to a student) are not directly comparable nor is a 1:1 correlation expected.

At the end of year 12, students, who have completed 240 hour courses of study satisfactorily in specific subjects and have sat for an external three hour examination, are awarded the Higher School Certificate (HSC). The HSC reports both an internal and an external measure of achievement. It reports:

• an assessment mark submitted by the school to the credentialing authority and produced in accordance with the credentialing authority's requirements for the internal assessment program

• an examination mark derived from the HSC external examinations prepared by, undertaken under the supervision of and marked by the credentialing authority.

While the Higher School Certificate has both an internal and external component, these are not reported separately using separate performance standards instruments as in the School Certificate. The HSC results are reported using a course report containing one scale that consists of performance bands that describe standards of achievement across the course.

The use of both internal assessment and external examinations of student achievement allows measures and observations to be made at several points and in different ways throughout the each course. Taken together, it is believed that the external examinations and internal assessment marks should provide a more valid and reliable assessment of the achievement of the knowledge, understanding and skills described for each course than either would by itself.

The internal assessment mark is submitted by the school to the accrediting authority and is intended to be a summation of each student's achievements measured by the school against the curriculum standards at points throughout the course. It reflects the rank order of students within each school in a course and relative differences between students' achievements. In science, in particular, the internal assessment provides a more valid assessment of students' practical skills than can be achieved by the external pen and paper examination instrument.

The state government's accrediting authority determines the assessment components, weightings and task-requirements to be applied to internal assessment. They are intended to provide commonality and consistency for internal assessment in the course across all schools, while allowing for flexibility in the design of tasks. Schools are required to use a variety of tasks in internal assessment to give students the opportunity to demonstrate outcomes in different ways and to improve the validity and reliability of the assessment. For each course the school is required to submit the internal assessment mark for each student to the credentialing authority towards the end of the course and before the external examinations are held.

The external examinations in each of the Higher School Certificate science courses are a three hour pen-and-paper test. They provide a measure of student achievement in relation to a range of syllabus outcomes that it is believed can reliably measured in a pen-and-paper examination setting, which are marked externally.

It is important for both the School Certificate test and, particularly for the Higher School Certificate examination that the questions are based on the curriculum standards as reflected in the course content and outcomes and are designed in such a way as to allow students to demonstrate the performance standards over the full wide range of descriptions. The process for ensuring this and for marking the examination scripts and aligning the student marks against the standards must be valid and stand up to strong scrutiny. It is rigorous, extensive and costly. The process includes:

• appointing an examination committee for each course

• developing a writing brief and exam specifications

• assessing the exam paper against the content and outcomes of the syllabus and against the exam specifications and brief

• developing marking guidelines

• appointing markers – the total number of markers involved in marking all the Higher School Certificate examinations across all course examinations is several thousand

• check the appropriateness of the marking guidelines through piloting

• marking the scripts and ensuring accuracy and consistency of markers throughout marking

• aligning student performance with performance bands through a judging process

• reviewing the outcomes of the judging process by expert committees.

The performance band for any course includes a description that summarizes the knowledge, skills and understanding typically demonstrated by students whose achievement meets that standard. The standards-based mark that is reported for each student on the performance band is determined through a standards-setting process in which students' raw examination marks are aligned (or transferred) to the performance scale.

To ensure comparability of assessment marks from each school, assessment marks submitted from each school for the Higher School Certificate are moderated to match the performance of each school group on the common external examination using the raw examination marks obtained by the group. There is no moderation of the grades awarded by schools to students in the School Certificate.

The reported Higher School Certificate mark is the average of the aligned school assessment mark and examination mark. It is reported together with the description of the standard achieved.

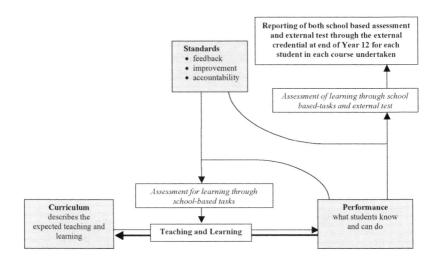

Figure 11:     How is assessment related to standards in the NSW Higher School Certificate?

For the Higher School Certificate, the external examination and its marking and reporting relate to curriculum standards and performance standards by:

• providing identified links to curriculum standards through the syllabus content and outcomes

• enabling students to demonstrate the levels of achievement outlined in the performance standards through the course performance scale

• applying marking guidelines that are related to the performance standards based on established criteria.

Student performance in any Higher School Certificate course is reported against performance standards on a course report. The course report contains a performance scale for the course describing levels (bands) of achievement, a Higher School Certificate examination mark and the internal assessment mark. It also shows, in graphical form, the state-wide distribution of examination marks of all students in the course. The distribution of marks are determined by students' performances against the known standards and not scaled to a predetermined pattern of marks.

### (iii) Function of assessing science standards in New South Wales

The majority of students in New South Wales continues on to post-compulsory education and undertakes the Higher School Certificate. There has, therefore, been pressure on the government to abolish the external test associated with the School Certificate. The government has clearly stated that it strongly believes that external examinations are necessary for the rigorous, independent and equitable evaluation of secondary school students' performance. It has stated that not only does it intends to keep the School Certificate test as part of the performance standards but to introduce a further external assessment based on curriculum and performance standards in Science for all year 8 students in 2007 (NSWBS, 2006).

These statewide' assessment programs are designed to provide systematic and regular measures of student learning. They are designed to investigate and monitor the 'health' of an education system and to improve student learning by providing information to stakeholders at different levels of the system. They provide the government with information to monitor standards over time, to monitor the impact of particular programs and to make decisions about resource allocation. They provide schools and teachers with information about whole school, class and individual pupil performance that they can use to make decisions about resource allocation and to support learning in the classroom.

The School Certificate recognizes eleven years of compulsory schooling and that students have completed all of the compulsory courses of study. The specific purposes of the School Certificate internal and external assessments are to:

- foster the intellectual, social and moral development of students in the compulsory study areas

- publicly acknowledge and reward students for the knowledge and understanding they have developed

- provide increased continuity between compulsory and post-compulsory secondary school studies

- provide that students who do not continue on to further study with an exit credential that details what they know and can do in foundation areas based on an external examination as well as information on the performance in relation to the outcomes across all the courses they have studies

- determine if there are any trends in student performance in particular schools or school systems

- determine if there are groups of students who underperform with respect to standards.

The Higher School Certificate recognizes thirteen years of schooling and offers a wide range of study areas to assist in providing greater career choices and increased opportunities at university and for other post-compulsory educational opportunities including university-recognized Vocational Education and Training (VET) in Schools Program[5] and courses through the NSW Technical and Further Education (TAFE)[6]. The purposes of internal and external assessment associated with the Higher School Certificate courses of study are to (McGaw, 1997):

- foster the intellectual development of students, in particular developing their

    – knowledge, skills, understanding and attitudes in the fields of study they choose

    – capacity to manage their own learning

    – desire to continue learning in formal or informal settings after school

- provide formal assessment and certification of students' achievements

- provide information about what they know and can do course of their own choice in relation to all the knowledge and skill outcomes in the each course

- publicly acknowledge and reward students for the knowledge and understanding they have developed.

5  http://www.bvet.nsw.gov.au/programs/vetschools.htm
6  www.schools.nsw.edu.au/media/downloads/schoolsweb/adminsupport/vetunits.doc

Teachers are able to use standards in science as a reference point for planning teaching and learning programs, and for assessing and reporting student progress. Where the curriculum and performance standards are clearly articulated in science, they help teachers and students to set targets, monitor achievement, and, as a result, make changes to programs and strategies to support and improve the progress of every student.

*(iv) Some side-effects of assessing science standards in New South Wales*

The testing of state standards has both positive and negative side effects:

- There is an increasing tendency for more consistent use of assessment terms by teachers, schools, education systems and the government authorities. Among other benefits this has meant that as students move from one school to another or from one system to another, government to/from non-government, the information provided in relation to a students progress is more likely to be based on common understandings.

- The use of assessment referenced to the standards has made schools more aware that they need to understand clearly the information that they receive, articulate why they need information, articulate what information they need, for whom the information is intended, what is the most efficient (and fair) way of collecting and interpreting it and how what is being assessed relates to the standards. It involves teachers, students and parents in reflecting on assessment practices and assessment data.

- Assessment for learning with reference to a common grade scale has affected teaching pedagogy at a school level as it recognises that assessment of the students requires making successive judgements about each student. It assists teachers in identifying the extent of each student's progress against clearly defined outcomes and in making judgments on their progress. It can also be used by teachers to determine any remediation needs and to assess the effectiveness of teaching strategies and their appropriateness to the learning needs of particular students.

- Using assessment referenced to standards helps students take responsibility for their own learning as it helps students know and recognise the standards for which they are aiming and providing feedback to help students understand the next steps in learning and plan how to achieve them.

- The cost of external statewide testing and marking is significant with major security issues to be considered at all stages of the tests and examinations – setting, distribution, sitting the exam and marking.

- The results of the Higher School Certificate are held in very high regard within the state by the general community, across Australia and internationally. Feedback indicates that the reports that include the performances scale and the detailed descriptions are also more easily understood by employers, parents and the community.

- The credentialing authority has had to produce clearer guidelines for schools concerning the range and balance of school-based assessments to be used, to ensure that school-based assessments focus on the aspects of curriculum content and outcomes not adequately assessed by external examination processes and do not simply mimic the external examination. Reports are provided to schools of the correlations between external and school-based assessment and while these are accompanied by interpretations that make clear that maximizing the correlation is not the goal of the school-based assessment, the very provision of such correlations sends a very different message.

- The inclusion of an external assessment means that the performance standards do not solely rely on internal teacher-based assessment .

- Teachers and students are developing a shared understanding of what is to be learned and the standards expected. Being explicit about standards also provides criteria for evaluating the effectiveness of the learning process and related assessment strategies.

- Students' marks are determined by their performance rather than predetermined distribution or scale. This means there is no limit on the number of students who can achieve a high score.

- Decisions about student achievement are based on more than a single performance and achieved in more than one context leading to more reliable data being acquired.

- The final Higher School Certificate marks are used by the universities to calculate a Tertiary Entrance Ranking for all students that determines entry into specific university courses. This leads to very significant pressures being placed on schools, teachers and students to perform. Tables of the top 500 students and their schools are published in newspapers and there is significant media interest around the results. Assumptions that are not always correct are made in relation to student performance and teaching at both school and community levels. The importance of the examination for the future of their children encourages many parents to employ outside tutors to try to ensure the child attains a high mark.

# References

Black, P., Harrison, C., Lee, C., Marshall, B. and Wiliam, D. (2003) *Assessment for learning: Putting it into practice.* Buckingham, UK: Open University Press.

Goodrum, D., Hackling, M. and Rennie, L. (2001) *The status and quality of teaching and learning of science in Australian schools.* Canberra: Department of Education, Training and Youth Affairs.
See also
http//:www.dest.gov.au/sectors/school_education/publications_resources/ profiles/ status_and_quality_of_science_schools.htm

Hackling, M.W., Goodrum, D. and Rennie, L. (2001) The state of science in Australia secondary schools. *Australian Science Teachers Journal*, 47(4), 6-17.

Killen, R. (2005) *Programming and assessment for quality teaching and learning.* Southbank, Victoria: Thomson Learning.

McGaw, B. (1997) *Shaping Their Future: Recommendations for reform of the Higher School Certificate.* Sydney: Department of Training and Education.

MCEETYA (Ministerial Council on Education, Employment, Training and Youth Affairs) (1999) *The Adelaide Declaration on National Goals for Schooling in the Twenty-first Century.* MCEETYA.
See also:
http://www.dest.gov.au/sectors/school_education/policy_initiatives_reviews/ national_ goals_for_schooling_in_the_twenty_first_century.htm

MCEETYA (Ministerial Council on Education, Employment, Training and Youth Affairs) (2002a) *The Context of Australian Schooling.* MCEETYA

MCEETYA (Ministerial Council on Education, Employment, Training and Youth Affairs (2002b) *National Year 6 Primary Science Sample Assessment: Assessment Domain and Progress Map.* Performance Measurement Taskforce. MCEETYA.

MCEETYA (Ministerial Council on Education, Employment, Training and Youth Affairs) (2003) *A Measurement Framework for National Key Performance Measures.* MCEETYA.

MCEETYA (Ministerial Council on Education, Employment, Training and Youth Affairs) (2005a) *A Measurement Framework for National Key Performance Measures.* MCEETYA.

MCEETYA (Ministerial Council on Education, Employment, Training and Youth Affairs) (2005b) *National Assessment: Program, Science, Year 6, 2003: Technical Report.* June 2005. MCEETYA.

NSWBS (NSW Board of Studies) (1999) *New Standards Brochure.* Sydney: NSW Board of Studies.

NSWBS (NSW Board of Studies) (2000) *Science Stage 6 Support Document, Part 1.* Sydney: NSW Board of Studies.

NSWBS (NSW Board of Studies) (2003a) *Science 7 – 10 Syllabus 2003.* Sydney: NSW Board of Studies.

NSWBS (NSW Board of Studies) (2003b) *Performance Band Descriptors – Science.* Sydney: NSW Board of Studies.

NSWBS (NSW Board of Studies) (2005) *Assessment, Course Performance Descriptors – Science.* Sydney: NSW Board of Studies.

NSWBS (NSW Board of Studies) (2006) *Assessment, Certification and Examinations Manual.* Sydney: NSW Board of Studies.

OECD PISA (OECD Programme for International Student Assessment) (1999) *Measuring student knowledge and skills: A new framework of assessment.* Paris: OECD Press.

Appendix 1

# National Goals for Schooling in the Twenty-First Century

1.  **Schooling should develop fully the talents and capacities of all students. In particular, when students leave schools they should:**

1.1 have the capacity for, and skills in, analysis and problem-solving and the ability to communicate ideas and information, to plan and organise activities and to collaborate with others.

1.2 have qualities of self-confidence, optimism, high self-esteem, and a commitment to personal excellence as a basis for their potential life roles as family, community and workforce members.

1.3 have the capacity to exercise judgement and responsibility in matters of morality, ethics and social justice, and the capacity to make sense of their world, to think about how things got to be the way they are, to make rational and informed decisions about their own lives and to accept responsibility for their own actions.

1.4 be active and informed citizens with an understanding and appreciation of Australia's system of government and civic life.

1.5 have employment-related skills and an understanding of the work environment, career options and pathways as a foundation for, and positive attitudes towards, vocational education and training, further education, employment and life-long learning.

1.6 be confident, creative and productive users of new technologies, particularly information and communication technologies, and understand the impact of those technologies on society.

1.7 have an understanding of, and concern for, stewardship of the natural environment, and the knowledge and skills to contribute to ecologically sustainable development.

1.8 have the knowledge, skills and attitudes necessary. to establish and maintain a healthy lifestyle, and for the creative and satisfying use of leisure time.

2.  **In terms of curriculum, students should have:**

2.1 attained high standards of knowledge, skills and understanding through a comprehensive and balanced curriculum in the compulsory-years of schooling encompassing the agreed eight key learning areas and the relationship between them:
- the arts
- English
- health and physical education
- languages other than English
- mathematics
- science
- studies of society and environment
- technology

2.2     attained the skills of numeracy and English literacy; such that, every stu-dent should be numerate, able to read, write, spell and communicate at an appropriate level.

2.3     participated in programs of vocational learning during the compulsory years and have had access to vocational education and training programs as part of their senior secondary studies.

2.4     participated in programs and activities which foster and develop enterprise skills, including those skills which will allow them maximum flexibility and adaptability in the future.

**3.     Schooling should be socially just, so that:**

3.1     students' outcomes from schooling are free from the effects of negative forms of discrimination based on sex, language, culture and ethnicity, reli-gion or disability; and of differences arising from students' socioeconomic background or geographic location.

3.2     the learning outcomes of educationally disadvantaged students improve and, over time, match those of other students.

3.3     Aboriginal and Tones Strait Islander students have equitable access to, and opportunities in, schooling so that their learning outcomes improve and, over time, match those of other students.

3.4     all students understand and acknowledge the value of Aboriginal and Tomes Strait Islander cultures to Australian society and possess the knowl-edge, skills and understanding to contribute to and benefit from, reconcilia-tion between Indigenous arid non-Indigenous Australians.

3.5     all students understand and acknowledge the value of cultural and linguistic diversity, and possess the knowledge, skills and understanding to con-tribute to, and benefit from, such diversity in the Australian community and internationally.

3.6     all students have access to the high quality education necessary to enable the completion of school education to Year 12 or its vocational equivalent and that provides clear and recognised pathways to employment and further education and training.

MCEETYA (Ministerial Council on Education, Employment, Training and Youth Affairs) (1999) *The Adelaide Declaration on National Goals for Schooling in the Twenty-first Century*. MCEETYA.
See also:
http://www.dest.gov.au/sectors/school_education/policy_initiatives_reviews/national_goals_for_schooling_in_the_twenty_first_century.htm

Appendix 2

# National scientific literacy progress map

| Level | Domains of scientific literacy | | |
|-------|-------|-------|-------|
| | Domain A Formulating or identifying investigable questions and hypotheses, planning investigations and collecting evidence | Domain B Interpreting evidence and drawing conclusions, critiquing the trustworthiness of evidence and claims made by others, and communicating findings | Domain C Using understanding for describing and explaining natural phenomena and for interpreting reports |
| 1 | Responds to the teacher's questions, observes and describes | Describes what happened | Describes an aspect or property of an individual object or event that has been experienced or reported |
| 2 | Given a question in a familiar context, identifies a variable to be considered, observes and describes or makes non-standard measurements and limited records of data. | Makes comparisons between objects or events observed | Describes changes to, differences between or properties of objects or events that have been experienced or reported |
| 3 | Formulates scientific questions for testing and makes predictions. Demonstrates awareness of the need for fair testing. Makes simple standard measurements. Records data as tables, diagrams or descriptions | Displays data as tables or bar graphs, identifies and summarises patterns in science data. Applies the rule by extrapolating or predicting | Explains the relationships between individual events that have been experienced or reported and can generalise and apply the rule by predicting future events |
| 4 | Identifies the variable to be changed, the variable to be measured and several variables to be controlled. Uses repeated trials or replicates | Calculates averages from repeat trials or replicates, plots line graphs where appropriate. Conclusions summarise and explain the patterns in the data. Able to make general suggestions for improving an investigation (eg. make more measurements) | Explains interactions, processes or effects that have been experienced or reported in terms of a non-observable property or abstract science concept |
| 5 | Formulates scientific questions or hypotheses for testing and plans experiments in which most variables are controlled. Selects equipment that is appropriate and trials measurement procedure to improve techniques and ensure safety | Conclusions explain the patterns in the data using science concepts, and are consistent with the data. Critiques reports of investigations noting any major flaw in design or inconsistencies in data | Explains phenomena, or interprets reports about phenomena, using several abstract scientific concepts |
| 6 | Uses scientific knowledge to formulate questions, hypotheses and predictions and to identify the variables to be changed, measured and controlled. Trials and modifies techniques to enhance reliability of data collection | Selects graph type and scales that display the data effectively. Conclusions are consistent with the data, explain the patterns and relationships in terms of scientific concepts and principles, and relate to the question, hypothesis or prediction. Critiques the trustworthiness of reported data (eg. adequate control of variables, sample or consistency of measurements), and consistency between data and claims | Explains complex interactions, systems or relationships using several abstract scientific concepts or principles and the relationships between them |

Note 1: It is anticipated that the national standard for scientific literacy for Year 6 students will be set in Level 3.
Note 2: This map was developed for the Primary Science Assessment Project and the Science Education Assessment Resources Project funded by the Australian Government's Department of Education, Science and Training.

MCEETYA (Ministerial Council on Education, Employment, Training and Youth Affairs) (2005b) *National Assessment: Program, Science, Year 6, 2003: Technical Report*. June 2005. MCEETYA

51

# Prescribed Focus Areas

The continuum is evident across each of the stages in the ways in which students demonstrate the knowledge, understanding and skills they have developed about each Prescribed Focus Area.

| PFA | Early Stage 1 – Stage 1 | Stages 2–3 | Stage 4 | Stage 5 | Stage 6: HSC |
|---|---|---|---|---|---|
| | A student: | A student: | A student: | A student: | A student: |
| History | appreciates contributions made by individuals, groups, cultures and communities to scientific and technological understanding | appreciates contributions made by individuals, groups, cultures and communities to scientific and technological understanding | identifies historical examples of how scientific knowledge has changed people's understanding of the world | explains how social factors influence the development and acceptance of scientific ideas | evaluates (discusses) how major advances in scientific understanding and technology have changed the direction or nature of scientific thinking |
| Nature and practice | exhibits curiosity and responsiveness to scientific ideas and the gathering of evidence related to these ideas | exhibits curiosity and responsiveness to scientific ideas and the gathering of evidence related to these ideas | uses examples to illustrate how models, theories and laws contribute to an understanding of phenomena | describes the processes that are applied to test and validate models, theories and laws | analyses the ways in which models, theories and laws in (area specified) have been tested and validated (applies the processes that have been used to test and validate models, theories and laws to investigations) |
| Applications and uses | initiates scientific and technological tasks and challenges and perseveres with them to their completion | initiates scientific and technological tasks and challenges and perseveres with them to their completion | identifies areas of everyday life that have been affected by scientific developments | evaluates the impact of applications of science on society and the environment | assesses the impact of particular advances in (area specified) on the development of technologies |
| Implications for society and the environment | shows informed commitment to improving the quality of society and the environment through science and technological activities | shows informed commitment to improving the quality of society and the environment through science and technological activities | identifies choices made by people with regard to scientific developments | discusses evidence supporting different viewpoints | assesses the impact of applications of (area specified) on society and the environment |
| Current issues, research and developments | appreciates the significance of Australian scientific and technological expertise across gender and cultural groups exhibits curiosity and responsiveness to scientific and technological ideas | appreciates the significance of Australian scientific and technological expertise across gender and cultural groups exhibits curiosity and responsiveness to scientific and technological ideas | describes areas of current scientific research | analyses how current research might affect people's lives | identifies possible future directions of (area specified) research |

# Knowledge and Understanding

| | Early Stage 1 | Stage 1 | Stage 2 | Stage 3 | Stage 4 | Stage 5 | Stage 6 |
|---|---|---|---|---|---|---|---|
| | A student: | A student: | A student: | A student: | A student: | A student: | |
| **Models, theories and laws; Structures and systems** | explores and identifies ways some forms of energy are used in their daily lives | identifies and describes different ways some forms of energy are used in the community | identifies various forms and sources of energy | identifies and applies processes involved in manipulating, using and changing the form of energy | identifies and describes energy changes and the action of forces in common situations | applies models, theories and laws to situations involving energy, force and motion | The outcomes of the Stage 6 in Biology, Chemistry, Earth and Environmental Science, Physics and Senior Science build upon the foundations laid in Stage 5 to extend students' knowledge and understanding in specific areas |
| | | | | recognises that the Earth is the source of most materials and resources, and describes phenomena and processes, both natural and human, that form and change the Earth over time | describes observed properties of substances using scientific models and theories | relates properties of elements, compounds and mixtures to scientific models, theories and laws | |
| | identifies ways in which living things are different and have different needs | identifies and describes ways in which living things grow and change | identifies and describes the structure and function of living things and ways in which living things interact with other living things and their environment | | describes features of living things | relates the structure and function of living things to models, theories and laws | |
| | | | identifies some of the features of the solar system and describes interactions that affect conditions on Earth | describe phenomena and processes, both natural and human that form and change the Earth over time | describes the dynamic structure of Earth and its relationship to other parts of our solar system and the universe | relates the development of the universe and the dynamic structure of Earth to models, theories and laws and the influence of time | |
| | explores and identifies ways the environment influences their daily lives | identifies and describes ways in which people and other living things depend upon the Earth and its environments | identifies and describes the structure and function of living things and the ways in which living things interact with other living things and their environment | identifies, describes and evaluates the interactions between living things and their effects on the environment | identifies factors affecting survival of organisms in an ecosystem | assesses human impacts on the interaction of biotic and abiotic features of the environment | |
| **Interactions** | | | | recognises that the Earth is the source of most materials and resources | identifies where resources are found, and describes ways in which they are used by humans | analyses the impact of human resource use on the biosphere to evaluate methods of conserving, protecting and maintaining Earth's resources | |
| | | | creates and evaluates products and services considering aesthetic and functional factors | creates and evaluates products and services, demonstrating consideration of sustainability, aesthetic, cultural, safety and functional issues | identifies, using examples, common simple devices and explains why they are used | relates the interactions involved in using some common technologies to their underlying scientific principles | |

# Skills

The K–12 continuum is also evident in the skills developed from Stage 1 through to Stage 6, and focuses on continually increasing students' expertise in planning and conducting investigations, communicating information and understanding, developing scientific thinking and problem-solving techniques, and working individually and in teams.

| | Early Stage 1 | Stage 1 | Stage 2 |
|---|---|---|---|
| **Skill** | A student: | A student: | A student: |
| **Planning investigations** | generates own ideas and designs through trial and error, play, modelling and making | develops own design ideas in response to an investigation of needs and wants | develops ideas using drawings and models |
| | identifies a limited range of equipment, computer-based technology, materials and other resources when undertaking exploration | selects a range of equipment, computer-based technology, materials and other resources to undertake investigation tasks | selects a range of equipment, computer-based technology, materials and other resources with developing skill to enhance investigation tasks |
| **Conducting investigations** | investigates their surroundings by observing, questioning and exploring | conducts guided investigations by observing, questioning, predicting and collecting data | conducts investigations by observing, questioning, predicting, testing and collecting data |
| | generates own ideas through trial and error, play, modelling and making | implements own design ideas in response to an investigation of needs and wants | implements ideas, uses drawings, models and prototypes |
| | uses a limited range of equipment, computer-based technology, materials and other resources when undertaking production tasks | uses a range of equipment, computer-based technology, materials and other resources to undertake an investigation task | uses a range of equipment, computer-based technology, materials and other resources to enhance investigation tasks |
| **Communicating information and understanding** | investigates their surroundings by reporting | conducts guided investigations by recording data | conducts investigations by recording and analysing data |
| | recognises and uses various means of communication | creates a range of information products and communicates using a variety of media | creates information products demonstrating an understanding of the needs of particular audiences |
| **Developing scientific thinking and problem-solving techniques** | | conducts guided investigations by suggesting possible explanations | conducts investigations by drawing conclusions |
| **Working individually and in teams** | | | |

54

|  | Stage 3 | Stage 4 | Stage 5 | Stage 6: HSC |
|---|---|---|---|---|
| **Skill** | A student: | A student: | A student: | A student: |
| **Planning investigations** | conducts their own investigations based on the results of planning<br><br>evaluates and selects a range of equipment, computer-based technology, materials and other resources to meet requirements and constraints of an investigation task | clarifies the purpose of an investigation and, with guidance, produces a plan to investigate a problem | identifies a problem and independently produces an appropriate investigation plan | justifies the appropriateness of a particular investigation plan |
| **Conducting investigations** | conducts their own investigations based on observing, questioning, predicting, testing and collecting data<br><br>uses a range of equipment, computer-based technology, materials and other resources to meet the requirements and constraints of investigation tasks | follows a sequence of instructions to undertake a first-hand investigation<br><br>uses given criteria to gather first-hand data<br><br>accesses information from identified secondary sources | undertakes first-hand investigations independently with safety and competence<br><br>gathers first-hand data accurately<br><br>accesses information from a wide variety of secondary sources | evaluates ways in which accuracy and reliability could be improved in investigations |
| **Communicating information and understanding** | conducts their own investigations based on the results of recording and analysing data<br><br>creates information products and processes, demonstrating consideration of the type of media, form, audience and ethical issues | evaluates the relevance of data and information<br><br>with guidance, presents information to a audience to achieve a particular purpose | explains trends, patterns and relationships in data and/or information from a variety of sources<br><br>selects and uses appropriate forms of communication to present information to an audience | uses terminology and reporting styles appropriately and successfully to communicate information and understanding |
| **Developing scientific thinking and problem-solving techniques** | conducts their own investigations and makes judgements based on the results of drawing conclusions | draws conclusions based on information available<br><br>uses an identified strategy to solve problems<br><br>uses creativity and imagination to suggest plausible solutions to familiar problems | uses critical thinking skills in evaluating information and drawing conclusions<br><br>selects and uses appropriate strategies to solve problems<br><br>uses creativity and imagination in the analysis of problems and the development of possible solutions | assesses the validity of conclusions from gathered data and information |
| **Working individually and in teams** | works cooperatively with others in groups on scientific and technological tasks and challenges | undertakes a variety of individual and team tasks with guidance | plans, implements and evaluates the effectiveness of a variety of tasks independently and as a team member | explains why an investigation is best undertaken individually or by a team |

# Values and Attitudes

By reflecting on the past, present and future involvement of science in society, students are encouraged to develop positive values and informed critical attitudes. In Stages 1–3, the main focus is developing positive values and attitudes towards themselves and others, and towards science and technology. In Stages 4 and 5, these are broadened to include lifelong learning and the environment. Stage 6 consolidates those values and attitudes developed in earlier stages to encourage students to justify both ethical behaviour and a desire for the critical evaluation of the consequences of applications of science.

Again, this continuum can be exemplified through the outcomes.

| | Stages 1–3 | Stages 4–5 | Stage 6: HSC |
|---|---|---|---|
| **Students will develop positive values about and attitudes towards:** | A student: | A student: | A student: |
| **themselves** | demonstrates confidence in themselves and a willingness to make decisions when investigating, designing, making and using technology<br><br>gains satisfaction from their efforts to investigate, to design, to make, and to use technology | demonstrates confidence and a willingness to make decisions and to take responsible actions | justifies informed values about, and attitudes towards, both the living and non-living components of the environment, ethical behaviour and a desire for critical evaluation of the consequences of the applications of science |
| **others** | works cooperatively with others in groups on scientific and technological tasks and challenges | respects differing viewpoints on science issues and is honest, fair and ethical | |
| **learning as a lifelong process** | exhibits curiosity and responsiveness to scientific and technological ideas and evidence<br><br>initiates and perseveres with investigations, and takes tasks to their completion | recognises the relevance and importance of lifelong learning and acknowledges the continued impact of science in many aspects of everyday life | |
| **science and technology** | appreciates contributions made by individuals, groups, cultures and communities to scientific and technological understanding<br><br>appreciates the significance of Australian scientific and technological expertise across gender and cultural groups | recognises the role of science in providing information about issues being considered and in increasing understanding of the world around them | |
| **the environment** | shows informed commitment to improving the quality of society and the environment through science and technology activities | acknowledges their responsibility to conserve, protect and maintain the environment for the future | |

NSWBS (NSW Board of Studies) (2000) *Science Stage 6 Support Document, Part 1.* Sydney: NSW Board of Studies.

Appendix 4

# Stage 5 Course Performance Descriptors – Science

**Areas for Assessment**

Knowing and understanding
Planning and conducting investigations
Problem-solving
Communicating

| Grade E | Grade D | Grade C | Grade B | Grade A |
|---|---|---|---|---|
| A student performing at this grade typically: | A student performing at this grade typically: | A student performing at this grade typically: | A student performing at this grade typically: | A student performing at this grade typically: |
| • recalls some examples of the impact of scientific research on science, society, technology and the environment. | • outlines some impacts of scientific research on science, society, technology and the environment. | • describes the impact of scientific research on science, society, technology and the environment. | • explains the impact of scientific research on science, society, technology and the environment. | • evaluates the impact of scientific research on science, society, technology and the environment. |
| • identifies some scientific models, theories and laws, and recalls some processes that can be used to test them. | • recalls scientific models, theories and laws to outline scientific phenomena, and identifies the processes that are used to test them. | • relates models, theories and laws to scientific phenomena, and outlines the processes that are used to test and validate them. | • describes scientific phenomena using models, theories and laws, and outlines the processes that are used to test and validate them. | • explains scientific phenomena using models, theories and laws, and describes the processes that are used to test and validate them. |
| • identifies some systems and structures of the living and non-living world. | • recalls some interactions within systems and structures of the living and non-living world. | • outlines interactions within and between systems and structures of the living and non-living world. | • describes interactions within and between systems and structures of the living and non-living world. | • explains interactions within and between systems and structures of the living and non-living world. |
| • with guidance, individually and in teams, plans and undertakes elementary first-hand investigations and draws simple conclusions from selected data. | • individually and in teams, develops elementary plans, and undertakes first-hand investigations and, with guidance, draws relevant conclusions from selected data. | • independently and in teams, uses identified strategies and problem-solving skills to plan and conduct first-hand investigations and draw relevant conclusions from the data collected. | • independently and in teams, selects strategies and problem-solving skills to plan and conduct first-hand investigations, gather and process data, and draw valid conclusions. | • engages, independently and in teams, in creative problem-solving processes to plan and conduct first-hand investigations, gather and process data, and draw valid conclusions. |
| • with guidance, locates information from provided resources to identify simple trends, patterns and relationships. | • locates and extracts information from provided resources to outline trends, patterns and relationships. | • independently locates and summarises information from a variety of sources to describe trends, patterns and relationships. | • independently locates and processes information from a variety of sources to explain trends, patterns and relationships. | • independently locates and processes information from a wide variety of sources to explain trends, patterns and relationships. |
| • with guidance, communicates information to an audience. | • communicates their scientific understanding to an audience. | • selects a suitable way to communicate their scientific understanding to an audience. | • selects suitable ways to communicate their scientific understanding to an audience. | • communicates their scientific findings, understanding and viewpoints in a variety of ways to an audience. |

NSWBS (NSW Board of Studies) (2005) *Assessment, Course Performance Descriptors – Science*, Sydney: NSW Board of Studies.

Appendix 5

## The NSW Board of Studies Common Grade Scale

| Grade | Common Grade Scale |
|---|---|
| A | The student has an extensive knowledge and understanding of the content and can readily apply this knowledge. In addition, the student has achieved a very high level of competence in the processes and skills and can apply these skills to new situations. |
| B | The student has a thorough knowledge and understanding of the content and a high level of competence in the processes and skills. In addition, the student is able to apply this knowledge and these skills to most situations |
| C | The student has a sound knowledge and understanding of the main areas of content and has achieved an adequate level of competence in the processes and skills. |
| D | The student has a basic knowledge and understanding of the content and has achieved a limited level of competence in the processes and skills. |
| E | The student has an elementary knowledge and understanding in few areas of the content and has achieved very limited competence in some of the processes and skills. |

NSWBS (NSW Board of Studies) (2005) *Assessment, Course Performance Descriptors – Science*, Sydney: NSW Board of Studies.

Appendix 6

# Science School Certificate Test
# Performance Band Descriptions

A typical performance in this band is demonstrated when a student:

| | |
|---|---|
| Band 6 | Demonstrates extensive and detailed knowledge and understanding of complex scientific concepts and the nature of science. Communicates logically, using correct scientific terminology and appropriate scientific formats, such as written text, diagrams, tables, graphs and flowcharts. Identifies and uses correct components of a scientific investigation. Demonstrates complex graphing skills, including locating information and identifying trends; uses information from graphs to solve complex problems. Interprets complex data from scientific processes, concepts and scales. Justifies the choice of appropriate scientific equipment to suit a hypothetical situation. Analyses and evaluates scientific relationships, synthesising information to draw conclusions. Applies scientific ideas to unfamiliar situations. |
| Band 5 | Demonstrates thorough knowledge and understanding of the nature of science. Communicates using correct scientific terminology and appropriate scientific formats, such as written text, diagrams, tables and graphs. Identifies components of a scientific investigation. Demonstrates competent graphing skills, including locating information and identifying trends; uses information from graphs to solve problems. Interprets data from scientific processes, concepts and scales. Justifies the choice of appropriate scientific equipment to suit a specific task. Explains scientific relationships and identifies patterns from information to draw conclusions. Applies scientific ideas to familiar situations. |
| Band 4 | Demonstrates sound knowledge and understanding of some scientific concepts and the nature of science. Communicates using correct scientific terminology and some scientific formats, such as written text, diagrams and tables. Recalls components of a scientific investigation. Demonstrates graphing skills, including locating some information and identifying trends. Uses data from scientific processes, concepts and scales. Selects appropriate scientific equipment to suit a specific task. Explains straightforward scientific relationships from information. Describes scientific ideas. |
| Band 3 | Recalls basic knowledge of some scientific concepts and the nature of science. Communicates using some scientific terminology and several scientific formats, such as written text and diagrams. States scientific observations from experimental data. Graphs data appropriately and locates some information in graphs. Uses data from scientific processes. Selects appropriate scientific equipment to suit general types of experiments. States straightforward scientific relationships. |
| Band 2 | Recalls basic knowledge of some straightforward scientific concepts and the nature of science. Uses fundamental communication relating to science using written text. Describes experiments in non-scientific terms. Demonstrates elementary graphing skills in science. Uses simple data from science processes. Recognises common scientific equipment. |
| Band 1 | |

NSWBS (NSW Board of Studies) (2005) *Assessment, Course Performance Descriptors – Science*, Sydney: NSW Board of Studies.

# Chapter 3

## Austria at the beginning of the way to standards in science

*Hubert Weiglhofer*

*Interfakultärer Fachbereich Fachdidaktik – LehrerInnenbildung*
*Universität Salzburg, Hellbrunnerstr. 34, 5020 Salzburg, Austria*

### The educational landscape in Austria

Education in Austria is organized according to the following compulsory school age groups. Pupils go to primary school from 6 to 10 and lower secondary school from 10 to 14 (secondary modern school or high school). From 14 to 18/19 they can continue on to either upper secondary school (high school, vocational school with secondary school leaving certificate) or vocational school without a secondary school leaving certificate from 14/15 to 17 (figure 1).

| Grade | 1 | 2 | 3 | 4 | 5 | 6 | 7 | 8 | 9 | 10 | 11 | 12 |
|---|---|---|---|---|---|---|---|---|---|---|---|---|
| Pupils'age | 7 | 8 | 9 | 10 | 11 | 12 | 13 | 14 | 15 | 16 | 17 | 18 |
| Level | primary school | | | | lower secondary school | | | | upper secondary school high school, vocational school | | | |
| Compulsory/ Optional | C | C | C | C | C | C | C | C | C/O | C/O | C/O | C/O |
| Scientific subjects | Environmental and natural studies is an integrated subject group comprising the fields of biology, geography, physics, health education. | | | | Separate: different distribution of lessons for each school subject and school year. Average sum of weekly hours during 4 school years Biology Ø 7 Physics Ø 5 Chemistry Ø 2 Geography Ø 7 Ø = average | | | | Separate: different distribution of lessons for each school subject and school year high school:   vocational school Biology Ø 6      Ø 0-6 Physics Ø 7      Ø 2-8 Chemistry Ø 4      Ø 2-8 Geography Ø 7      Ø 0-6 | | | |

Figure 1:    The educational landscape and science provision in Austrian schools

### Educational standards in Austria – general situation

Austria began to develop and implement educational standards in 2003. The Ministry of Education appointed working groups consisting of scientists, experts in science didactics and school teachers. The co-ordination takes place via a controlling group of the Ministry.

The first education standards developed were for grade 4 in German and Mathematics and for grade 8 in those two subjects and in English.

The published standards have a preamble which defines the contribution of the subject to general education (Lucyshyn, 2003). Then a set of competences is described and the standards are formulated. Tasks at different stages are developed.

The testing of these standards is being carried out over a period of four years (until 2007) at selected schools.

| Competences in Mathematics | Subject competences |
|---|---|
| Modelling | Mathematical numbers |
| Problem handling | Measuring |
| Arguing | Space and mode |
| Using mathematical representations | Functional connections |
| Dealing with mathematical symbols and formalism | Data and statistics |
| Communicating in, within, and through mathematics | |
| **Levels** Reproduce Represent correlations Generalize and reflect | |

Figure 2:    Examples of mathematical competences and levels at Grade 8

## Standards in science subjects

A start was made in 2005, by the Ministry of Education, to produce standards for science for upper secondary schools (grade 12). At present, a working group, consisting of school teachers, experts in science didactics and representatives of the Ministry of Education, is developing a set of competences including archetypal tasks.

It is expected that the standards will be introduced, nationwide, at the end of the school year 2008/09. The aim is to develop regular standards. In a first approach, the standard contents should be realised for approximately one third up to half of the instruction time. What is of immediate importance is not covering the contents of the syllabus, but advancing the dimensions of teaching and learning in natural sciences. Students should be enabled to use more complex stages of knowledge, to plan experiments and use concepts and models rather then just reproduce facts.

Assessment of standards will be carried out at the end of grade 12. However, many students finish their science courses in grade 10, and therefor it will only be possible to test for lastingly acquired competences. Considering these circumstances, test manuals will consist of information, facts and problems. Students have to observe, describe or

valuate them, create hypotheses, build connections and apply concepts.
The development of the standards which will involve the validation of the model of competencies and the testing and standardisation of the test instruments, will be introduced carefully starting with advanced training seminars for teachers. There will be a programme of monitoring and evaluation.

# 1    How are standards in science education defined?

Standards specify which competences pupils should have lastingly acquired up to a certain grade. Emphasis is put on the basics of a teaching subject and the expected learning results are described.

In Austria, standards will describe a regular level of demands. The starting point is the concept of Weinert (2001, p. 27f.) in which he describes competences as
*"cognitive abilities and skills possessed by or able to be learned by individuals that enable them to solve particular problems, as well as the motivational, volitional and social readiness and capacity to utilise the solutions successfully and responsibly in variable situations".*
The spectrum of competences includes proficiency in using one's abilities, gathering information, understanding connections, employing skills, collecting experiences, readiness and motivation for acting (Lackner and Timischl, 2005).

## *The model of competences*

In 2005, a model of competences was developed for biology, chemistry and physics combined. The working group was inspired by several international models (for example, National Research Council, 1996; CMEC, 1997; Bybee, 2002; KMK, 2005).

It is a three-dimensional model (figure 2):

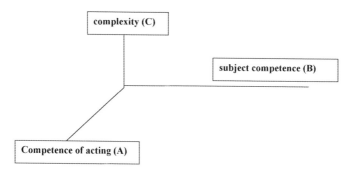

Figure 2:     A model to describe competencies

**Competence of acting (A)**

*A1: Observe and acquire* (at present, standards are not definitely fixed)
Includes the competence to observe procedures and manifestations in nature, to describe by formulas and symbols, to express themselves in the appropriate terminology and to arrange, present and describe these phenomena using basic concepts, facts and principles.

*A2: Inquire and work on*
Includes the competence to examine procedures and manifestations in nature and environment with specialist methods, to pose suitable investigative questions, to gather information and create hypotheses and for these results, a justified selection of methods (e.g. case studies, experiments, measurements and calculations).

*A3: Valuate and apply*
Includes the competence to document, present, value and apply and interpret data, facts and results, using a justified selection of valuation criteria, recognizing the limits of validity and applicability of scientific statements and prognoses. It further includes their applicability in personal and social areas.

Each area of competence of acting (A1–A3) is expressed by a varying number of "can do standards" (approximate 30). For example:

A1.2: I can describe procedures and manifestations in nature using the appropriate terminology.

A2.3: I can plan a simple experiment.

A3.1: I can indicate scientific criteria for the valuation of data and facts.

**Subject competence – Examples of basic concepts (B)**

B1: Substances, particles, structures
Structure and characteristics of matter, from molecule to cell, from cell to organism

B2: Interactions
Chemical, physical reactions, metabolism, sensation processing

B3: Evolution, processes
Transmission, evolution, chemical technology, physical development, science and society

B4: Systems
Periodic system of elements, space and time, ecology

**Complexity (C)**

Level 1: Reproduction
Reproducing scientific facts, reconstructing experiments, representing simple contexts
Level 2: Use in new connections, autonomous application
Analysing scientific processes, transfering to new applications, analogue reasoning, planning, arranging and evaluating experiments

## *A short example of a task derived from the model of competences*

The following illustrates the development of a task:

"The sensory organ, the eye" (subject competences B1, B2)
On the basis of an introductory text, the structure of the eye and the function of seeing are presented. Pupils have to mark the graphic presentation of a cross section of an eye (A1; observe).

Pupils reconstruct the causes of long-sightedness on aging, using as a basis, tables showing data concerning the changes of reading ability in the life cycle and the function of different lenses (A2: place suitable investigative questions, create hypotheses).

On the basis of different transmission curves the different filter effect and/or permeability of sunglasses are shown. Pupils interpret the transmission curves and deliver recommendations for high-quality sunglasses (A2, A3: interpret data, justified selection of valuation criteria).

The following are examples of some unanswered questions about the model of competences:

• The normative structure of the model of competence must be confirmed or adapted by empirical investigations. But the evaluation of the model of competences has not yet been decided.

• Does the model of competences cover the substantial knowledge and proficiency in the three scientific subjects? What can be done about areas which are not measurable?

• What characteristics actually determine the level of difficulty of tasks?

• What structure do the competences form among each other?

• How is cumulative learning made possible? At present, no model of developing competences is being worked on. Is hierarchization possible?

• Does a linkage take place with the results of PISA 2006 and with the European Qualification Framework (EQF)?

• How are the two levels of complexity adjusted to regular standards?

• Does the model of competences permit different solution profiles of the tasks?

• What effects do combined scientific standards have on curricula, teaching and teacher training (combined subject "science")?

## 2 How can the achievement of science education standards be assessed, and what function does assessment have?

The driving force behind the introduction of standards is the Ministry of Education.

The moderate results of the programs for international student assessments such as TIMSS and PISA have been discussed broadly in public and have put pressure on the Ministry. Compared to the year 2000, PISA brought weaker results throughout in 2003, which led to a slipping in the ranking of the countries from eighth to nineteenth in science. The function of standards is seen as an important instrument to score better in international comparison in the future.

The compliance with standards is to be examined on the basis of the existing school administrative structure. Test administration as well as evaluation occur at schools using specially trained teachers and will be guided by the Board of School control. Electronic data processing will take place centrally. The data obtained in the assessments will be available to pupils (individual diagnostic), to teachers (for their classes), to school management (data from their own school only) and to the school administration (aggregated data only). At regular intervals, a certain proportion of the pupils will be tested nationwide (system monitoring). Further, a freely accessible task pool will be built up, which should show clearly the purposes behind the standards.

The consequences for pupils who do not accomplish the given achievements have not been specified yet by the educational administration. Will it be for pupils, teachers, school; a 'promotion-model' similar to that used in some Scandinavian countries, where weak results lead to support or a 'market-model as in the US, where weak results can lead to a reduction of resources). Moreover, it has still not been decided whether or not, there will be a connection between the achievement of the standards-tests and the school marks.

Whether instruction quality and diagnostic competence can be raised by standards, will depend on the quality of the tasks (different ways of solution, assistance in realizing them in the classroom, assistance in interpreting data, etc.). Are standards to have a character of challenge and the character of a threat? If the learning culture is to be raised by standards – which is emphasized by the school administration – it is necessary to introduce 'opportunity-to-learn'-standards (class size, scale of foreign pupils, conditions of classroom work, location of the school, intensity of selection etc.).

## 3 What side-effects of testing standards are feared or observed?

A study – commissioned by the Ministry of Education – shows the following results (BMBWK, 2005a). 1000 secondary schoolteachers, who were involved in the development of standards in German, English and Mathematics were questioned.

The positive points raised included:
• Useful instrument for guaranteeing quality
• Goals of schools become more transparent
• More equal opportunities in school transitions.

The most important negative points were:
• Possible instrument of control and discipline of teachers
• Focus on results might neglect the dimension of the process of instruction and educational achievement
• Uncertainty on how to integrate standards into instruction.

The author recently held an advanced training seminar with 15 biology teachers about the introduction of standards in natural sciences. There was some hostility to the idea, and the following points were made:
• 'Teaching to the test'
• Unclear connection between school marks and standard examinations
• Misuse for school-rankings
• Control of the teachers
• Centralized final examinations
• Fewer liberties in the realisation of learning objectives
• Might push a narrowed concept of education (social, democratic, emotional aspects would be neglected)
• Limited integration of teachers into the standard development process (top-down).

These teachers were confronted with the ideas of standards for the first time, and with more information and preparation, their fear and opposition could be alleviated.

# 4    Can standards be implemented without centralized assessment?

The question arises about what goals should be reached by introducing standards.

If focus is put on comparability, centralized assessment will be inevitable. If the aspect of support is in the centre of attention, diagnostic quality, support of the weaker pupils, pupil-centred achievement examinations will become more important.

The motivation of teachers to integrate standards in their instruction will depend on which positive aspects (support in instruction and its preparation, transparency of achievement requirements etc.) they are able to see for themselves. Since, at present, it is not yet clear what the consequences of standard measurements will be, scepticism prevails among teachers.

According to statements of members of the Ministry of Education, standards should neither be used as an instrument for grading pupils, nor for rankings (BMBWK, 2005b).

The periodic examination of a certain proportion of all schools should assist the school administration. The standards should secure more readily the realization of the curriculum. Support systems (school supervision, educational institutes for advanced teacher training, educational offices) should make coordinated planning and realization of educational standards possible.

# References

BMBWK (2005a) *Bildungsstandards aus der Sicht der Anwender: Evaluation der Pilotphase I zur Umsetzung nationaler Bildungsstandards in der Sekundarstufe I* H. Freudenthaler, H. and Specht,W. Zentrum für Schulentwicklung, Graz-Klagenfurt, Abteilung Evaluation und Schulforschung. Graz: ZSE-Report; Nr. 69.

BMBWK (2005b) *Mathematik-Bildungsstandards – Eine Initiative von Bildungs-ministerin Elisabeth Gehrer.* http://www.bmbwk.gv.at/schulen/unterricht/ba/bildungsstandards_mathe.xml.

Bybee, R. W. (2002) Scientific Literacy – Mythos oder Realität? In W.Gräber, P. Nentwig, T. Koballa and R. Evans (eds) *Scientific Literacy. Der Beitrag der Naturwissenschaften zur allgemeinen Bildung.* Opladen: Leske + Budrich.

CMEC (1997) *Common Framework of Science Outcomes.* Council of Ministers of Education, Canada (CMEC) http://www.cmec.ca/science/framework/

KMK (2005) *Bildungsstandards im Fach Biologie für den Mittleren Schulab-schluss.* München: Luchterhand. http://www.kmk.org/schul/Bildungsstandards/Biologie_MSA_16-12-04.pdf

Lackner, J. and Timischl, W. (2005) *Bildungsstandards im Bereich der Berufsbil-dung.* Informationsvortrag im Rahmen der Auftaktveranstaltung des bmbwk. Wien, 27.4.2005.

Lucyshyn, J. (2003) *Bildungsstandards – Ein weiterer Qualitätssprung für das österreichische Bildungswesen.* http://land.salzburg.at/landesschulrat/service/standards/Standards_Projektbeschreibung.pdf

National Research Council (1996) *National Science Education Standards.* Washington D.C.: National Academy Press.

Weinert, F.E. (2001) Vergleichende Leistungsmessung in Schulen – eine umstrittene Selbstverständlichkeit. In F. E. Weinert (ed.) *Leistungsmessungen in Schulen.* Weinheim und Basel: Beltz Verlag, 17-31.

# Chapter 4

## Science education standards and science assessment in Denmark

*Jens Dolin*

*IFPR, University of Southern Denmark, 5230 Odense, Denmark*

### Introduction

There is a large gap in standards and assessment culture between Danish compulsory schools (which include primary and lower secondary classes) and the country's upper secondary school system. Thus, in order to give an adequate picture of standards and assessments in science education in Denmark, one has to examine both the compulsory school, the Folkeskole (i.e. the people's school), and the voluntary upper secondary schools with their two lines which include science. The latter have General Gymnasium (a general, academic oriented education catering for *ca.* 35 % of the year group in 2003, often just called the Gymnasium), and the Technical Gymnasium (oriented toward science and technical- related education and catering for *ca.* 4 % of the year group in 2003). In addition to this, we have commercial upper-secondary schools (15 % of the cohort) without any provision for science subjects, and a vocational training system.

The school systems are being subjected to radical changes these years, ostensibly to help students to better deal with the global challenges, the information society, new concepts of knowledge etc. These changes to the entire school system make it difficult to give an adequate picture of the present situation. It is more important to point out some fundamental aspects and the predominant directions of change.

### General information about the Folkeskole – and some new trends

The Folkeskole was founded in 1814. Since then, it has been regarded as one of the most important bearers of Danish identity and culture. It is a 9-year comprehensive school with a 10th year as an option. The preamble to the Act on the Folkeskole emphasized until 2006 that the Folkeskole shall

*… contribute to the all-round personal development of the individual pupil,*
*… endeavour to create such opportunities … that the pupils develop awareness, imagination and an urge to learn, so that they acquire confidence in their own possibilities and a background for forming independent judgements and for taking personal action,*

*... familiarise the pupils with Danish culture and contribute to their understanding of other cultures and of man's interaction with nature. The school shall prepare the pupils for active participation, joint responsibility, rights and duties in a society based on freedom and democracy.*

Thus the focus for the Folkeskole was on the development of the individual student and the preparation for participation in society. The so-called *Bildung* tradition still has a profound influence on the aims and everyday practice. Many critics claim that these values are obtained at the expense of specific professional knowledge. A new preamble to the Act on the Folkeskole passed in 2006 stresses proficiency aspects and the preparation for further education.

It is important to stress that the Folkeskole is not (or rather has traditionally not been) an examination-oriented school. It is a 9-year unified school system and the students are normally kept together throughout this time in the same school and often with many of the same teachers. The classes are unstreamed, the students being placed in a class according to age and not ability, and normally the children attend the local school. It is the class teacher (deep in the Danish school tradition) who has the main responsibility for monitoring and supporting the academic and social development of the pupils. School failure is an almost non-existing phenomenon in the Folkeskole.

About 13% of all students are matriculated in private schools, which follow the same sets of roles as the Folkeskole.

The Danish Parliament takes the decisions governing the overall aims of education, and the Minister of Education and the Ministry officials set the targets for each subject. However, the municipalities and schools decide how to reach these targets. Nevertheless, nearly all schools choose to use the centrally prepared guidelines as the basis for their curricula.

In forms 1–7, formative evaluations are given either in writing – or more usually – verbally in the form of meetings in which the pupil, parents and class teacher all take part. In forms 8–11, this information includes a written report, at least twice a year, giving the pupil's attainment in academic achievement and in application. This only applies to the leaving examination subjects, where pupils are marked on a 10-point scale. A new 7-point scale is being used from 2006.

Standard rules for all examinations ensure uniformity throughout the country. The examinations are both oral and written. An examiner, a teacher from another school, witnesses the oral examinations. The written papers are set and marked centrally. Examinations have not been, until now, compulsory. Students were free to decide whether or not to sit for them, after consultations with the school – in practice, their own teachers – and their parents. A new Act, which makes it mandatory to be examined, was passed by Parliament in 2006. Each examination subject is assessed on its own merit. Results cannot be summed up to give an overall mark.

The background to the changes reflects the assessment culture in the Folkeskole which has traditionally been weak. Most teachers have focused on the human development of the students and on the social functioning of the class, in order to build a strong foundation for the academic performance of the students – and thus (according to critics) give a low priority to subject specific knowledge. This is an attitude that has been generally accepted by the vast majority of parents and politicians – until now! Within the last few years, Denmark has witnessed some dramatic changes in political signals and public opinion. The rather disappointing results of the PISA tests have contributed towards this change, but in a larger perspective one might interpret it as a general shift towards considering the school as a part of the market. Politicians want it to be seen that the taxpayer is getting value for money, and it is more difficult to measure soft values, such as human development or the ability to participate democratically in society, than to see your ranking in a PISA league table.

As a reaction to the poor Danish results in PISA 2000, the government volunteered to participate in an OECD review of the Folkeskole (OECD, 2004). A team of examiners (from Finland, Canada and Great Britain – countries comparable with Denmark but with better PISA performances) set about to determine why Denmark did worse than expected and recommended a series of steps to better performance. One key suggestion was to build a stronger basis of student assessment and school evaluation. The government has launched a series of initiatives to follow up the report. Among these are more tests.

## General information about the Gymnasium

A major reform of the Gymnasium (year 10–12) began in 2005. The reform, as a political work, has a very complicated structure and some conflicting intentions. The politicians want to maintain the traditional academic virtues, but at the same time gear the students to the 21th century globalised information society. It put forward as the general aims: Enhanced subject content (professional/academic standard), enhanced study competencies, increased collaboration between disciplines and a contemporary concept of *Bildung*. The aims are to be achieved through a new structure, more interdisciplinary collaboration, new working methods and new assessment techniques.

All students start with a common semester followed by a choice between fixed combinations of subjects (study directions) and the possibility of adding a few optional subjects. Each student must take at least 4 subjects at level A (the highest level)(among which Danish literature and history are mandatory), normally 3 subjects at level B (mandatory: English and one natural science subject), and 7 at level

C (mandatory: mathematics, physics and 2 of the other 3 science subjects chemistry, biology, and natural geography). Natural geography is a new subject containing the earth science part of geography.

## The place of Science in the Folkeskole and the Gymnasium

Table 1 shows the provision of science in the school system years 1–12. The information about the upper secondarylevel is solely related to the Gymnasium. In the Technical Gymnasium, science accounts for a larger proportion of the time.

| Grade | 1 | 2 | 3 | 4 | 5 | 6 | 7 | 8 | 9 | 10 | 11 | 12 |
|---|---|---|---|---|---|---|---|---|---|---|---|---|
| Pupil's age | 7 | 8 | 9 | 10 | 11 | 12 | 13 | 14 | 15 | 16 | 17 | 18 |
| Level | primary lower secondary | | | | | | | | | upper secondary | | |
| Number of hours[1] | 2060 | | | 2230 | | | 2520 | | | 2470 | | |
| Mathematics | 150 | 150 | 150 | 120 | 120 | 120 | 120 | 120 | 120 | 125 | | |
| Nature/technics NSFC[2] | 30 | 30 | 60 | 60 | 60 | 60 | | | | 60 | | |
| Physics/chem[3] | | | | | | | 60 | 60 | 90 | | | |
| Physics | | | | | | | | | | 75 | | |
| Chemistry | | | | | | | | | | | 125[6] | |
| Geography[4] | | | | | | | 30 | 60 | 30 | 150[5] | | |
| Biology | | | | | | | 60 | 60 | 30 | | | |
| Total Science subjects[7] | 120 | | | 180 | | | 480 | | | 410 | | |
| Total humanistic subjects | 1000 | | | 955 | | | 1320 | | | | | |
| Total practical/creative subjects | 430 | | | 690 | | | 325 | | | | | |
| Class time | 70 | | | 70 | | | 85 | | | | | |

Figure 1:    The provision of science in Danish schools

The recent reform of the Gymnasium had the explicit purpose of strengthening the status of the natural sciences. However, the structure with its very complicated mixture of a common entry and later grouping in study lines, making it very difficult to decide whether the reform actually has given more muscles to science or not. Indeed, one can always interpret the meaning of the word 'strengthen' in many ways. Does it mean that more students are having more lessons in science subjects? Or that more students are having science at a higher level? Or that all students are having a certain minimum (higher than before)? Or does it mean something else? Maybe a more literacy-orientated science? Or maybe, on the contrary, more traditional science in order to focus on further education?

The experiences from the first year of the reform indicate that the students choice of study line results in fewer students taking science (especially physics) at either B or A-levels.

## The standards in science

The standards in science reflect the Danish *bildung* tradition. We do not have a fixed curriculum at any level or any authorized textbooks. Science education is steered by goals for the different levels and subjects and by some content demands, the more specific the higher the level.

**In the Folkeskole** each subject is described by the so-called "common goals". These consist of two sets of texts:

• The national binding goals for the subject, written in general phrases, and the so-called "core knowledge and skills" described for the final grades and for some intermediate grades.

• A guiding course of study with a description of how you can develop your teaching in order to allow students to obtain the core knowledge and skills. Every school has to formulate its own course of study in accordance with the Ministry's guidelines. When confirmed by the municipality these local curricula are binding for the school.

To give an idea of the details of these common goals, we can look at the three science subjects for year 7–9. For each subject the common goals are structured with some very general aims and core knowledge and skills within four areas.

The *general aims* for biology, for example, are (in brief):
Students must acquire knowledge about living organisms and the surrounding nature, the environment and health, and applications of biology – with emphasis on the understanding of connections.

The teaching must take the students' own experiences, investigations, and under-standing as a point of departure, and it must enhance their joy of nature and willing-ness to engage in biology and biological problems. It should develop the students' responsibility towards nature and provide a basis for attitude and action to environ-mental problems.

The *four areas* for the three subjects are:
For biology: Living organisms and their environments, environment and health, the application of biology, methods and ways of thinking in biology.

For physics/chemistry: The world of physics and chemistry (modelling), the devel-opment of scientific knowledge, the application of physics and chemistry in every-day life and society, methods and ways of thinking in physics and chemistry.

For geography: Global patterns, the natural conditions and their utilization, culture and conditions of life, methods and ways of thinking in geography.

Again taking biology as an example, the final core knowledge and skills for the area "environment and health" is to:
• describe and explain important functions of the body
• know different factors influencing the human health
• describe human exploitation of nature and know about sustainable development
• relate to contemporary environmental problems and their significance for human health and the nature.

*The guidelines* for teaching this area mention 10–12 problem areas or disciplines, such as:
• human reproduction and evolution
• different views on nature.

In summary, even the most detailed level allows latitude for the individual teacher and class; the student and the students' activities should be in the centre for the teaching; the practical and investigating aspects of the subjects should be the point of departure for the teaching.

In the Gymnasium, the reform has also meant significant changes. The traditional content demands (such as knowing the laws of Newton) and the traditional *Bildung* aspect have been supplemented with a set of *competence* goals, recommending the formulation of goals for the science subjects in terms of competencies (Andersen et al., 2003). Four science competencies are described (Dolin et al., 2003):

• An empirical competence: The ability to observe, describe, experiment, measure, etc.

- A representation competence: The ability to represent the phenomenon in different ways (graphs, figures, pictures, etc.) and to shift between the representations.

- A modelling competence: The ability to reduce complexity, determine causalities, build and use different kinds of models, etc.

- A perspective competence: The ability to put science into perspective, to reflect on the role of science in society, to assess scientific knowledge in relation to other knowledge, etc. (very much a competence formulation of the *Bildung* aspect).

The curriculum regulations for the science subjects (as for all subjects in the Gymnasium) now consist of some competence goals (the students should be able to …), a core curriculum (the central subject specific knowledge, concepts, etc.), and some other topics and problems you can choose among. They put more weight on epistemological aspects of the subjects and on the interplay between the subject and other subjects. This is, among other things, done by introducing a new subject (or collaboration frame) called 'general study competence'. All subjects must give 10% of their lessons to this new 'subject', which is mainly a frame for cross-curricular teaching with an epistemological and methodological aim, and with teaching organised very much as projects. Here the teachers (and the students) should be able to answer questions, for example, How can the subject contribute towards the examination of climate change or Life on Mars?

As an example, the goals for Physics C are:

The students should:
- know and be able to use simple models which qualitatively or quantitatively explains different natural phenomenon

- be able,by using examples, to put the contribution of physics into perspective, namely to understand natural phenomena and to understand developments in technology and science

- be able to describe and carry out simple qualitative and quantitative experiments, including the formulation and falsification of hypothesises

- be able to present experimental data in an appropriate way and to treat them in order to uncover simple mathematical connections

- be able to work with texts from the media, including identifying the specific scientific arguments

- be able to communicate an issue with a scientific content to a specific target group.

About 60 % of the total time in Physics C must be used on the three core curriculum areas:

1. Physics' contributions to the modern world picture (fundaments aspects of the universe, the earth as a planet in the solar system, the atomic explanation of different properties of matter)

2. Energy (energy conversion, different forms for energy, a quantitative treatment of a least one energy conversion)

3. Sound and light.

All students must in the first semester take a new foundation course in the natural sciences (the basic science course) There is no fixed academic content for this course, and emphasis is on epistemological and investigating issues. One of the main purposes of the course is to open the students' eyes to the possibilities and limitations of science, so they can appreciate how crucial it is to be familiar with and to understand the way natural scientists think and reason.

The reform documents mention some didactical principles, which the teacher has to follow (for example, students shall be given possibilities to experience physics as exiting, relevant and interesting). Generally speaking, the reform has given more degrees of freedom for the content of the courses and fewer degrees of freedom for pedagogical organization of the lessons.

## Assessment and examinations in science

As mentioned earlier, an OECD report has judged that the assessment culture in the Folkeskole is weak. However, the evidence for this claim was itself weak, but it more or less expresses the general opinion amongst some politicians and policy makers. But with some caution one may say, that so far the assessment has mostly been *formative assessment* of the instruction in order to improve teaching. The evaluation of the individual student's attainment has not been explored in depth. Teachers have evaluated students on the basis of a general impression and occasional tests. Much of the work is practical and project-oriented, and some importance has been given to the written assignments (often group based).

For the present, *the final examination* in science is an integrated examination in biology and physics/chemistry. It is a combined written and practical/oral examination. The written part consists of two sections each of 30 minutes duration with externally prepared assignments in the two subjects. No aids are allowed. The answers are marked externally. Schools can choose between two different forms for practical/oral examination. Version A is a two-hour work assignment involving both practical and theoretical aspects and with both biological and physics/chemical problems. While the student works on solving the problem, the teacher and the examiner (from another school) talk with the student in order to judge the student's understanding and use of concepts etc. Version B allows the student a day to prepare a known question followed by a 20 minutes conversation.

However, the assessment and examination system in the Folkeskole is under change. The government has introduced regular tests. In future, students will be tested, for the first time, by centrally designed problems in year 2 (Danish reading skills), year 3 (mathematics) etc. The first prescribed test in natural science, however, is interestingly enough at year 8. The guiding examples have so far been awful – simple computer based multiple choice questions which only test (more or less) rote learning.

The Gymnasium is by tradition more assessment and examination-oriented. The students are assessed (and given marks) in all subjects three times a year. Formal assessment is based on oral presentations, written tests, assignments (homework), and more process-oriented tools such as a portfolio. Subjects on C (lowest) and B (middle) levels are examined orally (with examiners from other schools), while the A level subjects are examined by written tests (centrally set and marked) and an oral examination. The exact format varies from subject to subject. For example, for

Physics C, the teacher, at the end of the year, works out a list of the issues that have been taught, and the ministry-appointed examiner must ensure that they are within the curriculum regulations. The student draws a question from the list and has 24 hours to prepare a presentation. The examination time is 24 minutes. The first 8 minutes is for the student's presentation and the last 16 minutes are a conversation where the teacher can include material relevant for the question.

For Physics B, there is first a 1½ hour session in the laboratory where the students work in groups with known experiments. The teacher and the examiner talk with each student during this work about both the practical problems and theoretical aspects. This is followed by a 24-minute individual, oral examination after the student has been allowed 24 minutes for preparation. The content of the oral part is different from the practical part.

For Physics A, there is a 5 hour written examination, based on the core curriculum. The oral examination is similar to Physics B, except that the laboratory work is for 2 hours.

## Functions and side-effects of the testing system

The official purpose of the formative assessment is to improve instruction and learning. The official purpose of the summative assessments and the examination is to evaluate the students' outcome of the education. An obvious – and official – function of final grades in the Gymnasium is as a mechanism of selection. The transition to tertiary level education is regulated by the final grades from the Gymnasium. Some studies demand certain subjects at middle or maximum level (B or A), passed with a minimum grade. The hope is to steer the students in certain – science orientated – directions, in order to compensate for the decline in the student interest in science related subjects.

But there are, of course, some other less official purposes. One of the most obvious is caused by the fact that summative assessment on one level can serve as formative assessment on another level. The examination results for the students in a class could, for instance, serve as an indicator for the teacher's teaching capability. This is not the case in Denmark on any level – at the moment. But you do see tendencies opening up for a closer link between student performance and individual teacher evaluation. However, the summative formative connection has been established on the school level (inspired by UK). The mean final grades for students in a school are now publicly accessible on the internet in order to facilitate the parents' free choice of school.

It is obviously a good idea to enhance the evaluation culture in the classroom. But there is a danger that more emphasis on summative assessment could be at the expense of some of the present good and productive sides of science education. Although some teachers in science are still rather transmissively orientated, the constructivist wave has been a strong influence in science education in Denmark. Many teachers work with a modern, often cross-curricular content, and with many alternative pedagogical approaches to science education such as an emphasis on language, role play, alternative written assignments, use of a portfolio, etc.). We have built a solid tradition for project-oriented work in science, and most important, we have founded the teaching on a practical, experimental approach. There is a great danger that we will see a backwash effect following the introduction of new tests in the Folkeskole. In meetings with science teachers throughout Denmark you hear how the test examples, recently published on the internet, makes them put more emphasis on the content areas covered by the test, and change their focus toward facts and the measurable. An increased focus on assessment *of* learning leads teachers to *teach for the exams* instead of *teaching and assessing for learning*.

As an overriding tendency you see a shift from the German/Nordic *didactic tradition* towards the Anglo-American *curriculum tradition* (Westbury, 1999). In didactic-oriented classrooms teachers autonomously interpret and translate the curriculum to make it fit to the specific class and the specific students in order to facilitate their *Bildung*. In curriculum-orientated classrooms teachers are seen as local implementers for the politically determined curriculum. In this tradition, one does not put particular weight on the transformation of the curriculum to the students, but one will rather understand curriculum as a relatively objective content to be presented for the students in a way so they are able to learn it. In such a light it might be easier to consider teaching as a societal service one can evaluate through tests of students.

## Problems and contradictions within assessment of science

The debate about the aims and the standards of the school has been sharp and there are conflicting opinions about the changes. The debate was largely initiated by the PISA results concerning reading and science literacy, which were relatively disappointing.

On one hand, new learning theories (situated cognition, communities of practice, etc.) and the more innovative parts of the business world argue for more creativity, more openness between school and society, new learning processes, focus on professional and personal competencies, etc. On the other hand, more conservative forces, and in Denmark these include many educational policymakers (among whom you can count the Minister of Education!), want to draw the teaching towards "the good old days". You see a new "back to basics" wave, with emphasis on rote learning, canonical content, solving the equations, more discipline, etc. Teachers are left with the task of developing the students' competencies in a broad sense and trying to ensure that the students perform better in the PISA test – all at the same time!

These contradictions are likewise expressed in the test system. Science teachers have built up experience, over many years, of formative evaluation, evaluation of collaborative processes, evaluation of complex competencies, etc. Instead of using this great source of experience in the reforms, the Government is forbidding collective examinations for the whole education system, more or less as an ideological action. On one hand, multiple-choice tests are being introduced at ever lower grades. Yet, on the other hand, the educational aims are expressed in broad competence terms.

It is a fundamental problem that the more you orientate the aims of science towards competencies, the more difficult it is to assess these competencies within the school system. With a sociocultural approach to teaching and learning, you aim to teach students to be able to deal with everyday situations involving science. But it is very difficult to assess such competencies in a (decontextualised) oral or written test. And we have no evidence (to my knowledge) for the relationship between traditional science knowledge (as tested by traditional tests) and the ability to cope with everyday problems involving science in a scientifically acceptable way. So we have a true dilemma. On one hand, we (many teachers and science education researchers) recommend a science education with a high degree of authenticity (everyday settings, all available artefacts, etc.) and on the other, the system wants cheap tests and a high PISA score.

# References

Andersen, N. O., Busch, H., Horst, S. and Troelsen, R. (2003) *Fremtidens natur-faglige uddannelse*. København: Undervisningsministeriet. In Danish (Science Education for the Future) with English summary.

Dolin, J., Krogh, L. B. and Troelsen, R. (2003) *En kompetencebeskrivelse af natur-fagene*. Nota nr. 2 til Fremtidens Naturfaglige Uddannelser. København: Under-visningsministeriet. In Danish (A competence-oriented description of the science subjects).

OECD 2004 *Denmark. Lessons from PISA 2000*. Paris: OECD Publishing.

Westbury, I. (1999) Teaching as a Reflectice Practice: What Might Didaktik Teach Curriculum? In: I. Westbury, S. Hopmann,. and K, Riquarts, (Eds.) *Teaching as a Reflective Practice. The German Didatik Tradition*. Mahwah, New Jersey, London: Lawrence Erlbaum Associates.

# Chapter 5

# How standards in science education are set and monitored in the English education system

*Robin Millar*

*Department of Educational Studies, University of York, York, YO10 5DD, UK*

## Introduction

The English education system, like many other national education systems, has a set of mechanisms for specifying the science curriculum that is offered to students at different ages, and monitoring its outcomes in terms of students' learning.

In approaching the question of how standards in science education are set and monitored, the distinction used in the TIMSS surveys (Robitaille, 1993) between the *intended* curriculum, the *implemented* curriculum and the *attained* curriculum provides a useful framework. As regards the *intended* curriculum, 'standards' relate to the content and emphasis of the science programme, the way in which its consistency and quality are ensured from school to school. 'Standards' of the *implemented* curriculum would then refer to the quality of the science programme actually experienced by students, including its match to the intended curriculum, and the ways in which this is monitored and maintained. Finally, there are the 'standards' of the *attained* curriculum, the knowledge and skills that students actually acquire as a result of following the programme of study provided, and the extent to which these meet our expectations.

To set the discussion of these in context, however, it may be useful first to outline the structure of the science curriculum in English schools.

## Background: the school science curriculum in England

Since the introduction in 1989 of a National Curriculum, all school students in England are required to study science from the age of 5 (when they enter primary school) to 16 (when they take a national examination, the General Certificate of Secondary education (GCSE) which marks the end of the compulsory phase of education). In the two years of upper secondary school, students who continue with academic study have a free choice of (usually) four subjects in the first year. They can choose at the end of the first year to take an Advanced Subsidiary level (AS-level) General Certificate of Education (GCE) qualification, or to continue to study the subject for a further year to A-level. The AS level course is, in effect, the first year of the two-year

A-level course, but designed to be self-standing and coherent in its own right. Most students continue with three subjects to the Advanced level (A-level) GCE at the end of the second year (around age 18). Performance in this examination, along with that in any AS-levels taken, is the basis for admission to university and other tertiary level courses.

This is summarised in table 1. Vocational subjects are also offered in upper second-ary school, leading to other kinds of qualifications and courses at tertiary level. These are not shown in table 1, and the focus of the remainder of this chapter is on the 'standards' of the science education 'pathway' that leads towards academic study of science at university level.

| School | Curriculum stage | Programme offered | Assessment of student attainment |
|---|---|---|---|
| Primary school (age 5-11) | Key Stage 1 (2 years) | Science (including biology, chemistry, physics) taught to all students. | Each student given a 'level' (1-8) based on teacher assessment |
| | Key Stage 2 (4 years) | | Each student given a 'level' (1-8) based on teacher assessment and a national test |
| Secondary school (age 11-16) | Key Stage 3 (3 years) | Science (biology, chemistry, physics) taught to all students. Taught as separate sciences in some schools. 15% of curriculum. | Each student given a 'level' (1-8) based on teacher assessment and a national test |
| | Key Stage 4 (2 years) | Science (biology, chemistry, physics) taught to all students. Most take double GCSE (20% of curriculum). A minority take single science (10%). Some schools offer separate sciences to some students (20- 30% of curriculum). | Students take GCSE examination in Science (Double or Single), or in Biology, Chemistry and Physics (3 subjects) |
| Upper secondary school (age 17-18) | AS-level (1 year) | Free choice of (usually) 4 subjects | GCE AS-level examination (optional if proceeding to A-level) |
| | A-level (1 year) | Free choice of (usually) 3 subjects | GCE A-level examination |

Table 1:      Overview of the science curriculum offered in English schools

A characteristic of the English education system which is particularly important to note in the context of any discussion about how standards are set and monitored is its long-established reliance on external examinations (i.e. examinations set and marked by someone other than the student's teacher and not seen by the student or teacher in advance). Historically, examinations in the UK have their origin in assessment pro-cedures for entry to the universities and the civil service in the 19th century, designed to avoid favouritism and the effects of patronage, and to replace these with a more meritocratic selection procedure (Black, 1998: 8-13). Some universities (Oxford, Cambridge, London) and groups of universities (the Northern Universities Joint Matriculation Board) set up their own bodies to produce and administer the tests used to identify students suitable to enter their courses. Having developed considerable expertise in managing examinations for university entry, these bodies (which had become known as Examining Boards) then took on the task of administering examinations for younger students when the General Certificate of Education (GCE) was introduced in 1951, with examinations at Ordinary level (O-level) for 16-year-olds, and Advanced level (A-level) for 18-year-olds. A wider range of organisations, some with weaker links to universities, managed the Certificate of Secondary Education (CSE), which was offered as an alternative qualification for less academic students at age 16, between 1965 and 1987 – until it was merged with GCE O-level into the General Certificate of Secondary Education (GCSE) from 1988.

Almost all of these qualifications were awarded on the basis of study of a prescribed syllabus laid down by the Examining Board, assessed by a terminal examination using an unseen written paper (or papers), set and marked externally (i.e. not by the student's own teacher). Some syllabuses (especially at A-level GCE) included a practical examination. A few included an extended project which was marked by the teacher, and then moderated by an agreed procedure to ensure comparability of standards and expectations across schools. These well-established procedures and the teacher expectations that grew from them are a very important part of the cultural background to the introduction of GCSE and of the National Curriculum. In particular, teachers were familiar with, and generally acceptant of, the idea of assessment by an unseen written examination, based on a clearly defined syllabus, marked by someone outside the school who did not know the identity or the school of the student whose work they were marking. Those responsible for selecting students for admission to more advanced courses, and to careers, were also used to having evidence from external examinations of this sort to inform their decisions.

When a National Curriculum was introduced in 1989, it adopted the GCSE as its terminal assessment, and added tests of a similar type (externally set and marked) at ages 11 and 14. The familiarity of teachers and others with this approach was a major factor in ensuring its acceptability.

## Standards and the introduction of a National Curriculum

A concern about educational standards was central to the introduction of a National Curriculum in England in 1989. Whilst a concern with standards is an almost permanent feature of educational discussion in England, the recent history of the 'standards debate' can be traced back to an influential speech in 1976 by the then Prime Minister, James Callaghan, at Ruskin College, Oxford. In it, he called (*inter alia*) for a 'great debate' about education. One consequence was the setting up of the Assessment of Performance Unit, to measure and monitor the performance in mathematics, science and English of students aged 11, 13 and 15 (APU, 1989). A series of publications by the Department of Education and Science and Her Majesty's Inspectors of Schools (HMI) (DES, 1979; DES/WO, 1981, 1982) were also exploring issues relating to the overall content and balance of the school curriculum, and the place of science within it. One criticism was of the wide variation in content and structure of courses that were nominally in the same subject, for students of the same age – a consequence of the proliferation of examining bodies for GCE O-level and CSE in the 1970s and 80s. A particular concern was the fact that students at age 14 typically chose to study one or two of biology, chemistry and physics in the final two years of compulsory education (age 15–16), and that their choices were strongly gender biased (a much lower proportion of girls than boys choosing the physical sciences). This was seen as closing down career options too early, and losing able students from the 'pool' of those who might go on to careers involving science. However, making all three sciences compulsory to age 16 was felt to require too high a proportion of total curriculum time, as the 'quantum' for each subject had become established as a course taking 10% of the school week. To do all three would then be 30% of the week, with mathematics, design & technology and information and communications technology (ICT) on top of that. The compromise, advocated by HMI and other influential voices in the Department for Education and Science (DES/WO, 1985) was a 'broad and balanced' science course that would require 20% of curriculum time for 15–16 year olds. 'Broad' meant coverage of all three major science, plus smaller amounts of astronomy and Earth science; 'balanced' meant that the curriculum should emphasise the processes of scientific enquiry alongside the acquisition of scientific knowledge. These developments were also supported by the major science teachers' organisation, the Association for Science Education, which had published several reports over the preceding decade advocating change (ASE, 1979, 1981). Fitting all three sciences (each of which, if studied, would have had 10% of a student's curriculum time) into a 20% time allocation for 'science' meant, however, an inevitable reduction in the amount of each science taught. In other words, requiring greater breadth meant somewhat less depth. This, as might be expected, led some to complain of a reduction in standards, and to see the 'double science' GCSE as less stimulating for able students, who had previously been able to cope with more content in the science they chose to study. Indeed, in many respects, this inevitable consequence of opting for breadth at the expense of depth has never been fully accepted by those who operate and comment on the education system – and has fuelled a continuing debate about 'falling standards' of the science curriculum offered to students.

At around the same time, as explained earlier, the examination system at age 16 (the end of the compulsory phase of education) was moving from Ordinary Level General Certificate of Secondary Education (GCE) for the more academic (or higher achieving), alongside Certificate of Secondary Education (CSE) for the less academic (or lower achieving) students, to General Certificate of Secondary Education (GCSE) for all students. For this new examination, subject criteria were published, the first attempt to regulate the content of examination courses at a national level. The National Curriculum was then based on the same 'double award science' model (20% of curriculum time) that had been implemented for GCSE a few years earlier.

# Setting standards: the *intended* curriculum

As outlined above, in the period before the introduction of a National Curriculum in England, the content of courses in the three main science subjects for 15/16-year-olds (GCE O-level and CSE) and for 17/18-year-olds (GCE A-level) was largely shaped by the examination syllabuses published by the various examining boards. Strictly speaking, these did not set out the programme to be taught but rather specified what would be examined in the end-of-course examination. In practice, as these were unseen examinations, externally set and marked, the examination syllabus largely determined the teaching programme. Content was specified at the level of main topics (or divisions of the subject) and major sub-divisions of these. (Although the specification (or syllabus) extract shown in table 2 is a more recent one, the level of detail is similar.)

In contrast to this, there was little specification of science curriculum content in lower secondary school (the age range now called Key Stage 3: 11–14 year olds) or in primary school. Practice was variable, and often shaped primarily by the school's choice of textbook or published teaching scheme. Some of these were developed by projects seeking to introduce specific emphases or approaches (e.g. *Science 5-13*; *Nuffield Junior Science*); others had no declared rationale. Many schools produced their own programmes of study for students of this age, often drawing on one or more published schemes and adding their own ideas to this. In primary schools, practice was particularly patchy and variable and tended to emphasise biology. Improving primary science, and broadening it to include routinely a mixture of the physical and biological sciences, was one major thrust of HMI lobbying in the late 1970s and 1980s (DES, 1983).

Against this background, the National Curriculum aimed to set standards for syllabus content and structure, by setting out in detail what students should learn. In the first version of the National Curriculum (DES/WO, 1989), this took the form of a series of statements about what students should know, understand or be able to do. For example, from the strand (or Attainment Target) on *Electricity and magnetism*:

Students should:
• know that may household appliances use electricity but that misuse could be dangerous (1)

• know that magnets attract certain materials but not others and can repel each other (2)

• understand that a complete circuit is needed for an electrical device, such as a bell or buzzer, to work (3)

• be able to construct simple electric circuits (4).

(DES/WO, 1989: 56)

Each statement was placed at one of ten ascending levels of demand, based on a model of progression in understanding (applying to all National Curriculum subjects) proposed by the Task Group on Assessment and Testing (DES/WO, 1988). The levels ascribed to the four sample statements above are in brackets after each. Children at primary school were expected to be working at levels 1–4 (or perhaps 5); at Key Stage 3 (age 11–14) at levels 4–7 (or perhaps 8), and at Key Stage 4 (age 15–16) at levels 5–10). The allocation of curriculum statements to levels was based on professional judgment, supported by such research evidence as was available of the relative difficulty of different ideas. I will return to the fate of this model of student learning when discussing standards of the attained curriculum, though some of the issues may be inferred from the discussion below.

In the first National Curriculum, there were 17 such Attainment Targets, one (AT1) on scientific enquiry allocated 25% of the overall assessment weighting for secondary school age students (and 50% at primary school level), and 16 dealing with different elements of science content. Largely because of problems of teacher workload relating to its assessment requirements (discussed in a later section), this was quickly found to be unworkable and a second version was published in 1991 which reduced the number of Attainment Targets (ATs) to four, by grouping those dealing with aspects of biology, chemistry/Earth science and physics/astronomy into ATs called 'Life and living processes', 'Materials and their properties' and 'Physical processes' respectively (DES/WO, 1991). The content remained much as before, and was simply re-arranged. Statements of what pupils should understand, or be able to do, were again grouped into levels from 1–10.

The 1995 revision of the National Curriculum (DFE/WO, 1995) made two significant changes to the way the curriculum was presented. First, statements were prefaced by the words 'Pupils should be taught' (rather than 'pupils should know/ understand/be able to') – reflecting a growing recognition that a statutory document could specify what schools were to provide, but not the learning outcomes. Second, the statements were grouped simply by sub-topic at each key Stage, with no division into levels. So, for example, the sub-section on 'Electricity and magnetism' in the Key Stage 4, Attainment Target on 'Physical processes', included the following statements:

Pupils should be taught:

a   how to measure current in series and parallel circuits

b   that energy is transferred from batteries and other sources to other components in electrical circuits

c   that resistors are heated when charge flows through them

d   the qualitative effect of changing resistance on the current in a circuit e how to make simple measurements of voltage

f the quantitative relationship between resistance, voltage and current

g how current varies with voltage in a range of devices (for example, resistors, filament bulbs, diodes, LDRs and thermistors)

h that voltage is energy transferred per unit charge

i the quantitative relationship between power, voltage and current.

(DfE/WO, 1995: 34)

The idea of levels of attainment did not, however, disappear. Instead a set of 'level descriptions' was added, providing thumbnail sketches of the sort of performance that might be expected of a student who was working at each level in a given attainment target. The range of levels was also reduced to 1–8, plus 'Exceptional performance' (i.e. beyond level 8). This approach was also followed in the 1999 version of the National Curriculum. In 2006, however, a revision of the Key Stage 4 National Curriculum came into effect which greatly reduced the amount of detail in the specification of content. The four Attainment Targets used since 1991 are collapsed into two components: 'Breadth of Study' and 'How science works', with the former having four strands: *Organisms and health*; *Chemical and material behaviour*; *Energy, electricity and radiations*; and *Earth and environment*. This fits on to one side of A4, compared with the nine sides of the previous version. On *Energy, electricity and radiations*, for example, all that is specified is that:

In [students'] study of science, the following should be covered:

a Energy transfers can be measured and their efficiency calculated, which is important in considering economic costs and environmental effects of energy use.

b Electrical power is readily transferred and controlled, and can be used in a range of different situations.

c Radiations, including ionising radiations, can transfer energy.

d Radiations in the form of waves can be used for communication.

(QCA, 2005)

The curriculum regulator, the Qualifications and Curriculum Authority (QCA), is currently consulting on proposed changes at Key Stage 3 which would result in a similarly slimmed-down specification of curriculum content.

In considering the level of detail to which the English National Curriculum specifies the programme that students should experience in class, it is important to bear in mind that assessment at the end of Key Stage 4 (age 16) has continued to be based on the GCSE examination – for which the examining boards (or Awarding Bodies as they are now known) continue to publish syllabuses (or specifications as they have come to be termed). These set out the content that can be covered in the examination at a level of detail similar to that which applied to examinations prior to the introduction of a National Curriculum. An extract from one current GCSE physics specification is shown in table 2. All GCSE specifications have to be approved by QCA as meeting National Curriculum requirements. They provide, however, rather more detail than the National Curriculum (and considerably more after the 2006 changes) – and provide for most teachers the template on which they base their own work programmes. They also act as guidelines for the authors of textbooks.

| 1 | identify cells, batteries and generators as electrical sources, and bulbs, resistors, bells, motors, LEDs, LDRs, thermistors and buzzers as parts of an electrical circuit where electrical energy is dissipated. [The electrical symbols for a cell, battery, power supply, filament bulb, switch, LDR, fixed and variable resistor, LED, motor, heater, thermistor, ammeter and voltmeter should be known.] |
|---|---|
| 2 | recall that resistors are heated when electric current passes through them |
| 3 | describe and explain the effect of a variable resist in controlling the brightness of a lamp and the speed of a motor |
| 4 | measure resistance by correctly placing a voltmeter and an ammeter in a circuit |
| 5 | state and be able to use the equation $V = IR$ |
| 6 | describe how current varies with voltage in a metal wire at constant temperature, a filament bulb and a silicon diode |
| 7 | describe how the resistance of an LDR varies with light level |
| 8 | describe how the resistance of a thermistor (ntc only) varies with temperature |

Table 2:    Extract from one of the GCSE physics specifications (OCR, 2002)

There is, however, no corresponding amplification of curriculum content at Key Stages 1–3. To fill this vacuum, QCA published in 1998 a sample *Scheme of Work for Key Stages 1 and 2* (QCA, 1998), which provided a lesson-by-lesson teaching scheme in science for each year of primary school. This was followed by a similar *Scheme of Work for Key Stage 3* (QCA, 2000). Neither of these has statutory force, but both have influenced practice considerably. Many schools and science departments feel more comfortable, and on 'safer' ground when their school is inspected, if they are following the QCA Scheme of Work rather than one of their own devising. And, equally significantly, publishers now clearly believe that only textbooks and teaching materials based directly on the QCA Schemes of Work will sell. So these detailed schemes, intended as illustrations and to help improve practice in weaker schools and departments, have had a significant constraining effect on practice – and have strengthened the already widespread view of teachers that their job is to 'deliver' a curriculum designed and specified by someone else, rather than to be thoughtful professional with a view on what they should be teaching as well as on how to teach it.

All of the preceding discussion has focused on curriculum content up to age 16. So how is curriculum content specified in the upper secondary school? For GCE AS- and A-level courses in the sciences, QCA (n.d.) specifies a subject core that is intended to constitute 60% of the curriculum, leaving the remainder to the discretion of Awarding Bodies. Specifications similar to those at GCSE level are published by all of the Awarding Bodies, again (technically) stating what may be covered in the end-of-course (or end-of module) examinations. The level of detail is similar to that for GCSE (see table 2). These specifications are the most important influence on the programmes of work followed in most schools – and on the authors of textbooks (which are increasingly being written to match a named specification, rather than claiming to be suitable for all specifications).

## Standards of the *implemented* curriculum

Statements of curriculum content such as those discussed in the previous section are, of course, simply statements about what someone wishes to happen. We might then ask what mechanisms ensure that the curriculum experienced by students is similar to that intended. In England, the most powerful of these mechanisms is the use of unseen externally set and marked examinations and tests to measure student attainment at different points. This will be discussed in more depth in the next section of this chapter, so I will make only a few very obvious points here. This assessment model strongly encourages teachers to cover all of the curriculum content, as they do not know which parts will be examined in any given year. And past examination and national test papers (which are not banked but enter the public domain after use) become key tools for many teachers, helping them to develop a clearer sense of the depth and detail to which they need to cover each topic than do the curriculum statements themselves. In addition to the papers, detailed mark schemes are also published, and an overall appraisal by examiners of each year's paper.

The influence of these examinations on practice is significantly strengthened by the fact that data on the performance of students in every school are published annually (in 'league tables') and are widely used to judge the quality of individual schools. For example, the proportion of students in a school who gain grades A*-C in five or more GCSE subjects is seen as a key indicator of the school's quality. This may influence, inter alia, parents' decisions about which school their child should attend.

A second important mechanism for ensuring standards of the implemented curriculum is the regular inspections of schools by the Office for Standards in Education (OfSTED)[1] OfSTED was developed from the former Inspectorate of Schools (HMI) to carry out regular inspections of all schools, using a consistent and precisely specified approach. An inspection involves a visit to the school by a team of inspectors

1 http://www.ofsted.gov.uk.

(which will include some former teachers and also lay-people with no professional involvement in education), during which they observe a sample of classes, inspect documentation on the school's policies and practices, and meet with teachers, students and parents. Until recently, schools were given several months' notice of inspection visits – which resulted in periods of considerable stress for school staff, and often ensured that what inspectors observed was not 'normal' practice. Inspections have more recently been slimmed down, to reduce stress on teachers and schools. Schools now only receive a few days' notice of an inspection visit. Inspectors' reports on schools are public documents, which are available online to anyone who is interested (cf. footnote 1, p. 91).

One function of the school inspection regime is also to identify common issues that might need to be addressed at a national level. In 2001, concerns about the quality of science teaching in lower secondary schools led to the setting up (by the Department for Education and Skills) of the National Strategy for Science at Key Stage 3 (Bunyan, 2006). This grew out of previous National Strategies for Literacy and Numeracy at primary school level, which were first extended to lower secondary, and then to include science as the other 'core' subject of the National Curriculum. In its first phase, the Key Stage 3 National Strategy developed packages for use in continuing professional development (CPD) short courses, focusing on generic aspects of science teaching. A second phase produced similar packages on the teaching of some specific topics, such as forces, energy and particle models of matter. Underlying the strategy can be detected a concern about the knowledge and confidence of the teaching force – and hence about its ability to provide an implemented curriculum of the desired standard. Surveys, for example, indicate that a majority of the teachers teaching physics topics to students in the 11–14 age range have tertiary level qualifications in biology and often no physics qualifications beyond GCSE level (Smithers and Robinson, 2005).

The setting up in 2004 of a National Science Learning Centre and a network of Regional Science Learning Centres (Holman, 2003) is another indication of the importance attached to the provision of CPD for science teachers, to enhance their subject knowledge, their pedagogic content knowledge, and the range of teaching and learning strategies they use.

## Student learning outcomes: ensuring standards of the *attained* curriculum

Finally, then, we turn to the question of how standards of student attainment are measured, evaluated and maintained (and perhaps indeed improved) in the English education system. As has been clear from the discussion in previous sections, external examinations play a central role. These were well established at ages 16 and 18 before the introduction of a National Curriculum. They continue to be centrally important ways of measuring educational outcomes at these ages – and the National Curriculum has also introduced similar external tests for students of ages 11 and 14.

The assessment model on which the first National Curriculum was based (elements of which still persist) was an ambitious one. It was proposed by a working group, the Task Group on Assessment and Testing (TGAT), set up to advise on assessment across the whole National Curriculum and chaired by Professor Paul Black. Many of its proposals were influenced by his earlier involvement in the Graded Assessments in Science Project (GASP), which had tried to introduce criterion-referenced assessment approaches in secondary school science in place of the dominant emphasis on norm-referencing (Swain, 1988). A short report for teachers on the TGAT's recommendations explained that:

*'The assessments proposed ... are like teachers' day-to-day assessments: they are directly concerned with what is being taught and they are designed to reveal the quality of each pupil's performance irrespective of the performance of other students. They rely on clear descriptions of the performance being sought'.* (DES/WO, 1988: 7)

TGAT proposed that student performance in each subject be described in relation to a 10-level model. External tests and teacher assessment would then locate each student on one of these levels for each Attainment Target, thus providing a means by which teachers, students, parents and others could see how students were progressing in knowledge and capability as they moved through the education system from age 5 to 16.

The reality of National Curriculum assessment, however, and in particular the part that was based on students' performance in the externally set and marked National Tests, fell some way short of this ambitious vision. Two relatively short test papers (as were used at age 14), consisting of structured short-response questions, could not provide a criterion-referenced assessment of student performance across the curriculum. Rather the test items sampled aspects of the curriculum. Students' responses to them rarely provided clear evidence that they had, or had not, attained specific learning objectives – and their identification with specific levels of performance was often tenuous. When marks attained on different questions were then aggregated to produce a total score for the student, criterion-referencing had all but disappeared. Levels became little more than the reporting grades for a norm-referenced examination.

Perhaps in implicit recognition of this, though it was not explicitly declared as a reason, the statements of the National Curriculum in its third version (DFE/WO, 1995) were not arranged in levels (as has already been explained). Instead the programme of study for each key stage (age bands 5–7, 7–11, 11–14, and 15–16) was presented as a series of statements about what students should be taught. Rather than attempting to allocate each statement to one of ten levels, a set of 'level descriptions' was provided. These were intended to 'describe the types and range of performance that students working at a particular level should characteristically demonstrate' (DFE/WO, 1995: 49). For example, in Attainment Target 4 (Physical processes) a student at level 5 was characterised as follows:

Students demonstrate an increasing knowledge and understanding of aspects of physical processes drawn from the Key Stage 2 or Key Stage 3 programme of study. They begin to apply ideas about physical processes to suggest a variety of ways to make changes, such as altering the current in a circuit or altering the pitch or loudness of a sound. They begin to use some abstract ideas in descriptions, such as forces being balanced when an object is stationary, or objects being seen when light from them enters the eye. They use models to explain effects that are caused by the movement of the Earth, such as the length of a day or year. (DFE/WO, 1995: 56)

The task for teachers in assessing students was to judge which of the level descriptions provided (levels 1–8, plus 'exceptional performance') best matched each individual student. In this way four levels were proposed for each student, for the four science attainment targets – and then averaged to produce a final teacher assessed level. This then formed one part of the assessment, alongside the level awarded on the basis of the national test taken at the end of the key stage. Both were said to be of equal weight. In practice, as the national test outcome was available before teachers had to finalise their internal grades, the former often came to dominate. And, as with the earlier ten levels, it was unclear how the criterion-referencing aspirations of the TGAT were realised in the testing procedures actually used. In other words, it was unclear what a 'level 5' actually signified in terms of specific understandings, as it could be arrived at in very many ways as marks on individual questions were aggregated.

Nonetheless, National Curriculum assessment levels are the principal tool of government in judging standards of students and of schools, and in seeking to raise these. So-called league tables are published annually, placing schools nationally in rank order of their students' attainment in National Tests and GCSE. These are reported in newspapers and are used to form views about the quality of provision in schools, and in local authority regions.

Unsurprisingly, national data in the early years of the National Curriculum showed an increase in the percentage of students reaching each of the levels. These data were used by government as evidence of the success of their policies, though some of the claims were questioned (Torrance, 2002, 2003; Tymms, 2004). One interpretation of improvements in the early years was teachers' growing understanding of the assessment approaches being used – leading to teaching to the test. But another doubt about evidence of rising attainment is the fact that national tests are released after use, so that each year's assessment uses a different set of test papers. There is no item banking. As attainment gains were well within the confidence limits of individual scores (due to the limited reliability of any test), they provided weak evidence that measured gains reflected a real underlying effect.

*Added value*

As the National Curriculum assessment system became established, concerns grew about the practice of comparing schools on the basis of their students' measured learning outcomes. A large and sustained body of research evidence, coming from work on school effectiveness, indicates that over 70% of the variation in student attainment at age 16 can be accounted for by the variation in student attainment on entry at age 11 – which in turn is strongly correlated with measures of the social and economic background of students (see, for example, Angus, 1993). It therefore seemed unfair to rank schools on their outcomes, when much of this was largely a function of the nature of their intakes.

This led to growing interest in the use of measures of added value, rather than outcome alone. These have been developed and promoted by a number of centres, most notably the Curriculum, Evaluation and Management (CEM) Centre at the University of Durham. This grew out of early work by Fitz-Gibbon with a small cluster of local schools into a national project in which hundreds of schools subscribe to participate in a testing system that gives them more detailed information on the performance of their subject departments against national norms (Tymms and Coe, 2003). The central idea of value added work is that a school's outcomes can be predicted from data about the students' attainment at the point of entry. The first such project used GCSE grades to predict A-level performance. The first stage was to collect data from many schools on their students' performance at the beginning and end of the period of interest (their GCSE and A-level grades). These correlate strongly, so a regression line can be drawn – and then used to predict the likely outcomes (A-level grades) of other schools from a knowledge of their input data (the students' GCSE scores). If a school's actual outcomes are better than this prediction, the school has 'added value' over the period; their students have done better than could have been predicted on the basis of their prior attainment alone. Conversely, a school may produce outcomes that are less good than their input would have predicted. This can be useful for internal planning – and may offer a fairer basis of comparison between schools. A recent study by Gorard (2006), however, shows that the correlation between schools' added value and output measures is very high – and questions whether anything useful is gained by basing comparisons of schools on added value. Several large assumptions are also built into added value measures, not least that the scales on which students are assessed are of interval level (rather than merely ordinal level). There is an untestable assumption – and it would be difficult to mount an argument that it is a valid one.

*PANDAs*

The availability of increasing amounts of data on student performance at different ages in the English education system has led to schools being provided with very large amounts of performance data. The most recent expression of this is the PANDA

(Performance and Assessment) report provided to each school by the Office for Standards in Education (OfSTED) (cf. footnote 1, p. 91). This takes into account a number of contextual and background factors about the school (social class of student intake, levels of parental income, etc.) in providing data on that school's performance in relation to that of other schools, both regionally and nationally, with similar characteristics. A PANDA report contains a large amount of detailed quantitative information, which the school is expected to use in planning its programmes, and which will form the basis for the periodic inspections carried out by OfSTED. Unlike a report on a formal inspection, it is not a public document; the information is provided only to the school itself. The PANDAs are an illustration of how far the collection of quantitative information on student performance can be taken, enabling individualised data to be provided annually to every school, including (for secondary schools) breakdowns of information by department

The overall result of the collection, publication and provision more privately to schools of very large amounts of quantitative data on student performance over the past 15 years in England has been to greatly increase schools' interest in, and concern about, the grades their students attain. One effect has been to stifle innovation; schools are reluctant to risk departing from the known, lest their results become worse. Teachers find it harder to get out of school to attend professional development courses – and are often reluctant even to ask as they have internalised the institutional concerns about student outcomes. The curriculum risks being narrowed down to those subjects which are assessed – and within subjects to the teaching of those topics which are most likely to feature on examinations and tests and the development of the kinds of knowledge that are most frequently tested.

## Intended and unintended outcomes

The mechanisms used in England to shape and monitor the science curriculum, and assess its outcomes, have both positive and negative aspects. Many teachers welcome the separation of roles of teacher and assessor, particularly in 'high stakes' situations where grades or marks awarded can significantly affect students' future opportunities. External assessment also provides greater assurance for many external 'users' of performance measures than teacher assessments – and are, *prima facie*, able to assure greater fairness of treatment and consistency of judgment for students from a range of schools and contexts. Conversely, assessment by external (mainly written) examinations has the significant negative characteristic of giving greater weight to attainments that can be assessed in this way – often resulting in an undue emphasis on the ability to recall information under examination conditions. This, in turn, can encourage forms of teaching that focus on these, rather limited, aspects of science learning.

The aspect of science National Curriculum assessment that is based on teacher assessment sends mixed messages. Student performance in Attainment Target 1 (Scientific enquiry) is largely based on teacher assessment of students' reports of an extended practical investigation. However, the criteria used in marking this have led to similar, rather dull, investigations being carried out in many schools, chosen to provide opportunities for students to display specific features, or mention specific points, that gain marks. In schools, a great deal of shaping and coaching goes on, to help students maximise their marks – and there is little sense that the outcomes tell you anything useful about the student's ability to engage thoughtfully in a practical scientific investigation (which is, presumably, the intention of including the Attainment Target in the first place). (For a fuller discussion of the issues raised by this Attainment Target and its assessment, see Donnelly et al., 1996.)

On the other hand, in some regions potentially valuable practices have evolved for dealing with teacher assessment of the other attainment targets at Key Stage 3 (which are assessed by both external test *and* teacher assessment). For example, teachers assemble portfolios of examples of student work that they think indicate that the student is at National Curriculum levels 4, 5, 6 and 7 – and then meet with others to review and discuss these. The aim is to achieve greater consistency in the criteria being used by teachers in different schools to allocate students to these levels. The work involved is much less than having to collect samples of every student's work. The intention is to 'calibrate' the teacher as a measuring instrument – and then rely on his or her judgment in other cases. This, it is argued (Assessment Reform Group, 2005), leads to assessments of individual students that are more valid and more reliable than external written examinations. The meetings involved are valuable forms of CPD, and help to build up professional expertise and judgment in critically important ways.

In a similar way, the publication of quantitative indicators of school performance has had both positive and negative effects. In many cases, it has acted as a spur to improving teaching. But is can also lead to a focus on specific sub-groups whose performance has the biggest impact on a school's public 'image'. For example, when the percentage of students obtaining five or more GCSEs at grades A*-C is used as a key criterion of a school's quality, there is strong encouragement to focus on students judged to be at the C-D boundary. Whilst this may be good for those who gain a C rather than a D, this can be at the expense of stimulating those performing well above this boundary – and those well below it. From a more general perspective, whilst few teachers favour the publication of 'league tables', many schools find the unpublished (and more detailed) PANDA data provided to each school useful in planning developments and monitoring their effects.

## Can educational standards be assured without external testing?

Historically the English education system has relied heavily on external examinations – seeing these (in line with their historical origins) as a protection against the effects of patronage and other potential biases. There is no discernable move, or wish among teachers and others, to alter this at GCSE and A-level – though some measure of teacher assessment (with external moderation) has also become an accepted norm in both. There is much less support for the continuation of a regime of external tests at ages 11 and 14. Here, many teachers and others believe that the monitoring of the attained curriculum could be more effectively achieved by teacher assessment, based on practices like the one described above – and that this would have positive effects on teaching, in eliminating the periods of revision leading up to each occasion of testing, and 'teaching to the test'. If, in addition to this, there is felt to be a need to use external testing to monitor the system as a whole (and to ensure that the intended curriculum is widely implemented), this might be more economically and effectively done by assessing samples of students in a sample of schools in any given school year – rather than making all sit an external test. Whilst such approaches have been suggested (e.g. Assessment Reform Group, 2005), there is still some way to go to persuade policy-makers that they offer the prospect of significant improvement in the professional role and engagement of teachers and in students' learning, whilst also monitoring the overall performance of the education system.

## References

Angus, L. (1993) The sociology of school effectiveness. *British Journal of Sociology of Education*, 14 (3), 333-345.

APU (Assessment of Performance Unit) (1989) *National Assessment: The APU Science Approach*. London: HMSO.

Assessment Reform Group (2005) *The Role of Teachers in the Assessment of Learning*. London: Institute of Education.

ASE (Association for Science Education) (1979) *Alternatives for Science Education*. Hatfield: Association for Science Education.

ASE (Association for Science Education) (1981) Education through Science. The policy statement of the Association for Science Education, 1981. *School Science Review*, 63 (222), 5-52.

Black, P. (1998) *Testing: Friend of Foe? Theory and Practice of Assessment and Testing*. London: Falmer Press.

Bunyan, P. (2006) The Secondary National Strategy: Science. In V. Wood-Robinson (ed.), *ASE Guide to Secondary Science Education* (pp. 63-70). Hatfield: Association for Science Education.

DES (Department of Education and Science) (1979) *Aspects of Secondary Education in England. A survey by HM Inspectors of Schools.* London: HMSO.

DES (Department of Education and Science) (1983) *Science in Primary Schools. A discussion paper produced by the HMI Science Committee.* London: HMSO.

DES/WO (Department of Education and Science/Welsh Office) (1981) *The School Curriculum.* London: HMSO.

DES/WO (Department of Education and Science/Welsh Office) (1982) *Science Education in Schools.* London/Cardiff: Department of Education and Science/ Welsh Office.

DES/WO (Department of Education and Science/Welsh Office) (1985) *Science 5-16. A Statement of Policy.* London: HMSO.

DES/WO (Department of Education and Science/Welsh Office) (1988) *Task Group on Assessment and Testing. A Report.* London/Cardiff: Department of Education and Science/Welsh Office.

DES/WO (Department of Education and Science/Welsh Office) (1989) *Science in the National Curriculum.* London: HMSO.

DES/WO (Department of Education and Science/Welsh Office) (1991) *Science in the National Curriculum.* London: HMSO.

DFE/WO (Department for Education/Welsh Office) (1995) *Science in the National Curriculum.* London: HMSO.

Donnelly, J., Buchan, A., Jenkins, E., Laws, P. and Welford, G. (1996) *Investigations by Order. Policy, Curriculum and Science Teachers' Work under the Education Reform Act.* Nafferton: Studies in Education Ltd.

Gorard, S. (2006) Value-added is of little value. *Journal of Educational Policy*, 21 (2), 233-241.

Holman, J. (2003) The National Science Learning Centre. *Education in Science*, 205, 8-13.

OCR (Oxford, Cambridge and RSA Examinations) (2002) *GCSE Physics specification.* Available online at URL: http://www.ocr.org.uk/qualifications/GCSE-Physics.html (accessed 01 August 2006).

QCA (Qualifications and Curriculum Authority) (1998) *Scheme of Work for Key Stages 1 and 2. Science.* London: QCA.

QCA (Qualifications and Curriculum Authority) (2000) *Scheme of Work for Key Stage 3. Science.* London: QCA.

QCA (Qualifications and Curriculum Authority) (2005) *National Curriculum. Science. Key Stage 4.* Available online at URL http://www.nc.uk.net (accessed 01 August 2006).

QCA (Qualifications and Curriculum Authority) (n.d.) *GCE Advanced Subsidiary (AS) and Advanced (A) level Specifications. Subject Criteria for Physics.* Available online at URL: http://old.accac.org.uk/uploads/documents/1335.pdf (accessed 01 August 2006).

Robitaille, D. (1993) *Curriculum Frameworks for Mathematics and Science. TIMSS Monograph No 1.* Vancouver: Pacific Educational Press.

Smithers, A. and Robinson, P. (2005) *Physics in Schools and Colleges. Teacher Deployment and Student Outcomes.* Buckingham: Carmichael Press, University of Buckingham.

Swain, J. (1988) GASP. The graded assessments in science project. *School Science Review*, 70 (251), 152-8.

Torrance, H. (2002) *Can testing really raise educational standards? Professorial Lecture, University of Sussex, 11 June.* Available online at URL: http://www.enquirylearning.net/ELU/Issues/Education/HTassess.html (accessed 01 August 2006).

Torrance, H. (2003) Assessment of the National Curriculum in England. In T. Kellaghan, and D. L. Stufflebeam (eds.), *International Handbook of Educational Evaluation.* Part 2 (pp. 905-928). Dordrecht: Kluwer Academic.

Tymms, P. (2004) Are standards rising in English primary schools? *British Educational Research Journal*, 30 (4), 477-494.

Tymms, P. and Coe, R. (2003) Celebration of success of distributed research with schools: the CEM Centre, Durham. *British Educational Research Journal*, 29 (5), 639-653.

# Chapter 6

# National science education standards and assessment in Finland

*Jari Lavonen*

*Department of Applied Sciences of Education, University of Helsinki*
*FIN-00014, Finland*

## Introduction

Finnish standards for science education as a part of *National Core Curriculum for Basic Education* are described and discussed. In the first part of the paper, some background about the Finnish education policy and the country's comprehensive schools is given in order to explain the Finnish approach to standards and assessment. Secondly, Finnish science education standards and assessment policy are described and discussed.

Further, some examples of how science teachers are supported in the assessment are given. Finally, some advantages and disadvantages of the assessment policy in Finland are described. In this paper, the focus is on physics and chemistry education and assessment at grades 5–9 in Finnish comprehensive schools.

## Finnish education policy and its implementation

The Finnish education system[1] consists of comprehensive school, post-comprehensive general (upper secondary school) and vocational education, higher education and adult education. In 2000, there were 65 000 seven-year-olds. About 60% of the students continue their studies in upper secondary school (gymnasium). Typically in Finnish schools there are fewer than 300 pupils in each one, with class sizes ranging from 20–30 students. Therefore, schools often forge close educational communities of teachers and pupils, including parental support and involvement.

The Ministry of Education (ME) controls education policy[2] and the Finnish National Board of Education (NBE)[3] takes care of its implementation. It is responsible for

---

1 A description of the Finnish comprehensive school can be found on the web-page of the Ministry of Education: http://www.edu.fi/english/SubPage.asp?path=500,4699
2 http://www.minedu.fi/minedu/education/general_education.html
3 http://www.oph.fi/english/frontpage.asp?path=447

development of education, preparation of the *National Core Curriculum for Basic Education* (NCCBE, 2004) and the organisation of national evaluations based on samples (figure 1).

According to the education policy documents, the most important features of the common, consistent and long-term policy, is a broad commitment to *a vision of a knowledge-based-society*. This vision is widely shared and accepted by the employers' and labour organisations as well as by industry and their interest groups. Representatives of these organisations have also been participating on the advisory boards of the national curriculum development projects. Furthermore, parents have appreciated education, school and teachers for a long time; even in 1800, when Finland was part of Russia, parents in rural areas wished to educate their siblings.

Another long-term objective of Finnish education policy has been to raise the general standard of education and to promote *educational equality*. In practice all Finnish young people complete the same nine-year comprehensive school education which is provided free of charge (including school books, meals, transport and health care). Learning the science, mathematics, our mother language as well as two foreign languages is required from everyone. Special-needs teachers help those with special educational needs and guidance counsellors give advice relating to studies and careers.

The third general education policy principle in Finland is *devolution of decision power and responsibility to the local level*. The local education providers (local authority or municipalities) have to plan the local curriculum with teachers based on the *National Core Curriculum for Basic Education* (NCCBE, 2004). They can focus teaching according to local needs and decide elective subjects. The local education providers are also responsible for organising the general assessment of schools and use the data for evaluating how well the goals has been achieved and education policy is working in practice. The role of headteachers is important in school development and evaluation and, moreover, in implementation of educational policy at the local level.

Schools and teachers are free to choose learning materials and teaching methods and there are several pathways by which to achieve the goals. There are no national or local school inspectors or national pre-evaluation of learning materials. Teachers are valued as experts in curriculum development, teaching and in assessment at all levels (NCCBE, 2004). The local curriculum is seen more of a process than a product and it has a central role in school improvement. Consequently, there is good and flexible interaction between national, municipal and school levels. *The culture of trust* means that education authorities and national level education policymakers believe that teachers, together with principals, headteachers and parents, know how to provide the best possible education for children and young people in certain region.

The Finnish comprehensive school system is very demanding on teachers, because versatile professional skills are needed in rather heterogeneous classes. Therefore, over 30 years ago, it was decided that all teachers (excluding kindergarten teachers) would be required to have a five-year Master's level University education. In addition to the general education policy, there have been and are several other strategies describing goals for teacher education, such as *Education and Research 2003–2008* (2004), *Teacher Education Development Programme* (2002) and *Education, Training and Research in the Information Society* (1999). These require that the teacher education programmes should help student teachers among other things to acquire: high-level subject knowledge and pedagogical content knowledge, and knowledge about how knowledge is constructed; knowledge about school as an institution and its connections to society (school community and partners, local contexts and stakeholders); and skills needed in developing one's own teaching, assessment and the teaching profession. Science teachers, at grades 7–9 are specialised in subject teaching and usually teach two subjects, such as mathematics and physics They have at least two years of university level studies (60 ECTS credits) in the subject. A research-based approach, emphasising the teacher's pedagogical thinking, is integrated into all teacher education programmes in Finland. The local education provider (local authority or municipalities) and NBE are responsible for teachers' in-service training.

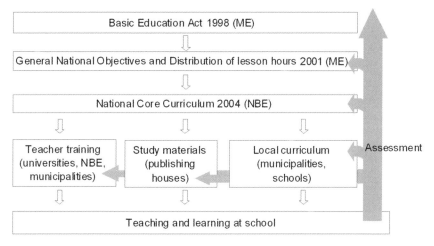

Figure 1:    Education policy, its implementation and feedback loop through assessment in Finland

# Finnish comprehensive school

The Government decides on the broad national objectives and the allocation of teaching time for different subjects and subject groups. The main objective of education in comprehensive schools is to support students' growth towards humanity and ethically responsible membership of society, and to provide them with the knowledge and skills necessary in life. Moreover, the instruction should promote equality in society and the students' abilities to participate in education and to otherwise develop themselves during their lives (Basic Education Act 628/1998).

The National Board of Education decides on the objectives and core contents of instruction by confirming the core curriculum. The core curriculum, general goals and subject specific goals, basic concepts in each subject (syllabus), integration and cross-curricular themes, and final-assessment criteria (standards) are described. In the core curriculum, all school subjects are emphasised giving equal value to all aspects of an individual's growth of personality, moral, creativity, knowledge and skills. The goals described in the national curriculum are, from the point of view of legislation, standards (compared to law) and the municipalities and the teachers have to follow these guidelines. Subject-specific minimum number of lesson hours (comprehensive school) and courses (upper secondary education) are determined by the government. Based on the national framework curriculum, each provider of education prepares the local basic education curriculum. There is not a subject called 'science' in the Finnish curriculum. Allocation of science-related subjects to grades in Finnish curriculum is described in figure 2.

In the Finnish science curriculum, the nature of the teaching/learning process is emphasized:

*"The starting points for physics and chemistry instruction are the students' prior knowledge, skills, and experiences, and their observations and investigations of objects, substances, and phenomena in nature. From these, the instruction progresses towards the laws and fundamental principles of physics and chemistry. The purpose of the experimental orientation is to help the students both (i) to perceive the nature of science and (ii) to learn new scientific concepts, principles, and models; (iii) to develop skills in experimental work and (iv) cooperation; and (v) to stimulate the students to study physics and chemistry (interest)."*

Experimental orientation means here physical (hands on) and mental activity (mind on) of the student emphasising empirical meanings of the concepts (see, for example, Lavonen et al., 2004). Of course, the role of a teacher is important in this process.

| Grade | 1 | 2 | 3 | 4 | 5 | 6 | 7 | 8 | 9 | 10 | 11 | 12 |
|---|---|---|---|---|---|---|---|---|---|---|---|---|
| Students' age | 7 | 8 | 9 | 10 | 11 | 12 | 13 | 14 | 15 | 16 | 17 | 18 |
| Level | primary school | | | | | | lower secondary school | | | upper secondary school, high school | | |
| | Comprehensive school, Basic education | | | | | | | | | | | |
| Science subjects | *Integrated environmental and natural studies is a subject group comprising the fields of biology, geography, physics, chemistry, and health education. Altogether 9 hours/week/4 year = 2.25 hours/week/year* | | | | | *Integrated Biology and geography 1.5 hours/ week/year*<br><br>Physics and chemistry *1 hour /week/year* | *Separate:* Biology *3,5 hours* Geography *3,5 hours* Physics *3,5 hours /week/3 year* Chemistry *3,5 hours /week/3 year* Health education *3 hours/week/3 year* | | | *Separate:* Biology *2+3 courses* Geography *2+2 courses* Physics *1+7 courses* Chemistry *1+4 courses* Health education (1 course = 1 hour/week/year) | | |
| Compul-sory/ Optional | C | | | | | | | | | C+O | O | |

Figure 2:     Allocation of science subjects to grades in comprehensive school [4]

## Science education standards in Finland

As it has already been described, there are actually two kinds of standards in the Finnish curriculum. The general and subject specific goals described in the national curricula are, from the point of view of legislation, standards (compared to law) and they are the guidelines municipalities and teachers have to follow. These goals describe what pupils are expected to learn in general and in each subject during their studies at comprehensive school. Therefore, the role of the assessment or evaluation is to take the measure of how well the goals have been reached. Thus the national curriculum states that

'The assessment is to address the pupil's learning and progress in the different areas of learning'.

As a summary, the goals for science education are the most important guiding principles for planning both teaching and assessment at local level.

4  http://www.minedu.fi/minedu/education/Perusopetuksen%20tuntijako%20(1435)%20engl.xls

However, the need for real standards, which would guide assessment in the final phase of the studies in the comprehensive school, was recognised soon after the implementation of the 1994 curriculum: *The Framework Curriculum Guidelines* (FCCS, 1994). The basic idea in the curriculum of 1994 was that it arouses a dynamic process in schools by continuously taking into account the changes in the environment and the information obtained through assessment. It was planned that the objectives given in the curriculum framework should not restrict teaching and the development of teaching, as well as participation of the teachers in the preparation of the school curriculum and other school level development activities. This 1994 framework curriculum has been, until now, most decentralised curriculum document in Finland.

Unfortunately, the ideas described in the 1994 framework curriculum were not completely realised in school practice and, for example, there was a variation in the assessment of standards obtained by pupils between schools and between teachers in a specific school. Authorities were especially worried about pupils' equality and comparison of pupil assessment at the end of their comprehensive school education. Therefore, it was decided to develop *final-assessment criterias* for the end of the ninth grade and, consequently, the 'pendulum swung' from decentralisation toward centralisation. These *criteria* were introduced in 1999 (FACEC, 1999) and they describe outcomes, what pupils should understand and be able to do, not the manner in which pupils will achieve the outcomes. In practice, the criterias described knowledge and skills required for grade 8 which is in the middle of the grading scale (4 … 10) used in Finland. Consequently, by introducing the *final-assessment criterias* it was hoped that teachers would use an absolute (criterion-referenced) assessment system at the end of the comprehensive school course and that teachers would compare students' performances with a described standard performance. The second aim was to help teachers to calibrate their assessment tools and to evaluate their own scale. The validity of this grading system depends, of course, on the teacher's ability to devise valid and reliable measurements of student performance. Later in this article some practical solutions are described on how teachers are supported in increasing validity.

When planning of the 2004 curriculum, *National Core Curriculum for Basic Education* (NCCBE, 2004), was started in 2001, it was decided that in the national curriculum for each subject goals, core contents (syllabus), *final-assessment criterias at the end of ninth grade*, and *descriptions of good performance at the end of fourth and sixth grade*, should be produced. Therefore, both goals of science education and final-assessment criterias are discussed here as standards.

*Goals as standards*

In the *National Core Curriculum for Basic Education* goals and contents are not allocated to a certain grade but between grades, for example, for grades 7–9. The goals for science education can be classified as follows (NCCBE, 2004). The goals and contents are classified by the author of this paper to the categories which are typically met in science education literature (e.g. Hodson, 1996; Millar et al., 1999: 42-47). The underlinings are also made by the author to demonstrate how a specific goal belongs to a specific category (table 1).

**Examples of goals for learning science subject matter:**
- In grades 5–6 progress is made towards the *basic concepts and principles* of physics and chemistry.
- The tasks of chemistry instruction in the seventh through ninth grades is to guide the pupil in *acquiring knowledge, and in applying that knowledge in different life situations.*
- In grades 7–9 the pupils will learn in physics *to use appropriate concepts, quantities, and units in describing physical phenomena and technological questions.*
- In grades 7–9 the pupils will learn in chemistry the physical and *chemical concepts that describe the properties of substances and learn to apply those concepts.*

**Examples of goals for learning scientific methods:**
The starting point for instruction in physics and chemistry in grades 5–6 are the pupils' observations and investigations of natural phenomena, objects, and materials. The pupils will learn in physics and chemistry in grades 5–6
- to *make observations* and *measurements*, to look for information on the subject of study, and to weigh the reliability of the information,
- to *carry out simple scientific experiments* clarifying the properties of phenomena, organisms, substances, and objects, as well as the correlations among them.

The *core task of physics instruction in the seventh through ninth grades is to strengthen pupils' skills in the experimental acquisition of information.* The pupils will learn in physics in grades 7–9
- scientific skills, such as the *formulation of questions and the perception of problems,*
- to *make, compare, and classify observations, measurements,* and *conclusions*; to present and test a hypothesis; and to process, present and interpret results,
- to *plan and carry out a scientific investigation* in which variables affecting natural phenomena are held constant and varied and correlations among the variables are found out,
- to *formulate simple models,* to use them in explaining phenomena, to make generalizations, and to evaluate the reliability of the research process and results,
- to *use* various graphs and algebraic *models* in explaining natural phenomena, making predictions, and solving problems.

The task of *chemistry instruction in seventh through ninth grades is to guide the pupil in acquiring knowledge from nature.* The experimental orientation must help the pupil to develop manual skills and abilities for experimental work and cooperation and stimulate the pupil to study chemistry. The pupils will learn in chemistry in grades 7–9

- to work *safely, following instructions,*
- to *use research methods typical* from the standpoint of acquiring scientific knowledge, ... and to *evaluate the reliability and importance of the knowledge,*
- to *carry out scientific investigation* and to interpret and present the results.

**Examples of goals for learning the nature of science:**

- In grades 7–9 the core task of physics instruction in the seventh through ninth grades is to *broaden the pupils' conception of the nature of physics.* The instruction guides the pupil in thinking in a manner characteristic of science, in acquiring and using knowledge, and in evaluating the reliability and importance of knowledge in different life situations. The purpose of the experimental orientation is to help the pupils to perceive the nature of science.
- In grades 7–9 the core task of chemistry instruction in the seventh through ninth grades is to guide the pupil in thinking characteristic of the (natural) sciences. The experimental orientation must help the pupil to grasp the *nature of science* and to adopt new scientific concepts, principles, and models, ...

**Examples of goals which affect the pupils' interest in studying science:**

- In grades 5–6 the instruction must *stimulate the pupils to study science.*
- In grades 7–9 the purpose of the experimental orientation is to *stimulate the pupils to study physics and chemistry.*

**Examples of goals for stimulating the pupils to become familiar with society:**

- In grades 5–6 the instruction must stimulate the pupils *to take care of their environment and act responsibly* in it.
- In grades 7–9 the instruction in physics helps the pupil understand the *importance of physics and technology in everyday life, the living environment, and society.* It also provides *capabilities for making everyday choices, especially in matters related to environmental protection and the use of energy resources.*
- In grades 7–9 the instruction in chemistry provides the pupil with material essential from the standpoint of personality development and the formation of a modern world view, and helps the pupil comprehend the importance of *chemistry and technology in everyday life, the living environment, and society.* Chemistry instruction must provide the pupil with the ability to make *everyday choices and to discuss, in particular, issues of energy production, the environment,* ...

**Examples of goals for cooperative skills development:**

- In grades 7–9 the purpose of the experimental orientation is to *help pupils to learn cooperation skills.* The pupils will learn in physics to work and investigate natural phenomena safely, together with others.

Table 1:     Examples of goals as standards in science

*Final-assessment criteria and description of good performance as standards*

In the national curriculum, the *description of good performance* at the end of fourth and sixth grade and the *final assessment (evaluation) criteria* at the end of ninth grade specify, on a national basis, the knowledge and skill levels that constitute the basis of pupil assessment. The *final assessment (evaluation) criteria* determine knowledge and skill levels for a grade of eight, on a scale 4 … 10. The criteria outline what a pupil should know, understand, and be able to do in science and are, therefore, a complete set of outcomes for pupils – they do not prescribe a curriculum.

The *description of good performance* in environmental and natural science at the end of fourth grade are classified as follows (examples are given in Appendix 1):
• science activities (scientific method and nature of science)
• organisms and environments
• natural phenomena and substances around us
• the individual and health
• safety

The *description of good performance* in physics and chemistry at the end of sixth grade are classified as follows (examples are given in the appendix 1):
• science activities (scientific method and nature of science)
• energy and electricity
• scales and structures
• substances around us

The *final evaluation's (assessment) criteria* at the end of ninth grade for physics are classified as follows (examples are given in Appendix 1):
• science activities (scientific method and nature of science)
• motion and force
• vibrations and wave motion
• heat
• electricity
• natural structures

The *final evaluation's (assessment) criteria* at the end of ninth grade for chemistry can be classified as follows (examples are given in Appendix 1):
• science activities (scientific method and nature of science)
• chemical processes and models for them
• properties of substances
• structure of matter
• chemical applications, environment and chemical industry

## Assessment in Science Education in Finland

*Role of Assessment in Science Education*

In Finland, pupil assessment forms a complete system, starting from pupils' self-assessment (evaluation) and ongoing feedback from the teacher and ending the course or summative assessment with tests or course evaluation instruments and, finally, with final assessment (evaluation) based on criteria at the end of grades 4, 6 and 9. Moreover formative and diagnostic assessments (evaluations) are used. The pupils' progress, work skills, and behaviour are assessed in relation to the curriculum's goals (objectives). With the help of assessment, the teacher guides the pupils, becoming aware of their thinking and actions and helping them to understand what they are learning. The teacher also uses the assessment data for developing his or her own teaching. Parents also use the data.

Simultaneously, *The Framework Curriculum Guidelines* (FCCS, 1994) was developed at the beginning of the 1990s education policy discourse focused on assessment (evaluation) as an essential tool of quality development of education. The Government saw assessment as a pivotal element in the new steering system since it 'replaced at the beginning of the 1990s the tasks of the old normative steering, control and inspection system' (Rinne et al., 2002; Simola et al., 2002). Thereafter, there has been no formal control system governing the work of schools and teachers in Finland.

In the *National Core Curriculum for Basic Education* (NCCBE, 2004), several goals are given to the *final assessment (evaluation) criteria*:
• The final assessment (and grading) must be nationally comparable and treat the pupils equally. In each core subject, the final grade is to be based on the pupil's performance in the final phase of comprehensive schooling. Criteria for final assessment in basic education have been prepared for all core subjects. The pupil's performance is assessed with those criteria, on the basis of diverse evidence.

• The final-assessment criteria define the level of knowledge and skill needed for a grade of eight (8), on a scale 4 … 10. The criteria have been drafted so that the pupil receives that grade if, on average, he or she demonstrates the performance level required by the criteria for the subject: failing to meet some criteria can be compensated for by surpassing the standard of other criteria.

• The pupil has acquired the knowledge and skills required in basic education adequately, earning a grade of five (5), if he or she is able to demonstrate to some degree the performance level required by the criteria.

• In the final assessment, the assessment of work skills is incorporated into the grade for the subject.

The several roles of assessment in Finland are rather similar to those described in the US *National Science Education Standards*: assessment is a primary feedback mechanism in the science education system (National Research Council, 1996). According to these US standards

> *"assessment data provide students with feedback on how well they are meeting the expectations of their teachers and parents, teachers with feedback on how well their students are learning, districts with feedback on the effectiveness of their teachers and programs, and policy makers with feedback on how well policies are working. Feedback leads also to changes in the science education system by stimulating changes in policy, guiding teacher professional development, and encouraging students to improve their understanding of science. "*

*Organisation of Assessment in Science Education*

Science teachers have the main responsibility for organising different kinds of assessment activities in the science classroom, like informal and formal assessment or diagnostic, formative and summative assessment. There are no national final examinations at the end of comprehensive schooling. Legislation ensures that at the local level (municipalities), school administrators and teachers have a duty to evaluate their education provision (self-evaluation) and to take part in external evaluations which are organised, for example, by the National Board of Education based on samples.

The Finnish National Board of Education evaluated in 1999 learning results in science (Rajakorpi, 1999). National evaluation was used to monitor students' science skills nationally and also in different parts of the country. There are plans to repeat this assessment in future. Local authorities also used these data to monitor how educational goals were realised in their areas. Some big towns have themselves the local assessment of pupils' science competence organised with similar aims. With these kinds of external evaluations the schools and the teachers are able to get regular updates about the skills of their pupils in relation to other schools and to the nationally set objectives. With the help of this information the schools performing below average have had the opportunity to take the steps needed to rectify the situation on a local as well as regional level. Evaluation findings are not used to brand and punish poorly performing schools.

Mathematics and science teachers have a pedagogical teachers' organisation MAOL[5], which works for the advancement of mathematics and science in Finnish society. The organisation annually prepares a physics and chemistry test for ninth grade pupils (see Appendix 2). Teachers, schools or even municipalities can purchase the tests voluntarily. On average, 30–40 % of comprehensive schools purchase and organise the tests at the end of April. The assessment data are used in several ways. The teachers can calibrate their own testing instruments and the pupils and parents get some feedback

---

5 http://www.maol.fi/index.php?id=161

about the pupils' learning results in science. The results of the tests usually improve the pupils' final grade in science.

It is common in Finland that teachers' guides and other resources such as test questions/test bank, transparencies/presentations and CDs are prepared simultaneously with physics and chemistry textbooks. These test-banks contain typically high quality tests with high content validity and large variation in items (item type and cognitive load) (Appendix 3). Teachers eagerly use these tests in their course assessment because they are geared to the goals in the curriculum.

*Challenges for teacher education and local level school administration*

The Finnish decision of *'standards without centralised assessment'* is not easy for teachers and local authorities. Therefore, this decision is taken seriously in teacher education programmes and student teachers are trained for organising assessments. Moreover, the National Board of Education is organising in-service training for teachers and giving support[6] for local level pedagogical decision making and local authorities and headteachers.

In the general national education strategy *Education and Research 2003–2008* (2004) and several earlier ones (e.g., Teacher Education Development Programme, 2002), teacher education study programmes in universities are expected to provide students, future teachers and headteachers, with knowledge and skills needed for independently operating as an expert and developer of the field. Especially, the teacher education programmes should help students to acquire:
• high-level subject knowledge and pedagogical content knowledge, and knowledge how knowledge is construed

• academic skills, like research skills; skills to use pedagogical information and communication technology, skills needed in processes of developing a curricula

• social skills, like communication skills; skill to cooperate with other teachers

• knowledge about school as an institution and its connections to society (school community and partners, local contexts and stakeholders)

• moral knowledge and skills, like social and moral code of the teaching profession

• skills needed in developing one's own teaching and the teaching profession.

---

6 An example of a web page for organising effective assessment at local level: http://www.edu.fi/itsearviointi/suomi/

Based on these strategies a research-based approach as the main organising theme of teacher education, emphasising teacher's pedagogical thinking, is usually integrated into the teacher education programmes in Finland. A teacher education programme is composed of four large content areas: subject knowledge, pedagogical content knowledge (subject didactics), the theory of education and practice. Teachers use this knowledge in their pedagogical thinking when they are making and justifying their pedagogical decisions about teaching and learning (including assessment) in the classroom (Kansanen et al., 2000). A teacher is seen as a reflective practitioner who has a strong personal-practical theory of education.

As mentioned earlier, all teachers and headteachers have a masters' level degree and write a masters' thesis. The aim of the thesis is to train students to find and analyse problems that they will face in their future work. Research studies give an opportunity to do a real project, in which students have to formulate a problem, seek information and data for the problem independently, to elaborate it with the latest research and to make a synthesis as a written thesis. This small scale research training improves teachers' competence to plan, teach and evaluate.

Guided by the national education policy and experiencing the research-based approach in teacher education, teachers are educated to be experts in their field and headteachers to be pedagogical leaders. This policy gives a lot of freedom and responsibility to teachers. They are, for example, responsible for developing a curriculum and for selecting learning materials for courses, which are based on national guidelines. Teachers are also expected to become experts in assessment.

*Side-effects of assessment in Finland*

Although, in Finland we do not compare pupils with standardised tests that are administered nationally, teachers usually purchase the physics and chemistry tests prepared by the Mathematics and science teachers' union or use tests in the teachers' guides of textbooks. Teachers are using these unofficial tests for calibrating their own assessment.

On the other hand, in Finland we have had experience of too flexible a curriculum and assessment from 1994–2000. As explained above, an ambition of the 1994 national curriculum was to arouse a dynamic process in schools which continuously evaluates and develops the local curriculum based on local experience. A consequence of this policy was a differentiation of goals and assessment based on goals. Therefore, the grading (assessment of the pupils) varied between teacher and schools. This was a threat to the pupils' equality and comparison of pupil assessment at the end of comprehensive school. This was the main reason why *'standards without non-centralised assessment'* was introduced to Finnish education as described in previous paragraphs.

# Discussion

In this paper, it has been described how standards have been implemented in Finland without centralised assessment. These decisions are different to those made in many other countries and they are difficult to understand and adopt to other societies. The assessment policy can be understood only as a part of general education policy. When Finnish education policy is compared to the education movements in other countries from the point of view of assessment, at least two opposing trends can be recognised (Hargreaves et al., 2001; Sahlberg, 2004).

First, the well-known movement, outcome-based education, became popular in the 1980s, followed in the 1990s by standards-based education policies, including centrally prescribed performance standards for schools, teachers and students, so favoured in Anglo-Saxon countries. On the contrary, in Finland, flexibility and diversity have been main guiding lines in implementation of the national framework curriculum and assessment at school level. Especially important in Finland has been the devolution of decision power and responsibility at the local level.

Secondly, one global trend in education has been consequential accountability systems for schools. Success or failure of schools and their teachers is often determined by standardized tests, school inspectors and external evaluations that only devote attention to limited aspects of schooling, such as student achievement in mathematical, science and reading literacy. In Finland, another direction has been chosen: *trust through professionalism*. Culture of trust within education system values teachers' and headteachers' professionalism in judging what is best for students and in reporting on progress of their learning.

As a summary, standards without centralised assessment have been implemented in Finland as a part of general education policy. The role of teachers and headteachers are important in both planning teaching and learning and organising assessment.

# References

*Basic Education Act* 628/1998: Available online: http://www.minedu.fi/minedu/education/translations/basicedu_act.pdf, visited 15.2.2006.

Education and Research 2003–2008; Development Plan (2004) *Publications of the Ministry of Education, Finland 2004:8*. Available online: http://www.minedu.fi/julkaisut/koulutus/2004/opm08/opm08.pdf, visited 15.2.2006.

*Education, Training and Research in the Information Society: A National strategy for 2000–2004*. (1999) Helsinki: Ministry of Education. Available online: http://www.minedu.fi/julkaisut/information/englishU/welcome.html, visited 15.2.2006.

FACEC (1999) *Final-assessment criterias for the end of comprehensive school (in Finland)*. Helsinki: National Board of Education.

FCCS (1994) *Framework curriculum for the comprehensive school (in Finland)*. Helsinki: State Printing Press and National Board of Education.

Hargreaves, A., Earl, L., Shawn, M. and Manning, S. (2001). *Learning to change. Teaching beyond subjects and standards*. San Francisco: Jossey-Bass.

Hodson, D. (1996) Laboratory work as scientific method: three decades of confusion and distortion. *Journal of Curriculum Studies, 28*, 115-135.

Kansanen, P., Tirri, K., Meri, M., Krokfors, L., Husu, J. and Jyrhämä, R. (2000) Teachers' Pedagogical Thinking. Theoretical Landscapes, Practical Challenges. *American University Studies xiv 47*. New York: Peter Lang Publishing.

Lavonen, J., Jauhiainen, J., Koponen, I and Kurki-Suonio, K. (2004) Effect of a long term in-service training program on teachers' beliefs about the role of experiments in physics education. *International Journal of Science Education, 26* (3), 309 – 328.

Millar, R., Le Maréchal, J.-F. and Tiberghien, A. (1999) 'Mapping' the domain: Varieties of practical work, pp. 33–59. In J. Leach and A. C. Paulsen (Eds.), *Practical Work in Science Education*. Roskilde: Roskilde University Press.

National Research Council (1996) *National science education standards*. Washington, DC: National Academy Press. [ED 391 690]

NCCBE (2004) *National Core Curriculum for Basic Education 2004*. Helsinki: National Board of Education. Available online: http://www.minedu.fi/minedu/education/translations/basicedu_act.pdf, visited 15.2.2006.

Rajakorpi, A. (Ed.) (1999) *Peruskoulun 9. luokkalaisten luonnontieteiden oppimistulosten arviointi. Keväällä 1998 pidetyn kokeen tulokset [Evaluation of the learning results in natural sciences of the 9th grade comprehensive school students. Results of the test that had been organised in the Spring of 1998].* Oppimistulosten arviointi 2/1999. Helsinki: Opetushallitus.

Rinne, R., Kivirauma, J. and Simola, H. (2002) Shoots of revisionist education policy or just slow readjustment? The Finnish case of educational reconstruction. *Journal of Education Policy*, 17(6), 643–658.

Sahlberg, P. (2004) Teaching and Globalization. *Managing Global Transitions*, 2(1), 65-83. http://www.fm-kp.si/zalozba/issn/1581-6311/2_1.htm (text/html)

Simola, H., Rinne, R. and Kivirauma, J. (2002) Abdication of the education state or just shifting responsibilities? The appearance of a new system of reason in constructing educational governance and social exclusion/inclusion in Finland, *Scandinavian Journal of Educational Research*, 46(3), 237–246.

*Teacher Education Development Programme* (2002) Helsinki: Ministry of Education, Department for Education and Research Policy. Available online: http://www.minedu.fi/julkaisut/OPEKO/opekoeng.pdf , visited 15.2.2006.

# The *description of good performance* in environmental and natural science at the end of fourth grade

**Science activities**

The pupils will

- know how to make *observations* with the different senses and how to direct their attention towards the essential features of the object of those observations

- know how to *describe, compare, and classify objects*, organisms and phenomena on the basis of their various properties

- know how, with guidance, *to carry out simple investigations* of nature, natural phenomena, and the built environment

- know how to use a variety of information sources and how to compare, by different means, the information they have acquired

- know how to express – orally, in writing, and by drawing – the information they have acquired about nature and the built environment.

**Organisms and environments**

The pupils will (examples)

- understand how living and lifeless nature differ from each other; know how to describe the features of different living environments, such as a yard, park, meadow and field, and identify those environments' most common species; and be able to give examples of vertebrate and invertebrate animals

- know how to describe the differences between the natural and the built environment; they will demonstrate an interest in, and a responsibility for those environments, they will know how to evaluate the beauty, diversity, and pleasantness of an environment.

**Natural phenomena and substances around us**

The pupils will (examples)

- know how to use central concepts and perceive concepts in their entirety

- know how to use simple measuring instruments such as a clock, linear measures, a thermometer, and a magnifying glass; and use self-made tools to make observations

- know how to connect up a simple electrical circuit using a battery, lamp, and wires; know the electrical devices used in a home; understand that using electricity is associated with dangers; and know how to use electrical devices safely

- know about various sources of light, sound, and heat; recognize and know how to investigate light-, sound- and heat-related phenomena such as the propagation of sound, the propagation and reflection of light, the flow of heat, and heating

- know how to investigate the properties of air and water, and changes of state of water, and how to describe the cycle of water in nature

- know how to sort wastes, avoid littering, and know how to spare water, electricity, and heat.

**The Individual and health**

The pupils will (examples)

- know about day-to-day practices and habits that promote health – a daily rhythm, adequate sleep and rest, nutrition, regular meals, daily exercise, proper working positions at school and home, posture, oral health, hygiene, and dressing.

**Safety**

The pupils will

- know and recognize factors that threaten safety in the immediate environment.

# The *description of good performance* in physics and chemistry at the end of sixth grade

**Science activities**

The pupils will

- know how to work and act safely, while protecting themselves and their environment, and will follow the directions given

- know how to make observations and measurements with different senses and measuring instruments, and how to direct their observation at the target's essential features, such as motion or temperature, and at changes in those features

- know how to draw conclusions from their *observations* and measurements; to present their measurement results with the aid of tables, for example; and to explain causal relationships associated with fundamental natural phenomena and the properties of objects – for example, the greater the mass a body has, the more difficult it is to put it into motion or stop it

- know how to perform simple experiments, for example, to investigate what factors affect the dissolving of a solid
- know how to use concepts, quantities, and their units in describing, comparing, and classifying the properties of substances, objects, and phenomena
- know how to assemble the information they have found in different sources, and to weigh its correctness on the basis of their prior knowledge, their investigations, and discussions with others.

## Energy and electricity

The pupils will

- know about different voltage supplies, such as a battery and an accumulator, and know how to do experiments in which electricity is used to produce light, heat, and motion
- know that electricity and heat can be generated from various natural resources, and know how to classify natural resources as renewable or non-renewable.

## Scales and structures

The pupils will

- know how to investigate forces, such as gravity, friction, and air and water resistance, and how to recognize different types of motion
- know how to investigate how force changes the motion of an object, and how to apply scientific knowledge in traffic or moving about
- recognize phenomena caused by the motion of the earth and moon, such as times of the day, seasons, phases of the moon, and eclipses; know about the structure of the solar system; and be able to make observations about the night sky
- know how to describe dangerous situations in traffic and other everyday environment.

## Substances around us

The pupils will (examples)

- know about the composition of air and the chemical symbols of atmospheric gases and understand the importance of the atmosphere in sustaining life
- know how to investigate the various properties of water and know how water is purified
- know how to classify substances.

## The *final evaluation (assessment) criteria* at the end of ninth grade for physics

**Science activities**

The pupils will

- know how to work safely, following directions, alone and with others

- know how to *carry out a science investigation* according to the instructions given, to plan simple experiments, to agree on tasks and the allocation of tasks, and to set objectives or goals together with other pupils

- know how to prepare small-scale research reports, to present results with the help of tables and graphs, for example, and to interpret those results

- know how to perform a controlled experiment and to evaluate the functionality of the experimental arrangement and the reliability, precision, and meaningfulness of the results

- know that physics is a basic science, and that physical knowledge and experimental methods of information acquisition are used in other sciences, and in technology.

**Motion and force**

The pupils will

- know how to investigate various phenomena connected with interactions and motion and to use quantities such as time, distance, velocity, acceleration, and force in describing them

- know how to make graphic presentations, for example, about the results of measuring uniform and accelerating motion; to interpret those results; to use a model of uniform (rectilinear) motion to make predictions concerning motion; and to employ the equation of average velocity to estimate and calculate distance or time

- understand the functioning principle of simple mechanical devices such as a lever and know about applications of mechanical devices and various structures

- know how to use quantities that describe the properties of objects and substances and to explain, with the aid of those quantities, the phenomena the pupils have observed – for example, to compare the densities of substances and to use density in explaining various phenomena, such as floating and the function of a hot-air balloon,

- know the relationship between work and energy

- understand the physical basis of rules concerning traffic safety.

## Vibrations and wave motion

The pupils will

- recognize wave motions and the phenomena characteristic of them, including for example, the production, progression, detection, reflection, and refraction of wave motion

- recognize various periodic phenomena and sources of vibration in their environment, and the properties of those phenomena and vibration sources, and be able to characterize the phenomena in question with depictive quantities

- know how to investigate the reflection and refraction of light and to explain, using rays of light as a model various vision-related phenomena and the functioning of mirrors and lenses

- understand the importance of sound and light to the individual and the community, as in the case of noise, protection from noise, or light in data transmission.


## Heat

The pupils will

- recognize phenomena related to the flow and storage of heat in nature and know how to interpret those phenomena

- know how to characterize basic phenomena of thermodynamics, such as thermal expansion and the heating of an object, with the aid of quantities and experimental laws that describe those phenomena

- know how to use the laws of heating, changes of state, and thermal expansion when examining and explaining thermal phenomena in nature.


## Electricity

The pupils will

- know the principles of using electrical and heat-producing devices safely and economically, and know how to estimate and calculate the costs of utilizing electrical devices of various power levels

- understand the relationship between potential difference and the electrical current in a closed circuit, as well as the effect of resistance on the magnitude of electric current; and know how to make predictions about the functioning of a circuit and how to use a circuit diagram as a model of the circuit

- know about applications such as electrical devices and electronic communication

- know about the processes associated with production and transmission of electricity, such as the functioning of a transformer, and know how to explain the conversion of energy at a power plant and evaluate the advantages and disadvantages of different types of power plants.

**Natural structures**

The pupils will

- know the types and effects of radiation, be able to distinguish between harmful and harmless types, and know how to protect themselves against radiation

- perceive the chain and proportions of structural parts, from elementary particles to galaxies, and know how to illustrate these structures and systems with appropriate models

- know how to use key concepts of physics, such as energy, interaction, and radiation, in their discussions

- understand the conservation law of energy and be able to give examples of the conversion of energy in various processes, such as the burning of wood and the falling of a stone.

## The *final evaluation (assessment) criteria* at the end of ninth grade for chemistry

The pupils will

- know how to work safely, individually and in a group, according to the instructions given

- know how to carry out simple science experiments, for example, to investigate the combustion of a substance, the dissolving of a combustion product in water, or the acidity of the aqueous solution formed

- know how to present and interpret the results of their experiments

- know about the cyclical processes of substances and the phenomena those processes give rise to in nature and the environment, these including the carbon cycle, the greenhouse effect, and acidification

- know about the importance of chemical phenomena and applications to the individual and society – for example, the importance of photosynthesis to living nature's energy resources, and the importance of corrosion and protection from corrosion in construction and the metal industry

- know about substances that affect the environment, and their sources, ways of spread, and effects on the well-being of people and nature – heavy metals and fossil-fuel combustion products, for example

- know about different industrial sectors, such as the metal and wood-processing industries, and about their products and importance in everyday life

- know how to interpret product descriptions, to explain the lifecycle of a product, and to make choices as a consumer

- know how to use the proper concepts in describing chemical phenomena and the properties of substances, such as acidity, electrical conductivity, and changes of state

- know how to investigate the properties of substances and use the results in classifying, identifying, and distinguishing among elements and compounds, such as precious and non-precious metals

- know how to describe an atom, chemical bonds, and compounds, using the proper models

- know how to interpret simple reaction equations and write, for example, the equation for the combustion of carbon

- know how to draw conclusions about a substance's reactivity on the basis of electronic structure of the atom or an element's location in the periodic table.

Appendix 2

## Examples from the annual test prepared by MAOL
## (the Finnish mathematics and science teachers union).

**1.** Choose right alternatives.

A. Particle radiation is
a) a -radiation
b) b -radiation
c) g -radiation

B. Consequence of the rotation of the earth around the axis is
a) a day
b) a month
c) a year

C. Joule is
a) the unit of work
b) the unit of power
c) the unit of energy

D. Absolute zero is equal to
a) 0 °C
b) 0 °F
c) 0 K

E. Boiling point of water will increase if
a) pressure increase
b) salt is dissolved to the water
c) adjusting the knob of the hotplate is turned

F. The gravity on the moon is smaller than on the earth. On the moon the weight of an astronaut
A) the weight of an astronaut increases
b) the weight of an astronaut becomes smaller
c) the mass becomes smaller

G. The effect doubles when
a) the work doubles
b) the time doubles
c) the time is halved

H. The voice is
a) a longitudinal wave motion
b) a transversal wave motion
c) both wave motion and particles

**4.** A certain material was warmed 60 minutes. In the investigation, the results given above were obtained:
a) Present the measurement results in the grid (time-temperature).
b) What is the boiling point of the warmed material?
c) How long does it take for the warming of the fluid from the melting point to the boiling point?
d) What is the form of the material when it has been warmed for 13 minutes?

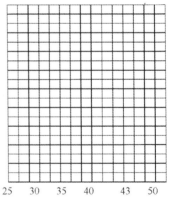

| time [minutes] | 0 | 4 | 13 | 22 | 25 | 30 | 35 | 40 | 43 | 50 | 60 |
|---|---|---|---|---|---|---|---|---|---|---|---|
| temperature [°C] | -10 | 5,5 | 5,5 | 5,5 | 16 | 33 | 50 | 69 | 80 | 80 | 80 |

7. It is your task to study factors which affect the resistance of the wire. You can use the following tools and meters: the voltage supply, the ammeter, the insulator pillars, cables and separate thick copper wires of different length.
a) Explain how you can study the phenomena. Write and use drawings?
b) What you can say about the resistance base to different values of the electric current?
c) How do the properties of the wire have an effect on the resistance of the wire?

Appendix 3

# Typical examples of the test questions/test bank from the teachers' guide of a science textbook.

10. a) Name the parts of the diagram of the power plant: turbine, condenser, generator, pot, power-distribution network, cooling water.
b) What is the task of each part in the power plant?
c) Why is an alternating voltage produced in the power plant?

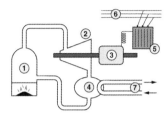

17. Draw the circuit diagrams, of connections the **A**, **B**, **C** and **D**. Which connection will the biggest *lighting power* have when all the lamps and batteries are alike?

a)   b)   c)   d)

26. a) The voltage between the poles of the *metal cable* is 4,5 V. A 0.15 **A** electric current goes through the cable. Calculate the resistance of the cable.
b) A microwave oven, connected to the mains voltage, is used for 5 min. How much energy will the oven use when the electric current needed by it is 2.0 **A**?

31. In the science lesson it was investigated how the voltage between the ends of the cable affects the electric current which goes through the cable. The results were presented graphically
a) Draw the circuit diagram of the used connection.
b) Determine the resistances of cables.
c) Determine the voltage caused by 200 mA electric current?

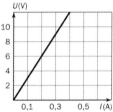

4. Combine the substance and the *ball model* which describes the component of material.
a) ozone molecule
b) nitrogen molecule
c) water molecule
d) oxygen atom
e) hydrogen molecule

10. The carbon dioxide was made with the help of acetic acid and of baking soda in a glass. The burning splinter of wood was taken to the *glass* which contains carbon dioxide. a) What happens to the burning splinter of wood? b) The burning magnesium tape was taken to the same glass. What happens to the magnesium tape? Write also possible reaction equations.

125

# Chapter 7

## Science education standards in France

*Pierre Malléus*

*Groupe des sciences physiques et chimiques, Ministère de l'Education nationale de l'enseignement supérieur et de la recherche, 107, rue de Grenelle, 75007 Paris, France*

### Some clarifications

Although the term 'standard' is of French origin, it is now mainly used in French industry to point out norms or state of a process. The word "*norme*" is preferred (the same as in the German language). In France, we speak of official syllabus (*programme officiel*), official recommendations (comments on the syllabus) or official time schedule for pupils (*horaires officiels*).

The word curriculum appears to be an English word (although of Latin origin) and has no equivalent in the French language in education. The notion of a curriculum is unclear: does it encompasses syllabi, time schedule for students, assessment of students, type of learning activities (courses, practical work), necessary resources (including lists of material, classroom fittings, appliances for practical activities), textbooks, official recommendations?

In the description of the French system I will avoid, whenever possible, the imprecise (from a French point of view) term 'curriculum'.

### The French system of education

Secondary education spans from the age of 11 to 18, compulsory education ending at 16. The table in Appendix shows the general structure and figure 1 gives the time of study in science and technology for secondary students.

| Grade | 6 | 7 | 8 | 9 | 10 | 11 | 12 |
|---|---|---|---|---|---|---|---|
| Form | 6th | 5th | 4th | 3rd | 2nd | 1rst | Final Class |
| Age | 11-12 | 12-13 | 13-14 | 14-15 | 15-16 | 16-17 | 17-18 |
| Level | Lower secondary | | | | Upper secondary For grade 1 and final scientific track only | | |
| Physics & Chemistry | 0 | 1.5 | 1.5 | 2 | 2 + 1.5 | 2.5 + 2 | 3 + 2 |
| Biology & Geology & Earth Science | 1.5 | 1.5 | 1.5 | 1.5 | 2 + 1.5 | 2 + 3 | 2 + 3 |
| Technology | 1.5 | 1.5 | 1.5 | 2 | 0 | 0 | 0 |

Teaching sessions per week on an annual basis. They last 55 min.
The time after " +" relates to half-size classes for laboratory work.
Optional subjects in upper secondary schools are omitted.

Figure 1:     Grades and time allocation in science subjects in secondary education.

# A historical insight into French education

## The tradition of a centralised system

The French system of education has a long tradition of centralisation dating back to the political centralisation exerted by the kings of France and Napoleon. Some positiv consequences arose for the international community: for example, it led to the metric system and a relatively unified set of laws in Continental Europe. However, another consequence for France, and perhaps less desirable, was the development of a centralised civil service making decisions for schools in the minutest detail. A caricature of this type of management is the famous phrase of a minister of education: "I know what all French pupils are learning at each hour of each day". The trend became all the more pervasive as modern societies tended to become more and more sophisticated and had a wider diversity of needs and expectations.

A French tradition inherited from the Roman Empire is the constant need to refer to written law. This state of mind permeates all through our everyday life. One consequence is what is called 'official texts inflation'. Thus most French teachers want a syllabus that tells them what to do in minute detail. The phenomenon is even more visible in the form which has to be completed before an official exam such as the *baccalauréat*.

1  I remember a conversation in 1998 with Poul Tomsen of Aarhus University. Poul read some French syllabi and asked me how it was possible that French teachers accepted so detailed instructions, adding that Danish teachers would take to the streets for that. I answered that, unfortunately, French teachers would take to the street for the absence of that.

*A tradition of change and reform*
Another characteristic of modern French education is the rapid succession of reforms. The French have high expectations of their system of education and the money that has been invested during the last thirty years testifies to that. At the same time, these high and contradictory expectations, combined with social problems, lead to perpetual change. Systemic reforms combined with modest changes in syllabi have resulted in different physical science syllabi every 5 years, on average, over the last thirty years. The consequence of this needs to be considered. On average, no more than three cohorts of students have had the same syllabus and the same structures at upper secondary level (3 years).

It is well known that the political time is far shorter than the educational time. A physicist would say that the system is solicited at a frequency higher than its highest mode. Therefore, it is difficult or even impossible to draw conclusions about the consequences of any particular reform.

Up to now, the changes in the syllabi were generally content-oriented and top-down driven, giving teachers little chance to be listened to and giving them almost no time to reflect on their practices.

## How are standards in education defined in France for the next years?

The law promulgated in April 2005 (*Loi d'orientation pour l'avenir de l'École*)[2] is the result of a large debate and consultation across the entire country conducted during the 2004–2005 school year.

This law is a real novelty for France: for the first time in our history, the choice of the contents, knowledge and competencies to be attained and the measure of their attainment are not left to the specialists alone but are put under direct scrutiny of parliament.

*The legal framework: the principle of accountability*
The law states that a High Council of Education is created and that it contains nine members appointed for six years by the President of the Republic, the Presidents of the National Assembly and the Senate and the President of the Social and Economic Council.

The High Council of Education gives advice and can make proposals at the request of the Minister of Education on questions related to pedagogy, syllabi, assessment of knowledge, organisation and results of the system of education and teacher training. Its advice and proposals are made public. Each year, the Council delivers a report on

2  See: http://www.legifrance.gouv.fr/WAspad/VisuArticleCode?commun=&h0=CEDUCATL.rcv&h1=2&h3=3

the results of the system of education to the President of the Republic, and this, in turn, is sent to Parliament.

Obviously, the law lays stress on the results of the system of education and gives the final decisions on the budget to Parliament. Through this mechanism it, in effect, gives a larger say on pedagogy and syllabi to society at large[3]. The notion of results is now clearly linked to the financing. The instruments to identify results are being built in the present time in accordance to the 'Organic Law on the Laws of Finances', which is the mechanism that evaluates the performance of all parts of the civil service. All this requires cooperation between two ministers, that of the budget and of education and placed under the scrutiny of parliament. A Senate commission has already criticised the Ministry of Education about the choice of pedagogical indicators.

### The legal framework: the content
The objectives that must be attained by the end of compulsory education (16-year-old), and which are laid down by statute, are summarised thus:
"Compulsory education must guarantee an equal opportunity to all to attain a foundation constituted by a set of knowledge and competencies that must be mastered to pursue one's training, build one's personal and occupational future and be a successful member of the society". The core compulsory subjects are French language, a foreign language, mathematics and scientific and technological culture, ICT, humanistic culture, social and civic competencies.

The knowledge and competencies are specified by a decree[4]. It is interesting to underline that for each subject what is expected from the students is listed in three paragraphs, namely knowledge, abilities and attitudes.

The Government presents a report to the Parliament, every three years, which explains how the syllabi meet the rules for the common core together with the assessment results of students throughout the years of compulsory education.

Additionally to the foundation, other courses are taught during the period of compulsory education, for instance, physical education and sports.

### The legal framework: how to assess educational results
One exam is described here in more detail. The law specifies that a diploma (the "Brevet des collèges") is given on the basis of an examination at the end of compulsory education together with an element of coursework assessment and validation of

---

3 Officially, the pedagogy is left to the teachers but the standards of knowledge and competencies and their assessment are under scrutiny of the society at large as they have never been before. It has inevitably some consequences on the pedagogy.
4 « Décret n° 2006-830, 11 July 2006 relatif au socle commun de connaissances et de compétences ». See: http://www.legifrance.gouv.fr/WAspad/Visu?cid=421785&indice=1&table=LEX&ligneDeb=1#

a wide range of activities that the students take part in, including sport. Their behaviour is also taken into account.

Special grades are given to the best students who can be awarded a scholarship (to support them in further studies at the "lycée") on the basis of their results and their socio-economic background.

## How Standards in Education have been defined up to now in France?

The State is responsible for the syllabi (*"Programmes officiels"*). Once published, these syllabi are mandatory for the whole country. Each year of schooling and each discipline have their own syllabus. From the first year of primary school to the baccalaureate, several books of official instructions and comments are necessary to cover the entire spectrum. Many *baccalaureates* exist for the different tracks: general (science, literature, social and economic studies), technical (mechanical engineering[5], electrical engineering…), vocational (industry, services, handicrafts …).

The Minister of Education has always been the driving force for establishing standards. The Minister used to choose a scholar who would then invite experts (mainly university professors and teachers) to form a steering committee. A short letter from the Minister gave terms of reference for the committee in very broad terms. This decision rarely used any of the evidence produced about the previous syllabus.

Separate official texts specify the time devoted to each subject and the class size (e.g. half size classes for practical work (figure 1)). The process of implementing a syllabus reform is shown in figure 2.

The example below illustrates, using the physical sciences for lower secondary school students as the model, what can be found in a syllabus. It is worth noting that the same teacher teaches both physics and chemistry. These excerpts are not intended to cover the whole topic, but rather to give an idea of what an official syllabus consists of.

The introduction gives the broad goals of the syllabus, at some length, and the state of mind in which they should be taught. This introduction is meant to be valid for the upper secondary too.

5  At a basic level.

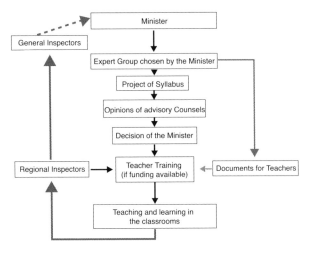

Figure 2:     The process of implementing syllabus reform


Physics and chemistry teaching and learning have their own objectives which are as follows [6]:

1. Teaching chemistry and physics aims at developing, for pupils, elements of science literacy that are indispensable in the world of today and encourage scientific career choices (technicians, engineers, researchers, doctors …): in this respect, it must be exciting and anchored in the everyday environment and contemporary techniques.
2. Through the practice of scientific experiences, it must train the mind to exactness, to the methods of science, to critical thinking and intellectual honesty. With attractive themes and fascinating experiences, it must excite curiosity; it should be noted that scientific inquiry itself is a factor of motivation.
3. Physics and chemistry teaching and learning must train students to reason from both quantitative and qualitative points of view. The study of matter and its transformations is one of the best areas for this where using mathematical tools is less important than detecting predominant factors under the complex of phenomenon. The qualitative way is not the easiest: it is far easier to do a correct computation than to elaborate an appropriate reasoning.
4. It must be open to techniques that, for the most part, are grounded in physics and chemistry.
5. At the same level as other scientific disciplines, physics and chemistry intervene in social, political or even ethical choices. Physics and chemistry teaching and learning must contribute to the "direction of use for science and technology" so that pupils are prepared for these choices.

6 See (in French): ftp://trf.education.gouv.fr/pub/edutel/bo/2005/hs5/annexe4_1.pdf

6. This teaching must emphasize that physics and chemistry are essential parts of our culture because they show that the world is understandable. The extraordinary variety and complexity of nature and technology can be described by a small number of universal laws which give a coherent vision of the universe. In this spirit, the historical evolution of ideas should be emphasized. Provision must be made for the sciences of the universe, astronomy and astrophysics.
7. It must show that this coherent representation is rooted in experience: experimental activities find an essential place, specific to these disciplines. (Not other sciences?)
8. Teaching and learning is largely open to applications. It is necessary that pupils know that thanks to research and fundamental knowledge, essential technological applications were born and, conversely, applications can motivate research.
9. The future citizen and consumer must be trained to use beneficially technical devices and chemical products in everyday life. This education opens up naturally to the learning of safety, protection of health, and respect for the environment. In order to allow the future citizen and consumer to understand future choices for society and be able to take part in these choices, modest notions on energy, history of science and statistics should be introduced in the teaching. These themes are annexed to the syllabus (see "themes of convergence") and precise references are given in this syllabus.
10.Rooted in everyday life, teaching and learning must use the best tools of communication and modern ways of expression. The teaching and learning of physics and chemistry gives preference to observation, experimentation and measurement. The use of the computer is complementary to these practices, being a vital tool for data acquisition, analysis and simulation. Its use should be integrated in the pedagogy.

More details may be found in excerpts related to the 2nd form (15/16-year-old).[7]

Figure 3 shows a small part of the syllabus and suggests a particular balance between full size class courses and practical work with half-size classes. The themes are supposed to allow for more free choice and to represent 20% of the school year.[8]

The introduction of the syllabus explains why practical work is necessary and what types of competencies are expected from this work and the help that can be given by ICT.

Figure 4 gives an example, extracted from a more comprehensive table, of which competencies are involved in each practical work. This is meant primarily to help teachers diversify their approach.

Competencies relative to other disciplines necessary for the study of the physical sciences are specified, namely in mathematics, French language and ICT.

7  The original document in French, can be found at: http://www.education.gouv.fr/bo/2001/hs2/default.htm
8  The reality may be far from this ideal. The time that should be devoted to "Themes" is often used to teach more content in a classical way, paying lip service to the interests and autonomy of the students.

| THEMES | |
|---|---|
| PHYSICS and CHEMISTRY: *6 practical works and 12h full class* | |
| CHEMISTRY<br>About 3 practicals and 6h full class | PHYSICS<br>About 3 practicals and 6h full class |
| COMMON CORE | |

CHEMISTRY
I. "Chemical or natural products?"
   4 practical works and 8h full class
II. Structure of matter
   4 practical works and 8h full class
III. The transformation of matter
   4 practical works and 8h full class

PHYSICS
I. Exploring space
   5 practical works and 10h full class
II. Universe in movement and time
   4 practical works and 8h full class
III. The air around us
   3 practical works and 6h full class

Figure 3:    Example showing the level of detail given in the official program of studies (15-16-year-olds)

| GRID FOR THE FOLLOW-UP OF COMPETENCIES INVOLVED IN PRACTICAL WORK | | | | | | | | | | | |
|---|---|---|---|---|---|---|---|---|---|---|---|
| Experimental competencies | TP 1 | TP 2 | TP 3 | TP 4 | TP 5 | TP 6 | TP 7 | TP 8 | TP 9 | ... | .... |
| I- COMPETENCIES LINKED TO LAB WORK | | | | | | | | | | | |
| Analysing evidence and comparing it to theoretical results | | | | | | | | | | | |
| Determining the domain of validity of the model | | | | | | | | | | | |
| II – PRACTICAL COMPETENCIES | | | | | | | | | | | |
| Obeying order: personal safety and environment | | | | | | | | | | | |
| Acting following a protocol (text or schema) | | | | | | | | | | | |

Figure 4:    Part of a grid intended to guide teachers in ensuring that a range of competencies and abilities are practiced over a series of practicals

Figure 5 shows a now well established layout in all science syllabi: three columns describe the type of activity specific to the discipline that should be conducted in the classroom, the content itself, and the abilities required in an assessment of the student.

| EXAMPLES OF ACTIVITIES | CONTENT | KNOWLEDGE AND ABILITIES TO BE REQUIRED |
|---|---|---|
| Synthesis (or semi-synthesis) of one or several chemical compounds, implying simple techniques such as reflux, heating, filtration, separation. Synthesising a compound existing in nature and, as far as possible, one that can be extracted. Verify with previously acquired knowledge that a synthesised chemical compound is identical to the same compound contained in a natural extract. | 3.1 Necessity of chemical synthesis. Some examples of synthesis in heavy chemical industry and fine chemistry (high added value) from raw natural materials to satisfy the needs of the consumers. 3.2 Synthesis of a chemical product. 3.3. Characterising a synthetic chemical compound and comparing it with a natural extract including the same chemical compound. | *Following a protocol of synthesis, obeying orders (safety, environment), proposing an experimental way of comparing two chemical compounds.* Interpreting, discussing and presenting results of a **comparative** analysis. |

Figure 5:     Part of the chemistry syllabus for 15/16-year-old students. The title of this part is 'The world of chemistry: synthesis of chemical compounds in the laboratory and in industry'

The content of the syllabi is dominated by concepts and little room, if any, has been left to the broader concepts of competency advocated by, for example, the European Union (Commission of European Communities, 2002) and OECD (2005). Due to the very recent changes in the French legal framework referred to earlier, one could expect significant advances, at least for compulsory education.

## The assessment of educational achievement in France

### Coursework assessment
Nowadays, there are very few guidelines given in the syllabi about assessment of students. In secondary education, coursework assessment is the responsibility of the teacher, and thus the tests may vary from school to school. In the year of the *baccalauréat*, a more unified assessment is proposed to students by their teachers on the basis of their previous examinations.

135

An significant feature of the students' assessment is the mark, on a 20-point scale, for each test, with a possibility of compensation between the different exercises of one test and between tests of the same discipline. An overall score is produced for a discipline every three months, often including a variable proportion of marks for work done in class and at home. Sometimes marks are awarded for behaviour in the classroom. This score, together with some basic comments, is given to the parents in the form of a report card. There is one score for each subject and these scores are used by the teachers' council to decide the fate of the student for the following year of schooling.

After the end of the year all marks are forgotten and the process begins all over again for the new school year.

No precise link is made with competencies stated in the syllabus and so there is no way for teachers to know what competencies their students attained in previous years.

The assessment of students is mainly summative and the practice of formative assessment remains sketchy.

The harsh criticisms arising from the General Inspection, have made little impact. Changes to the assessment and the teaching have been very limited.

***Examinations***
At the moment, there are two examinations for the whole secondary education and both rely mainly on paper and pencil tests. Successful candidates are given a diploma in each case. French teachers are fond of such anonymous tests because they believe that they guarantee the objectivity of the marking and help to make their lives easier.

*Grade 9: 'Diplôme national du brevet'*
At the age of 15, students sit the "*Diplôme national du brevet*" which consists of tests in mathematics, French, and history and geography. The marks are combined with coursework marks in all disciplines. The exam papers are set and marked at a regional level. Until now, the diploma has had a poor reputation and has been considered of little value either inside or outside the education system.

A new form of this examination is to be introduced in June 2007. Among the changes, the papers will be set at a national level but the examiners who mark the tests will be local. Also, a science exam can be selected instead of the paper on history and geography.

Studies, independent of this examination, will be conducted to inform the parliament of the level of attainment of the competencies and knowledge.

*Grade 12: 'Baccalauréat'*

The *baccalauréat* is the first grade delivered by the University and allows the laureates to apply for any university in any kind of tertiary studies regardless of the type of track previously followed. For nearly two centuries, the *baccalauréat* has been regarded as the only route to higher education. The French seem to be very fond of this exam and it appears to be regarded as a kind of initiation ritual and cultural landmark at the end of adolescence, made all the more important since compulsory military service disappeared few years ago.

The papers are set nationally but marked locally. The marking is, at least in theory, monitored nationally but too little time is allowed for this moderation and small discrepancies may arise between one local authority and another.

### The myth of uniqueness

Under the same name, many different brands of *baccalauréat* coexist from the best considered (the scientific *baccalauréat*) to the least conducive for further studies, namely the '*Baccalauréat Professionnel*' for vocational studies. Using this one term may give the illusion to young people and their families that all brands are equivalent but one year later, all illusions are lost, at considerable cost to the students and their families. The socio-economic differences are strong from one brand to another.

### Unnecessary complexity

The *baccalauréat* is very costly. Due to the sheer numbers of candidates and the extraordinary variety of the optional disciplines that can be sat, thousands of different papers have to be prepared. Further, because staff and rooms are required, many upper secondary schools (lycées) stop all courses in the first week of June. The loss due to uncompleted courses is high.

### Limited information on performance

Grades (very good, good, and good enough) are awarded to the best students but these grades are global and cannot inform on the degree of attainment of the student in any particular discipline. The achievement measured in each discipline is not published and does not provide information on the attainment of separate competencies.

### Redundant testing

Many tests seem to be redundant and, therefore, add to the cost. An example is the scientific *baccalauréat* (series S with 60% of the global score given to mathematics or science). The candidates sit ten written tests in different disciplines. A recent study by the statistics division of the Ministry of Education (the DEPP) shows that three tests are sufficient to forecast 90% of the results[10]. The importance of reviewing and simplifying the structure of the exam cannot be overemphasised.

---

10 See: ftp://trf.education.gouv.fr/pub/edutel/dpd/ni/ni2005/ni0538.pdf

One obstacle to the simplification is the wide-spread concern among teachers of all disciplines that their subject matter is put in jeopardy if it disappears from the set of written tests of the *baccalauréat*. Resistance also arises because it is felt that the exam helps to exert pressure on the students and make them work harder. One could ask, did they not work in the lower classes or is learning now so boring that students cannot work without strong external constraints?

### The assessment of experimental abilities
A remarkable innovation occurred three years ago when an examination on lab work was introduced into the physical science score, of up to 20% of the total mark. The test, one hour long, is sat during the second semester. The 25 questions of the year are drawn at random from a national pool of 100 questions. Then a limited set of questions, adapted to the possibilities of their laboratory, is chosen by the schools. The candidate draws a question at random from this set. A teacher examines at most four candidates and two teachers are present in the room, one of whom does not know the candidate. Experience shows that this practical test helps physical sciences to be the most discriminate of the science tests, spreading the spectrum of capacities towards the upper end. Biology and Earth Science followed suit in 2005.

The change was not easy. The experiment started eight years ago and spread gradually to a majority of local educational authorities. It took about five years of experimentation and hard work to prepare all teachers for this new exam. The decisive argument convincing the diehards of some teachers' unions was the fact that practical teaching requiring half-size classes and a lot of money could catch the eye of the tax payer. One good way to insure the durability of lab works was therefore to introduce a paper into the *baccalauréat* exam. Curiously, turned the other way, it is the same argument that is used to raise severe criticism against the complexity of the *baccalauréat* (see previous section).

### The baccalauréat is hardly useful for the selection of the elite
Most of selective sectors in tertiary education select students from reports given by the schools, particularly the report cards, which contain their marks. The selections are made before the *baccalauréat* results are known. The preparatory classes for the Engineering Schools and the Institutes of Technology are examples. However, medical schools wait until the end of the first year of the university to filter the best students through a highly competitive exam.

The French Jesuits in the seventeenth century brought from China a system of competitive exams to recruit civil servants. It was quickly extended to students. The French system of education has ever since thought it could select an elite effectively. The highly hierarchical structure of the French society agrees wholeheartedly with this system. There lies perhaps the origin of the practices of assessment in the secondary school: the teachers tend to rank the students more than help them to learn. The 'teach to test' type of learning is always present even in the forms without an exam at the end of the year, although at a lesser extent. The goal for well-informed students is not only to pass the *baccalauréat* but to go to the best tracks, to go to the best schools and to get the best teachers within the school. The need to compete is pervasive at least for the knowledgeable parents and students. The mark is considered by many students as the payback for their schoolwork, not the indicator of what they really know or are able to do. This consumerist attitude explains why the fine by grained analysis of competencies is generally not one of concern for the student, the parents or indeed the teacher.

The system could have endured for more centuries if our modern society had not found it necessary for a majority of the population to have a better overall level of education and training. As long as a small elite was needed, it was unnecessary to bother about sophisticated competencies for all: a basic literacy was enough for the majority of French peasants at the end of the nineteenth century. But times are changing as France faces increasing competition from other countries.

In stark contrast to the secondary schools, French primary schools appear to be less competitive and pay more attention to the development of competencies, including creativity and autonomy.

## The diagnostic assessment

Each year the statistics department of the Ministry of Education conducts two full scale assessments of pupils in primary schools, one at the end of Grade 3 (8/9-year-olds) and the other at the end of Grade 5 (for 10/11-year-olds). The goals is to help teachers to identify which competencies, in the French language and in mathematics, are attained by individual pupils and which are not. Parents are informed of the results of their child. A computer program makes it easier for the schools to extract important information from the data.

These assessments are designed to inform the teachers on the competencies attained by each student, and as training to formative assessment for the teachers as well. Banks of exercises have been prepared and are available to teachers on a website to complete this training[11].

Unfortunately, the local authorities are more prone to misuse this information in the form of league tables than the teachers are to adapt their teaching and assessments to the needs of their pupils.

A few years ago, the diagnostic assessment was also applied at the beginning of the 2nd form (grade 6) but the cost proved to be too heavy.

---

11  http://www.banqoutils.education.gouv.fr/

## Testing Standards

This wording needs to be clarified. One can test standards through achievement of a whole population of students in an examination, such as the baccalaureate. From these results, it is possible to trace back the performances of individual schools. If the standard for a school is the proportion of success, then the information is relatively easy to access.

If the standard is the mastering of specified competencies, the exam paper must be written for this goal. Even using this assumption, two ways are open. If the goal is to know to what extent an individual or a school performs, all the students should be tested. If the objective is to inform the national educational system or reform, then samples of the overall population will suffice.

The attainment of some competencies implying higher order cognitive skills may need longer studies and the follow-up of a cohort. It may be particularly the case for competencies revealed in the working life. The need for long-term trend studies is obvious and rarely satisfied.

Unfortunately, newspapers are rarely interested in this type of result unless they imply international comparison.

## A qualitative but not systematic assessment

The general inspectors in each discipline may decide to study the consequences brought about by changes in a syllabus or in the structure of some level of the system. This sort of study, often conducted with the help of the network of regional inspectors concerned with this particular subject matter, gives a qualitative view, which is made public [12].

The minister does not specifically ask for this work and many reforms are decided without considering this evidence. Thus it is not surprising that each change of a science syllabus is criticised by teachers in terms of content overload and consequently the lack of time to complete the syllabus properly.

## A quantitative but not permanent assessment

In the past, the evaluation of existing syllabi, structures and types of student assessment was of no concern to the policy makers. Up to the 1980s, the explosion in the number of pupils due to the generalisation of secondary education put quantitative

---

12  See: http://www.education.gouv.fr/syst/igen/rapports.htm

concerns in first place. The quality of the system of education is a more recent pre-occupation but it cannot be effectively addressed without the necessary instruments giving the adequate data.

The recent law on the system of Education (discussed earlier in this paper) lays stress on qualitative outcomes. As a consequence, the DEPP is preparing, with the help of teachers and inspectors, a summative assessment of students (*évaluation-bilan*), at the end of compulsory education, with a sample of 15 000 students. Following a field trial, the science tests will be administered during 2007. No link is attempted with previous work and no trend can be analysed in the near future. The results will be sent to the minister and to parliament.

## The side-effects of testing standards

The detrimental side-effects of high stakes examinations, which are found, are very similar to those reported in other countries (Harlen, 2004). However, they may be different in their intensity because in France the stakes are high for the students and/or parents but not for the teachers. Unlike their peers in the U.S. and U.K., French teachers do not risk their jobs on the grounds of the results of the students' examination results.

Another side-effect may be the tilting of competency-based assessment towards a content-based assessment. The systems of education tend to lay more and more stress upon competencies, often defined in broad and general terms. Teachers know well how to assess content but the assessment of competencies remains a real diffi-culty. Moreover, the reporting scale of competencies needs a reliable form of taxon-omy. Unfortunately it seems that there is no unique or universal taxonomy, although science is universal. Teachers have not been trained to identify and/or measure com-petencies and naturally tend to rely on old habits. The exercises supposed to show competencies are gradually transformed into content exercises in the following exams. It is a well known cause of 'content inflation'.

As competition between students is pervasive at all levels, the proportion of failing students is high. Although recognised, this phenomenon has been tackled with limited success. Some indication can be gauged from the large numbers of young people leaving school with no qualification and the high proportion of students repeating classes.

Another consequence is the consumer state of mind that leads parents to heed the league tables published by the newspapers and, from this evidence, try their best to choose the school they deem appropriate for their siblings.

# Can standards be implemented without centralised assessment?

*Are there differences between centralised and decentralised countries?*
The question of centralised assessment calls for comparison between different existing educational systems, those which are centralised and those who are not. The results from TIMSS in 1995 (Gonzales and Smith, 1997) shed light on the three levels of curriculum: the intended curriculum, the implemented curriculum and the attained curriculum. From this point of view, it does not seem that any difference was noticed between the two types of systems.

The 2003 PISA study draws no clear conclusion on the performances of students according to the methods of assessment, be it standardised tests, student portfolios, teachers' judgemental ratings, teacher-developed tests or student projects and homework (OECD, 2004).

Centralised assessment in science may be helpful to get homogeneous and efficient equipment in the school's laboratories or align the teaching content on a new curriculum. However the more complex question of attainment remains unresolved.

*Can a centralised assessment be limited to a particular country?*
The European Commission seems to use the PISA indicators as a reference for the 'key competencies' (Commission of European Communities, 2005). Even in France, the Ministers of Education are becoming more and more sensitive to the PISA results.

*How to report to society?*
The importance of standards may be linked to the way attainment is reported and central examinations are not the only way and may not be the best way of reporting the results to the nation[13].

It is important that people and organisations (including universities) who build on the knowledge and competencies of students having just completed their secondary education understand the new system of standards and competencies. At present, they tend to set their own standards without referring to the National Education Standards. The situation may be different in technological studies in the two first years after the *baccalauréat* and in school of engineers where the link with employers is fairly strong.

There is little dialogue between employers and the educational authorities[14], but the transition between education and work is worth careful and detailed study and analysis.

---

13 The USA is facing some counterproductive consequences of the bipartisan law "No Child Left Behind" voted in January 2002.
14 The phenomenon is not very different in the USA. Think to the role of SAT in the student's entrance applications to American universities and colleges.

Students should know whether the education they receive will be helpful to prepare them for what is now, inevitably, life-long learning. Feedback from society should be valued and solicited through the tools of democracy and first of all, through parliament and the living forces of the economy.

Do we know how to assess, in a classic examination, scientific curiosity, creativity, autonomy, courage and perseverance? New ways of reporting need to be invented by the schools, the local educational authorities and the State. Not all disciplines are assessed in PISA or in Brevet and a different subset of disciplines to be assessed could be chosen each year.

## Provisional conclusion

France has practiced national standards for nearly two centuries. The form of students' assessment that prevails is mainly written and summative, with stress on the ranking of students inside the classroom and limited to one school year. The continuity of learning over years and schools is hardly taken into account. The examinations themselves are of the type 'fail or pass'. No provision is made for using the evidence that comes from studying the results in examination results over the years.

Noticeable progress was made when the assessment of experimental abilities was introduced few years ago in the physical sciences tests in the science *baccalauréat*.

Assessments focused on student's knowledge and competences may be more valued in the future mainly to inform parliament about educational outcomes. But the status of science is still modest at the end of compulsory education and the status of science education has proven unstable in the recent past [15].

The question of measuring higher order cognitive skills remains open. The dwindling enrolment of science and engineering students in the developed world could lead to a renewal of science syllabi and of the assessment and career counselling of students.

Meanwhile, it is possible that international studies such as PISA will impose their own framework and agenda.

15  The teaching of physics and chemistry in grades 6 and 7 'disappeared' in 1992.

# References

Commission of European Communities (2002) *Eurydice*. Directorate General for
Education and Culture.
http://www.eurydice.org/Documents/survey5/en/FrameSet.htm

Commission of European Communities (2005) *Progress towards the Lisbon Objectives in Education and Training*. Commission Working Paper, 2005 Report.
http://europa.eu.int/comm/education/policies/2010/doc/progressreport05.pdf

Gonzales, E. J. and Smith, T. A. (1997) User Guide for the TIMSS International
Database, Primary and Middle School Years. TIMSS Study Center, Boston College
September 1997; http://timss.bc.edu/timss1995i/database/UG_1and2.pdf

Harlen, W. (2004) *The role of assessment in the implementation of science in the
primary school*. Science is Primary: European Conference on Primary Science
and Technology Education, Amsterdam. http://www.science.uva.nl/scienceisprimary/

OECD (2004) *Learning for Tomorrow's World: First Results from PISA 2003*. Paris:
OECD Publishing.

OECD (2005) *Definition and Selection of Key Competencies*.
http://www.portal-stat.admin.ch/deseco/news.htm

# The French system of education

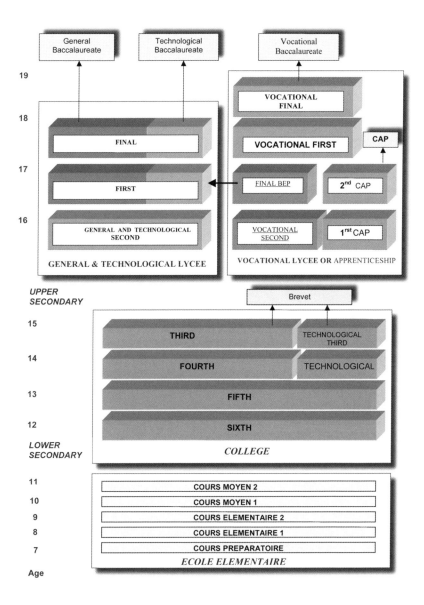

# Chapter 8

## Standards and competence models: The German situation

*Horst Schecker\* and Ilka Parchmann[#]*

*\* Institut für Didaktik der Physik, Universität Bremen, Postfach 33 04 40, 28334 Bremen, Germany*

*# Chemiedidaktik, Carl-von-Ossietzky Universität Oldenburg, Postfach 2503, 26111 Oldenburg, Germany*

### Introduction

*The PISA-shock*

In 2001, the results of the first PISA-Study (Programme for International Student Assessment) were published in Germany (Baumert et al., 2001). Compared to 31 other countries, German students only reached achievement levels that were below the international average in all three test domains (reading comprehension, mathematics, and science). The distance to the top ranking countries (e.g. Japan, Finland) was more than one standard deviation, or – expressed in terms of teaching time – more than one school year. In Germany, the spread of abilities between the highest scoring 5% of students and the lowest 5% was broader than in any other participating country. An additional national survey compared student achievements within Germany (Baumert et al., 2002) and revealed big differences between the federal states.

These findings confirmed results of the series of studies, now known as the Trends in International Science and Mathematics Study (TIMSS), beginning in the 1990s. Against the background of the 1997 study (Baumert et al., 1997), researchers had already demanded changes for the teaching of science (e.g. Schecker and Klieme, 2001). One large initiative that had been started after TIMSS was the SINUS-programme[1], in which eleven areas of demand for innovation were described, such as learning with problem-based tasks and the development of a better understanding of the nature of science. Based on these modules, groups of teachers started to work on the optimization of the teaching and learning of maths and sciences.

---

1 The SINUS project, http://www.ipn.uni-kiel.de/projekte/blk_prog/blkstefr.htm;

In 1999, the German Conference of the Ministers of Education (Kultusministerkonferenz)[2] decided to develop common criteria for educational quality and instruments to assess student achievements. It was, nevertheless, only after the PISA results, which again delivered unsatisfactory results for the German school education, that policy makers put more weight on revising the formal framework of teaching, i.e. the curricula and standards.

However, with respect to any school and curriculum innovation, the complexity of the German education system (figure 1) has enormous consequences for there are three to five types of schools in 16 federal states all with different curricula! Therefore, the decision to produce some common achievement standards for all states and schools which describe goals for the end of lower secondary education can be seen as a major step forward for German school education.

| age | grade | | | College University | Tertiary level |
|-----|-------|---|---|---|---|
| 19 -<br>18 -<br>17 -<br>16 - | - 13<br>- 12<br>- 11<br>- 10 | Part-time vocational school (50%) | Technical-business-school (12%) | Gymnasium<br><br>(20%) | Upper secondary level |
| 15 -<br>14 -<br>13 - | - 9<br>- 8<br>- 7 | Hauptschule (42%) | Realschule (24%) | Gymnasium (24%) | Secondary level |
| 12 -<br>11 -<br>10 - | - 6<br>- 5<br>- 4 | | | | Orientation phase |
| 9 -<br>.8 -<br>.7 - | - 3<br>- 2<br>- 1 | Grundschule (Primary School) (almost 100%) | | | Primary level |
| ..6 -<br>..5 - | | Vorschule (Preschool) | | | Elementary level |
| ..4 -<br>..3 - | | Kindergarten (Nursery School) | | | |

Figure 1:     The School System in Germany

The German school system is organised in a federal system and the structure varies from state to state. For example, Berlin and Brandenburg have six years of primary education, while all other states start with their secondary schools in year 5. This phase is marked as "orientation phase" in figure 1. Another change which has just begun in some states is the reduction from 13 down to 12 years of schooling.

2 KMK (Kultusministerkonferenz): Bildungsstandards:
  http://www.kmk.org/schul/Bildungsstandards/bildungsstandards.htm  (22/11/06)

Consequently, the amount of science education also differs enormously between states. For example, Schleswig-Holstein only offers two years of chemistry for secondary education, while students in Niedersachsen get the chance to learn chemistry for four or even five years, one or two lessons a week. The curricula in all states start with biology or an integrated science course, followed by physics and chemistry. At least, a number of science courses as part of secondary education are mandatory in all states. For primary education, the German school system does not offer science as a subject, but a low number of scientific ideas are integrated into a subject called "Sachunterricht", which also contains aspects from history, geography, technology and other areas.

A framework for the development of national education standards was laid out in the work of Klieme et al. (2003). Following these guidelines, groups of teachers from all federal states and types of schools, together with an advisory educational researcher, developed achievement standards at first for the main subjects German, maths, and the first foreign language, followed by the science subjects, biology, chemistry, and physics in 2003. The separate teaching of three science subjects is another peculiarity in Germany, compared to many other countries.

In reaction to the 'shocks' caused by TIMSS and PISA, where German students only reached mediocre results, the German federal ministers of education agreed upon the development of common national educational standards and assessment procedures. In a country with up to five different types of schools and 16 different curricula, this is an ambitious and important undertaking.

## Defining Educational Standards – Competencies and Competence Models

The new German National Standards of Education (Nationale Bildungsstandards, NBS) are *achievement standards*. They describe the abilities that students are expected to have attained at the end of lower secondary education (grades 9 or 10, students about 16 years old). Before 2003, teachers were told by curricula and syllabi what they had to teach in a detailed manner. Now, they are told what their students are meant to be able to do at the end of a certain grade. In comparison with the US and some other countries, the German NBS include neither system standards nor teaching standards. Hence, the decisions for the realization of these achievement standards are left to the federal states and their teachers. Approaches to transfer the standards into ideas for teaching and learning will be described in the chapters on operationalization and implementation.

*Competencies*

We use the term 'competencies' in the way that Weinert (2001, p.47) described 'specialized cognitive competencies' as "clusters of cognitive prerequisites that must be available for an individual to perform well in a particular content area". This notion is opposed to general cognitive abilities, often referred to as 'key competencies'. Specialized cognitive competencies require long-term learning, a broad experience, a deep understanding of the topic, and automatic action routines that must be controlled at a high level of awareness (cf. Weinert 2001, p.47). Weinert also points out that competencies do not only include cognitive abilities but also the motivation and willingness to apply knowledge in different situations.

*Types of competence models*

Achievement standards are either based on an explicit model of competence in a certain domain, or they carry at least an implicit model. In order to test the achievements of such standards, models which describe the structure and the development of competencies are necessary. Klieme et al. (2003) characterize the function of a competence model as the link between the abstract goals of education (in German, *Bildung*) and the concrete problems that students should be able to solve.

For an analysis of competence models, we propose the following distinctions (figure 2):
• models of competence *structure* versus models of competence *development*
• normative models versus *empirical* models

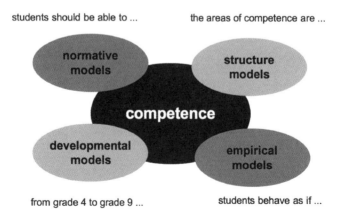

Figure 2:    Types of competence models

A *normative* competence structure model is based on norms and traditions in an educational domain, e.g. science education. It can be defined as a *set of categories* (e.g. areas of competence, levels of expertise) that systematize the competencies that a learner is *expected to have acquired* (c.f. Klieme et al., 2003, p.74). The German standards for the science subjects (physics, chemistry, biology) express four areas of competence: Subject knowledge, epistemological and methodological knowledge, communication, and judgement. Similar domains can be found in other countries (e.g. Canada). They mainly result from the educational goal to develop a scientific literacy for all students and to form a basis for further studies. This goal cannot be realized by the learning of facts and experiments only. It also requires competencies in the areas of communication, decision making, or the understanding of the special characteristics of scientific investigations.

An *empirical* model of competence structure is based on empirical evidence. It consists of a set of categories that are useful to organize findings about students' abilities, i.e. to distinguish between sub-structures of students' cognitive systems. The aim is to reconstruct typical achievements and failures of students in a specific domain. The structures of normative and empirical models are not necessarily compatible. Rost et al. (2005), for example, found in a German national study accompanying the PISA 2003 survey that the content areas (which play an important role in the structure of normative models) played only a minor role for the modelling of students' science competence. More important were more general cognitive competencies such as convergent thinking, working with mental models, or working with numbers (see also Senkbeil et al., 2005).

Further distinctions can be made between normative and empirical models of competence development. *Developmental models* describe assumptions about the growth of competencies and about stages in the process of learning science which can be determined (for example, Hammann (2004)). In a time-perspective, empirical models describe age-levels where students reach an understanding of certain concepts like e.g. the particle model or the idea of scientific modelling. In a structural perspective, the dynamics of competence development is considered. Normative models following a hierarchical notion often try to derive competence progression from the subject logics of a domain.

The relationship between normative models as they are used in educational standards on the one hand and models gained from empirical investigations on the other hand is a highly interesting field of science education research. Normative models can be taken as starting points for the development of assessment instruments. Whether the cognitive systems of students can be adequately described in the same way as curriculum experts structure the aims of teaching remains to be seen.

Normative models are frequently used in educational standards and assessments. A good example is Bybee's normative structure model of scientific literacy (1997) that was adapted for the PISA studies. However, there are only few examples of models resulting from empirical research (e.g. Klieme, 2000).

## The German national educational standards

The German educational standards are contained in booklets that specify the aims of and indicators for the quality of education in specific subjects. These indicators shall serve as a basis for system monitoring in large-scale assessments (accountability of all the participants in the domain of education). They are also used as starting points for handbooks of 'good teaching practice'.

The German standards for the three science subjects at the end of lower secondary schools are based on a *normative structure model* of competence, which uses three structural elements that we call 'dimensions' (see also Schecker and Parchmann, 2006):

1) *Areas of competence*: Expected abilities are structured by four categories: subject knowledge, application of epistemological and methodological knowledge, communication, and judgement.

2) *Basic concepts*: The content domain is organized by the description of basic concepts of a subject, e.g. the connection between matter and particle models, or the energy concept.

3) *Levels of competence*: Three levels are used as guidelines: reproduction, application, and transfer.

In the NBS paper the basic concepts are represented as a sub-division of subject knowledge. Another way is to visualize the competence model as a three-dimensional matrix (figure 3).

The standards for the pre-university level (final year of upper secondary school) are structured in a very similar way (cf. Leisen, 2004). Both papers about the standards in physics and chemistry include large sets of concrete problems that exemplify what is expected of students. So far there has been neither an empirical evaluation of this model structure nor of the items [3]. It is thus not clear whether the demands on students are comparable to what is actually achieved by teaching science.

> The German National Education Standards (for the sciences) describe achievement standards for students. The NBS are based on a normative model of competence structure. Empirical research is needed to evaluate whether the model categories used to describe students' proficiency are compatible with students' cognitive structures.

[3] For mathematics, a first national survey was carried out in 2006.

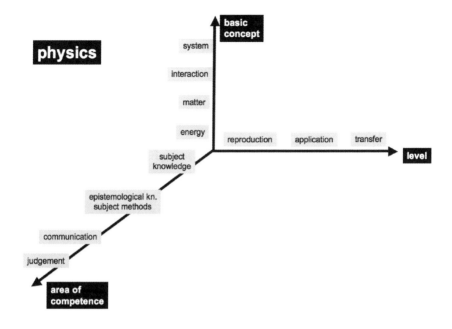

Figure 3:     3D-representation of the Competence model used in the national education standards for physics. The dimensions area, basic concept, and level span a three-dimensional competence-space

## Operationalization of Standards

The operationalization of the German achievement standards has been organized in several steps. As the standards only describe expected goals (for example, table 1), teachers still need support and guidance on how to reach these goals. Up to now, fairly detailed curricula and syllabi stipulated what topics had to be taught in each school year. Now, the idea is to describe core curricula, which only specify a limited amount of compulsory content and give some advice on how the standards could be transformed into a cumulative development of competence. Therefore, core curricula have to point out sub-levels for the goals stated in the standards. These sub-levels also serve as an orientation until empirical studies may or may not prove that the expected sub-levels and final levels of expected competencies can be achieved by a majority of learners.

The next step will have to be realized by the teachers themselves. The core curricula must be transformed into lesson plans, ideally in co-operation with all science teachers at a particular school. Unfortunately, the tradition in German schools is more or less that of 'lonely fighters'. Time will tell whether the implementation of standards can have the side effect (see below) of enhancing co-operation among teachers (and maybe even between teachers and researchers).

*The role of exemplary tasks*

In addition to core curricula and school decisions, the most effective way to demonstrate and to operationalize standards are exemplary tasks and sample items. Teachers are very experienced in posing questions and problems (though traditional tasks do have hardly involved open problem-solving activities so far!) to design their own assessments. Consequently, the biggest part of a German standards-booklet consists of concrete problems. In the physics volume (for the final year of lower secondary schools), the competencies that students are to attain are defined on less than two pages. There are rather general formulations like 'students distinguish between physics language and everyday-life language to describe phenomena' (communication) or 'students use physics knowledge to assess risks and security measures while experimenting, in everyday-life, and in connection with modern technologies' (judgement).

Students use bonding models to interpret spacial structures of matter.

Students draw conclusions about the use of substances from their knowledge about properties of matter and discuss advantages and risks.

Students recognize and formulate questions which can be investigated by the use of chemical knowledge and methods.

Students [...] interpret and translate chemical and daily-life presentations.

Students discuss and evaluate important decisions in a society from different perspectives.

Table 1:    Examples of standards in chemistry

Six more pages describe the areas of competence, the basic concepts and the competence levels. Sample problems and their solutions are then spread out on 17 pages. Each item is characterized according to the competence model (figure 4).

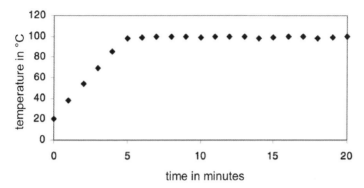
Figure 4:    Sample problem unit No. 10 from the German physics standards
             (end of lower secondary school)

Using problems to illustrate competencies is fully compatible with the "outcome-approach" for steering educational systems (cf. Klieme et al., 2003). In an extreme form one might even think of presenting standards completely as commented sets of problems that students are expected to be able to solve and the end of their school days.

The first German NBS were agreed by the Kultusministerkonferenz for the main school subjects German, English, and mathematics in 2003. Large sets of items for nation-wide large-scale assessments in theses domains are being developed by the newly founded Institute for Quality Development in the Educational System ("Institut zur Qualitätsentwicklung im Bildungswesen", IQB)[4] (this book, Chapter 10). The development of a science item database starts in 2007. Items are proposed by groups of teachers. After revision by experts they are characterized according to the categories of the competence model (cf. figure 3).

The intended function of the tests is to evaluate the efficiency of the educational system ('system monitoring'); Is it able to reach the goals set by the NBS? What are its strengths and deficits? The data may also be used for empirical research on the structure of the competence model itself and on students' understanding of subject concepts. Empirical data also offer advice on developing a better support for students. However, these are no focal issues so far, diagnostic testing in order to give individual support for low or high achievers is not intended by the IQB.

Concurrently to the IQB-assessments, the federal states have developed or are still preparing their own standard-related performance tests which are used as part of the grading process for the final exams in upper and lower secondary schools. During the last five years more and more federal states in Germany have shifted from exams developed by a school or an individual teacher to central exams.

Benchmarking between schools is also intended. Some policymakers plan to use benchmarks as an instrument to increase competition among schools. This could lead to a situation where the 'quality' of a school would simply be expressed by the achievements of its students in the final exam. However, from a pedagogical point of view as well as under psychometric aspects, a school's quality can only be fairly assessed by considering the entrance competencies of its students and as well as the background variables of the school (Baumert et al., 2002).

Recapitulating the situation, there is a strong need for good assessment tools. Still, until now, several worries accompany this process of assessment. There is little expertise in test development and evaluation in the federal states compared to the IQB, at the same time central exams – with the national standards as a point of reference – play an increasing role. Additionally, it must be feared that school benchmarking will become more important than the use of careful empirical investigations for a general quality development process and for changes in educational policy based on system monitoring data.

---

4 Institut zur Qualitätsentwicklung im Bildungswesen (Institute for Quality Development in the Educational System): http://www.iqb.hu-berlin.de (2006/01/31)

The German science standards are operationalized by sets of sample problems. The items are characterized according to the dimensions of the competence model. This helps teachers to find access to the standards.

Development of large-scale assessment instruments is under way. The use of such assessment data is still uncertain and worrying to some point, if data will be used for benchmarking only instead of taking it as a starting point for more general educational reforms.

## Side Effects: Teaching to the Test – Problem or Chance?

Standards connected with assessments relevant to exams directly affect the teaching. Teachers who feel responsible for their students' future career will try to prepare them in the best possible way for their exams. Some of the federal states in Germany have a long tradition of central assessments. Significant parts of teaching time in the final year before the Abitur is devoted to practicing exam questions from previous years. Other states that are introducing central exams provide the teachers with sample problems, so that they get an idea of what to expect at the end of their school year.

*Chances*

'Teaching to the test' usually has a negative connotation (at least in Germany), often being associated with just testing routines, as these are much easier to mark (rote learning). On the other hand, assessment could become an efficient way of influencing classroom activities and in particular the so-called 'problem-posing cultures'. The results from TIMSS showed the relative strengths of German students in solving formal equation-based quantitative problems, whereas huge deficits were revealed in qualitative argumentation (cf. Klieme, 2000). Obviously, students have not been taught to deal with this kind of requirement (such demands) in physics lessons. PISA items, where the relevant information had to be extracted from longer texts or science-process questions like 'Can this conclusion be drawn from the given data?', were unfamiliar to German students. This led to the debate about a 'new problem-posing culture' in science classrooms, including both the contents and the types of problems. This issue became important in teachers' training. Programmes for improving the educational quality and measures to enhance the efficiency of science teaching were set up (see below the section on Implementation). Booklets with 'PISA-like' problems were developed for schools (for example, Petri and Einhaus, 2006). The 'new culture' had a strong impact on the illustrative problems given in the NBS.

Consequently the new problem-posing culture must also become evident in the assessments and the exam questions, or else there would be a contradiction between what is (to be) taught and what is tested. Such inconsistencies would shortly lead to the dominance of what is tested. It would be disastrous if teachers, trying to meet the new demands in their teaching found the conventional problems in the final exams as there were before the NBS.

Therefore, in a positive sense standard-based assessments can 'force' teachers to change their classroom-activities in a more preferable direction from a science education perspective. With good standards and well chosen problems teaching to the test is a chance rather than a risk. However, there are at least four prerequisites needed for the success of such a process:

• *Quality*: The standards must be compatible with science education research and development.

• *Accessibility*: The standards must be within reach – i.e. the gap between prevailing and new teaching aims must not be too wide. There should e.g. be a 'roadmap' describing the steps for the transition from 'conventional' to 'new-culture' exams problems.

• *Support*: Teachers must be supported in working out the new standards for themselves and in changing their teaching (teacher training, teaching materials).

• *Consequence*: The standards must in fact be applied by administrators, e.g. in central exams.

*Restrictions*

Some problems are inherent in the central assessments in the sciences. Important science method competencies are the abilities to plan experimental investigations, to carry out experiments, to work with scientific apparatus, to gather and document data, to evaluate data, and to assess the results critically (NBS competence area 'epistemological and methodological knowledge'). Only a few parts of this process can be included in (paper and pencil) written exams. In some local settings it was possible to integrate experiments into the exam. For example, the physics-Abitur in those federal states without central exams sometimes included small experiments like finding out the distance between tracks on a CD-ROM by light diffraction and interference. Unfortunately, central assessments will not be able to provide identical experimental apparatus for all exam classes but will be restricted to paper and pencil tests. This is certainly a negative side effect, if it becomes true.

As mentioned above, there is no strong culture of co-operation between teachers in German secondary schools, and particularly not in Grammar schools (Gymnasium). Now, the change from detailed curricula towards standards and core curricula is asking for its further operationalization at schools. Teachers have to produce the necessary student-oriented lesson plan, aiming at the cumulative development of competencies (progression of content and skills). Frameworks and materials can be and will also be developed by science educators, delivered by text-books and other services. However, there are hardly any such materials available at present that directly meet the new standards. Teachers will have to come up with and produce a lot of ideas themselves for quite some time. This might be a burden but also a chance to foster co-operation among the concerned teachers and a better culture of in-service training. Talks and workshops to present the new standards and especially to discuss and develop competence oriented tasks are being organized in many federal states at the moment, additionally supported by in-service training centres (e.g. in chemistry, workshops are funded by the German Chemical Society) or by projects, such as SINUS[1] (see below). First results do not only show high interest and need for further information and support, they also underline the chance and importance of co-operation (Parchmann et al., 2006).

---

The assessment of standards – in particular if connected with central exams – directly affects the teaching. "Teaching to the test" does not necessarily carry a negative meaning if the test is based on sound educational standards. Assessment can effectively be used to influence classroom activities in the aspired way, given that teachers are supported in changing their "problem-posing culture" by special trainings and resources.

Additionally, the realization of standards might enhance the co-operation among the teachers of a certain school and between teachers and researchers in general through in-service trainings and projects.

---

## Implementation

The question of implementation again points out the difficult structure for the German school system: the Kultusministerkonferenz initiated the development of standards and the ministers in all federal states have agreed on using them as guidelines in their states. However, the implementation is now left to the states themselves, so there are no nationwide measures and activities. An ongoing exchange between the members of the group that developed the standards even shows that in some states, no measures at all were undertaken yet. Therefore, the side effects described in the chapter above might become important tools for the implementation of the standards.

*Implementation through a new culture of tasks for teaching, learning and assessing*

Nation-wide assessment of the new science standards in Germany will not start before 2007. However, several federal states have already started to produce their own central assessments and there is a clear shift towards central exams at the end of lower and upper secondary education. The successful implementation of standards will depend crucially on the development of suitable assessment tasks, as discussed above.

Additionally, if the standards are taken seriously, many teachers will have to modify their teaching practices as well as the focus of their teaching. A good starting point for this process would be to contrast the problems posed in their own teaching tradition and tests so far with the sample problems given in the standard papers. First experiences from projects and in-service training workshops have shown the efficiency of such discussions and high quality of commonly produced tasks and test items. Only the exchange between teachers and science educators can assure a shared fundament of the development and interpretation of tasks and of the students' results. According to our own still ongoing studies, there are discrepancies between teachers' expectations of their students' performance in tests and the actual test results analysed by researchers. Therefore, a successful implementation of standards needs a better and more conscious culture of problem posing, assessing, and evaluating students' capabilities. This would also provide the necessary support for teaching towards a continuous development of competencies. Hence, a new culture of problem posing tasks does not only include the tasks themselves but also an intensive exchange about the transported goals, the demands and the interpretation of students' answers. Possible questions for such an exchange might be the following:

i) Which of the sample problems will our students presumably be able to solve? Where do we expect failures? Which areas of the competence model and which levels of competence are particularly deficient (cf. figure 2)?

ii) How do our traditional items fit into the competence model of the NBS? Which areas of competence do we usually assess on which level?

iii) By comparing steps i and ii: In which way do we have to develop our teaching and the support for students' learning?

The second question should be answered by reviewing the tests that were used by the teachers in their classes over the last years. From a psychometric point of view, an ideal item would get a single parameter for each of the three competence dimensions (area, basic concept, level). However, it is often difficult to assign an item to a single cell of the three-dimensional competence space. Items from classroom tests usually get more than just one parameter-triplet.

Looking at question i, experiences from training courses show that teachers do not always agree with the characterization of sample items in the standards. We also find a fruitful discussion among the group members about the focus of certain problems. Reasons can be given as follows:
• It takes time to develop a clear understanding of the four competence areas, in particular of the sub-dimensions 'communication' and 'judgement'. (Even experts obviously have difficulties: Some NBS-sample items rated as 'judgement' do not fulfil the definition of this competence area as given in the NBS.)

• Whether the solution of a problem needs reproduction, application or transfer of knowledge depends on the previous content of teaching. When teachers rate an item, they take into account if and in which way they normally deal with similar problems in their classes.

Our first experiences encourage the idea to use the discussion of tasks among teachers and between teachers and researchers to implement the idea of standards.

*Implementation through new approaches for teaching and learning*

Following the TIMSS results, several projects have been initiated, the large ones being funded by the central Ministry of Education and the federal states. These projects, such as SINUS[1] and *Chemie im Kontext*[5], *Physik im Kontext*[6] and *Biologie im Kontext*[7] have been and still are producing conceptual frameworks and resources for teaching and learning sciences which are different from the traditional approaches.

In the SINUS project, groups of teachers chose different modules as starting points to improve their teaching and learning, supported by in-service training workshops. The so-called 'context projects' develop and test the teaching units and learning material through learning communities (Parchmann et al., 2006). Groups of teachers and science education researchers work together on the realization of a context-based framework to bridge the gap between situated learning and the systematic and cumulative development of basic concepts and competencies. The *Chemie im Kontext* (ChiK) project for example has produced a series of units and materials which can be used to focus on certain standards and to describe 'learning lines' for the intended development of competencies. Within the project, instruments to check students' conceptions

5 Chemie im Kontext: http://www.ipn.uni-kiel.de/abt_chemie/chik.html: (22/11/06)
6 Physik im Kontext: http://www.uni-kiel.de/piko/; (22/11/06)
7 Biologie im Kontext, http://www.ipn.uni-kiel.de/abt_bio/projekte_bio.htm (22/11/06)

and abilities at different stages of a learning process are also tested. Research results have underlined the special value of co-operation and support given by learning communities and the exchange of ideas and materials for further developments (Parchmann et al., 2006). Consequently, the structure realized in such projects could be used as further instruments for the implementation of standards.

A good way to implement the German achievement standards for the science subjects would be to support teachers in comparing the tasks and tests they normally use with the sample problems in the NBS.

Another instrument could be the establishment of co-operation structures, such as learning communities, between teachers from different schools and researchers to develop and evaluate teaching and learning materials, including tasks, which aims at the development of competencies described in the standards.

## Conclusions

The process of developing national standards to describe the expected achievements of students by the end of certain school levels is a huge step forward for the diverse German educational systems. However, without accompanying implementation measures the description of expected learning outcomes alone will have no effect on the teaching and learning in the science classrooms. So far, the development of such measures is left to the federal states and to personal initiatives.

One effect that has already become evident is the shift towards more assessments and centralised exams. The assessment of achieved competencies is necessary. It can even enhance standard-oriented teaching (positive side effects). On the other hand, the risk of misinterpretation is high when tests are of low quality and influencing factors such as the social background of the students are not taken into consideration for benchmarking.

To adjust goals and teaching strategies, an important consequence must be the development of an advanced 'problem posing culture' among teachers and researchers. This also demands more research on the adequacy of the competence models used in the standards. Additionally, support must be given to the individual teachers who have to ensure that their students get the best assistance during their learning processes. Core curricula only set the frame, materials and exemplary units will be other important tools to foster a successful implementation of standards in Germany.

# References

Baumert, J., Lehmann, R., Lehrke, M., Schmitz, B., Clausen, M., Hosenfeld, I., Köller, O. and Neubrand, J. (1997) *TIMSS: Mathematisch-naturwissenschaftlicher Unterricht im internationalen Vergleich. Deskriptive Befunde.* Opladen: Leske + Budrich.

Baumert, J., Klieme, E., Neubrand, M., Prenzel, M., Schiefele, U., Schneider, W., Stanat, P., Tillmann, K.-J. and Weiß, M. (2001) *PISA 2000 – Basiskompetenzen von Schülerinnen und Schülern im internationalen Vergleich.* Opladen: Leske + Budrich.

Baumert, J., Klieme, E., Neubrand, M., Prenzel, M., Schiefele, U., Schneider, W., Stanat, P., Tillmann, K.-J. and Weiß, M. (2002) *PISA 2000 – Die Länder der Bundesrepublik Deutschland im Vergleich.* Opladen: Leske + Budrich.

Bybee, R. (1997) Toward an Understanding of Scientific Literacy. In W. Gräber and C. Bolte, (Hrsg.): *Scientific Literacy.* Kiel: IPN, 37-68.

Hammann, M. (2004) Kompetenzentwicklungsmodelle, Merkmale und ihre Bedeutung – dargestellt anhand von Kompetenzen beim Experimentieren. *Der mathematische und naturwissenschaftliche Unterricht,* 57(4), 196-203.

Klieme, E. (2000) Fachleistungen im voruniversitären Mathematik- und Physikunterricht: Theoretische Grundlagen, Kompetenzstufen und Unterrichtsschwerpunkte. In: J. Baumert, W. Bos and R. Lehmann, *TIMSS – Mathematisch-naturwissenschaftliche Bildung am Ende der Sekundarstufe II.* Opladen: Leske + Budrich, 57-128.

Klieme, E., Avenarius, H., Blum, W., Döbrich, P., Gruber, H., Prenzel, M., Reiss, K., Riquarts, K., Rost, J., Tenorth, H.-E. and Vollmer, H. J. (2003) *Zur Entwicklung nationaler Bildungsstandards.* Bonn: Bundesministerium für Bildung und Forschung.

Leisen, J. (2004) Einheitliche Prüfungsanforderungen Physik. *Der mathematische und naturwissenschaftliche Unterricht,* 67(3), 155-159.

Parchmann, I., Gräsel, C., Baer, A., Nentwig, P., Demuth, R., Ralle, B. and the ChiK project group (2006) *Chemie im Kontext* – a symbiotic implementation of a context-based teaching and learning approach. *International Journal of Science Education,* 28 (9), 1041-1062.

Petri, J. and Einhaus, E. (2006) Aufgabenbeispiele zur naturwissenschaftlichen Grundbildung gemäß der PISA-Konzeption). *Der mathematische und naturwissenschaftliche Unterricht* 59, 300-301.

Rost, J., Walter, O., Carstensen C.H., Senkbeil, M. and Prenzel, M. (2005) Der nationale Naturwissenschaftstest PISA 2003. *Der mathematische und naturwissenschaftliche Unterricht* 58 (4), 196-204.

Schecker, H. and Klieme, E. (2001) Mehr Denken, weniger rechnen. *Physikalische Blätter* 57 (7/8), 113-117.

Schecker, H. and Parchmann, I. (2006) Modellierung naturwissenschaftlicher Kompetenz. *Zeitschrift für Didaktik der Naturwissenschaften* 12, 45-66.

Senkbeil, M., Rost, J., Carstensen, C. H. and Walter, O. (2005) Der nationale Naturwissenschaftstest PISA 2003. *Entwicklung und empirische Überprüfung eines zweidimensionalen Facetten-Designs*: Empirische Pädagogik, 19 (2), 166-189.

Weinert, F. E. (2001): Concept of competence – A conceptual clarification. In: D. S. Rychen and L. H. Salganik (Eds.): *Defining and Selecting Key Competencies.* Göttingen: Hogrefe and Huber , 45-65.

# Chapter 9

# Standards for a lower secondary biology course in Germany: A contribution from MNU

*Jürgen Langlet*

*Förderverein MNU, Am Hang 17, 21403 Wendisch Evern, Germany*

After the publication of standards by the KMK (the Standing Conference of German Ministers of Education) for mathematics, German and English, standards for biology, chemistry and physics were published in late 2004 (KMK, 2004).

It was intended, by developing national standards, to effect a general change from an input- to an output-orientation of teaching. However, the responsibility for implementing them remains with the 16 Bundesländer (federal states). While teachers generally appreciate the flexibility in the way that the standards have been written, there is a danger that this could lead to different, and perhaps erroneous, interpretations with respect to basic concepts, competences and levels of achievement.

The German Association for the Promotion of Mathematics and Science Education (MNU), with its ca. 6000 members, and devoted, as it is, to the improvement of mathematics and science education in Germany, has supported, right from the beginning of these discussions, the national development of output- and competence-oriented standards in science teaching.

Thus, MNU is promoting the national standards for the three science disciplines in the Länder, starting with biology, by producing specific teaching-aids to show:
• how to find the elements of a competence
• how to relate the elements to the levels of competence[1]
• how to distinguish between disciplinary and transdisciplinary competences
• how to work with the basic concepts (see below)
   and last but not least
• how to promote students' understanding of science.

It is the aim of MNU to encourage teachers and teacher groups in schools to begin structuring their own biology curriculum in line with these competences and standards and to improve it by means of self-evaluation.

---

[1] For a more detailed explanation of the competence model, as it is used in the German National Standards, see Schecker and Parchmann (2007).

The recommendations presented in this paper were agreed at a conference, organised by the MMU, in April 2005, between experts from different Bundesländer, from biological research and from biology education (MNU, 2006).

## Standards as competencies

The standards published by KMK are aiming at

*'existing or achievable cognitive abilities and skills of individuals to solve specific problems, as well as motivational, volitional and social tendencies to successfully and responsibly apply such problem-solving skills in variable situations.'*

This definition of a 'competence' (Weinert, 2001) is being generally used in German speaking countries in the development of competences and standards in science education. Such a general problem-solving competence, however, like other general competences (e.g. 'methodological', 'personal' and 'social' competences), resists any attempt of a well-defined validation. It rather implies, as teaching practice and educational research demonstrate, a preamble-like generality and vagueness – and hence ineffectiveness.

However, developing specific descriptions of levels of performance such as the following, should more effectively encourage acceptance of competences and standards by schools and teachers:

*'Competences are abilities attributed to a person formulated by means of achievable standards and thus can be evaluated. In order to reach this goal, dimensions and operators of activity have clearly to be indicated in the core curriculum'.*

This is graphically represented by a matrix (figure 1):

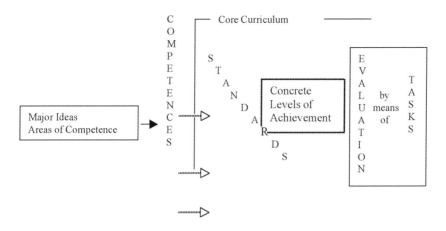

Figure 1:     From major educational ideas to the evaluation of competences required


Four areas of competence have been deduced from major educational ideas such as the expectation that adolescents learn to know about the world (knowledge), to make the world accessible for themselves (acquisition of knowledge), to share their knowledge and their questions about the world (communication), and to judge the relevance of their knowledge and of the answers to their questions (judgement). Certainly, these areas of competence are still too broad to be manageable for teaching. They have, therefore, to be broken up into their elements. For the 'judgement' area of competence, for example, it had to be clarified which elements constitute the judgement competence in the science classroom. Reitschert et al.(2007) have suggested the following:

• to perceive and to be aware of one's own attitude
• to perceive and to be aware of moral relevance
• to judge
• to reflect on consequences
• to change perspective
• to argue.

In the next steps these elements of the competence must be operationalized as standards, related to a core curriculum, and attributed to different levels of achievement. That means that competences have to manifest themselves as specific operations in specific tasks. Only then can they be evaluated. Thus it is the actual ability of the learner that is in the focus of interest. The teacher wants to know which learning process students actually have acquired in the process of teaching. It is *The discovering of ability!*'

The recommendations presented in this paper are restricted to the competence areas of 'Subject knowledge' and 'Epistomological competence' (acquisition of knowledge). For the area of 'Evaluation', nine levels of achievement have been published, while an elaboration of the area of 'Communication' will be considered later.

Elements of 'Subject knowledge' and 'Epistomological competence' are differentiated into different levels, and exemplary tasks are attributed to each level. A flow chart (figure 2) for part of the area 'Subject Knowledge', using 'Thinking in terms of evolution' as an example, demonstrates the general procedure:

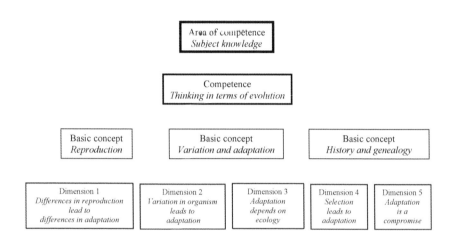

Figure 2:     An example of defining a basic competence in the area of ' Subject knowledge'

## Levels of achievement

Competence- and standard-oriented teaching relies on appropriate models of competence. It is crucial that teachers are able to identify minimum, average and maximum levels, to define the grade of ability that the student should have acquired at the end of a teaching period.

> *"Models of competence development play a key role hereby. They help planning implementation of competences over age levels in such a way that existing levels of competence are picked up and systematically can be developed further (cumulative promotion of competences). Furthermore, such models offer good orientation with respect to feedback and assessment of competence growth by specific examples regarding possibilities of operationalizing levels of competence."* (Hammann, 2004)

Hence such 'models of competence' are understood as descriptions of competence and levels. The more clearly defined they are, the more educational improvement can be achieved and levels checked.

However, tests with large populations, so-called 'comparative studies' like those planned by IQB[2], underlie statistical criteria so that their tasks will be less inter-related with the actual teaching process. In addition, in the IQB studies, tasks are being created which can be localized post hoc in a specific competence model. This procedure has already been used in the PISA study where competence levels were defined afterwards on the empirical basis of answers given by the examinees. Hereby, the ranking scale was analogized afterwards using the grading system of Bybee (Bybee, 2002). This procedure discloses a central problem, which occurs when attempting to establish models of competence. It points at a specific dilemma, with specific consequences. There are hardly any empirical data (except those of Hammann (2004)), that shows how competences develop, or which human achievements can be reached by means of which competences. This is the old distinction between concrete and abstract-operational thinking made by Piaget. However, it has been shown that children, with appropriate support and on the basis of solid primary knowledge, are capable of abstract-operational thinking much earlier than Piaget suggested. (Gräber and Stork, 1984)

The dimensions within the competence areas are further subdivided into qualitatively different 'levels'. This development of descriptions of performance links the tentative classification of levels of scientific literacy with first approaches towards a 'theory of meaningful learning' (Langlet, 2005) implying the following levels: Pre-conception – Knowledge – Application – Reflection and Understanding – Meta-reflection.

| Level | | Description of Ability | Tasks |
|---|---|---|---|
| A | Pre-conception | Follows the preconception that everything is well adapted or could be perfectly adapted at will and with practice | |
| I | Knowledge | Attributes specific physical features (e.g. of a mole) to characteristic patterns if living | |
| II | Application | Explains physical features of an organism (e.g. a bat) with the concept of adaptation | |
| III | Reflection and Understanding | Explains limited adaptation of an organism with a change in environmental conditions or in the pattern of living (e.g. back problems of humans) | |
| R | Meta-reflection | Explains differentness of organisms (e.g. mole and shrew) with the concept of adaptation | |

Figure 3:     Levels of achievement

2 Institute for Educational Progress (Institut zur Qualitätsentwicklung im Bildungswesen, IQB), see Rupp and Vock (2007).

Students who perform at an average level of achievement are expected to reach competence levels I and II in the development of their scientific understanding. Levels III and R are seen as goals for higher achievers.

Table 1 describes the competence levels for the two competence areas 'Subject knowledge' and 'Epistemological competence' in more general terms. The levels are here referring to Bybee's terms.

| Competence level | Subject knowledge | Epistemological competence |
| --- | --- | --- |
| **A Pre-conceptions**<br>Description of natural biological phenomena on the basis of everyday understanding | Using everyday knowledge to describe biological phenomena | Using intuitive strategies of problem-solving and logics |
| **I Nominal scientific literacy**<br>Knowledge and definition of biological (scientific) concepts and "facts" | Reproducing (basic) knowledge acquired by teaching | Reproducing steps of scientific (problem-solving) procedures and other skills |
| **II Functional scientific literacy**<br>Rational application of knowledge acquired by teaching | Applying knowledge acquired by teaching to new unknown phenomena | Applying steps of scientific (problem-solving) procedures and other skills |
| **III Conceptual and procedural scientific literacy**<br>Understanding of basic biological and scientific concepts and processes | Understanding subject-specific basic concepts and applying them appropriately | Understanding specific modes of exploration in biology, as compared with those of other sciences |
| **R Multidimensional scientific literacy**<br>Understanding trans-disciplinary biological and scientific concepts and processes (meta-reflecting) in social and scientific contexts | Understanding trans-disciplinary basic concepts in social and scientific context | Understanding specific modes of science exploring the world as compared with those of other sciences, in the view of philosophy of science |

Table 1:      Competence areas and levels of competence in a two-dimensional model

Table 2 illustrates the levels of achievement in more specific detail for the area of judgement using Preimplantation genetic diagnosis (PGD) as an example. PGD involves testing the early embryo, after in vitro fertilisation, for genetic risks in a very early stage of their development. Problematic ones are discarded and only those without problems are transplanted into the mother's uterus. This procedure is outlawed in Germany, but there is much discussion on whether the law should be liberalized, posing a complex ethical conflict. The levels of judgmental competence are delineated below.

Discussions are frequently characterized by a simple exchange of opinions. Also students often think just expressing opinions and arbitrarily indicating reasons (which often have no concrete relation to statements) can be considered as proper debate. Only implicit norms and values underlying the statements are being conveyed by opinions. Proper debating, however, means basing one's own statements on consistent reasons and reacting directly to other peoples's statements.

| Level | Meaning of Levels | Competence appropriate to level can be recognized by ... *Exemplary statement of students' judgement about preimplantation genetic diagnosis (PGD)* |
|---|---|---|
| A | Opinions | ... expressing opinions without giving reasons and without recognizing the necessity for reasoning. *"I am for PGD"* |
| I | Knowing and recognizing reasons | ... giving reasons, but without relating them specifically to the statements. *"I am for PGD because other European countries do the same"* |
| II | Supporting statement with reasons | ... consistent reasoning of statements. *"I think PGD should also be allowed in our country to counteract PGD-tourism into other European countries and thus to keep money in our own country"* |
| III | Giving reasons from different contexts to back up one's case | ... recognizing generally accepted principles of reasoning and being able to apply them in different contexts. *"I support PGD, because money flowing, by PGD-tourism, into our country could essentially contribute to the welfare of the own society. And welfare of the society is a generally accepted principle"* |
| R | Reflecting ones own reasoning | ... understanding and acknowledging necessity as well as limits and scopes of reasoning. *"I know quite well the principal difference between argument and expressing opinions, but I also know that general principles always have to be questioned again."* |

Table 2: Competence levels within the 'judgement' dimension

# References

Bybee, R.W. (2002) Scientific Literacy – Mythos oder Realität? In W. Gräber, P. Nentwig, T. Koballa and R. Evans (Hrsg.) *Scientific Literacy.* Opladen: Leske + Budrich, 21-43.

Gräber, W. and Stork, H. (1984) Die Entwicklungspsychologie Jean Piagets als Mahnerin und Helferin des Lehrers im naturwissenschaftlichen Unterricht. MNU, 37 (4), 193-201; *MNU*, 37 (5), 257-269.

Hammann, M. (2004) Kompetenzentwicklungsmodelle. Merkmale und ihre Bedeutung – dargestellt anhand von Kompetenzen beim Experimentieren. *MNU*, 57 (4), 196-203.

Klieme, E., Avenarius, H., Blum, W., Döbrich, P., Gruber, H., Prenzel, M., Reiss, K., Riquarts, K., Rost, J., Tenorth, H.-E. and Vollmer, H. J. (2003) *Zur Entwicklung nationaler Bildungsstandards.* Bonn: Bundesministerium für Bildung und Forschung.

KMK (Kultusministerkonferenz) (2004) *Vereinbarung über Bildungsstandards für den Mittleren Schulabschluss (Jahrgangsstufe 10) in den Fächern Biologie, Chemie, Physik.* http://www.kmk.org/doc/beschl/RV-jg10nawi-BS308KMK.pdf.

Langlet, J. (2005) *Arbeiten mit den Bildungsstandards im Fach Biologie, fachspezifisch und fachübergreifend, elementarisiert und niveauvoll. Tagung von Vertretern der Bundesländer wie Experten aus der Fachdidaktik und aus der Schulpraxis zur Erstellung von Empfehlungen für die Umsetzung der KMK-Standards Biologie S I.* Unpublished manuscript.

MNU (2006) *Arbeiten mit den Bildungsstandards im Fach Biologie, fachspezifisch und fachübergreifend, dimensioniert und niveauvoll. Empfehlungen für die Umsetzung der KMK-Standards Biologie S I. MNU* 59(2) 2, Beihefter.

Reitschert, K., Langlet, J., Hößle, C., Mittelsten Scheid, N. and Schlüter, K. (2007) Dimensionen Ethischer Urteilskompetenz. – Dimensionierung und Niveaukonkretisierung. *MNU* 60 (1), 43-51.

Rupp, A and Vock, M. (2007) This book, Chapter 10.

Schecker, H. and Parchmann, I. (2007) This book, Chapter 8.

Weinert, F. E. (2001) Vergleichende Leistungsmessung in Schulen – eine umstrittene Selbstverständlichkeit. In Weinert, F. E. (Hrsg.). *Leistungsmessung in Schulen.* Weinheim: Beltz, 17-31.

# Chapter 10

## National educational standards in Germany: Methodological challenges for developing and calibrating standards-based tests

*André A. Rupp and Miriam Vock*

*Institut zur Qualitätsentwicklung im Bildungswesen, Humboldt-Universität zu Berlin, 10099 Berlin, Germany*

## Introduction

This chapter is about the methodological challenges that were encountered in the development of test items for standards-based assessments that serve to provide national proficiency scales in the context of the current standards-based movement in Germany. This is done by describing the national item development process at the *Institute for Educational Progress (Institut zur Qualitätsentwicklung im Bildungswesen, IQB)* in Berlin, Germany, and by highlighting the specific interventions that were taken to address the challenges that were encountered during the process. While the context is specific to Germany, we believe that many of the consequences of the decisions that were made in this process can prove valuable and useful to specialists from other countries engaged in similar processes. The primary objective of the chapter is, thus, to raise awareness about the complexity of this process and to provide methodological recommendations that might aid others in saving often expensive resources, particularly manpower, money, and time.

## The genesis and implications of national educational standards in Germany

To understand some of the rigorous demands that underlie the development and subsequent calibration of test items for standards-based assessments in Germany, which have led to the challenges that were encountered, a brief overview of the historical context in which these assessments are placed is necessary (see Schecker and Parchmann (2006) for a more detailed discussion of these developments).

*From Input- to Output-orientation*
In contrast to some other countries, outcomes of school education processes in Germany had not been systematically and continually examined before the 1990s. Instead, the major frameworks that had informed curriculum development had been

didactic theories, which resulted in numerous suggestions for an effective sequencing of instructional units, an effective development of instructional approaches and an effective preparation of suitable instructional materials. In other words, curricula were characterized by rather detailed descriptions for *what content to teach and how to teach the content* (i.e., an *input* orientation), but lacked a consensus on *what students should have learned* at certain points in their educational careers (i.e., an *output* orientation).

Recently, however, a public interest in what types of classroom teaching are actually effective in bringing about higher rates of student achievement has emerged due to the unexpectedly weak performance of German secondary students in the *Trends in International Math and Science Study* (TIMSS) (e.g., Baumert et al., 2000; Martin et al., 2004) and the *Programme of International Student Assessment (PISA)* (e.g., Baumert et al., 2001; OECD, 2005). The so-called 'PISA-shock' led to a process of rethinking educational goals and the establishment of subsequent measures to monitor the attainment of these goals, which was nothing short of a paradigm shift towards empirical research for accountability and student support in educational research and practice. Consequently, it is now more widely accepted in the German educational community that the outcomes of school education processes have to be evaluated through periodic assessments of student competencies, which represents an explicit focus on objectively measurable results of classroom teaching.

This is important also because there is ample evidence for ethnic and social disparities in the essentially four-tiered German school system consisting of *Hauptschule* (general secondary school), *Realschule* (intermediate secondary school), Gesamtschule (comprehensive school), and *Gymnasium* (grammar school) that were revealed through the international large-scale studies and their national extensions. These disparities need to be quickly overcome if Germany wants to catch up to the achievement and equality standards already attained by other countries.

*The Development of National Educational Standards*

In October 1997, the *Standing Conference of the Ministers of Education and Cultural Affairs* of the 16 federal states in Germany (*Ständige Konferenz der Kultusminister der Länder, KMK*) agreed on a regular evaluation of the performance of students across all major school types and grades in the German school system via large-scale assessments. These evaluations allow for continual international benchmarking and are supplemented by national evaluations with larger samples that allow for a reliable comparison of student performance across the 16 federal states.

In addition, the KMK commissioned the development of *National Educational Standards (NES)* that were based, in part, on recommendations from an expert committee that included specialists in didactics, educational researchers, and school practitioners from all 16 federal states (Klieme et al., 2003). In 2003 and 2004, standards documents were developed and all federal states officially accepted the NES. The NES are tied to school-leaving qualifications and currently exist for the primary level ('Primarbereich') and the lower secondary level ('Mittlerer Abschluss' and 'Hauptschulabschluss') in German, English and French as first foreign languages, mathematics, biology, physics, and chemistry.

To support the federal states in their efforts to ensure and improve the quality of schooling, the *Institute for Educational Progress (Institut zur Qualitätsentwicklung im Bildungswesen, IQB)* at the Humboldt University in Berlin was founded in December 2004. The primary mandate of the IQB is to develop normative national proficiency scales based on the NES, to illustrate the standards through tasks for implementation in classrooms, and to develop the standards further. The IQB is conceived as a scientific research institution of the 16 federal states and, thus, develops and engages in several research programs that evaluate programs based on standards-based assessment and implementation systems. With respect to the operationalization of the NES, one can distinguish two different types of task that are developed at the IQB.

One type of tasks serves the implementation of standards-based instruction in schools (i.e., 'classroom or implementation tasks'). These tasks can be used freely by teachers in classrooms to align their instruction to the NES and are intended to lead to a higher degree of implementation of standards-based educational principles in classroom practice (see Blum et al., 2006). The second type of task is needed for the development of national proficiency scales and associated norms of student achievement (i.e., 'standards-based test items'). The purpose of the test items is to provide a snapshot of student performance at different times in their educational careers with respect to the NES, which allows for an estimation of the proportion of students that are able to comply with each individual standard within each federal state or school type. The focus of this chapter is on key methodological challenges that have been encountered in the process of developing, piloting, and calibrating the standards-based test items and the subsequent measures that have been put into place to respond to them.

## Challenges in the item development process

As stated above, the primary objective of the item development process at the IQB is to establish, for each subject-matter domain and each grade level, a proficiency scale that is reliable and meaningful so that it allows educational stakeholders to report to each teacher the level of proficiency of his or her students with respect to a certain area of competence. Ideally, it the scales would be functioning well enough so that information could not only be provided at an aggregate level (i.e., for accountability purposes at the school or state level) but also at an individual student level (i.e., for diagnosing areas of deficiency that can inform the development of remedial programs). Therefore, the test items that need to be developed have to conform to strict test-theoretic criteria so that they allow for an objective, reliable, valid, and economic measurement (for an overview of professional testing standards that specify such criteria see, e.g., AERA/APA/NCME, 1999).

Importantly, in order for likely interpretations on the basis of the standards-based assessments to be defensible in the end, it is necessary that the entire process from the operationalization of the standards through test items to the setting of cut scores that determine proficiency classes on the resulting proficiency scales are defensible from the beginning. This requires that multiple aspects of the validity of likely interpretations such as face validity, criterion-related validity, and construct validity be considered throughout the process and that empirical as well as rational information be amassed to support them (see, e.g., Messlck, 1989, Buisboom et al., 2004; Mislevy et al., 2003, for a discussion of validity).

*Overview of the item development process*

In contrast to other countries, national structures for the development of standards-based assessments had not existed in Germany before the creation of the IQB. Nevertheless, some experience had been amassed from the participation of Germany in international large-scale assessment studies such as TIMSS, TOSCA, PISA and PIRLS (e.g., Köller et al., 2004; PISA Konsortium, 2005; Bos et al., 2003) as well as national large-scale assessment studies such as DESI (e.g., Klieme and Beck, in press) and from the development of standardized achievement tests for use within and across several federal states. Before the IQB was established, invaluable groundwork concerning the development of test items in alignment with the NES for the lower secondary level in mathematics was laid by the German PISA consortium and the *Leibniz Institute for Science Education (IPN)* at the University of Kiel. Many features of this process of item development for mathematics were adapted by the IQB for item development in all subject areas.

Yet, national structures, which require a larger amount of logistics related to communication and travel as they bring together practitioners and experts from various domains, had to be established from first principles. This meant especially that numerous people from different backgrounds partook in the process, whose different frames of reference had to be made commensurate to a degree that allowed an efficient item development process to be put into place. Figure 1 provides an overview of this process.

Put simply, item developers are charged to write tasks for classroom implementation and items for national tests. The primary utilization of the standards-based classroom tasks is to obtain student solutions, which are confidentially collected, coded,

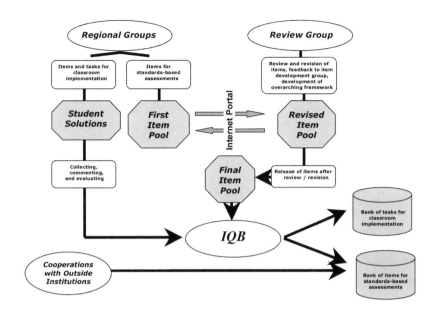

Figure 1:     Overview of the item development process at the IQB

and analyzed at the IQB to learn about the functioning of the classroom tasks and to provide suggestions for their revision. This helps to develop instructional materials and strategies that are empirically tested. The test items go through an even more complex evaluation process as follows.

Item writers are trained by national and international experts through a series of workshops, which are discussed in more detail below. The item writers are initially encouraged to try their items informally with their own students in their own classrooms before bringing the items to their regional group where they can be discussed further. First experiences with an item and empirical data from these experiences are seen as the necessary basis for the initial discussions about item quality to protect this process from remaining hypothetical in nature. One example that shows the importance of early pre-trials of items is that many item writers are often very motivated to construct innovative and interesting items. At the beginning, however, this frequently results in too many difficult items. For a good measurement of competences in the whole student population, easy items that require only a very basic competence level are also needed and the empirical feedback from the classroom helps to raise consciousness among the item writers for this issue.

Items that are developed are also shared with members of the regional groups through an internet portal at the IQB and are, at some point, released to an item review group for evaluation. The group of reviewers, which provides comments through the internet portal and either revises or releases the items, consists of university teachers in didactics, educational scientists and psychometricians. Once the items have been released, they are collected in an item bank at the IQB. In addition, due to the large numbers of items that are needed, the IQB has commissioned part of its item development process to outside institutions (e.g., the CIEP in Sèvres, France), who work in close collaboration with the German experts from the item review group. The items that are provided by those institutions are also added to the overall item pool at the IQB.

Once a suitable number of items are available for a particular domain, the items are more systematically pre-trialled in classrooms using convenience and random samples. On the one hand, this is done to obtain first empirical information about their psychometric properties. Analyses, therefore, focus on classical item parameters such as item difficulty, item discrimination, and the functioning of distractors. On the other hand, this is done to obtain information about administration characteristics such as the comprehensibility of instructions, the clarity of the scoring instructions, and the time allotments for items and booklets. Once these data have been evaluated, the items are looped back into the same item development process for revision, while, in some cases, they are simply discarded.

In the next step, the items are administered in a pilot study to larger random samples of about 6000 – 8000 students from different states across Germany, which provides more reliable calibration data and more extensive data on student perceptions via questionnaires. Time permitting, the pilot study is also used to perform qualitative validation studies using think-aloud protocols or experimental manipulations on subsets of items to learn how their functioning can be optimized. These data are evaluated and items are, again, revised or discarded. The remaining items are then administered in a field trial to another large random sample of 6000 – 8000 students. Those items that 'survive' this calibration from a psychometric perspective, which is described in more detail further below, are the ones that are used as the basis to develop the proficiency scales.

All in all, this is an expensive and time-consuming process, because the size of the desired initial item pool that is needed to establish the final proficiency scales is fairly large. On average, several hundred items are required that need to 'survive' the strict process of quality control for the creation of a single proficiency scale. Due to the fact that many items have to be discarded in the process, especially when item writers are less experienced, around 1000 items need to be developed for each subject-matter domain.

The entire process from initial meetings with item developers and didactic experts to developing final proficiency scales takes about three years for each subject-matter domain. Importantly, supplementary information is collected throughout the process. For example, item developers and experts in didactics rate items according to their difficulty and selected features that might account for this difficulty. Information from students about the attractiveness, familiarity, and functioning of the items is collected via questionnaires and interviews. Further, statistics about item characteristics from the pre-trial, the pilot study, and the field trial are collected and updated in the item bank, whose structure is necessarily complex.

Due to the complexity of this process, a large number of challenges were encountered that needed to be overcome in order to ensure that it ran as smoothly as possible and that the quality of the items that were developed remained as high and as suitable as possible for the final calibration with sophisticated statistical models. Some of the key challenges are described in the following.

*Challenges in the Selection of the Item Writers*

One attractive option for developing test items that can be linked to the NES is to ask experienced item writers to provide such items. However, this approach is difficult to realize in Germany for several reasons.

A main reason is that there had not been a long tradition of standardized achievement tests in German schools; thus, there is a lack of experts in the field of item writing for standardized achievement tests and expertise had to be built up during the process. While insightful expertise was available from researchers that had collaborated on other large-scale assessment studies in terms of methodology, these approaches could not be adopted directly, because these studies were typically not linked to the NES and used instruments that were either too specific or too general for the objectives of the IQB. Similarly, the option of working only with international experts that had extensive knowledge and experience in item writing and test development was discarded mainly because knowledge about German curricula and the German NES were crucial for the process. Another important reason was that the process also needed to lead to a high level of acceptance from educational stakeholders who would be using the resulting standards-based assessments in their daily work.

For these reasons – and to make the most use of the competences that already existed in the country – it was decided that teachers should be the ones who are primarily responsible for writing the items. Since an experienced but neutral group of experts was additionally needed to review the items, experts in didactics and test development were selected to form these item review groups. All groups were coordinated by members of the IQB in collaboration with additional stakeholders to have a representative set of persons with different levels of expertise engaged in the process. Moreover, an important challenge was not only to establish a single item bank for the initial proficiency scales, but, rather, to set in motion a continual production process for item writing so that the pool can be maintained and refreshed over time.

The teachers were carefully selected for the process by the 16 federal states, because they needed to possess many years of teaching experience, ideally coupled with experience in developing standardized assessments for use within and across federal states. Despite this experience, it was encountered that most teachers found it easier to write standards-based classroom tasks than items for standards-based assessments, because the classroom tasks resemble, in many respects, the tasks that they had always been using and developing for their lessons. Hence, despite existing expertise the teachers needed to be extensively trained so as to minimize the number of items that might have to be discarded later in the process.

*Challenges in the training of the item writers*

Apart from developing expertise in writing items for standardized assessments, some important challenges in the training of item writers were neither logistical nor conceptual, but rather psychological. To overcome these psychological barriers, a time-consuming process was put into motion that involved a lot of repetition, transparent communication, and comprehensive argumentation on part of the experts who trained the item writers as well as the members of the IQB. Experience with this process has shown that it is indispensable to get item writers to accept and internalize – not merely apply – the core principles of item development for standards-based assessments because they are the ones who will go back to their federal states and train other teachers in this process once their work for the IQB is completed. Hence, from the perspective of professional development, it is paramount to look beyond the immediate horizon of item development to the larger national context right from the beginning.

*Psychological barriers toward certain item types*

One particularly noticeable challenge was that many cautions about the use of standardized assessments exist among German teachers, which are, in part, grounded in prejudices about such assessments. For example, many teachers are reluctant to accept professional standards for item writing – in particular multiple-choice items – because constructed response items – in particular those that allow for extended responses – are viewed as indispensable for a sound and differentiated diagnosis of student competencies. While this line of reasoning can, of course, be correct under certain circumstances, it neglects the specific constraints that exist for standards-based assessment at a national level in contrast to classroom assessment.

180

For national assessments, each open-ended response requires coding instructions that need to be detailed and flexible enough to be applicable to all possible responses that could be given by students. It also requires that numerous coders need to be trained to apply these instructions reliably. Consequently, large amounts of time and money are needed to score individual answers and automatization of these processes is essentially impossible except for constructed response items in very limited domains and contexts. Even if software programs for an automatic evaluation of student responses were purchased and adapted for use with a limited set of items, this would require substantial financial investments.

Moreover, since it is intended that part of the items will be released to schools for their own evaluations, it is indispensable for a sound and fair measurement that the items can be scored objectively by teachers who were not extensively trained in coding theses items. For the primary level in German, for example, it was, thus, agreed that a rate of about 50% of items with closed answer format should be targeted. It is also worth noting, however, that one of the benefits of the negative preconceptions about standardized test items of many teachers was that many creative selected-response formats were utilized as a reaction to the constraints.

Hence, through gradually teaching the item writers the core concepts and by illustrating the benefits of well-constructed items and problems of poorly constructed items with many examples, item writers became slowly more open to the specifics of standards-based test development at a national level and empowered to transfer their acquired knowledge to other contexts.

*Psychological barriers toward assessing different competencies in separate items*

Another challenge for the item writers was to try to write items that did *not* require many different competencies at the same time. From their experience in designing good tasks for use in their classroom instruction, they often preferred to construct integrative tasks that require a bundle of different skills and competencies. Therefore, in the beginning, many teachers believed that only integrative tasks would be able to provide an accurate picture of students' competencies. Here, again, extensive training and ongoing communication was necessary to change this preconception and to clarify the benefits of measuring only one competence with one item.

*Psychological barriers toward rejecting items*

Another important psychological barrier that needed to be overcome concerned the frustration and negative impact on motivation among item writers caused by unexpected poor psychometric properties of single items and the need to discard these items. Hence, item writers were informed at the beginning and throughout the training, that a large proportion of items usually do not pass the strict psychometric tests. The primacy of psychometric criteria was particularly challenging to communicate whenever items possessed high face validity and were viewed as exemplary for the creativity and engagement that item writers had put into the process. One solution that was chosen to alleviate this source of stress for item writers was to keep these items as classroom implementation items.

*The necessity of appropriately tailored training materials*

One structural aspect of training given to item writers involved providing numerous examples that illustrated central principles of item construction for standardized assessments. Apart from essential item writing guidelines such as how to write questions that are unambiguous and distractors that are plausible, several key aspects of item quality were new to item writers and needed to be trained extensively. Of particular importance were means by which items could be constructed in a way that allowed for a fair assessment of students with different ethnic backgrounds, sexes, or types of background knowledge, which are potential sources for item bias (e.g., Clauser and Mazor, 1998; Penfield and Lam, 2000) in the statistical analyses for deriving the proficiency scales.

While numerous guidelines for item writers are available in the literature (e.g., ALTE, 2005; Mullis et al., 2004; Neuhaus and Braun, in press), it was necessary to compile the relevant information anew for the item writers to tailor them to their specific needs. This was done primarily for two reasons. One, not all item writers were able to read the languages in which existing manuals or guidelines were written. Two, due to the time constraints that the item writers faced from their job as teachers and the parallel item development work for the IQB, several manuals or guidelines proved to be too extensive. As a result, the most important item writing principles were synthesized and continually updated for different item development groups, which required additional resources within the IQB (see, e.g. Köller et al., (2005a, 2005b), for German and mathematics at the primary level).

*The necessity of intensive training sequences*

Effective training for item writers was provided predominantly by national or international experts outside of the IQB who were commissioned to plan, conduct, and document the training. Importantly, this training was periodic, intensive, and focused on particular sets of competencies. For example, in English as a first foreign language, the item writers were trained in seven week-long workshops where approximately every two workshops focused on one set of competences such as reading comprehension or writing. Teachers were, thus, able to form coherent teams that work collaboratively in a constructive manner. Furthermore, they were able to sequentially build up overarching item-writing skills necessary for writing high-quality items across all competency areas as well as specific item-writing skills necessary for writing high-quality items in a particular competency area.

Moreover, the sequencing also allowed for the relatively flexible integration of new item writers into the process due to the fact that some item writers that had already been trained had to drop out due to other commitments. From the perspective of the IQB, however, drop-outs are always a difficult phenomenon to deal with. On the one hand, from a professional development perspective, it is desirable to have well-trained specialists working autonomously in the federal states for a reintegration of well-trained item writers into their local communities is important. On the other hand, if the departure takes place in the middle of the process, the item writers that replace the departed ones are not sufficiently trained yet, which sets the process back to some degree and requires additional resources to be invested. Hence, there was no ideal solution to completely prevent any risk of drop-outs other than to have a sufficiently large number of item writers be engaged in the process so that the system was able to buffer the loss of a few members. Again, this is why it is important to construct the item development process as iterative and ongoing, well beyond the creation of the initial proficiency scales.

*Challenges in construct selection and operationalization*

Due to the psychometric demands for test items in terms of reliability and an objective scoring, the range of competencies or constructs that can be assessed with them has to be necessarily limited. Indeed, certain competency areas such as intercultural or methodological competencies in the first foreign language are impossible to assess with standards-based assessments. These can only be assessed in their full complexity through observations that involve authentic contexts and an interaction among many students and native speakers, which is prohibitive for assessment at a national level for economic and logistical reasons. It is, thus, not the standards-based assessments that have to adapt to the need for assessing broader competency areas, but the culture of evaluation more generally so that alternative assessment formats such as performance assessments or portfolios are developed, accepted, and weighted properly.

The first challenge in deciding which competencies to measure through standards-based assessments was rooted in the freedom that the verbal statements in the standards documents leave for their operationalization. In fact, this is one of the advantages of the NES for classroom practice, because the standards documents deliberately refrain from lists of statements that are too numerous and detailed to be practically useful to teachers. Yet, it is also one of their disadvantages, because there are many potential tasks and items that could require students to activate the cited competencies to some degree and any set of items is subject to legitimate criticisms of exclusion. Again, the groundwork that had been laid by the PISA consortium and the IPN was instrumental in this regard, because their operationalizations of constructs and competence models could be used as an important starting point.

In general, all NES distinguish between competencies at different levels of detail such that there are broad *competency areas*, which are broken down further with specific *sets of competencies*. Additionally, the NES define different levels of cognitive demand for tasks and items. One of the challenges for teachers was to think about multiple competencies simultaneously and in isolation when writing items while also being able to write a variety of items at different levels of difficulty that activate different combinations of competencies. One helpful instrument in this regard is a *table of specifications* for prototypical assessments, which lists the different content domains, levels of cognitive demands, and number of items for each combination and helped structure the thinking of the item writers.

An inspection of the NES across subject-matter domains shows, however, that there are a large number of competency descriptions, especially when the lists of specific competencies are viewed in conjunction with the general preambles at the beginning of the standards documents. This is in conflict with the desire by stakeholders to obtain, ideally, reliable information on each specific competency, because it is not possible to have an equal number of items in each cell of the matrix or even to write items for each possible combination of competency, difficulty level, and content area. As a consequence, not all possible combinations could be assessed and large numbers of items were needed to cover at least the selected competencies. These items had to be distributed in various booklets using a *multi-matrix design*, where different students respond to different sets of items. This, in turn, created a challenge for the statistical modelling that could be conducted, because it placed restrictions on the statistical models that could be used for the calibration of item data.

## Psychometric challenges in the creation and validation of proficiency scales

There are three key challenges for creating the proficiency scales for the resulting standards-based assessments and the subsequent validation of inferences about learner competencies that can be made with them that were encountered,
(i)   the selection of a statistical model for calibration
(ii)  the process of setting cut scores on the resulting statistical dimensions, and
(iii) the development of complex performance profiles for individual learners on the basis of multiple classification models.
Since data for most subject-matter domains are currently in the pilot-study phase, the explanations in this section refer partially to first experiences with such data sets, partially to research projects, and partially to strategies for the future.

184

Data that have been collected for large-scale standards-based assessments are typically calibrated with models from *item response theory* (IRT) (e.g., Embretson and Reise, 2000; Rost, 2004a; van der Linden and Hambleton, 1997). The advantages of models developed within this statistical framework over models in classical test theory (e.g., Lord and Novick, 1968) are manifold and include their ability to place learners and test items on the same scale, to handle complex data-collection designs including nested and rotated designs, to estimate learner and item characteristics properly when missing data are present, to accurately estimate item characteristics for item bundles or testlets, and to efficiently include additional explanatory variables into the model structure (see, e.g., Adams et al., 1997; deBoeck and Wilson, 2004; Wainer et al., 2006).

In order to understand the challenges properly as well as the resulting consequences and compromises of a particular model choice that are faced by the IQB, it is useful to remember that there are, in fact, a large number of models that have been developed within an IRT framework. All such models use latent variables that are supposed to represent the latent characteristics of the learners (i.e., the competencies in the NES) about which inferences are desired (e.g., Borsboom et al., 2003; Edwards and Bagozzi, 2000). Some dimensions that are useful for organizing these models are the following (see also McDonald, 1999; Muthén, 2002; Rupp, 2002; Skrondal and Rabe-Hesketh, 2004).

First, models can be distinguished by whether they model dichotomous, polytomous, or continuous item responses, which can all arise out of different item formats. Second, models can be distinguished by whether they model one latent dimension or multiple latent dimensions simultaneously; in the latter case, the latent correlations between the latent variables can be estimated without measurement error. In the case of multidimensional models, it is useful to separate models that combine the multiple competences in a compensatory fashion so that an excess in one competence can compensate for a lack in another competence or in a non-compensatory fashion where this is not possible. Third, models can be distinguished by whether the mathematical functions they utilize are parametric (i.e., result in smooth item characteristic curves reflecting the relationship between the latent variable and the probability of obtaining a certain item score) or nonparametric (i.e., result in empirically approximated item characteristic curves). Fourth, they can be distinguished by whether the latent variables are continuous-leading to norm-referenced interpretations about learners- or categorical-leading to criterion-referenced interpretations about learners. Fifth, they can be distinguished by whether they allow for the inclusion of explanatory variables at the level of the learner, the item, or higher structural levels in the case of multi-level designs (e.g., students within schools within states).

Given the complexity of the model space within IRT, it is important to recognize that the choices of calibration models utilized in large-scale assessments, including standards-based assessments, appear rather limited at first sight. Among the prototypical models that are often discussed for calibrating data are unidimensional IRT models, which include the one-parameter or Rasch model, the two-parameter and three-parameter models, and their compensatory multidimensional extensions. In many studies that use large-scale achievement tests, which resemble standards-based assessments in their design and objective, such as PISA, TIMSS, or DESI, the unidimensional Rasch model is used. Moreover, it is not uncommon in these studies to estimate separate unidimensional scales even for multidimensional tests and then to compute and correct the observed correlations between the latent dimensions in a separate step.

This theoretically rather restricted choice has many important practical reasons. One of the most important factors that drive the application of the Rasch model is not only its theoretical property of specific objectivity but also the easy of interpretability of item and learner characteristics, because both are represented by a single number and estimates of precision. This is of particular importance for standards-based assessments, because achievement profiles of learners at different levels of aggregations and the resultant political decisions have to be easily communicated to different stakeholders, which are typically not well trained in measurement and statistics.

Another factor is the complex design structure of these assessments. For most of the tests developed at the IQB, the items for an individual competence such as reading comprehension or mathematical ability are distributed to over 100 hundred booklets that random samples of learners are working on. The booklets are designed under content and competence constraints. They contain common items, so-called anchor items, in such a way that all booklets can be sequentially connected to one another and all learners and items can be placed on one common scale using an IRT model.

This design induces, first and foremost, data that are missing by design, because not all students work on all items. However, the problem of missing data by design gets overlaid with the occurrence of data that are missing at random due to reasons like general fatigue, time pressure or a lack of intrinsic motivation. The missing data have to be modelled correctly within a multilevel structure so that accurate and precise effect sizes at class and school levels can be obtained. Since achievement can be strongly influenced by background variables of the learners such as ethnicity and sex as well as school variables such as class size and opportunities-to-learn (see, e.g., Neubrand, 2004; Schiefele et al., 2004; Schümer et al., 2004; PISA Konsortium, 2005), these variables need to be collected through additional questionnaires and need to be, ideally, included in the measurement models to obtain purified effect sizes.

These desiderata for data calibration result in the need for software programs that can not only handle these kinds of data, but can do so within reasonable timeframes.

One popular program for estimating such complex data structures is *ACERConQuest* (Wu et al., 1998) where calibrations with unidimensional Rasch models take less than one hour for many scales. However, even with this powerful software, the calibrations can even take a few days, if not weeks, if multidimensional Rasch models with predictors are used. While the program is very flexible in estimating different classes of measurement models including the *linear logistic test model (LLTM)* (e.g., Fisher, 1997), it is further constrained to estimate models in the Rasch family. Hence, other assessment institutes such as CITO in the Netherlands or ETS in the U.S. have developed their own software programs that can accommodate their particular needs, but that is an expensive process that requires extensive programming and statistical expertise that a team of researchers needs to be able to commit to over several years.

In sum, while the theoretical model space in IRT is rich and contains many models that are well suited to complex data structures, it is practical constraints, required statistical expertise, and established traditions that result in most large-scale assessment institutions, including the IQB, making modelling choices that may appear somewhat restricted but serve the practical needs for decision-making reasonably well. However, as one means to tackle the challenges imposed by the data structures, the IQB also engages in research programs that seek to investigate multiple novel statistical models. In particular, one research group investigates the theoretical properties and practical limitations of modern statistical models that can address the desire of stakeholders to obtain reliable classifications of students according to multiple competencies.

*The development of complex performance profiles for individual learners*

While many operational standards-based assessments are designed to provide accurate and efficient information about groups of learners at an aggregate level such as classes and schools, the development of the NES suggests a need for individualized feedback for the purpose of developing remedial training and suitable intervention programs. In psychometrics, biometrics, and mathematical psychology, statistical models that can estimate such complex performance profiles for individual learners have been refined significantly since about the mid-1990s. For reviews of these models and related considerations for their use, the interested reader may consult Junker (1999), Leighton and Gierl (in press), Rupp and Mislevy (in press), Rupp (in press), or Rupp, Leucht, and Hartung (2006) as well as the sources cited therein.

Put simply, the chief advantage of these models is that they classify each learner as either having or not having learned each competence on the basis of probabilistic estimates that take into account potential aberrant response behaviour such as slipping (i.e., responding incorrectly when they should respond correctly) and guessing (i.e., responding correctly when they should respond incorrectly). These models are, thus, termed *multiple classification models*. Technically, they are *restricted latent class models*, because the number of latent classes that a learner can belong to is restricted by the number of competences that are postulated to underlie performance on the test and the possible gradations of each competence (e.g., absent-present vs. absent-in development-fully developed). This also makes them multidimensional IRT models with binary latent variables that can estimate a complex item structure.

The most prominent models for multiple classifications are the *DINA and NIDA models* (e.g., de la Torre and Douglas, 2004; Junker and Sijtsma, 2001), the *reparametrized unified / fusion model* (e.g., Hartz, 2002; Templin and Henson, 2005), the *general diagnostic model* (e.g., von Davier, 2005), and *Bayesian inference networks* (e.g., Williamson et al., 2006). The first four models can essentially be distinguished by the types of parameters they estimate for items, learners, or competences with the fusion model being the most complex of the three. Bayesian inference networks are more of an umbrella term for a wide variety of measurement models and allow the specification of complex competence dependencies that can be flexibly adapted to different task demands within a test. Just like more traditional IRT models, the objective is to view each individual item as the unit of analysis for which a particular model can be specified so that various models can be estimated within a single test. In recent years, researchers have, thus, developed multiple classification models that can accommodate polytomously scored items (e.g., Bolt and Fu, 2004; Templin et al., 2003a), can distinguish between ordinal competence gradations (e.g., Templin et al., 2003b; von Davier, 2005), and can map hierarchical competence structures (e.g., de la Torre and Douglas, 2004).

To illustrate the advantages of these models for standards-based assessments, consider, for example, the content standards for mathematics in Germany (KMK, 2003, 2004), which distinguish between six broad competence sets. Using multiple classification models, one could obtain performance profiles such as the one shown in figure 2 for each learner, which shows the probability of mastery for each of six competence sets. This profile shows that the first, fifth, and sixth competence sets have probably not been mastered to a satisfactory degree by this learner, while the opposite is true for the second, third, and fourth competence sets. Such estimates can be used to develop competence profiles for groups of learners that provide information about how difficult it is to learn them. An example of such a relationship is shown in figure 3, which shows that the first competence set is much harder to learn than the second, because even with higher ability on a global measure of proficiency the probability of mastering that competence set is lower than for the other competence set.

While such information is practically useful to distinguish among learners at a more fine-grained level of detail, the practical implementation of these models can pose various challenges. For example, the models require as input the specification of which items require which sets of competences for all items on the test in a so-called *Q-matrix* (Tatsuoka, 1983). If the classification should be defensible to stakeholders,

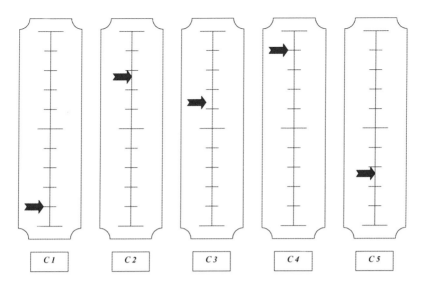

Figure 2:    A competency profile for an individual student

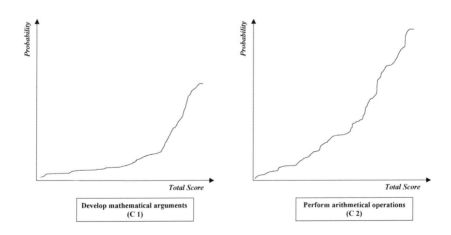

Figure 3:    The probability of mastery for two competencies as a function of the total score on an assessment

this information needs to be meticulously specified by committees of experts and sources of disagreement need to be identified and resolved, if possible. The grain size of the information in the Q-matrix (i.e., the nature of the variables represented by the models) depends on the application in which the multiple classification is embedded and can reach from classification of learners on the basis of rather broadly defined competence sets (e.g., six different aspects of mathematical ability as in the example above) to classifications on the basis of very finely defined competences (e.g., different competences involved in number subtraction). This level of detail comes at the price of higher development costs for items. Specifically, Q-matrices have to be developed by committees of experts anew each time a certain diagnostic statement at a new level of granularity or for a new subject-matter domain is desired. At the IQB, item writers are thus asked to provide classifications of items according to the competencies they measure early on in the process and the item review committees can be used as initial sources of Q-matrix specification and verification.

As with the continuous multidimensional models discussed in the first part of the section, the computation time for these models can be prohibitive for timely feedback. A simple model with two competences that underlie four items and 200 learners, for example, may calibrate within a few seconds or minutes, whereas a simple model with seven competences that underlie 40 items and 3000 learners already takes several days to estimate. These examples are further for simple data structures that do not include data missing at random or by design, in which case such times can increase even more. This requires efficient software programs for their estimation, which, until recently, has not been easily accessible for testing institutes due to the fact that researchers either wrote their own code, which might require a user to learn new programming languages, or that companies had developed their own software for in-house research purposes only.

In sum, the theoretical objective of multiple classification models fits snugly with the objective of standards-based assessments in that diagnostic feedback about multiple competences is provided to individual learners. Yet, the practical limitations that currently exist in terms of calibration time, available software programs, and statistical expertise may hamper the exciting potential these models hold for standards-based assessments. The following section now describes additional challenges in the process that typically follows the unidimensional or multidimensional calibration of the data, namely the setting of cut scores to create proficiency levels, which also requires many principled choices to be made.


*The setting of cut scores*

Stakeholders generally wish to communicate and receive results about student achievement in simple and understandable terms that allow them to make decisions in a fair and defensible way (see Kohler and Schrader, 2004). While the creation of

190

unidimensional scales uses the response data for a comparison of learners with one another or an outside norm, the quantitative location on a scale, especially a latent-variable scale, is not as easy to communicate as distinct performance levels such as 'basic', 'proficient', or 'advanced'. Hence, once the statistical dimensions have been created, it is often necessary to divide the continuum into adjacent categories that reflect different ordered levels of achievement, which is also required for the national proficiency scales in Germany (for an overview of such procedures see, e.g., Cizek et al., 2004; Haertel and Lorié, 2004; Zieky and Perie, 2006).

In the psychometric literature, various quantitative approaches to determining the boundaries between the performance categories, the so-called cut scores, have been proposed. According to Rost (2004b), most procedures for setting *cut-scores* can be viewed as belonging to one of three broad categories,

(i)   procedures that utilize the difficulty parameters of the items or item response categories,
(ii)  procedures that utilize characteristics of the items that are indicative of the response processes they induce,
(iii) procedures that define differing solution profiles for different groups of learners.

Consequently, the range of models employed for these approaches ranges from explanatory item response models such as the LLTM and its extensions (e.g., Hartig and Frey, 2005) to mixture models (e.g., Rost, 1990).

Despite the wish to inject the process of determining a cut score with objectivity through the use of quantitative methods, it remains essentially a consensual process based on expert judgment (Cizek et al., 2004). That is, the setting of multiple cut scores by committees of experts can be systematized through the use of a particular standard-setting method, but there are no 'true' cut-scores that are determined by this process in the way that true population parameters are estimated in statistical models by unbiased sample statistics. Among the most popular methods for setting cut scores are the *Bookmark* and *modified Angoff* methods, which are examples of *test-centered methods* (i.e., methods that require judgments about items), and the *Contrasting Groups* and *Body-of-work methods*, which are examples of learner-centered methods (i.e., methods that require judgments about learners).

All methods, however, require iterative rounds of judgments, which can include discussions among panellists and feedback about the inter- and intra-judge consistencies. Further, they all make use of the notion of a *borderline*, rather than a typical learner, which is a learner that is at the transitioning point between two performance levels.

Not surprisingly, there are numerous practical challenges that need to be addressed for setting cut scores for standards-based assessments. Overall, while the process of holding the standard-setting sessions is relatively compact and can typically be done within a few days, it requires comprehensive preparation and the significant expertise so as to avoid undue influences of extraneous factors on the judgments of the panellists. It is also a rather expensive process, because it is typically necessary to determine cut scores for each scale and each grade level separately (see Cizek et al., 2004, for an illustrative example). As with most methodological endeavours, it is important to document each aspect of the process meticulously and to situate it within theoretical frameworks so that the decisions that were made are defensible to stakeholders on both empirical and rational grounds.

One particular challenge in this process is the synthesis of quantitative and qualitative information about where cut scores should be set. It is worth remembering that the process of determining cut scores by means of expert panel will always lead to some form of disagreement, which is typically resolved by averaging cut score levels across judges, rounds, or both. Importantly, the process of determining cut scores by means of statistical models will always lead to some form of disagreement also, because different statistical models and different sets of variables used within them will influence the results. The boundary of where qualitative processes end and quantitative processes start is obviously arbitrary as judges may utilize item properties to inform their decisions and can also produce sets of variables to predict item characteristics such as difficulty that can be used in explanatory modelling. It is clear, however, that robustness analyses need to be conducted for the resulting classification of learners even though the final decision of where cut-scores should be set has to be made by political bodies that weigh the cost of different kinds of classification distributions and not methodologists.

At the IQB, due to the high-stakes political context for which the national proficiency scales are developed, expert panels consisting of diverse groups of stakeholders are utilized in conjunction with multiple standard-setting procedures. Members of the expert panels include selected students, teachers, principals, politicians, and other decision-makers. The standard-setting process is conducted in coordination with national and international experts for the purpose of triangulating data, borrowing strength from the individual methods, and achieving higher levels of acceptance from policy makers and stakeholders. Some peculiar challenges arise in addition to the ones listed above such as when the standards for the first foreign language are linked to the *Common European Framework of Reference for Languages* (Council of Europe, 2001) and evidence for both the defensible linking of items and proficiency statements to the European framework and the associated standard-setting procedure has to be amassed.

## Conclusion and summary

In this chapter, we have discussed selected key challenges that were encountered at the IQB during the item development for large-scale standards-based assessments that operationalize the NES in Germany. It became apparent that this process is complex, iterative, and full of compromises. While it is clearly possible to avoid certain obvious mistakes, it is not possible to arrive at a single solution that remains optimal under all possible practical and theoretical perspectives. One of the most important considerations for building the argument that inferences about learners can be validly drawn from the proficiency scales is the meticulous, comprehensive, and precise documentation of all pieces of empirical and rational information that could be considered evidence in this regard. Guidelines for which aspects may be most relevant for the acceptance of such arguments by a wide community of stakeholders can be found in testing standards (e.g., AERA/APA/NCME, 1999) and need to be explicitly referenced. Moreover, the process needs to be planned with a long-term perspective and with multiple back-up strategies in mind so that there are less unexpected events that arise and the ones that do arise can be buffered by the development system.

While the recommendations presented in this chapter are relevant for many kinds of standardized assessments, they are especially important for developing standards-based assessments, because their uses are high-stakes from a political and educational perspective. Decisions about learners within school contexts can affect funding decisions by local authorities and may, in the long run, lead to litigation in cases where parents disagree with the evaluation of their children. Therefore, it is imperative that any validity argument be defensible as best possible within the resource constraints that an institution such as the IQB has to work.

## References

AERA/APA/NCME (1999) *Standard for educational and psychological testing.* Washington, DC.

Adams, R. J., Wilson, M. and Wang, W. (1997) The multidimensional random co-efficients multinomial logit model. *Applied Psychological Measurement,* 21, 1-23.

ALTE (2005) *Materials for the guidance of test item writers* (1995, updated July, 2005). Available online at www.alte.org

Baumert, J., Bos, W. and Lehmann, R. (2000) *TIMSS/III. Dritte Internationale Mathematik- und Naturwissenschaftsstudie. Mathematische und naturwissenschaftliche Bildung am Ende der Schullaufbahn* [TIMSS/III. Third International Math and Science Study. Mathematical and scientific education at the end of the secondary level]. Opladen: Leske & Burich.

Baumert, J., Artelt, C., Klieme, E., Neubrand, M., Prenzel, M., Schiefele, U., Schneider, W., Stanat, P., Tillmann, K.-J. and Weiß, M. (Eds.) (2001) *PISA 2000. Basiskompetenzen von Schülerinnen und Schülern im internationalen Vergleich* [PISA 2000. Elementary competencies of students in an international comparison]. Opladen: Leske + Burich.

Bolt, D. and Fu, J. (2004, April) *A polytomous extension of the fusion model and its Bayesian parameter estimation.* Presentation at the annual meeting of the National Council on Measurement in Education, San Diego, CA.

Borsboom, D., Mellenbergh, G. J. and van Heerden, J. (2003) The theoretical status of latent variables. *Psychological Review,* 110, 203-219.

Borsboom, D., Mellenbergh, G. J. and van Heerden, J. (2004) The concept of validity. *Psychological Review,* 111, 1061-1071.

Bos, W., Lankes, E.-M., Prenzel, M., Schwippert, K., Walther, G. and Valtin, R. (2003) *Erste Ergebnisse aus IGLU. Schülerleistungen am Ende der vierten Jahrgangsstufe im internationalen Vergleich* [Initial results of IGLU. Comparison of elementary school students' academic achievement at the end of the 4th grade]. Münster: Waxmann.

Blum, W., Drüke-Noe, Ch., Hartung, R. and Köller, O. (2006) *Bildungsstandards Mathematik: Konkret* [National educational standards: Concrete illustrations]. Berlin: Cornelsen Scriptor.

Cizek, G. J., Bunch, M. B. and Koons, H. (2004) Setting performance standards: Contemporary methods. *Educational Measurement: Issues and Practice,* 23, 31-50. Available online at www.ncme.org

Clauser, B. and Mazor, K. (1998) Using statistical procedures to identify differentially functioning test items. *Educational Measurement: Issues & Practice,* 17(1), 31-44.

Council of Europe (2001) *Common European reference framework for languages.* Available online at www.coe.int

de Boeck, P. and Wilson, M. (Eds.) (2004) *Explanatory item response models: A generalized linear and nonlinear approach.* New York: Springer.

de la Torre, J. and Douglas, J. (2004) Higher-order latent trait models for cognitive diagnosis. *Psychometrika,* 69, 333-353.

Edwards, J. R. and Bagozzi, R. P. (2000) On the nature and direction of relationships between constructs and measures. *Psychological Methods,* 5, 155-174.

Embretson, S. E. and Reise, S. P (2000). *Item response theory for psychologists.* Mahwah, NJ: Erlbaum.

Fisher, G. H. (1997) Unidimensional linear logistic Rasch models. In W. J. van der Linden and R. K. Hambleton (Hrsg.), *Handbook of modern item response theory* (pp. 225-244). New York: Springer.

Haertel, E. H. and Lorié, W. A. (2004) Validating standards-based test score interpretations. *Measurement: Interdisciplinary Research and Perspectives, 2,* 61-103.

Hartig, J. and Frey, A. (2005, July) *Application of different explanatory item response models for model based proficiency scaling.* Presentation at the 14th international meeting of the Psychometric Society, Tilburg, NL.

Hartz, S. M. (2002) *A Bayesian framework for the Unified Model for assessing cognitive abilities: Blending theory with practicality.* Unpublished doctoral dissertation, University of Illinois, Urbana-Champaign, Department of Statistics.

Junker, B. W. (1999) *Some statistical models and computational methods that may be useful for cognitively-relevant assessment.* Unpublished manuscript. Available online at http://www.stat.cmu.edu/~brian/nrc/cfa

Junker, B.W. and Sijtsma, K. (2001) Cognitive assessment models with few assumptions, and connections with non-parametric item response theory. *Applied Psychological Measurement, 25,* 258-272.

Klieme, E. and Beck, B. (Eds.) (in press). *Sprachliche Kompetenzen – Konzepte und Messung* [Linguistic competences – concepts and their measurement]. Weinheim: Beltz

Klieme, E., Avenarius, H., Blum, W., Döbrich, P., Gruber, H., Prenzel, M., Reiss, K., Riquarts, K., Rost, J., Tenorth, H.-E. and Vollmer, H. J. (2003) *Zur Entwicklung nationaler Bildungsstandards: Eine Expertise* [The development of national educational standards]. Berlin: Bundesministerium für Bildung und Forschung.

KMK. (2003) *Beschlüsse der Kultusministerkonferenz – Bildungsstandards im Fach Mathematik für den mittleren Schulabschluss (Beschluss von 04. Dezember 2003)* [Resolutions of the KMK – National educational standards for mathematics for the 'Mittlerer Schulabschluss']. München: Wolters Kluwer Deutschland.

KMK. (2004) *Beschlüsse der Kultusministerkonferenz – Bildungsstandards im Fach Mathematik für den Hauptschulabschluss (Beschluss von 15. Oktober 2004)* [Resolutions of the KMK – National educational standards for the 'Hauptschulabschluss']. München: Wolters Kluwer Deutschland.

Köller, O., Watermann, R., Trautwein, U. and Lüdtke, O. (2004) *Wege zur Hochschulreife in Baden-Württemberg. TOSCA – Eine Untersuchung an allgemein bildenden und beruflichen Gymnasien* [Pathways to school-leaving qualifications in Baden-Württemberg. TOSCA – A study of general and vocational grammar schools]. Opladen: Leske + Budrich.

Köller, O., Böhme, K., Winkelmann, H., Bremerich-Vos, A., Granzer, D., Vock, M., Pöhlmann, C., Robitzsch, A. and Würfel, K. (2005a) *Hinweise zur Erstellung von Testaufgaben für das Projekt „Evaluation der Standards Deutsch in der Grundschule"* [Guidelines for the development of test items for the project "Evaluation of standards in German at the primary level"] (Working paper GS-2005-01). Berlin, Germany: Institute for Educational Progress, Humboldt University Berlin.

Köller, O., Böhme, K., Neubrand, J., Walther, G., Winkelmann, H., Robitzsch, A., Vock, M., Granzer, D., Pöhlmann, C. and Würfel, K. (2005b) *Hinweise zur Erstellung von Testaufgaben für das Projekt „Evaluation der Standards Mathematik in der Grundschule"* [Guidelines for the development of test items for the project "Evaluation of standards in mathematics at the primary level"] (Working paper GS-2005-02). Berlin: Institute for Educational Progress, Humboldt University Berlin.

Kohler, B. and Schrader, F.W. (Hrsg.) (2004) Ergebnisrückmeldung und Rezeption – Von der externen Evaluation zur Entwicklung von Schule und Unterricht. Sonderheft der Zeitschrift *Empirische Pädagogik, 18.*

Leighton, J. and Gierl, M. (Eds.) (in press). *Cognitive diagnostic assessment in education: Theory and practice.* Cambridge: Cambridge University Press.

Lord, F. M. and Novick, M. R. (1968) *Statistical theories of mental test scores.* Reading, MA: Addison-Wesley.

McDonald, R. P. (1999) *Test theory: A unified treatment.* Mahwah, NJ: Erlbaum.

Martin, M. O., Mullis, I. V. S. and Chrostowski, S. J. (Eds.) (2004) *TIMSS 2003 technical report.* Chestnut Hill, MA: TIMSS & PIRLS International Study Center, Boston College. Available online at http://timss.bc.edu/timss2003i/technicalD. html

Messick, S. (1989) Validity. In R. Linn (Ed.), *Educational measurement* (pp. 13-103). New York: Macmillan.

Mislevy, R. J., Steinberg, L. S. and Almond, R. G. (2003) On the structure of educational assessments. *Measurement: Interdisciplinary Research and Perspectives, 1,* 3-67.

Mullis, I. V. S., Martin, M. O. and Kennedy, A. M. (2004, March) *Item-writing guidelines for the PIRLS 2006 field test.* Paper presented at the 2nd PIRLS 2006 NRC Meeting, Bratislava.

Muthén, B. O. (2002) Beyond SEM: General latent variable modeling. *Behaviormetrika, 29,* 81-117.

Neubrand, M. (Ed.) (2004) *Mathematische Kompetenzen von Schülerinnen und Schülern in Deutschland: Vertiefende Analysen im Rahmen von PISA 2000* [Mathematical competencies of students in Germany: Supplementary analyses for PISA 2000]. Wiesbaden: Verlag für Sozialwissenschaften.

Neuhaus, B. and Braun, E. (in press) *Testkonstruktion und Erhebungsstrategien – praktische Tipps für empirisch arbeitende Didaktiker* [Test construction and assessment strategies – practical tips for empirically working didacts]. Innsbruck: Studienverlag.

OECD (2005) *The PISA 2003 technical report.* Paris: OECD Publishing. Available online at www.pisa.oecd.org.

Penfield, R. D. and Lam, T. C. M. (2000) Assessing differential item functioning in performance assessment: Review and recommendations. *Educational Measurement: Issues and Practice,* 19, 5-15.

PISA Konsortium (Eds.) (2005) *PISA 2003. Der zweite Vergleich der Länder in Deutschland: Was wissen und können Jugendliche?* [PISA 2003. The second comparison of the federal states in Germany. What do our students know and what can they do?]. Münster: Waxmann.

Rost, J. (1990) Rasch models in latent classes: An integration of two approaches to item analysis. *Applied Psychological Measurement,* 14, 271-282.

Rost, J. (2004a) *Lehrbuch Testtheorie und Testkonstruktion.* Bern: Huber.

Rost, J. (2004b) Psychometrische Modelle zur Überprüfung von Bildungsstandards anhand von Kompetenzmodellen [Psychometric models for the empirical investigation of national educational standards via theoretical models of competence]. *Zeitschrift für Pädagogik,* 50, 662-679.

Rupp, A. A. (2002) Feature selection for choosing and assembling measurement models: A building-block-based organization. *International Journal of Testing,* 2, 311-360.

Rupp, A. A. (in press). The answer is in the question: A guide for describing and investigating the conceptual foundations and statistical properties of cognitive psychometric models. *International Journal of Testing.*

Rupp, A. A. and Mislevy, R. J. (in press) Cognitive psychology as it applies to diagnostic assessment. In J. Leighton (Ed.), *Cognitive diagnostic assessment in education: Theory and practice.* Cambridge: University Press.

Rupp, A. A., Leucht, M. and Hartung, R. (2006) Die Kompetenzbrille aufsetzen: Verfahren zur multiplen Klassifikation von Lernenden für Kompetenzdiagnostik in Unterricht und Testung. *Unterrichtswissenschaft,* 34(3), 195-219.

Schecker, H. and Parchmann, I. (2007) This book, Chapter 8.

Schiefele, U., Artelt, C., Schneider, W. and Stanat, P. (Eds.) (2004) *Struktur, Entwicklung und Förderung von Lesekompetenz: Vertiefende Analysen im Rahmen von PISA 2000* [The structure, development, and remediation of reading comprehension ability: Supplementary analyses for PISA 2000]. Wiesbaden: Verlag für Sozialwissenschaften.

Schümer, G., Tillmann, K.-J. and Weiß, M. (Eds.) (2004) *Die Institution Schule und die Lebenswelt der Schüler: Vertiefende Analysen im Rahmen von PISA 2000* [Schooling and the personal background of students: Supplementary analyses for PISA 2000]. Wiesbaden: Verlag für Sozialwissenschaften.

Skrondal, A. and Rabe-Hesketh, S. (2004) *Generalized latent variable modeling: Multilevel, longitudinal, and structural equation modeling.* Boca Raton, FL: Sage.

Tatsuoka, K. K. (1983) Rule-space: An approach for dealing with misconceptions based on item response theory. *Journal of Educational Measurement, 20,* 345-354.

Templin, J. L. and Henson, R. A. (2005) *The random effects reparametrized unified model: A model for joint estimation of discrete competences and continuous ability.* Manuscript submitted for publication.

Templin, J. L., Roussos, L. and Stout, W. (2003a) *An extension of the current fusion model to treat polytomous attributes.* Unpublished Technical Report for the ETS External Diagnostic Group.

Templin, J. L., He, X., Roussos, L. and Stout, W. (2003b) *The pseudo-item method: A simple technique for analysis of polytomous data with the fusion model.* Unpublished Technical Report for the ETS External Diagnostic Group.

van der Linden, W. J. and Hambleton, R. K. (1997) *Handbook of modern item response theory.* New York: Springer-Verlag.

von Davier, M. (2005) *A general diagnostic model applied to language testing data* (Research Report RR-05-16). Princeton, NJ: Educational Testing Service.

Wainer, H., Brown, L. M., Bradlow, E. T., Wang, X., Skorupski, W. P., Boulet, J. and Mislevy, R. J. (2006) An application of testlet response theory in the scoring of a complex certification exam. In D. M. Williamson, R. J. Mislevy and I. I. Bejar (Eds.), *Automated scoring of complex tasks in computer-based testing* (pp. 169-200). Mahwah, NJ: Erlbaum.

Williamson, D. M., Almond, R. G., Mislevy, R. J. and Levy, R. (2006) An application of Bayesian networks in automated scoring of computerized simulation tasks. In: D. M. Williamson, R. J. Mislevy and I. I. Bejar (Hrsg.), *Automated scoring of complex tasks in computer-based testing* (pp. 201-258). Mahwah, NJ: Erlbaum.

Wu, M. L., Adams, R. J..and Wilson, M. R. (1998). ACERConQuest [Software Program]. Melbourne: Australian Council for Educational Research.

Zieky, M. and Perie, M. (2006) *A primer on setting cut scores on tests of educational achievement.* Princeton, NJ: Educational Testing Service.

# Chapter 11

# 'Science and Technology for All' – an Israeli curriculum based on new standards in science education

*Rachel Mamlok-Naaman*

*Department of Science Teaching, Weizmann Institute of Science, Rehovot, 76100, Israel*

## Provision of science in Israeli schools

The science curriculum for primary, secondary and high school students, in Israel, is defined by special committees, which operate in a centralized system. Each committee consists of approximately ten members – the superintendent who chairs the committee and is appointed by the Ministry of Education, scientists, science educators, and teachers.

The compulsory science curriculum for high school students consists of at least one-credit course, three hours per week for each scientific discipline (biology, chemistry and physics), dispersed over the $10^{th}$ grade, or a three credit course – nine hours per week for an integrated new science curriculum: "Science and Technology for all" for those who are non-science oriented students, dispersed over the $10^{th}$ to $11^{th}$ grades. For students who would like to continue and study one or more of the scientific disciplines in the $11^{th}$ grade (a three credit course for each), a timeframe of three periods (each period consists of 45 minutes) per week in the $10^{th}$ grade and six periods per week in the $11^{th}$ grade is recommended. For those who choose to expand their knowledge in any of the scientific disciplines, there is an addition of a two-credit course during the $12^{th}$ grade (six periods per week).

In the secondary schools (junior high schools), technology and integrated science (biology, physics, earth sciences, environmental science, etc.) are dispersed over the $7^{th}$ to $9^{th}$ grades, within a timeframe of approximately 600 periods. Each school has the autonomy to break up the 600 periods over the three years. For example, in one of the junior high schools, the team of science teachers decided upon a timeframe of 4 periods per week in the $7^{th}$ grade, 5 periods per week in the $8^{th}$ grade, and 4 hours per week in the $9^{th}$ grade.

Science studies in the primary school start at the 1st grade and end at the $6^{th}$ grade. The students study two periods per week and the curriculum comprises of integrated scientific disciplines, e.g., biology, geography, physics, chemistry, health and environmental science. Table 1 presents the current timeframe of study in science and technology in primary, secondary and high schools, compiled by the curricula committees and influenced by the reform in science and mathematics education in Israel which started in 1992.

| Level | Primary | Secondary | High school | | | |
|---|---|---|---|---|---|---|
| | | | Science-oriented students | | | Non-science oriented students |
| Age | 6-12 | 12-15 | 15-16 | 16-17 | 17-18 | 15-17 |
| Grade | 1-6 | 7-9 | 10 | 11 | 12 | 10-11 |
| Periods per week | 2 | 13-14 | 9 (3x3) * | 6 for each of the scientific disciplines ** | 6 for each of the scientific disciplines *** | 9 |
| Scientific subjects | Integrated scientific disciplines, e.g., biology, geography, physics, chemistry, health and environmental science. | Technology and integrated science (biology, physics, earth sciences, environmental science, etc.) | Biology, chemistry and physics, as separate disciplinary sciences (Basic concepts). | A three credit course (together with the 10th grade studies) for each of the separate disciplinary sciences: Biology, chemistry or physics. | A five credit advanced course (together with the 10th and 11th grade studies) for each of the separate disciplinary sciences: Biology, chemistry or physics | A three credit course for an integrated new science curriculum "Science and Technology for all". |

*Compulsory for high school science-oriented students
**Optional for high school non-science-oriented students
***Optional for high school science-oriented students who choose expand their
 knowledge in any of the scientific disciplines

Table 1:     The timeframe of study in science and technology in primary, secondary and high schools in Israel

## Reform in science and mathematics education in Israel

Reform in science and mathematics education in Israel started in 1992 when the Ministry of Education and Culture published the "Tomorrow 98" report (Tomorrow 98: Superior Committee on Science, Mathematics and Technology Education in Israel, 1992). The report gave 43 recommendations for changes and improvements to the existing programs and referred to the educational and structural areas of curriculum development and implementation, pedagogy of science and mathematics teaching, as well as directions and actions to be taken in the professional development of science and mathematics teachers (table 2).

- Experience the richness and excitement of knowing about and understanding the natural world

- Use appropriate scientific processes and principles in making personal decisions

- Engage intelligently in public discourse and debate about matters of scientific and technological concern

- Increase students' economic productivity through the use of knowledge, understanding, and skills of the scientifically literate persons in their careers.

- Science education should aim at preparing students to become scientifically literate citizens, e.g., science for personal needs, social issues, career awareness, academic preparation

- The science curriculum should be relevant to everyday life, and should change dramatically from focus on the disciplinary approach to a multidimensional approach

- Different programs should be taught to science and non-science-oriented students, namely high-school students (grades 10–12), who did not choose to major in any of the scientific disciplines

- New instructional strategies should be developed

- Preparation and professional development of science teachers should take place in different teachers' centers.

Table 2:    The goals and recommendations of the 'Tomorrow 98' report

The recommendations of the committee were accepted and the government committed itself to ensure that science is taught to all high-school students in the country, not only to prepare students for academic careers in science, but also to prepare them to become scientifically literate citizens in a society that is highly affected by scientific advances and is aware of its technological manifestations (Bunce, 1995; Hofstein et al., 2000). Consequently, science would be taught with appropriate emphasis on its relevance to everyday life and its role in industry, technology, and society. In recent years, the science curriculum has been changing dramatically from a focus on the structure of the discipline approach to a multidimensional approach.

It was also decided that a different curriculum would be taught to non-science-oriented students, namely high-school students (grades 10–12), who did not choose to major in any of the science disciplines (biology, science, or physics). The reasons for this are numerous and diverse among which is the assumption that some of these students have a poor attitude toward science, which declines further from junior to senior high school (Neathery, 1997; Weiss, 1987). The goals of this curriculum followed those of the U.S. National Science Education Standards (National Research Council, 1996), aiming to educate students who will be able to:

• Experience the richness and excitement of knowing about and understanding the natural world;

• Use appropriate scientific processes and principles in making personal decisions;

• Engage intelligently in public discourse and debate about matters of scientific and technological concern;

• Increase their economic productivity through the use of knowledge, understanding, and skills of the scientifically literate person in their careers.

As mentioned before, the science curriculum in Israel is centralized, and defined by special committees. The committees meets several times a year, to check the implementation of the different curricula, the relevance to every day life, and the alignment to innovations and developments in science. As a result, the curriculum of each of the scientific domains used to change every 10–12 years. Recently, the committee, which is in charge of the primary science curriculum, started to work on the definition of national standards. The other committees have yet to discuss national standards, but rather determined goals and recommendations regarding the subject matter, the pedagogical issues and the assessment methods. The "Tomorrow 98" report (Tomorrow 98: Superior Committee on Science, Mathematics and Technology Education in Israel, 1992), had a great impact on the committee's decisions, and the different curricula became more structured and more detailed than they used to be, in defining the subject matter topics as well as in suggesting pedagogical strategies and didactic tools.

As part of the reform in science education that has been evolving in Israel since 1992, a different curriculum, for non-science-oriented students (i.e. for those who do not choose to major in any of the three school science disciplines) has been developed. This paper is principally concerned with this course, 'Science and Technology for All'.

## 'Science and Technology for All' in Israel

The 'Science and Technology for All' program is a multidisciplinary integrative subject aimed at students who are not majoring in any of the scientific disciplines. The topics in the program do not focus on a specific discipline, but rather on various aspects of scientific fields impacting on technology and society. Teaching the subject enables diversifying "traditional" teaching methods and incorporating others. The program's structure is modular. Each module focuses on a specific scientific topic (Dori and Hofstein, 2000) and the following are some examples:

*(i) Energy and the Human Being* (Ben-Zvi, 1998, 1999) clarifies some issues concerning many beliefs and misconceptions about energy (Ben-Zvi, 1999).

*(ii) Science: An Ever-Developing Entity* (Mamlok, 1998) develops an understanding of the nature of science by using historical examples. In this way, science is presented as a continuously developing enterprise of the human mind (Erduran, 2001; Mamlok et al., 2000).

*(iii) Brain, Medicine, and Drugs* (Cohen, 2000; Cohen et al., 2004) focuses on several selected aspects of brain research and its relationship to human behavior and emotions.

The team of science high school teachers select five to seven modules from a database of modules (some 30 have been developed as of now, 35–40 hours each), including a diversity of disciplines and skills, all having an STS-type structure and content, tackling a specific problem in the interface between science, society and technology (Hofstein and Mamlok, 2001).

### How do teachers choose the modules of 'Science and Technology for All'?

As mentioned above, each student should study five modules during the 10th and 11th grades. The five modules must include at least one of the life sciences (biology) modules and two material science modules – one, chemistry-oriented and the other, physics-oriented. Selection of the subjects is based on the decision of the science teaching team at school – the knowledge and interests of the teachers, as well as on the preferences of the students. No hierarchy exists among the modules. When making the module selection, modules should be included that enable linking scientific and technological developments with social, ethic and moral processes and aspects. The science teachers' team at school should decide upon a group of core skills which should be embedded in the program, e.g., critical thinking in scientific technological fields, locating and analyzing scientific technological information, processing, discussing and presenting scientific technological information, or applying scientific technological knowledge.

### Teaching methodology

When teaching the modules, the teachers are expected to use a wide range of pedagogical interventions and instructional techniques in order to cope with a wide range of student abilities, interests, and means of motivation. Moreover, the implementation of such an STS program with a wide spectrum of learning goals necessitates matching to each learning goal its instructional technique as well as an assessment tool to measure students' achievement and progress (Hofstein et al., 2006).

There is no doubt that the new content standards call upon implementation of new and varied pedagogical interventions and instructional techniques, tailored for a diverse student population. Hofstein and Walberg (1995) and Tobin et al. (1988) suggested that instructional techniques in science must be matched with the learners' characteristics, learning style, and interests, in order to maximize the effectiveness of the teaching and learning processes as well as to increase student motivation (Hofstein and Kempa, 1985). Clearly, in practice, it is difficult to respond to each student's needs and learning style, but much can be achieved if science teachers use a wide repertoire of instructional strategies in their classroom. This will enable many students to study science using an approach that is more aligned with their own interests and learning style. In the science classroom, the teacher can vary the classroom learning environment by implementing various instructional techniques, e.g., learning in small groups, simulation games, debates (role-playing), critical reading of articles in newspapers and scientific journals, inquiry-type laboratories, using computer-assisted instruction (CAI), student projects, and educational field trips to chemical industries.

The teaching strategies of 'Science and Technology for All' consist of:

• Critical reading and analysis of popular scientific articles.

• Learning through teamwork.

• Guided viewing of video tapes.

• Experience in laboratories.

• Presenting different types of learning outcomes in fairs or exhibits: constructing a model for a project, planning and preparing a poster or presentation, writing a paper and presenting it to peers.

• Utilizing the computer as a tool for achieving the learning objectives beyond the technical aspect – information science investigation of a scientific nature via databases.

• Field trips – conducting periodical tours as part of the annual and multi-annual teaching program, entailing: preparations, actual tour, and summary of the field-trip.

• Implementing special scientific-content-dependent projects while studying the modules and constituting the process.

• Active involvement of the students in the community.

• Practical experience in gathering data through various means: observation, interviews, surveys.

We believe that the combination of varied teaching methods with learning science and technology subjects has an enormous importance and makes a unique contribution to the students' education. The variety of activities allows the students to express intelligences beyond the cognitive, such as meta-cognitive, emotional, and social spheres (Armstrong, 1996).

## *The preparation of 'Science and Technology for All' teachers*

In order to implement STS-type curriculum materials effectively, mainly in the upper secondary level of schooling, we must consider the preparation and the professional development of the science teachers.

The STS characteristics of 'Science and Technology for All' differ from all other high school subjects taught in Israel, and therefore each team of teachers that joins the 'Science and Technology for All' teaching program has to participate in an in-service workshop. 'Science and Technology for All' is based on multidisciplinary teaching teams in biology, chemistry, physics and technology-engineering subjects. The belief is that teachers who teach one of the science or technology disciplines and, at the same time, teach 'Science and Technology for All' – will be teaching riche and better in both tracks. The main goal of the in-service workshops is to prepare the teaching teams through a multidisciplinary approach to scientific-technological concepts learned via various teaching methods. It also imparts skills intended for a wide range of students and develops criteria to evaluate the students' achievements using alternative methods. The in-service workshops are usually conducted in teacher centers.

The following issues are dealt within the framework of the 'Science and Technology for All' in-service workshops:

* Rationale of the 'Science and Technology for All' Teaching Program

• Providing scientific technological knowledge to students who choose not to specialize in the sciences

• Teaching sciences by an integrative and multidisciplinary approach 'Science, Technology and Society' (STS)

* Imparting 'Science and Technology for All' teaching/learning skills

* Inculcating and expanding broad multidisciplinary information relevant to 'Science and Technology for All' to teachers who were prepared to teach one scientific discipline (biology, chemistry or physics)

* Diversifying methods of teaching/learning

* Developing and adapting evaluation methods for different teaching methodologies

* Developing multidisciplinary teamwork patterns

## How can the achievement of science education standards be assessed?

The implementation of a wide spectrum of instructional techniques in the science classroom necessitates matching an appropriate assessment tool for each learning goal to measure the students' achievements and progress (Trowbridge and Bybee, 1996; Hofstein et al., 1997). Indeed, as has been so cogently expressed

> *"Assessment policies and practices should be aligned with the goals, student expectations, and curriculum frameworks. Within the science program, the alignment of assessment with curriculum and teaching is one of the most critical pieces of science education reform".* (NRC, 1996: 211)

The assessment of students should therefore, be multidimensional, drawing information from various sources and based on a variety of teaching and learning techniques. The need to match assessment tools to the learning goals has received support in studies conducted in science by Ben-Zvi et al. (1977), and in biology by Tamir (1974). Their work clearly shows that achievement in written examinations is not highly correlated with achievements requiring inquiry abilities, which are manifested by laboratory work. Moreover, Shavelson and co-workers (1990) compared multiple-choice tests with hands-on performance assessment and found that the correlation between these variables is only moderate.

Different ideologies and different research agenda led to the development of some research tools that try to assess students' learning regarding the STS programs. Enger and Yager (2001) offer several methods for assessing science standards, with grade-level examples, rubrics, teacher assessments, and examples of student work. The Views on Science-Technology-Society (VOSTS) instrument (Aikenhead and Ryan, 1992), for example, measures students' understanding of the nature of science, and students' understanding and attitudes toward STS topics. VOSTS is derived directly from students' own views on various issues of STS. It consists of a pool of 114 multiple-choice items surveying a wide variety of STS topics, different from traditional instruments that are derived from researchers' conceptual schemes (Aikenhead et al., 1989). Another tool, developed by Zuzovsky (1997), measures the ability to apply scientific principles in non-academic contexts. One of the tasks describes a family's use of an electrical appliance. The students were asked to calculate the cost of electricity used through the provided data, decide upon several daily issues such as the heating methods, compare several types of power stations, and identify commonalities and differences, and finally, to critically analyze a newspaper advertisement regarding environmentally friendly actions undertaken by the electricity company.

In the past, before the 1992 reform (Tomorrow 98: Superior Committee on Science, Mathematics and Technology Education in Israel, 1992), only a small fraction of student learning and activities were assessed (Lazarowitz and Tamir, 1994). Final grades given to students were mainly based on their ability in paper and pencil tests. Moreover, students' achievement using other learning techniques such as inquiry in the science laboratory, students' group and personal projects, reading of scientific articles and many other more effective instructional activities were rarely assessed and included in students' final grades. This was usually due to lack of valid and reliable criteria as well as appropriate assessment tools for these learning activities. Another problem is that teachers are less confident in using alternative assessment methods and there is a need to prepare teachers to change their methods of teaching science, in general and their methods to assess their students' achievements and progress, in particular.

The goals of the 'Science and Technology for All' evaluation processes were defined as:

* To evaluate the students' achievements at different stages of the learning process. The evaluation includes 'Formative Assessment' that enables identification of difficulties the student has in order to provide support, advance and improve the subsequent teaching and learning, and 'Summative Assessment' that usually describe the students' achievements for grading and certification purposes.

* To foster a culture that is appropriate for a student-centered perception that places the responsibility for the learning process, involvement in the evaluation and its results as well as self-evaluation on the student. The advantage of this method is that it encourages learning through the success and involvement of the students, not only in understanding the course material, but also in evaluating the learning process reflectively.

* To encourage the involvement of the teachers in the process of selecting the most suitable method to evaluate the achievements and skills that are otherwise impossible to assess by conventional methods. This approach encourages mutual respect between and among the teachers and the students and enhances individual attention to each student.

Students' evaluation, which is formative, takes place from the first lesson, from the very beginning of the 'Science and Technology for All' studies:

• Evaluation through a variety of means enables mapping students' achievements at different-functioning levels of thinking: basic cognitive thinking (knowledge and understanding), advanced cognitive thinking (application, analysis, synthesis and evaluation), emotional (attitudes and values), social (personal communication skills) and meta-cognitive (reflection).

• Ongoing evaluation, in a variety of ways, improves the learning environment and enhances learning motivation.

• By employing alternative evaluations – evaluation of activities such as individual and group projects, analysis of articles accompanied by increasingly harder assignments, guided viewing of films, developing a model to demonstrate a concept or process, report on experience in lab work, scientific investigation via information science research, report on a fieldtrip, presentation of learning outcomes, including: poster, presentation or model presented at fairs or exhibits, presentation to the students, written and oral expression, preparation of a portfolio, etc., in addition to the cognitive sphere, meta-cognitive, emotional and social spheres, as well as the quality of the implementation, can be assessed too.

The evaluation is based mainly on the school assessment alternative tools, but has also an external component. Evaluation of the students' achievements is conducted by each school and carried out in ways that reflect the teaching and learning methods. The judging process entails an evaluation of learning outcomes through 'Judging Panels'. At the first stage, two teachers carry out the evaluation. A discussion session is held with the teaching team. At the second stage, an external evaluation is taking place.

The control mechanism for the school evaluation process addresses the need for a non-uniform objective evaluation component. The following report components are sent by the school science team to the department of 'Science and Technology for All' in the Education Ministry in Jerusalem at the end of each school year.

• Report on the evaluation tool for the relevant school year/

• Samples of each assignment. One sample only for each evaluation tool. Each evaluation tool sample has to include:

  a) Instructions for the students for the assignment.

  b) Description of the answer sheets employed in evaluating the students' work. The guidelines will include criteria for assessing the performance level (high, intermediate, low).

208

c) Photocopied samples of student projects in the three performance levels: high, intermediate, low.

This mechanism has two stages:

(a) Sending a representative sample of the students' work (at high, intermediate and low levels, with the answer sheet and the grades attached). This sample is sent at the end of the school year.

(b) A comparison of the school's average student grades with the expected national achievements. It is carried out by an external party and includes the school's national standing.

As mentioned above, students' achievement using other learning techniques such as inquiry in the science laboratory, students' group and personal projects, reading of scientific articles and many other more effective instructional activities were rarely assessed and included in students' final grades. This was usually due to lack of valid and reliable criteria as well as appropriate assessment tools for these learning activities. Thus, in the framework of the program 'Science and Technology for All', tools were developed aimed at attaining as many criteria as possible for reliability and validity of students' assessment. The validity is checked through the evaluation of the achievements related to the teaching goals, including the subject concepts of the module selected and the skills imparted. These teaching goals are examined at the cognitive, emotional and social levels, at different levels of difficulty and complexity. The reliability of the evaluation (ability of different examinations to conduct an independent and identical evaluation of the same assignment) is weakened due to diminished standardization of the achievement assessment and to a lack of tradition regarding the quality of the outcomes in different types of evaluations. The tools for obtaining reliability consisted of:

a. Definition of the teaching goals including concepts in the subjects studied (modules), by the team of developers and the teaching teams in the schools.

b. Development of answer sheets and experiments in a pilot group; scales to evaluate implementation levels according to specific criteria.

c. The answer sheets will be developed through:

    i.  Teamwork by teachers
    ii. Including students in determining the evaluation criteri
    iii. Explaining the criteria to the students, teachers and external evaluators (through examples).

Table 1 presents a recommended evaluation model for 'Science and Technology for All' students.

| Relative weight | Recommended Evaluation Tool | Evaluator |
|---|---|---|
| 25%-35% | Quizzes and examinations: Multiple-choice questions<br>• True or False statements<br>• Completion and Matching<br>• Defining concepts/terms<br>• Open-ended problems<br>• A two-stage evaluation test:<br>Stage A - Examinations<br>Stage B - Correcting the examination according to the teacher's instructions<br>• Interpretation of data in a popular scientific text, in a table or a graph | The teacher, after discussions with the school teaching staff |
| 30%-40% | **Evaluating individual and group activities (some are included in the examinations and quizzes).**<br>• Developing a model that demonstrates an idea or process<br>• Reporting on laboratory work experience<br>• Conducting an information investigation of a scientific-technological nature: databases, interviews of experts, surveys<br>• Reporting on a fieldtrip, including preparations, actual tour and summary of the fieldtrip. Evaluating special projects related to science content studied in the module and individual or group work in the module studies:<br>    • Carrying out the project<br>    • Presenting the learning outcomes: poster, presentation or model at exhibits or fairs<br>    • Making a presentation before the students | The teacher, after discussions with the school teaching team |
| 10% | Overall participation | Subject teacher |
| 25% | Tool for evaluating skills:<br>50% Evaluation of core skills<br>50% Evaluation of elective skills | Uniform external evaluation for all "Science and technology for all" |

Table 3:    A recommended evaluation model for 'Science and Technology for All' students

## Development of alternative assessment methods

Science teachers participated in the development of alternative assessment methods for the 'Science and Technology for All' course (Dori and Hofstein, 2000). Further, we developed a model for the professional development program for teachers who implement the curriculum. The workshop participants consisted of 10 science teachers, each from a different high school. Each taught the Science and Technology for All' program in one class and had at least 10 years of highschool science teaching experience, mainly in grades 10–12. All of them had already participated in several in-service professional development workshops. Their scientific backgrounds differed, and included areas such as chemistry, biology, agriculture, nutrition, technology, and physics. The teachers had already taught some Science and Technology for All' modules previously mentioned but had difficulties in using a variety of teaching strategies in general, and in grading and assessing their students in particular. Each of the teachers who participated in the workshop had taught at least one of the modules in one class consisting of about 30 students. The workshop coordinators focused on guiding the participating teachers in using a variety of teaching strategies, and in the development of auxiliary assignments for their students, together with assessment tools. The assessment tools used in this workshop consisted of detailed checklists (rubrics) and rating scales (tables 1 and 2). In the first three meetings, the teachers partook in lectures and in activities related to alternative assessment tools and methods, and especially to the way in which they should get used to working with rubrics.

Each teacher prepared the assignments for their students, followed by assessment tools. The assessment tools included tests, quizzes, and assessment guides for carrying out mini-projects, writing essays and critical reading of scientific articles. All the assignments were developed in stages, each of which required consideration and an analysis of assessment criteria as well as scoring. These assignments were then administered stage-by-stage at school. The students were involved in the assessment methods and their respective weights. This continuous assessment provided them with more control over their achievements, since they were aware of the assessment method, the weight percentage for each of the assessment components, and the final grade. At each stage, the students submitted their papers to the teacher for comments, clarification, and assessment. The students met the teachers before and after school for extra instruction and consultation. The detailed checklist given to each student after each assignment compelled them to address the comments with the greatest seriousness if, of course, they wanted to improve their grade. The students reflected on their work and ideas at each stage, and followed their teachers' comments on a detailed checklist and corrected them accordingly. Thus, they were able to improve their grades. The teachers revised the rubrics related to the assignments at each stage. Samples of the students' assignments were brought to the workshop for further analysis, involving both the coordinators and their colleagues – the participating teachers. The group discussed the revision of the rubrics, and agreed on the percentage (weight) allocated to each of the assignment's components. They also agreed on the criteria for levels of performance, in order to grade the students as objectively as possible.

The rubrics can be applied to a variety of teaching situations. If you take advantage of all the possibilities inherent in the format, your students will have a rich and powerful experience. If an assignment falls between categories, feel free to score it with in-between points.

| Instructions | Accomplished 5 points | Developing 3 points | Beginning 1 point |
|---|---|---|---|
| **Identify at least five scientific concepts** the meaning of which you do not know. Use reference books including dictionaries. Indicate the reference of each explanation. | Identification and explanation of at least five scientific concepts that are new to the student, indicating the reference to each explanation. | Identification and explanation of at least five scientific concepts that are new to the student, without indicating the reference to each explanation. | Identification and explanation of less than five scientific concepts that are new to the student, and lack references to each explanation. |
| **Compile questions that raise criticism of the article's contents:** *The questions should be formulated clearly *The questions should link the article's contents with other fields of knowledge studied in class. *The answers should appear in the article. | The questions are formulated clearly, link the article's contents with other fields of knowledge studied in class, and the answers appear in the article. | The questions are formulated clearly, link the article's contents with other fields of knowledge studied in class, but the answers do not appear in the article. | The questions are not formulated clearly, do not link the article's contents with other fields of knowledge studied in class, and the answers do not appear in the article. |
| **Answer the questions that you compiled:** Use precise, complete answers. | All the questions that the student compiled are answered clearly and precisely. | 75% of the questions that the student compiled are answered clearly and precisely. | 50% of the questions that the student compiled are answered clearly and precisely. |

Comment: Only those students meeting the deadline are eligible for a temporary grade, the possibility of correction, and a final grade.
Enjoy your work!

Table 4: Rubrics given to the students for 'Critical reading of scientific articles'

Table 4 presents rubrics for 'Critical reading of scientific articles'. Each student in class had to choose an article from a collection of diverse articles provided by the teachers. The students were also provided with a written guide for reading the paper critically (Levy Nahum et al., 2004). Table 5 presents rubrics given to the students for the essay '*The person behind the scientific endeavor*'. To help students in writing this essay, the teachers introduced them to the biographies of numerous eminent scientists from different periods. These scientists developed scientific theories that often contradicted those that had been previously accepted (Mamlok, 1998). The students were asked to describe in detail the lives of the scientists and the discoveries made by them. They also produced work characterizing "their" scientists: a picture of the scientist accompanying an article that the students had written. The students used internet resources, and the teachers helped them with references dealing with the history of science (Rayner-Canham and Rayner-Canham, 1998).

The rubrics can be applied to a variety of teaching situations. If you take advantage of all the possibilities inherent in the format, your students will have a rich and powerful experience. If an assignment falls between categories, feel free to score it with in-between points.

| Instructions | Accomplished 5 points | Developing 3 points | Beginning 1 point |
|---|---|---|---|
| **Give a detailed background of the scientist's era**, consisting of scientific, technological, and societal aspects | A broad picture of the era, consisting of scientific, technological, and societal aspects | A partial picture of the era, lacking one of the aspects | A partial picture of the era, including only the scientific aspect |
| **Write about the scientist's life story** (The Person Behind the Scientific Endeavor), consisting of the following aspects: *The scientist's scientific work and discoveries, and their contribution to society *The impact of society on the scientist's work *The scientist's personal life and its impact on his / her work | A description consisting of all the three aspects – scientific, societal, and personal | A partial description, consisting of only two of the aspects | A partial description, consisting only of the scientist's scientific work |
| **Present an accurate list of references**, according to those that appear in the text, in alignment with your teacher's instructions, and organize them alphabetically | A full list of references, matched with those that appear in the text, according to the teachers' instructions, and organized alphabetically | A full list of references, which is not in alignment with the teacher's instructions, and not organized alphabetically | A partial list, which is not in alignment with the teacher's instructions, missing some references and not organize alphabetically |
| **Organize** your essay in a rational and aesthetic way. The essay should include: *All the chapters that were defined in the instructions given to the students *The ideas are presented rationally *The citations are placed correctly in the text | The essay is organized according to the given instructions, and is presented aesthetically | The essay lacks one of the components required | The essay lacks one of the components required, and is not presented aesthetically |

Table 5:     Rubrics given to the students for the essay 'The person behind the scientific endeavor'

We have also evaluated its impact on the attitudes of teachers and students (Mamlok-Naaman et al., in press). The science teachers who usually taught the traditional scientific disciplines (namely, chemistry, biology, agriculture, nutrition, technology, and physics), and who were not familiar with the interdisciplinary subject matter as well as with the alternative assessment methods, felt that the best way to cope with an unfamiliar interdisciplinary subject was to be involved in its development, and by working in a group and cooperating with colleagues. Interviews with them revealed their satisfaction with the curriculum, a significant change in the relationship with their colleagues, and a change in the general climate in school. Most of the teachers mentioned and noted that the continuous assessment of students' progress and achievements provides a valid and reliable picture of the students' knowledge and abilities. They also claimed that teaching this curriculum changed their teaching habits. They felt that they actually guided the students in the learning process and did not just provide the students with information. Indeed, we have evidence that shows that in this school the teacher-student interactions were improved; this in turn improves the learning environment in this particular class. However, the teachers claimed that the new system of assessment was more time-consuming, a lot of work with students and with their assignments, and involved in a heavy responsibility in assessing students' portfolios.

We found that the students who participated in the project generally expressed satisfaction with the way they had learned chemistry. Indeed, there is some evidence based on the results of the action-research that was conducted by the team, indicating that a healthy learning environment was established in the science classroom. These findings are especially important in an era in which creating an effective and improved classroom learning environment is becoming a major goal. Moreover, there is no doubt that this approach to assessment caused a significant decline in students' anxiety that accompanies final examinations in Israel. On the other hand, although in general, students expressed satisfaction with the way they studied chemistry as well as in the way they were evaluated, they felt that they had to work harder than usual compared with other subjects to obtain high grades

Since this approach allows for more intensive and effective interaction between students and learning materials, students and their peers, and students and their teachers, there is great potential to create an effective classroom-learning environment. We suggest that this could eventually increase the motivation to learn and therefore result in the enhancement of learning.

# Summary

In the framework of reform in science education an extensive, dynamic, and long-term professional development of the science teachers should take place (Loucks-Horsley and Matsumoto, 1999; National Research Council, 1996). Teachers need to receive guidance and support throughout the various teaching and implementation stages involving changes in the curriculum (Harrison and Globman, 1988). On the one hand, it is not easy for the teachers to undergo modifications that include changes in the content and in the way they teach. On the other hand, it has been noted that teachers, in general, are excellent learners, and are interested in trying to teach a new curriculum, as well as in improving and enriching their teaching methods (Joyce and Showers, 1983). An integrated science curriculum differs from a traditional science curriculum. Science teachers usually receive good preparation in teaching the traditional science curriculum – one or two science disciplines, but not integrated science. However, they need to learn the knowledge, skills, attitudes, and teaching skills to teach such an interdisciplinary topic (Bybee and Loucks-Horsley, 2000). They should be encouraged to expand their repertoire of student assessment strategies to include such techniques as observation checklists, portfolios, and rubrics (Wiggins, 1988).

One of the ways of overcoming the anxiety of teachers regarding reforms such as STS, requires their active involvement in the development of learning materials, instructional techniques, and related assessment tools (Loucks-Horsley et al., 1998; Parke and Coble, 1997). Similarly, Sabar and Shafriri (1982) claimed that

> "Participation in curriculum development, which is a protracted process, is likely to take the teacher from a conscious phase to one of greater autonomy and internalization phase". (p. 310)

It is generally believed that involving teachers in the process of curriculum development leads to a wide variety of pedagogical ideas regarding instructional techniques and their related tools (Connelly and Ben-Peretz, 1980).

Teachers' knowledge of science is based on previous experiences (von Glasersfeld, 1989) and on doing and experiencing (Gilmer et al., 1996). Therefore, it is recommended that teachers should be involved in the *development* of new learning materials according to new standards as well as in the assessment procedures. It was shown that personal involvement helps to reduce their anxiety in teaching an unfamiliar subject (Joyce and Showers, 1983). Therefore, teachers who actually develop the teaching strategies and assessment materials get a better understanding of how it should be taught and experience some kind of involvement: they are part of the curricular process (Parke and Coble, 1997), feel pride in their work, and become producers rather than consumers (Sabar and Shafriri, 1982). The new curriculum materials also appear to be effective vehicles for teachers' learning (Bybee and Loucks-Horsley, 2000). They should be involved in the development of learning materials as well as the teaching strategies and assessment tools, which must be tailored adequately to the students' cognitive and affective characteristics, as mentioned by Ben-Peretz (1990).

The active learning for which we strive in order to stimulate and motivate our students also stimulates and motivates the teachers. They understand better that the traditional paper and pencil assessment tools frequently used in science courses are inadequate for such an interdisciplinary program that is accompanied by a wide range of pedagogical interventions. As a result, the interest of these teachers' students in the process of learning increased, as well as their satisfaction from the learning materials, the learning strategies, the assessment methods, and the ongoing dialogue with their teachers. Since the students who studied the STS program were not science-oriented and their interest in scientific topics was limited, the variety of assignments enabled them to succeed with certain assignments and to do less regarding other activities. It is in alignment with the main goal of the reform in science education in Israel – the need to make science an integral part of the education of all citizens (Tomorrow 98: Report of the superior committee on science mathematics and technology in Israel, 1992):

> "Modern socioeconomic problems require an understanding of their scientific background. Other questions arise when we discuss the division of resources and world wealth, different environmental issues and other topics that require the individual to demonstrate an understanding based on having acquired a basic education the sciences."
> (p. 3)

To attain a wide range of assessment models, clearly time is needed in order to construct a supporting framework for science teachers (Westerlund et al., 2002). Indeed, the teachers in the workshop were continuously supported and assisted by the workshop coordinators.

Teachers who implement a new curriculum should receive sustained support in order to gain knowledge of different teaching strategies and of assessment skills. This can be done by attending professional development workshops that deal with those topics, which will consequently stimulate their creativity and diversify their instructional strategies in the classroom. Such skills should improve their ability to teach and understand their students' learning difficulties. Since they will understand the goals, strategies, and rationale of the curriculum better, they will feel more qualified to modify the curriculum as needed. We believe that such workshops help more teachers become producers rather than just consumers. Such efforts and reform in the way students are assessed (school-based assessment) necessitate support from other people not directly connected to the program, namely school headteachers, science coordinators, and government regional consultants (Krajcik et al., 2001).

Moreover, such efforts and reform necessitate the release of national science standards rather than the structured different curricula which consist of goals and recommendations for each scientific discipline' age and grade. It should define the science content that all students should know and be able to understand, and provide guidelines to assess the degree to which students have learned that content. The national standards should also include the teaching strategies, the professional development, and the support necessary to provide high quality science education to all students.

# References

Armstrong, T. (1996) *Multiple Intelligences in the Classroom*. Jerusalem: Ministry of Education, Culture and Sport, Branco Weiss Institute for the Development of Thinking.

Aikenhead, S. G. and Ryan, A. G. (1992) The development of a new instrument: Views on "Science-Technology-Society" (VOSTS). *Science Education*, 76, 477-491.

Aikenhead, S. G., Ryan, A. G. and Desautels, J. (1989) *The development of multiple-choice instrument for monitoring views on science-technology-society topics.* Ottawa: Social Sciences and Humanities Research Council of Canada.

Ben-Zvi, R. (1998) *Energy and the human being.* Rehovot: Weizmann Institute of Science (in Hebrew).

Ben-Zvi, R. (1999) Non-science oriented students and the second law of thermodynamics. *International Journal of Science Education*, 21, 1251-1267.

Ben-Zvi, R., Hofstein, A., Samuel, D. and Kempa, R. F. (1977) Modes of instruction in high school science. *Journal of Research in Science Teaching,* 14, 433-439.

Ben-Peretz, M. (1990) Teachers as curriculum makers. In T. Husen and N. T. Postlethwaite (Eds.), *The International Encyclopedia of Education* (2nd ed.) (pp. 6089-6092). Oxford: Pergamon Press.

Bunce, D. M. (1995) The quiet evolution in science education – teaching students the way students learn. *Journal of College Science Teaching,* 25(3), 169-171.

Bybee, R. W. and Loucks-Horsley, S. (2000) Supporting change through professional development. In B. Resh (Ed.), *Making sense of integrated science: A guide for high schools* (pp. 41-48). Colorado Springs, CO: BSCS.

Cohen, D. (2000) *Brain, medicines, and drugs.* Rehovot, Israel: Weizmann Institute of Science (in Hebrew).

Cohen, D., Ben-Zvi, R., Hofstein, A. and Rahamimoff, R. (2004) On brain, medicines, and drugs: A module for "Science for All" program. *The American Biology Teacher,* 66(1), 9-19.

Connelly, F. M. and Ben-Peretz, M. (1980) Teachers' role in the using and doing research and curriculum development. *Journal of Curriculum Studies,* 12, 95-107.

Dori, Y. J. and Hofstein, A. (2000, April) *The development, implementation and initial research findings of 'Science for All' in Israel.* Paper presented at the National Association for Research in Science Teaching, New Orleans, LA.

Enger, S. and Yager, R. (2001) *Assessing Student Understanding in Science: A Standards-Based K-12 Handbook.* Iowa City: The University of Iowa.

Erduran, S. (2001) Philosophy of science: An emerging field with implications for science education. *Science & Education,* 10, 581-593.

Gilmer, P. J., Grogan, A. and Siegel, S. (1996) Contextual learning for premedical students. In: J. A. Chambers (Ed.), *Selected papers from the 7th National Conference on College Teaching and Learning* (pp. 79-89). Jacksonville, FL: Florida Community College at Jacksonville.

von Glaserfeld, E. (1989) Cognition, construction of knowledge, and teaching. *Synthese,* 80, 121-140.

Harrison, J. and Globman, R. (1988*) Assessment of training teachers in active learning: A research report.* Ramat-Gan: Bar-Ilan University (in Hebrew).

Hofstein, A. and Kempa, R. F. (1985) Motivating aspects in science education: an attempt at an analysis. *European journal of Science Education,* 7, 221-229.

Hofstein, A. and Walberg, H. J. (1995) Instructional strategies. In: B. J. Fraser and H. J. Walberg (Eds.), *Improving science education* (pp. 70-89). Chicago: National Society for the Study of Education.

Hofstein, A., Mamlok, R. and Carmeli, M. (1997) Science teachers as curriculum developers of Science for All. *Science Education International,* 8(1), 26-29.

Hofstein, A., Kesner, M. and Ben-Zvi, R. (2000) Students' perception of an industrial classroom leaning environment. *Learning Environments Research,* 2, 291-306.

Hofstein, A. and Mamlok, R. (2001) From petroleum to tomatoes: Attaining some of the content standards using an interdisciplinary approach. *The Science Teacher,* 68(2), 46-48.

Hofstein, A., Mamlok, R. and Rosenberg, O. (2006) Varying instructional methods and students assessment methods in high school chemistry. In: M. McMahon, P. Simmons, R. Sommers, D. DeBaets and F. Crawley (Eds.), *Assessment in Science* (139-148). Arlington, Virginia: NSTA press.

Joyce, B. and Showers, B. (1983) *Power and staff development through research on training.* Alexandria, VA: Association for Supervision and Curriculum Development.

Krajcik, J. S., Mamlok, R. and Hug, B. (2001) Modern content and the enterprise of science: Science education in the 20th century. In: L. Corno (Ed.), *Education across a century: The centennial volume* (pp. 205-238). Chicago, IL: National Society for the Study of Education.

Lazarowitz, R. and Tamir, P. (1994) Research on using laboratory instruction in science. In D. L. Gabel (Ed.), Handbook of research on science teaching (p. 94-127), New York: *Research and Practice,* 5, 301-325. Retrieved April 6, 2005, from http://www.uoi.gr/cerp/

Levy Nahum, T., Hofstein, A., Mamlok-Naaman, R. and Bar-Dov, Z. (2004) Can final examinations amplify students' misconceptions in chemistry? *Chemistry Education: Research and Practice,* 5, 301-325. Retrieved April 6, 2005, from http://www.uoi.gr/cerp/

Loucks-Horsley, S., Hewson, P. W., Love, N. and Stiles, K. (1998) *Designing professional development for teachers of science and mathematics.* Thousand Oaks, CA: Corwin Press.

Loucks-Horsley, S. and Matsumoto, C. (1999) Research on professional development for teachers of mathematics and science: The state of the scene. *School Science and Mathematics*, 99, 258-271.

Mamlok, R. (1998) *Science: An ever-developing entity.* Rehovot, Israel: Weizmann Institute of Science (in Hebrew).

Mamlok, R., Ben-Zvi, R., Menis, J. and Penick, J. E. (2000) Can simple metals be transmuted into gold? Teaching science through a historical approach. *Science Education International*, 11(3), 33-37.

Mamlok-Naaman, R., Hofstein, A. and Penick, J. (In press) Involving Teachers in the STS Curricular Process: A Long-Term Intensive Support Framework for Science Teachers. *Journal of Science Teachers Education.*

National Research Council (1996) *National science education standards.* Washington, DC: National Academy Press.

Neathery, M. F. (1997) Elementary and secondary students' perceptions toward science: Correlations with gender, ethnicity, ability, grade, and science achievement. *Electronic Journal of Science Education,* 2(1). Retrieved April 6, 2005, from http://unr.edu/homepage/jcannon/ejse/ejse.html

Parke, H. M. and Coble, C. R. (1997) Teachers designing curriculum as professional development: A model for transformational science teaching. *Journal of Research in Science Teaching*, 34, 773-789.

Rayner-Canham, M. and Rayner-Canham, G. (1998) *Women in chemistry.* Washington, DC: American Chemical Society and the Chemical Heritage.

Sabar, N. and Shafriri, N. (1982) On the need for teacher training in curriculum development. *Studies in Educational Assessment*, 7, 307-315.

Shavelson, R. J., Baxter, G. P. and Pine, J. (1990) Performance assessments: Political rhetoric and measurement reality. *Educational Researcher*, 21(4), 22-27.

Tamir, P. (1974) An inquiry-oriented laboratory examination. *Journal of Educational Measurement*, 11, 23-33.

Tobin, K., Capie, W. and Bettencourt, A. (1988) Active teaching for higher cognitive learning in science. *International Journal of Science Education*. 10, 17-27.

*Tomorrow 98: Report of the superior committee on science mathematics and technology in Israel* (1992) Jerusalem: Ministry of Education and Culture (English Edition: 1994).

Trowbridge, L. W. and Bybee, R. W. (1996) *Teaching secondary school science.* Columbus, OH: Merrill.

Weiss, I. R. (1987) *Report of the 1985-86 national survey of science and mathematics education.* Research Triangle Park, NC: Research Triangle Institute.

Westerlund, J. F., Garcia, D. M., Koke, J. R., Taylor, A. T. and Mason, D. S. (2002) Summer scientific research for teachers: The experience and its effects. *Journal of Science Teacher Education*, 13, 63-83.

Wiggins, G. (1998) *Educative assessment: Designing assessments to inform and improve student performance.* San Francisco, CA: Jossey-Bass Publishers.

Zuzovsky, R. (1997) Assessing scientific and technological literacy among sixth graders in Israel. *Studies in Educational Evaluation,* 23, 231-256.

# Chapter 12

# Development and evaluation of standards in secondary science education in the Netherlands

*Heleen Driessen*

*SLO (Netherlands National Institute for Curriculum Development) Postbus 2041, 7500 CA Enschede, The Netherlands*

## Introduction

A new wave of science curriculum development in secondary education, including the development of new forms of assessment, began in the Netherlands in 1998. The reforms include basic secondary education and senior secondary education and involve both different governmental advisory committees and different time schedules.

New educational structures for post-fifteen education were introduced, including a simultaneous didactic reform and the national implementation of a novel Science for Public Understanding course for higher vocational and pre-university level students.

Shortly after the introduction of the 1998 reform, the Ministry of Education, Culture and Science reduced the extent and assessment specifications of most examination programs. A detailed evaluation, by the Ministry, of the educational structure and all examination programs took three years, including a series of monitoring reports from the schools inspectorate and much additional research. The government took a further two years to make decisions about the new structure for higher vocational and pre-university level schools and this will only be introduced during 2007. Between 2000 and 2007, most temporarily arrangements, made in 2000, were continued. This new structure will bring simultaneous changes in the examination programs of all school subjects, the specifications for school assessment and the introduction of several new school subjects e.g. Nature, Life and Technology.

In 2002, the Ministry of Education appointed an exploratory committee of eminent scientists, teachers and experts in curriculum development. This committee made an inventory of the problems in science education. In 2003, the Ministry then commissioned an advisory committee for chemistry to propose a blueprint and development structure for a renewed chemistry curriculum for senior secondary education. This committee consisted of experts from chemical research and industry, teachers and curriculum development. This was followed, in 2005, by the appointment by the government, of three different advisory committees for biology, physics and mathematics, and, in 2006, a steering group, commissioned to develop a curriculum for the new school subject, Nature, Life and Technology. These five new curricula, including far reaching changes in scientific content and didactic approach, will be implemented nationally around 2010.

In 2004, a government-appointed committee, comprised of experts in school development and school inspection, advised on the reform of basic secondary education for all levels. This committee involved many school principals and teacher teams in the development of a new structure for the first two years of secondary education, which was implemented in 2006.

Another special national committee has been advising the government, since 2004, on the mid-term (2007) and long-term (2010) structure of secondary science education including the role of assessment for higher vocational and pre-university level students. The long-term advice may influence the new curricula and assessment specifications of the 2010 reform of the science curricula.

## Educational landscape in the Netherlands

### Primary education

Dutch children start their compulsory school life at the age of 4 (table 1). Parents are free to choose a school. Children stay in the same group till the end of primary education.

| Group | | 1 | 2 | 3 | 4 | 5 | 6 | 7 | 8 |
|---|---|---|---|---|---|---|---|---|---|
| Age | 3 | 4/5 | 5/6 | 6/7 | 7/8 | 8/9 | 9/10 | 10/11 | 11/12 |
| | voluntary playgroup or crèche | compulsory | comp. | comp. | comp. | comp. | comp. | comp. | comp. |

Table 1:     Structure of primary education in the Netherlands

### Secondary education

Schools for secondary education base their decision for choosing the level of basic secondary education for a student on the advice of the group 8 class teacher and on a national test (in 85% of the schools). There are generally three levels of secondary school: vmbo, mixed vmbo-havo and mixed havo-vwo (table 2). Schools are free to place students in classes of sub-specified levels e.g. vwo/gymnasium, etc.

| Class | 1 | 2 | 3 | 4 | 5 | 6 |
|---|---|---|---|---|---|---|
| Age | 12/13 | 13/14 | 14/15 | 15/16 | 16/17 | 17/18 |
| Nieuwe onderbouw* | ▓ | ▓ | | | | |
| Vmbo** | | | ▓ | ▓ | ▓ | ▓ |
| Havo*** | | | ▓ | ▓ | ▓ | ▓ |
| Vwo/gymnasium**** | | | ▓ | ▓ | ▓ | ▓ |

\*     Nieuwe onderbouw – junior secondary education
**    Vmbo – pre vocational education
***   Havo – senior secondary general education
****Vwo – pre-university education, gymnasium – pre-university education with Latin and/or Greek

Table 2:      Structure of secondary education in the Netherlands


*Junior secondary education*

Since 1993, the curriculum of years 1 and 2 is described in targets that students should have attained at the end of the first two years of secondary education. These targets are prescriptions of skills and subject knowledge. At the end of year 2, schools decide on the student level for year 3 (table 2), based on school assessment. Before 2004, the attainment targets were highly specific and the school organisation of basic secondary education for all levels was compulsory. The 2006 reform includes a small number of attainment targets in a global prescription, meeting both the need of a less fragmentated school curriculum for pupils at vmbo-level and the need for a greater challenge for pupils at havo-vwo level. From 2006, schools became relatively autonomous and could organise their own structure and content of these first two years of basic secondary education. Schools define their own standards for promotion of students to the next class, either to vmbo-level or to havo/vwo or a more highly specified sub-level.

All schools have made decisions about the focus of the innovation path for the development of basic secondary education. This can be characterised by one of four future scenarios. The key point in these scenarios is that for a successful innovation path, schools have to integrate the development of school curricula for the subjects, of assessment, of school organisation and continuous professional development of teachers. School development can only be sustainable when all stakeholders are involved during the innovation phase.

In *scenario 1*, schools keep close to the former organisation with 15 different school subjects and traditional timetables. Scenario 1 schools may take small steps to integrate curricula of a few subjects e.g. instead of physics/chemistry and biology, there is an integrated science curriculum. Or a few small scale school projects may be introduced.

In *scenario 2*, schools make parts of the time table more flexible, so that teachers are no longer subject teachers but coach students in project work in which attainment targets of several subjects are integrated. For example, a project may be undertaken, which includes national language, science and math.

In *scenario 3*, schools redesign the school organisation and the pedagogical view underpinning the school curriculum. This includes a shift towards far more responsibility of teachers for the school curriculum and timetables. For example, a school in an urban environment might develop a school curriculum based on an integration of education and participation of students in societal environment. Teachers develop projects in cooperation with local stakeholders and all are involved in the coaching of students.

In *scenario 4*, a new school stream for basic secondary education is created. This is based on a total reorganisation of teaching and learning, with individual learning programmes for students, supported by highly integrated e-learning and coaching. In a scenario 4 school, students may have individual week programs with scheduled times in a learning centre and for group projects. Study results are monitored by a tutor and for problems the students can go to a study assistant. Learning materials are mostly digital.

After two years of junior secondary education, 65% of the pupils enter one of the streams of pre-vocational education (vmbo). Nearly all students leave pre-vocational education with a certificate including the attained levels, specified in the national curriculum for that stream.

The third year of havo/vwo (35 % of the pupils) is either an extension of the first two years of junior secondary education or a preparation for the second stage of secondary education. Schools are autonomous to organize the third year of havo/vwo in integrated or more sub-specified classes.

Large schools may have a gymnasium stream parallel at vwo, starting up in year 1 of basic secondary education, with additional Latin and Greek. Many gymnasia are small schools with only gymnasium students.


*Upper secondary education*

The traditional senior secondary education (havo, vwo and gymnasium) was restructured significantly in 1998. A second stage of upper secondary education was introduced with an educational approach including more independent learning. All levels follow a national curriculum in which the study load (lessons, homework and assessment) is expressed in hours (table 3). Roughly 60% of the student study load is spent in lessons.

Within each level, students have a compulsory general program, a chosen subject profile and a free part with one or two subjects of their own choice and school projects. Students start the curriculum of the second stage in year 4.

| | Havo | Vwo | Gymnasium |
|---|---|---|---|
| Totally including homework | 3200 hours | 4800 hours | 5280 hours |
| General part | 1640 hours (51%) | 2120 hours (44%) | 2980 hours (56%) |
| Profile part | 1160 hours (36%) | 1840 hours (38%) | 1840 hours (35%) |
| Free part | 400 hours (13%) | 840 hours (18%) | 460 hours (9 %) |

* Last cohort students starting in year 4 in 2006

Table 3:     Senior secondary education in the Netherlands (1998-2006)

The subject profiles are:
• Culture & Society (C&M), languages, art and culture, mathematics
• Economy & Society (E&M) economics, geography, history, mathematics
• Science & Health (N&G) biology, chemistry, physics, mathematics
• Science & Technology (N&T) with extended programs physics, chemistry and mathematics

An evaluated structure with an adapted profile structure including adapted national curricula for the subjects will be compulsory from 2007 (table 4).

| | Havo | Vwo | Gymnasium |
|---|---|---|---|
| Total including homework | 3200-3280 hours | 4800-4920 hours | 5400 hours |
| General part | 1120 hours (ca 35%) | 1920 hours (ca 40%) | 2520 hours (47%) |
| Profile part | 1400-1480 hours (ca 44%) | 1880-2000 hours (ca 41%) | 1880-2000 hours (37%) |
| Free part | 680 hours ( ca 21%) | 880 hours (ca 19%) | 880 hours (16%) |

**First cohort students starting in year 4 in 2007

Table 4:     Senior secondary education from 2007

The changes in the national curriculum for all subjects of senior secondary education in 2007 involve:
1     Globally prescribed examination programmes for all subjects
2     Part of the examination programmes for most science subjects (25–40%) is only assessed by the school. Schools are autonomous in their interpretation of the content corresponding tot the items in globally prescribed examination program for school assessment. The other part is assessed in national exams. Until 2007 the whole curriculum for all science subjects was assessed twice, in school and in national exams.

3   All national specifications for the form of school exams are replaced by the following three criteria:
  • The authority of the school is responsible for the form, organisation and standards of the school exams
  • Part of the program for the national exam can be assessed in the school exams in addition to the compulsory program for the school exams
  • The authority of the school can decide to add additional subject knowledge to the school exams. This may be different from school to school.

Schools will become far more autonomous in the organisation and assessment of upper secondary education.

From 2010, students will start in year 4 with profoundly renewed subject curricula for mathematics, biology, chemistry, physics and Nature, Life and Technology. From 2010, the profile structure and study load of school subjects will only be influenced by the long term advice of the special national committee and conclusions of monitoring reports of the schools inspectorate.

With a certificate of havo or vwo/gymnasium, students can enter either higher vocational education (havo/vwo) or university (vwo/gymnasium) in studies in their chosen subject profiles.


## Science education from 12–19 in the Netherlands

### Junior secondary education

In years 1 and 2 of secondary education (junior secondary education), all science is integrated in the global prescription of the characerics and 12 attainment goals of the learning framework 'Human & Nature'. This includes skills and knowledge of the former subjects biology, physics, chemistry, design and technology and personal care.

Some examples of these attainment goals are:
33 The student learns to use theories and models in scientific investigations of physical and chemical phenomena such as electricity, sound, light, movement, energy and matter.

34 The student learns to understand the main issues of the structure and functions of the human body, to relate this knowledge to the benefit of physical and psychological health and to express an individual responsibility concerning health.

Students of pre-vocational education (vmbo) choose one out of four streams (Techniques, Health, Economics and Agriculture). Three streams include some compulsory science education and all students can choose a science subject as one of their additional subjects (table 5). Pre-vocational education of each subject can be followed in four levels.

|  | Techniques | Health | Ecomomics | Agriculture |
|---|---|---|---|---|
| Compulsory | physics/chemistry<br>mathematics | biology<br>mathematics | economics<br>mathematics | mathematics<br>physics/chemistry<br>or biology |
| Additional subjects | biology | physics/chemistry | physics/chemistry<br>or biology | biology |

Table 5: Streams of pre vocational education

In upper secondary education (havo, vwo and gymnasium), the science subjects are compulsory in two of the profiles, Nature and Health and Nature and Technology. In the 1998 scheme, havo-students have to choose one additional subject. Biology is popular for students in non-science streams. In the 2007 streams, havo-students have to choose one profile subject and an additional subject of their own choice. Schools are allowed to offer fewer than the possible three or four profile subjects.

The numbers in tables 6 and 7 express the study load in hours for lessons, homework and assessment in the schemes for 1998 and 2007.

The free choice of two school subjects for vwo-students in the scheme of 1998 is narrowed to one profile subject and one free chosen subject. Nature and Health students are allowed to choose between two different mathematics programs.

|  | Havo 1998 | Havo 2007 | Vwo 1998 | Vwo 2007 |
|---|---|---|---|---|
| Science for Public Understanding | 160 | --- | 200 | 120 |
| Mathematics | 320 | 320/400 | 600 | 520/600 |
| Biology | 320 | 400 | 480 | 480 |
| Chemistry | 280 | 320 | 400 | 440 |
| #Physics or | 240 (mandatory) | *400* | 360 (mandatory) | *480* |
| #Nature, Life and Technology or | -- | *320* | -- | *440* |
| #Geography | -- | *320* | *360* | *440* |
| **Final project** | 40/80 | 40/80 | 80 | 80 |

Table 6: Upper secondary education subject profile, Nature and Health (1998 and 2007)

| | Havo 1998 | Havo 2007 | Vwo 1998 | Vwo 2007 |
|---|---|---|---|---|
| Science for Public Understanding | 160 | -- | 200 | 120 |
| Mathematics | 440 | 400 | 760 | 600 |
| Chemistry | 280 | 320 | 520 | 440 |
| Physics | 440 | 400 | 560 | 480 |
| #Nature, Life and Technology or | -- | 320 | -- | 440 |
| #Biology or | | 400 | | 480 |
| #Computer science or | | 320 | | 440 |
| # Mathematics D | | 320 | | 440 |
| Final project | 40/80 | 40/80 | 80 | 80 |

Table 7:     Upper secondary education subject profile, Nature and Technology (1998 and 2007)


## Standards for science education

The standards for the national curricula havo and vwo from 1998 are very detailed and are specified and grouped within a structure of several domains. Each domain is divided into subdomains, each subdomain contains a number of specific terms. Table 8 gives an overview of the structure of the national curricula for biology, chemistry, physics and Science for Public Understanding. Table 9 specifies the domains, subdomains and number of terms per subdomain of the chemistry curriculum vwo (1998).

There is a rather large variation in the level of specification of the terms in the examination programs for 1998. This because of the relative emphasis given on renewal by the different advisory subject committees for the 1998 reform. Biology and chemistry still follow the traditional level of specification (tables 8, 9 and 11) and for physics the number of terms was halved (tables 8 and 11). The global prescription of the terms in the national curriculum of Science for Public Understanding (table 8) was a pilot for the curriculum changes in 2007. Domain A skills (tables 8 and 10) are identical for havo and vwo and nearly all science subjects.

| Havo 1998 | Science for Public Understanding | Biology | Chemistry | Physics |
|---|---|---|---|---|
| **Skills** | | | | |
| - number of domains | 1 | 1 | 1 | 1 |
| - number of subdomains | 7 | 7 | 7 | 7 |
| - number of terms | 34 | 47 | 47 | 47 |
| **Subject knowledge** | | | | |
| - number of domains | 5 | 4 | 7 | 5 |
| - number of subdomains | 11 | 15 | 26 | 13 |
| - number of terms | 27 | 167 | 111 | 69 |

| Vwo 1998 | Science for Public Understanding | Biology | Chemistry | Physics |
|---|---|---|---|---|
| **Skills** | | | | |
| - number of domains | 1 | 1 | 1 | 1 |
| - number of subdomains | 7 | 7 | 7 | 7 |
| - number of terms | 34 | 47 | 47 | 47 |
| **Subject knowledge** | | | | |
| - number of domains | 5 | 4 | 7 | 5 |
| - number of subdomains | 14 | 18 | 30 | 19 |
| - number of terms | 33 | 216 | 202 | 74 |

Table 8:     An overview of the structure of examination programs in havo and vwo (1998)

| Domain | Sub-domain | Title | Number of terms |
|---|---|---|---|
| **A** | | **Materials, structure and bonding** | |
| | A1 | Language skills | 1-8 |
| | A2 | Arithmetical/mathematical skills | 9-14 |
| | A3 | Information skills | 15-22 |
| | A4 | Technical-instrumental skills | 23-27 |
| | A5 | Design skills | 28-34 |
| | A6 | Research skills | 35-43 |
| | A7 | About science, society and future profession | 44-47 |
| **B** | | **Materials, structure and bonding** | |
| | B1 | Applications | 1-4 |
| | B2 | Processes/reactions | 5,6 |
| | B3 | Atomic structure and Periodic Table | 7-12 |
| | B4 | Bonding, types and properties | 12-20 |
| | B5 | Names and formulas | 26,27 |
| **C** | | **Chemistry of carbon compounds** | |
| | C1 | Applications of synthetic polymers | 28-32 |
| | C2 | Other applications of carbon compounds | 33-40 |
| | C3 | Reactions of carbon compounds | 41-50 |
| | C4 | Structures of carbon compounds | 51-68 |
| **D** | | **Biochemistry** | |
| | D1 | Industrial applications of biopolymers | 72-74 |
| | D2 | Metabolism | 75-81 |
| | D3 | Structures of biochemical materials | 83-90, 92 |

| D | | Biochemistry | |
|---|---|---|---|
| | D1 | Industrial applications of biopolymers | 72-74 |
| | D2 | Metabolism | 75-81 |
| | D3 | Structures of biochemical materials | 83-90, 92 |
| E | | Properties of chemical reactions | |
| | E1 | Applications | 94-99, 102-105 |
| | E2 | Energetic effects | 106-109 |
| | E3 | Reaction speed | 107, 110-114 |
| | E4 | Equilibra | 118-123 |
| | E5 | Calculations about chemical reactions | 125-128 |
| F | | Chemical technology | |
| | F1 | Syntheses of materials | 129-133 |
| | F2 | Separation and purification of materials | 134-138 |
| | F3 | Identificaton of materials | 139-141 |
| | F4 | Analysis toohnology | 142-145 |
| | F5 | Process industry | 146-151 |
| | F6 | Bulk products | 152-153 |
| G | | Acids and bases | |
| | G1 | Applications | 154-156 |
| | G2 | Research | 157-162 |
| | G3 | Properties, reactions and the Brønsted-theory | 163-174 |
| | G4 | Calculations | 175-178 |
| | G5 | Names and formulas | 179-181 |
| H | | Redox | |
| | H1 | Applications | 182-187 |
| | H2 | Redox as a process | 188-190 |
| | H3 | Redox reactions | 191-202 |

Table 9 :    Domains and subdomains for chemistry vwo (1998)

---

**Subdomain A5 Design skills**

*The student can*
*A28 identify and specify a technical problem*
*A29 convert a technical problem into a design brief*
*A30 identify priorities, alternatives and specifications for the development of a design*
*A31 make a work scheme for the development of a design*
*A32 build a prototype of the design*
*A33 evaluate design product and prototype, related to the priorities and*
*    specifications*
*A34 make suggestions for improvement of the design.*

Table 10:    An example of the specification of a subdomain of domain A Skills

Table 11:    Examples of specified terms in the chemistry and physics national curriculum (1998)

The standards for science education in vmbo are less specific than the havo-vwo standards and are strongly related to the future employment of these students. These standards were introduced in 2000 and evaluated in 2006. The new standards for the next period of five years will be more generally specified and schools will be more autonomous to develop their interpretation for the school curriculum and forms of school assessment.

## Assessment

The entire of the national curriculum for havo, vwo and gymnasium in biology, chemistry and physics is assessed twice, both in a national exam and in a set of school exams. The student's result is determined by the national exam (50%) and the average result of the school examination portfolio (50%). Science for Public Understanding is assessed only by school exams.

The school examination portfolio must consist of:
• Written tests. The school decides how, when and how many.
• Course work. At least one experimental investigation (not in Science for Public Understanding) and using some of the following techniques:
    - a scientific enquiry
    - a technical design
    - a literature survey
    - a project on decision making
    - a project of free choice.

The coursework has to be presented in a variety of ways. At least one piece of coursework assessment must be derived from group work. A piece of coursework may take between 5 and 20 hours of study.

The examination of skills in the portfolio is spread over the four science as well as general subjects. The specifications for school assessment only prescribe that skills have to be assessed, not how and to what extent. This is contradictory to the specification level of the assessment forms of subject knowledge in school assessment. Most schools put emphasis on research skills and include information and technical/instrumental skills. Presentation skills are mostly assessed in the final project.

In addition to the tests for the examination portfolio, teachers give advancement tests, which influence the promotion to the next school class.

## The functions of assessment

All assessment in junior secondary education determines the promotion of pupils to the next class and the determination of what is considered to be the most appropriate type and level of secondary education commensurate with their capabilities. Students can stay down in a class only once in the first three years. Teachers are themselves responsible for all advancement tests. Within a school all pupils of the same level of junior secondary education may have different teachers but the same advancement tests.

Teachers offer additional support to the lower achievers in the preparation of the tests. Some schools offer special additional programs for the higher achievers.

National tests take place at the end of the last school year of vmbo, havo, vow and gymnasium. The functions of these tests are:
• Validation of the level to the vocational or university education to be followed
• Benchmarking of overall school quality
• Benchmarking of teacher quality

The number of certificated and non-certificated students of all schools are published on the website of the national inspectorate. Schools are also obliged to publish their results in information leaflets for parents of their (future) students. For a small number of schools, the results may be so poor that there follows a programme designed to improve the results from the school, supervised by the national school inspectorate.

The benchmarking of teacher quality within schools is characterized by implicit or more explicit judgement processes, involving school managers and other teachers of the same school.

If there is a large difference between the results of the national exams and school portfolio, the school inspectorate investigates the forms and quality of the school assessment. The school management is responsible for the monitoring and improvement of the quality of school assessment.

## Side effects of the national testing

In 2002, the Exploratory Committee on Chemical Education mapped out the problems encountered currently in chemistry education in the Netherlands. The conclusions are also relevant for biology and physics education.

'The exam requirements for chemistry are a constraining straitjacket. Practical assignments and personal research receive too little attention. The examination programme makes it impossible to have extramural activities such as an introductory visit to a university, a school for vocational education, a laboratory or a company.'

The most important side effect of the national test is that teachers emphasize the teaching for the national test. In the construction of written tests for the school examination, most teachers copy questions from former national exams instead of developing questions, which are congruent to the learning, classroom activities and teaching. Most teachers doubt the quality of their own school exams and do not have confidence in school exams of their colleagues from other schools. In initial teacher training and continuos professional development the development and evaluation of assessment in written tests and other forms receive hardly any attention.

On a national scale, the difference between the average result of the school exams, a mark between 1 till 10 (maximum), and national exam, is less then 1.0 although individual and school differences might be larger.

Some schools start the 'training' for the national exam in school exams two years before the national exam is taken.

The second side effect is that teachers feel trapped by requirements of the final examination programme. The Exploratory Committee noted that teachers are afraid to exercise any personal classroom freedom and do not dare let go of parts of the programme.

Their lessons are strongly dictated by the schoolbooks. They feel very little freedom for personal professional input in subject matter or in lesson periods that can be injected from the teacher's personal ideas and experience. In an endeavour to reduce the overload in teaching and learning in havo, the Ministry of Education, in 2002, cut 20% off the number of examination terms in subject knowledge. However, they left a disconnected curriculum.

The third side effect is the emphasis on teaching and testing of subject knowledge at the expense of skills such as experimental chemistry laboratory studies, seen by many students as one of the most appealing aspects of their chemistry course.

The fourth side effect is that the emphasis given on teaching the assessable discourages students from engaging with modern developments, especially in biochemistry, material science and associated technology and the important and profound significance of chemistry in society today. In the curriculum overview only the chemistry at the end of the 19th century and the first half of the 20th century is addressed. Before the educational reform in 1998, most schools were involved in final projects as part of the school assessment in cooperation with universities. This good practice got lost in the last few years but will be rehabilitated when the next reform is initiated in 2007

The fifth side effect is that science education in the Netherlands is strongly dictated by the textbooks of different educational publishers. The targets of the examination programme are extensively injected into subject matter and rarely in a novel way. As has already been stressed, teachers are faithful to their textbooks and do not have the courage to drop or change anything. This teaching method offers little leeway for current developments in science and science education. Changes in textbooks require a time span of at least four years. This means that curriculum renewal in a subject such as chemistry can only enter classroom practice very slowly and does not keep pace with rapidly changing and increasing chemical knowledge. With the introduction of the 2007 standards, schools are also invited to make their own decisions about parts of the curriculum for school assessment. Thus teachers are encouraged to substitute some chapters in the textbook about the applications of science with investigation projects based on contemporary science. Many projects have already been developed in cooperation with universities, research institutes and industrial companies, with government funding.

## Science standards without centralized assessment

In 1998, the Science for Public Understanding course was introduced as a mandatory school subject for all students in the second stage of havo and vwo. It was intended to be the laboratory for science curriculum renewal of the disciplinary subjects biology, chemistry and physics. The examination program was in global prescribed terms and assessed in school exams. Unfortunately this new school subject was a political plaything, a representative of all the problems that accompanied the reform of the structure of secondary education since 1998. After the student demonstrations in 1999, the Minister of Education cancelled the course but the Parliament could not agree with this decision. After a debate over three years, Parliament has agreed that, from 2007, the mandatory part of Science for Public Understanding course for vwo will be reduced by 40% to 120 hours. Further from 2007, the Science for Public

Understanding course will no longer be a mandatory subject for havo, although parts of the course can be integrated in the curricula of chemistry, physics and biology.

Teachers, school managers, students and parents strongly value results of national exams. Teachers are vulnarable according to the acceptance and quality standards of school based assessment.

Some motives for the deciding on school assessment for science are:

1   An essential precondition for further development of teaching and learning in the first years after the introduction of a novel school subject.

2   A chance for science education starting with present-day examples of the development and application of science knowledge and the societal and ethical issues related to science and technology.

3   A precondition to encourage students' interest and motivation in science.

4   A chance to engage more teachers in continuous professional development and thus close the gap between their personal disciplinary subject knowledge and the state of the art of science and technology.

However, there are also possible concerns about solely depending on school assessment without some form of national benchmarking, which include:

1   Large differences between good practices and very bad practices in school assessment.

2   Large differences between the teaching qualities of strongly motivated and less motivated teachers.

3   Large differences between the contribution of this school subject to the entire program of havo and vwo.

# References

*Annual reports on implementation and further development of science and science for public understanding* (2000, 2001, 2002, 2003, 2005) Enschede: SLO, www.slo.nl

*Building Chemistry, A Blueprint to initiate Renewal of Chemistry Programme in Upper Secondary Education in the Netherlands* (2003). The Exploratory Committee on Chemical Education. Enschede: SLO .

*Concept examination programs 2007.* www.slo.nl and www.tweedefase-loket.nl

*Chemistry between context and concept, designing for renewal* (2003) Committee for the Renewal of Chemistry Education in HAVO and VWO. Enschede: SLO.

*Examination programs* 1998. www.cevo.nl and www.tweedefase-loket.nl

*Guide working students through SPU.* www.slo.nl

*Natuurkunde left* (2005) Committee for the Renewal of Physics Education in HAVO and VWO. www.nieuwenatuurkunde.nl

*Specifications for national exams.* www.slo.nl, www.cevo.nl and www.tweedefase-loket.nl

*Working guide for school assessment 2007.* www.slo.nl and www.tweedefase-loket.nl

*Vernieuwd biologie onderwijs van 4 tot 18 jaar (2005).* Commissie Vernieuwing Biologie Onderwijs. www.nibi.nl (CVBO)

# Chapter 13

# Science curriculum in Portugal:
# From the development to the evaluation of students' competences

*Cecília Galvão\*, Pedro Reis, Ana Freire, Teresa Oliveira*

*Faculty of Sciences, University of Lisbon, Campo Grande, C6, Piso 1, 1749-016 Lisbon, Portugal*

## Introduction

The concept of standards is not an easy one, but even more complex is the concept of competence, at a conceptual level and in terms of national traditions and cultures. In international discussions on standards, the use of the words 'competence' and 'standards' can create misunderstandings, since some countries have different definitions and different notions are involved.

In Portugal, the science curriculum and the associated concepts of competence for basic education (from the age of 6 to 14) was implemented in 2002. The development of a new curriculum for secondary education (15 to 17), in which several competences, besides content, were introduced, started later, in 2004-05.

The following scheme illustrates the Portuguese educational system (figure 1):

| Level | Basic education (compulsory) | | | | | | | | | Secondary education (non-compulsory) | | |
|---|---|---|---|---|---|---|---|---|---|---|---|---|
| | 1st Cycle | | | | 2nd Cycle | | 3rd Cycle | | | | | |
| Grade | 1 | 2 | 3 | 4 | 5 | 6 | 7 | 8 | 9 | 10 | 11 | 12 |
| Pupils' age | 6 | 7 | 8 | 9 | 10 | 11 | 12 | 13 | 14 | 15 | 16 | 17 |
| Scientific subjects | "Estudo do Meio" – Integrated environmental, natural and social studies, comprising the fields of biology, geography, physics, chemistry, health and environmental education and history. | | | | Natural sciences – Integrated biology geology, physics, chemistry; health and environmental education. | | Physical and natural sciences – Two subjects for each grade: 1) Integrated biology, geology, environmental and health education; 2) Integrated physics, chemistry and environmental education. | | | Two years* of biology and geology (as one subject) Two years* of physics and chemistry (as one subject) | | biology **or** geology **or** physics **or** chemistry § |

\* Each student can begin this two-year subject at 10th or 11th grade
§ Each student must choose only one subject

Figure 1: Science provision in Portuguese schools

238

# 1 How are science education standards defined?

## 1.1 Basic Education

For basic education, which is compulsory, there is a National Curriculum (NC) whose standards are defined in the form of general and specific competences. The concept of competence is based on the definition by Perrenoud (1997) as 'the integration of knowledge and skills developed in complex learning situations'. This notion is one of 'wide-ranging competence, comprising knowledge, capacities and attitudes, which may be considered as knowledge in action or in use' (DEB, 2001). Therefore, the issue is to promote the integrated development of both capacities and attitudes that enable the use of knowledge in different situations, especially problematic situations. As regards science, it also refers to a definition of scientific literacy competences, which includes *what do people know*, *what can people do* and *what do people value* (Gräber and Nentwig, 1999).

The National Curriculum defines competences considered to be essential, distinguishing those that are general and correspond to a basic education profile – which are then taken as a starting point for all subsequent formulations – and those that are specific to each subject area. The work of interpreting and implementing such guidelines is the teachers' responsibility, especially within the scope of each class council, teachers' council or curriculum department.

### 1.1.1 General competences

The Portuguese National Curriculum (DEB, 2001) states that, by the end of basic education, students should be able to:
1. Mobilise cultural, scientific and technological knowledge in order to understand reality and to deal with daily life situations and problems

2. Use the languages from the different areas of cultural, scientific and technological knowledge in order to express themselves

3. Master the Portuguese language in order to communicate in a suitable manner and to structure their own thinking

4. Use foreign languages in order to communicate effectively in daily life situations and for the appropriation of information

5. Adopt personalised work and learning methods appropriate to the intended objectives

6. Research, select and organise information so as to turn it into transferable knowledge

7. Adopt problem-solving and decision making strategies

8. Carry out activities in an autonomous, responsible and creative manner

9. Co-operate with others on common tasks and projects

10. Relate body with space, harmoniously from a personal and interpersonal perspective promoting health and quality of life.


### 1.1.2 Specific competences for students' scientific literacy by the end of basic education

These competences include *knowledge* (substantive, procedural or methodological, epistemological), *reasoning*, *communication* and *attitudes*. Students must be involved in the teaching-learning process through the differentiated educational experiences a school must provide.

*(a) Knowledge*
*Substantive knowledge* – involving the analysis and discussion of evidence or problematic situations that ensures appropriate scientific knowledge. This contributes to the interpretation and understanding of scientific laws and models and recognition of the limitations of science and technology in solving personal, social and environmental problems.

*Methodological knowledge* – experienced by carrying out bibliographic research, observation, experiments, individually or in groups, assessing the results obtained, planning and carrying out research, designing and interpreting graphs based on statistical and mathematical data.

*Epistemological knowledge* – involving the analysis and discussion based on the reports of scientific discoveries, which should highlight successes and failures, the persistence and working patterns of different scientists and societal influences on science.

*(b) Reasoning*
Whenever possible, learning situations should be planned which are focused on problem-solving, including interpretation of data, formulation of problems and hypotheses, research planning, prediction and assessment of results, establishment of comparisons, carrying out inference, generalisation and deduction. Such situations should seek to promote creativity, relating evidence and explanation, confronting

different perspectives on scientific interpretation, building and analysing alternative situations that require response and the use of diverse cognitive strategies.

*(c) Communication*
Educational experiences that include the use of scientific language in interpreting the different sources of information are recommended. It is important to distinguish the essential information from the complementary information and to use different modes of representing this information. Situations in which students can discuss issues should be included, providing them with an opportunity to present and defend their own ideas, to analyse and summarise arguments and to create written or oral texts. These educational experiences should also include co-operation in the sharing of information, and presentation of research results, thereby using different means, including new information and communication technologies.

*(d) Attitudes*
Educational experiences should take place where the student is able to develop attitudes inherent to work in science. Such attitudes consist of curiosity, perseverance and dedication, respect for and questioning of the results obtained, critical reflection on the work carried out, flexibility to accept errors and uncertainty, reformulation of student's own work, development of an aesthetic sense so as to admire the beauty of objects and physical and natural phenomena, respecting ethics, and awareness of the scientific impact on society and on the environment.

### 1.1.3  Learning experiences in basic education

So that students understand that scientific knowledge is in close relation to their surrounding reality, it is important to undertake learning experiences such as those set out below:

• Observing the surrounding environment. This necessarily involves planning walks in the countryside; drawing up observation routes, devising simple instruments to record information, field diaries; using instruments (such as the compass, magnifying glass, stopwatch, thermometer, geological hammer, sensors)

• Gathering and organising material, classifying it into categories or themes. This involves taking the protection of the environment into consideration, gathering only a small sample of natural material or recording only by drawing, photography or film. Making a portfolio registering all the steps, from gathering to classification, is recommended

• Planning and developing different types of research. Problem solving situations are essential for understanding science, as they imply different forms of research, gathering, analysis and organisation of information

- Designing projects, predicting all the steps to be taken from defining the problems onwards. This implies different forms of research and environmental intervention. Students should participate actively in the project and get involved from its design to its final stage

- Carrying out experimental activities and using different instruments for observation and measurement. Experimental activities, planned with students, should result from issues to be investigated, and which do not merely represent the application of a set of 'recipes'. Formulating hypotheses, predicting results, observing and explaining should be included

- Analysing and criticising newspaper and TV news, applying scientific knowledge to everyday situations

- Carrying out debates on controversial and contemporary issues, where students have to provide reasons for and/or against a given problem and make decisions, thereby stimulating the capacity for argument and fostering respect for different points of view from one's own

- Reporting the results of research and projects, setting out one's own ideas and those of his or her group, using audiovisuals, models or the new information and communication technologies

- Carrying out cooperative work in different situations (in extra-curricular projects, in classroom situations, for example, problem-solving) and independent work.

## 1.2 Secondary Education

The curriculum for secondary education is developed through different subjects, all of which point out the development of competences and suggest different sorts of activities to promote and assess these competences. The competences and learning experiences mentioned in this point of the paper refer to biology-geology and physics-chemistry (two year subjects that can begin at 10th or 11th grade; (figure 1) and biology or geology or physics or chemistry (grade 12).

### 1.2.1 Competences

The competences suggested by these curricula are organized in three domains: (a) *Knowledge*, (b) *Reasoning* and communication and (c) *Attitudes*.

(a) *Knowledge* – The acquisition, understanding and use of data, concepts, models and theories

(b) *Reasoning and communication* – The development of learning and reasoning skills (such as researching, analysing, organising, critically evaluating, understanding and communicating information; interpreting, critically discussing, judging, deciding and responsibly acting upon the surrounding reality)

(c) *Attitudes* – The adoption of attitudes and values related to personal and social awareness and to grounded decision-making (concerning problems that involve interactions between science, technology, society and the environment), aimed at an education for citizenship (for instance, attitudes and values pertaining to the nature of science and its social implications; rigour; curiosity; humbleness; scepticism; critical analysis; reflection; responsibility; cooperation and solidarity).

### 1.2.2 Learning experiences in secondary education

The secondary curricula for the above mentioned subjects recommend a set of activities for promoting and evaluating the competences already discussed:

• Promoting practical activities (viewed as a broad concept that comprises activities of a diverse nature, such as lab activities or field trips). Through these activities, students can develop and/or enhance competences as: a) using optical instruments and those of automatic systems to gather data (e.g. sensors); b) presenting and interpreting data; c) writing up reports about practical activities; d) researching information; e) reinforcing communication abilities; and f) using information technologies. Special attention is paid to the development of activities that imply students in the planning of experimental procedures. These approaches require the integration of theory and practice as well as collaborative work among students

• Using students' daily life situations or scientific applications with social interest to explore the relations between science, technology and society

• Promoting the identification of problematic situations, meaningful to students, whose understanding implies the formulation of questions that may steer research processes, with the planning and execution of intentional learning processes, involving the confrontation and evaluation of arguments and a summary of information

• Discussing aspects of the history of science in order to review the fundamental steps of the construction of scientific knowledge and to present science as an enterprise with personal and social dimensions

• Using non-formal learning situations to stress the importance of science in everyday life.

The basic and the secondary education curricula require that the assessment of the activities should be considered part and parcel of educational processes, making teaching, learning and assessment three interdependent and inseparable processes. Thus assessment is an ongoing, complex task implying the use of different techniques and instruments, namely observation grids, checklists, tests and questionnaires, activity reports, portfolios and concept maps.

## 2 How can the achievement of science education standards be assessed?

In the Portuguese educational system, it is now considered essential that students' assessment focus on several competences besides content.
In an official document dating to January 2005, the following is expressed (Ministério da Educação, 2005):
Assessment regards the learning and competences defined in the National Curriculum for the several areas and subjects, should ensure
(i) Consistency between the assessment processes, learning and the competences which students are intended to achieve, according to the contexts where they are developed
(ii) Use of different techniques and instruments of assessment
(iii) Value of formative assessment including processes of self-assessment
(iv) Value of students' learning evolution.

Although this document concerns basic education, the principles are also true for secondary education. This assumption is based on the principle that the competences defined are those we consider necessary for a citizen of the 21$^{st}$ century. This means that there has to be a strong connection between the learning situations created by the teacher and the assessment of the students involved in these situations. Several authors and studies reveal that one of the main causes of student failure is the divorce between what teachers do with students and what is assessed.

If we consider Portuguese PISA results (OECD, 2004a; 2004b), we can see that the main difficulties encountered by our students lie in reasoning and in the ability to communicate their ideas. Thus the most important change that we can make, if we are to succeed is by placing assessment at the centre of a reflective process for teachers and students.

It is expressed, in the National Curriculum, that science assessment must go beyond remembering facts and laws but also value the holistic knowledge of scientific ideas and the critical understanding of science and scientific thinking. It is therefore essential that students distinguish evidence from explanation and identify gaps in scientific knowledge. It is also important that they use their own words to present scientific ideas to their colleagues and teachers. The substantive knowledge of science is extremely important and is revealed, above all, in the explanations about phenomena given by the students themselves, in the way they communicate their ideas and in the arguments they use to defend their points of view. It is vital to develop in students, throughout their school career, attitudes inherent to the nature of the construction of scientific knowledge. These attitudes include curiosity, scepticism, perseverance, critical analysis, discussion and argumentation, are part of scientific research and discovery, and they are extremely important for the development of a stance of active and critical citizenship. When considered both in learning strategies and in evaluation strategies, they promote critical thinking and creativity.

The following are examples of the recommendations included in the science curriculum for students' assessment in basic education:
• Interpretation of scientific news in the media
• Demonstration of the understanding of the main scientific ideas, through explanations using their own words
• Formulation of questions based on data, and corresponding answers
• Recognition of the importance of evidence in problem solving, arguing and using different theoretical frameworks
• Use of scientific language in different situations.

We know that all these areas can be included in tests. But only by expressing different learning situations such as the discussion of controversial issues, research, the planning and development of projects, can students become involved in a particular learning environment, leading to the comprehensive understanding of what science is, and giving teachers different contexts in which to assess their students. In this sense the science curriculum recommends, for example, that teachers value what students write as well as the process and product of project work they are involved. It also recommends the assessment of practical work as a global process, including planning and communicating the results. The curriculum suggests that we acknowledge, using the ideas of Aikenhead (2002), assessment not only as a matter of testing, but as being related to daily classroom work where we can verify that there is better learning when instruction and evaluation are integrated.

As the association between educational experience and evaluation is one of the guidelines of both national and foreign official documents, it is natural that teachers are faced with the difficulty of assessing increasingly open products, such as reports, texts, posters, elaborated individually or in a group. By defining criteria that are appropriate for the tasks and clarifying discriminating levels of performance, the evaluation of what students do becomes more objective and fairer and, at the same time, students are provided with precise instructions how to improve their work.

Currently, the final secondary education exams in biology or geology or physics or chemistry (table 1) are written and last 120 minutes (GAVE, 2005). The exam includes sets of items based on information that may be given in the form of texts (newspaper articles, scientific texts, description of experiences, interviews), figures, tables, graphs and so on. The items of each set may be closed questions (for instance, true/false, association or multiple choice) or open questions (a short composition or a long composition with instructions), according to the competences being assessed. For example, a set of items can be based on the description of a situation/experience related to the process of science construction, to daily life, to the environment or to technology.

With the information provided, there can be many different questions: interpreting this information; justifying certain situations/results; formulating hypotheses; critically analysing procedures and subsequently suggesting changes; identifying the social and technological applications of a given concept/process; elaborating short texts that explain a certain situation scientifically or that demonstrate knowledge of important landmarks in the history of biology or geology or physics or chemistry; predicting results in different experimental situations from those presented. We give an example of an item and its assessment from a12th grade biology exam (GAVE, 2006):

Item
A couple with fertility problems, under medical advice, undertook several clinical examinations in order to identify the possible causes of their problem. The tests provided the following results:
• Spermigram with normal values
• Both individuals have shown normal hormonal levels
• Cervical mucus hostile for sperm cells
• Normal oogenesis
• Normal anatomy for both reproductive systems

After a first diagnosis, the doctor considered one of the two techniques of assisted reproduction:
1. Artificial insemination, using husband's sperm
2. Artificial insemination, using a donor's sperm

However, in accordance with the results, the doctor suggested the first technique. Justify this medical option and give a reason for the infertility of that couple.

Assessment criteria
The assessment of this item considers: scientific content; logical-thematic organisation; use of scientific language; and communication in Portuguese language.

The answer must include the following aspects:
• the infertility reason is due to the fact that the cervical mucus is not favourable to the husband sperm cells

- the artificial insemination technique puts the sperm cells directly inside the uterus and they do not need to cross the cervical mucus barrier
- once the spermigram shows normal values it is not necessary to use a sperm donor.

The following table (figure 2) presents the quotation to each level of performance:

| Levels of performance in the specific scientific domain of the subject | | | Levels of performance in the domain of communication in the Portuguese language Levels* | | |
|---|---|---|---|---|---|
| | | | 3 | 2 | 1 |
| Levels | 5 | The answer includes all the three topics. The writing is coherent (the discourse is logical and in accordance with the question); use of adequate scientific language | 15 | 14 | 13 |
| | 4 | The answer includes all the three topics. The writing is coherent (the discourse is logical and in accordance with the question); occasionally use of non-adequate scientific language Or The answer includes all the three topics. Occasionally incoherent writing even with adequate scientific language | 12 | 11 | 10 |
| | 3 | The answer includes two out of three topics. The writing is coherent (the discourse is logical and in accordance with the question); use of adequate scientific language | 9 | 8 | 7 |
| | 2 | The answer includes two out of three topics. The writing is coherent (the discourse is logical and in accordance with the question); occasionally use of non-adequate scientific language Or The answer includes two out of three topics. Occasionally use incoherent writing although with adequate scientific language | 6 | 5 | 4 |
| | 1** | The answer includes only one topic. The scientific language is adequate to the understanding of the answer | 3 | 2 | 1 |

*
– Level 3 – Well-structured composition, without syntax, punctuation or spelling mistakes, or with some occasional mistakes which do not lead to the loss of intelligibility and/or coherence and meaning.
– Level 2 – Sufficiently structured composition, with some syntax, punctuation and spelling mistakes which do not lead to the loss of the intelligibility and/or coherence and meaning.
– Level 1 – Low structured composition, with serious syntax, punctuation and spelling mistakes which involve the loss of the intelligibility and/or coherence and meaning.

** In the case that level 1 of performance in the scientific domain is not reached the answer quotation given to it is Zero.

Figure 2:    Assessment criteria for the item example

In the exam, classification criteria vary according to the type of item. For example, in open-question items (as the example above), criteria are organised by levels of performance. In order to fit answers into a given level of performance, several aspects are kept in mind, such as content-related elements, the logical sequence of ideas, the use of suitable scientific language and adequate Portuguese language mastery.

## 3    What function does the assessment of science education standards have?

In the paper written for the second International Symposium on Scientific Literacy (Galvão and Abrantes, 2005), we stated:

> *Our major concern now is to deal with many issues related to science curriculum implementation and evaluation: how to know more about the processes of curriculum evolution both at local and national levels; how to help teachers experimenting with the new way of organising learning environments, creating materials, selecting content and learning experiences with respect both to local contexts and to student needs; how to argue against the influence of conceptions in favouring the perpetuation of a technique-oriented curriculum; and how to rebuff old political arguments that 'pure science' leads to better performance from our students in international testing.* (p. 192)

In fact, curriculum evaluation in basic education did not exist in the sense of a real understanding of the impact of the new proposal. It is not enough to write coherent documents and give them to the teachers saying "Do it". Innovations need to be created with others, explained, discussed and followed in order to reorient and correct what is going on in practice. Curriculum in basic education was created to be implemented according to Freudenthal's (1991) concept of 'educational development'. We can say that the curriculum implementation followed the idea of an *enactment strategy* (Snyder et al., 1992) where teacher education, counselling, assessment and opinion shaping were not later phases of the process but aspects that should be incorporated from the beginning. Political changes made this impossible, so, what happened in Portugal was the multiple interpretations of curriculum, and the evaluation we can do now is "everything can happen in our schools". We will try to summarise this in a few examples.

The results of a questionnaire submitted to 59 secondary teachers reveals that there is a faulty interpretation of what is proposed in the official documents (Galvão, et al., 2004). There are different reasons for this, such as:

• the implementation process itself – lack of communication, where discussion concerning fundamental issues did not reach all teacher groups

• the lack of understanding of the language of the official documents, due to difficulties in clarification and reaching a consensus about the meaning of the concepts

• the resistance against changing traditional views in science teaching, which is why, for example, the Curricular Guidelines are read in the light of the previous programmes and its contents are seen more as a set of lists rather than viewed in terms of a global, integrative perspective.

Basically there is a lack of understanding of what is now required of them as science teachers. In their criticism, teachers reveal a static perspective of science, overvaluing the products of science and undervaluing other components. The objections of some teachers demonstrate their criticism of the proposed educational experiences, because they feel these undervalue the transmission of scientific knowledge and give more importance to the learning experiences that are more pupil-centred, based on a constructivist perspective of learning. Thus they criticise the guidelines in the national curriculum which they perceive, correctly, as not valuing previous practices and not seeming open to the potential of teaching steered towards the development of competencies. They adopt different language, but do not change their practices. And if we concentrate our attention on the assessment perspectives, the problem remains. Old practices are connected to old ways of assessment and this does not match with official international and national specifications.

In another study (Martins, 2005), in which 398 teachers of Primary education (6 to 12 years old) took part, only 29 % correctly defined competence as it is used in the national curriculum. For most of them (23%) competence and objective are one and the same. Generally speaking, this study confirms the idea that teachers are aware of the official discourse but have not appropriated its underlying meaning and implications. Often they are unfamiliar with the official documents and simply use student textbooks. So it is understandable that many of them continue to say they feel no need to change their practice. And if teaching is not oriented towards the development of competences, then these can hardly be assessed.

## 4 What side effects of testing standards are feared or observed?

In the Portuguese educational system, science subjects are only assessed, at national level, at the end of the secondary when they take national exams. These exams have been used both to evaluate the science education carried out in Portugal and to choose the students who are to go on to university. For Portuguese language and mathematics, however, students are assessed at the end of the 1st and 3rd cycles of basic education, and at the end of secondary education (through national exams). The evaluation of the first cycle, focused on the assessment of competences, has had an interesting effect on the Portuguese educational system in that it encourages a shift in classroom practices in the direction of activities that have more to do with the items proposed in these exams.

Both our personal experience and several research results show that formal evaluation (namely the kind of national exam that is proposed) is crucial in establishing the importance and priority given to teaching specific topics and to using certain classroom practices (Craveiro and Neto, 1999; Millar and Osborne, 1998; Reis and Galvão, 2004). In Portugal, it is disturbing to see that the type of 12th grade national exam proposed some years ago, instead of seeking to induce a change in classroom practices in the sense recommended by curricular documents, has had a harmful (and undesired) effect on the organisation and management of the 12th grade classes in the subjects already mentioned. These exams were mainly focused on specific details (terms, structures, facts).

Over the years, that type of national exam proposed has led teachers to prepare their students for a type of assessment that is strongly centred on memorisation instead of critical analysis. So many students entered higher education burdened with terms but lacking in various competences considered to be essential by secondary education curricular documents.

In the school year of 2005–2006, in which national exams were supposed to evaluate the new secondary education curricula, the Ministry of Education cabinet responsible for the construction of examinations actively promoted a wide-ranging discussion (involving teachers and evaluation experts) in order to introduce new types of items that would allow the assessment of the various competences determined in the curricula. The evaluation of the impact of this process will only take place after the first exams are made public, which will be at the end of this school year. Meanwhile, following an earlier dissemination of a few examples of items, there has already shown significant improvement through:
(i) highly rating the logical sequence of discourse and the use of appropriate scientific jargon used in open-question items
(ii) highly rating Portuguese language written communication skills in open-question items
(iii) reinforcing the items concerning the capacities of critical thinking and planning of experimental activities.

However, the examples that were made public did not include any item regarding the discussion of the social, economic, ethical and moral implications of scientific and technological enterprise (an important dimension of the secondary education curricula in biology and geology and in physics and chemistry). In our opinion, using items on these dimensions is indispensable, if one is to evaluate subjects that are meant to be heavily marked by the analysis and discussion of the different implications of biotechnology and of interactions between science, technology, society and environment.

If the 12th grade exam does not include this type of item, once again it will be limiting and overthrowing the curricular objectives of the scientific subjects. Once again, we will have exams that instead of inducing a change in classroom practices in the sense recommended by curricular documents (calling for argumentation and discussion, for example), will have a negative (and restrictive) effect on class organisation and management, inducing teaching practices strongly centred on memorisation (of terms, concepts and facts) instead of on critical analysis.

## 5    How can standards be implemented without imperative testing?

In Portugal, the lack of a system to evaluate on the work carried out by teachers in their classes has been at the root of many situations of non-completion of the proposed curricular guidelines and objectives. Each teacher has total freedom regarding approaches, methodologies and activities in his/her classes and it has been student's assessment on a national level that plays a regulating part. But is it only through external evaluation that competences can be implemented? The answer to this question should be: no, absolutely not. We could put the question another way: regardless of national-level evaluation, how can we promote a practice of teaching through competences?

We know that in all learning situations there must be a previously defined corresponding form of evaluation, both of the process and of the product, so that teachers and students have full knowledge of the scope of what was learned with the development of the situation, allowing for the necessary reflection for changing objectives and strategies.

But it is not easy to begin to create new evaluation processes, countering decades of action in a given direction. And if the new evaluation processes are suited neither to the learning situations nor to the students, and the instruments that are elaborated are not the best for that which is to be evaluated, the consequences are serious and unfair. That is why teamwork between teachers is imperative, so they can discuss objectives and techniques, experimenting and evaluating in a critical way, under the assumption that this evaluation must always have a formative finality. Fully aware of how difficult it has been to implement competences and their assessment in Portugal, the Basic Education Science Curriculum designers have constructed materials for teachers (Galvão et al., 2006). These materials include examples of learning situations, of competences whose development they enable and of the respective assessment.

Successive political changes have hindered the possibility of stability in implementing educational reforms. Evaluating teacher performance has been one of those cases where there has been neither will nor strength to fight against the establishment of the last few decades. During the last three decades, teachers' work has not been evaluated. However, valuing good practices and a strong evaluation of teacher performance are indispensable measures to accomplish the implementation of competences. Until then, exams and students' textbooks continue to lead the way, despite their perverse effects.

# References

Aikenhead, G. (2002) *Renegotiating the culture of school science: scientific literacy for an informed public*. http://www.usask.ca/education/people/aikenhead/procsci.htm (17/05/2002)

Craveiro, C. L. and Neto, A. (1999) Das concepções curriculares e metodológicas dos professores de ciências ao ensino CTS: um estudo descritivo. *Actas do VII Encontro Nacional de Educação em Ciências*. Faro: Universidade do Algarve, Escola Superior de Educação (pp. 307-317).

DEB (Departamento de Educação Básica) (2001) *Currículo nacional do ensino básico. Competências essenciais* Lisboa: Ministério da Educação.

Freudenthal, H. (1991) *Revisiting mathematics education*. Dordrecht: Kluwer Academic Publishers.

Galvão, C., Freire, A.M., Lopes, A. M., Neves, A., Oliveira, T. and Santos, C. (2004) Innovation in Portuguese science curriculum: some evaluation issues. In ME-DEB (Coord). *Flexibility in curriculum, citizenship and communication/Flexibilidade curricular, cidadania e comunicação* (pp 49-64). Lisboa: DEB.

Galvão, C. and Abrantes, P. (2005). Physical and natural sciences – a new curriculum in Portugal. In P. Nentwig & D. Waddington (Eds.), *Making it Relevant: Context-based learning of science* (pp. 175-194 ). Münster: Waxmann.

Galvão, C., Reis, P., Freire, A. and Oliveira, T. (2006) *Avaliação de competências em ciências. Sugestões para professores do ensino básico e do ensino secundário*. Lisboa: ASA.

GAVE (Gabinete de avaliação educacional) (2005) *Informação de exames do ensino secundário*. http://www.gave.pt/infoexame_es_novo_2005.htm

GAVE (Gabinete de avaliação educacional) (2006) *Exame de Biologia do 12º ano, 1ª Fase*. Lisboa: Ministério da Educação.

Gräber, W. and Nentwig, P. (1999) *Scientific Literacy: Bridging the gap between theory and practice*. Paper presented at ATEE Spring University in Klaipëda/Lituânia.

Martins, I. F. (2005) *Competências em Ciências Físicas e Naturais. Concepções e práticas de professores do ensino básico*. (Unpublished thesis). Aveiro: Universidade de Aveiro.

Millar, R. and Osborne, J. (1998) *Beyond 2000: Science education for the future*. London: King's College.

Ministério da Educação (2005) Despacho normativo [Normative dispatch] nº 1 de 2005. *Diário da República* Iª Série-B, 71-76.

OECD (2004a) *Learning for tomorrow's world – First results from PISA 2003.* Paris: OECD Publishing.

OECD (2004b). *Problem solving for tomorrow's world – First results from PISA 2003*. Paris: OECD Publishing.

Perrenoud, Ph. (1997) *Construire des compétences dès l'école.* Paris: ESF éditeur.

Reis, P. and Galvão, C. (2004) The impact of socio-scientific controversies in Portuguese natural science teachers' conceptions and practices. *Research in Science Education*, 34(2), 153-171.

Snyder, J., Bolin, F. and Zumwalt, K. (1992) Curriculum implementation. In P. W. Jackson (Ed.), *Handbook of Research on Curriculum*, (pp. 402-435). New York: Macmillan Publishing Company.

# Chapter 14

## Standards in science education: The situation in Scotland

*Tom Bryce*

*Department of Educational and Professional Studies, University of Strathclyde, Glasgow G13 1PP, Scotland*

## National (centralised) prescription

Scotland is a small country of some 5 million people and has its own education system, separate from the rest of the United Kingdom. State schools are the norm (only about 4% of pupils attend private schools) and we are long used to national prescription of the curriculum of primary (5–12 year olds) and secondary (12–18 year olds) schools. This can be understood in terms of the general, socialist outlook amongst Scots where uniformity of provision is seen to be in the interests of equity/equal opportunities and perceived fairness. Schooling is compulsory to 16 years old but staying-on rates have risen dramatically in recent years and some 50% now enter Higher Education, post-school.

There is one national examination board, the Scottish Qualifications Authority (SQA), serving upper school pupils and students in Further Education. Although moves are afoot to change things, the pattern has been for school pupils to take national Standard Grade courses between 14 and 16 years (anything up to eight subjects, at least one of which must be a science, and more typically two are science subjects) and National Qualification courses between 16 and 18 years (often up to five subjects where pupils are not required to take a science, but many do, and some do more than one). Both Standard Grades (S grades) and National Qualifications come at different levels (of ability/achievement) and the 'gold standard' is the Highers (H grades), though in the final year of school there is the opportunity for the most able to take Advanced Highers. In 2004 the proportions of school leavers gaining these qualifications in physics were:
59% no qualification; 29% Standard Grade, 10% Higher; 2% Advanced Higher.

(The figures for chemistry and biology were similar: respectively 53%, 35%, 10%, 2%; and 55%, 35%, 8% and 2%.) These figures can be read with some satisfaction, approximately one third of the cohort achieving science qualifications at Standard Grade and around ten percent at Higher Grade; equally, the two percent figures at Advanced Higher might surprise and disappoint many teachers, the proportions being very low nationally.

# The nature of prescription in the sciences

Each of the subjects in the school curriculum evolves (slowly) under the leadership of a group of experienced teachers and other experts and the SQA plays an important part in ensuring that the prescriptive detail is commensurate in format and kind. For each level there is detailed documentation which therefore specifies the standards to be achieved. These documents are readily available[1] and are known as *The Arrangements* … (in whatever subject at whatever level). They are affectionately known by teachers as 'the bibles' which says a lot about their importance.

To illustrate, physics at Higher level (a course which fits into one school session, typically for 16–17 year olds, but also for FE College students) is specified in a 43 page document and a lot of the detail expresses the objectives/standards/criteria under three broad headings (referred to as 'Outcomes'). These are that pupils should:

1. Demonstrate knowledge and understanding related to … (the content of the Unit).
2. Solve problems related to…(the content of the Unit).
3. Collect and analyse information related to Higher Physics obtained by experiment.

At the heart of the Arrangements document are 16 pages of
• Content statements (specifying what the pupil/student should be able to do in demonstrating knowledge and understanding associated with each of the three Units ('Mechanics and Properties of Matter'; 'Electricity and Electronics'; and 'Radiation and Matter'); and

Contexts, Applications, Illustrations and Activities which provide suggestions as to where and how these may be addressed, ie. worthwhile observations, experiments. Appendix 1 is an extract from these pages from the first unit.)

An indication of the balance of 'knowledge and understanding' (Outcome 1) to 'problem solving' (Outcome 2) is given by the weighting in the written test papers (partly multiple choice, partly structured questions) which is about 40:60.

There is, in addition to these specifications, a considerable amount of support material available to teachers (and pupils). First of all, the three units are tested compulsorily at the level of basic competence using a unit assessment which must be passed with a score of 60% before the candidate is allowed to sit the national (external) examination. These tests are drawn from an item bank devised by the SQA and are known as National Assessment Bank items (NABs). So the class teacher has guidance of standards in this form. Secondly, with regard to the external examination, there are specimen papers (which can be downloaded from the SQA website – see above).

1 http://www.sqa.org.uk

Thirdly, past papers are available from the SQA and are commonly bought by schools/pupils and are used as practice materials, often in the lead up to the national examination diet. Thus the whole thing is assessment-driven; teachers teach towards the examination, rather unashamedly.

## Other levels in Scotland, particularly stages earlier than certification

In the past fifteen years or so efforts have been made to provide national prescription for the earlier years of schooling and these are contained in documents known as 5–14 (a deliberate attempt to link up the primary school (5–12y) curriculum with the first two years of secondary (12–14y) despite the structural shift at 12y. Learning outcomes for the sciences are provided in Environmental Studies 5–14 and it has been quite a strain on primary teachers in particular (for they are generalists and cover all aspects of the curriculum; very few will have science expertise in their own higher education) to cope with the detail of the specification. The net effect has been to ensure that more science is taught in primary schools than pre-1990 but the amount and quality of it is a little varied across the country, dependent upon teachers' enthusiasms.

A very recent initiative by the Scottish government, 'A Curriculum for Excellence', (Scottish Executive, 2006) has been to signal the admission that the 5–14 curriculum in particular has been over-specified; is cluttered and needs some simplification; schools need some flexibility. This is long overdue and working parties have been set up to consider how this might be done. This is not a move against standards or specification *per se*, but it is a concession that too much has not been wholly effective, particularly when the full range of pupil abilities are taken into account. For example, Scotland has created legislation in recent years to mainstream the educational provision for children with special or 'additional support' needs (previously such pupils tended to be educated separately) so the curriculum has to be differentiated much more and that does require local considerations to be considered and implemented. More generally, the government's mantra that every child should receive an education which demonstrates 'breadth, balance and coherence,..' might have to be adjusted if the current developments do lead to more variations within the curriculum!

Specifically looking at the questions put as guidance for the Symposium, from a Scottish perspective:

## How are standards in science education defined?

We have played about with various terms; objectives, outcomes, criteria (as in grade-related criteria), competences, standards (though that term is not usually equated to the others), endeavouring to get clarity; always falling short of complete behavioural specification; usually achieving consensus amongst the teachers, but as argued above, largely because there is a huge amount of support of different kinds which helps to target their teaching and assessment, with the obvious consequence being fairly considerable uniformity of teaching across the country. 'Standards' in Scotland is more typically taken to mean what is required to be achieved for the level at which a set of outcomes (or criteria or competences) have been set (and that implicates content and therefore values and choices).

## How can the achievement of science education standards be assessed, and what function does the assessment have?

In Scotland, there is the usual range of assessment formats in school science education, much of it conventionally written but with effort spent to make it appropriate to the cognitive demand (multiple-choice and short structured questions for more factual recall; extended, more open-ended tasks with novel features for problem-solving and application, etc...). Practical assessment still features at Standard Grade levels in the sciences (and the objectives read accordingly).

The definition of grade-related criteria (GRC) (the different criteria you have to meet in order to be judged to have reached the grade) began in the 1980s in Scotland with Standard Grades. They are certainly used by teachers and by the assessment system to articulate various levels and qualifications. (eg. A pupil must achieve a Standard Grade at level 1 or 2 (of 7) to enter a Higher course; an entrant to Medicine at University will be expected to have 5 Highers including chemistry and biology at the top level (A); ...). From the accountability perspective, 'league tables' of schools are assembled by newspapers from the national (SQA) data on the numbers of pupils gaining, say, five Highers, etc ... So the effect is to define 'good schools' in conventional academic achievement terms. Past governments explicitly drove legislation to do this (and fought off serious efforts to have raw data modified by statistical indicators of the socio-economic factors pertaining to the context in which a school operates). Similarly, concerted local government action persuaded national government to make national testing at the discretion of teachers, thus preventing crude national comparisons of primary schools on achievement data. So, while educators have a feel for the extent to which a school's examination success is a reflection of its pupil intake, naïve (or not-so-naïve) politicking has been used considerably to judge educational policy and provision.

## What side effects of testing standards are feared or observed?

As indicated above, the direct effect in Scotland of 'testing standards' has been to unify or standardise teaching across the country; much of this is arguably good, though it has to be judged that some originality in teachers/teaching has been a casualty. It would be difficult to weigh up the pros and cons. Good practice does spread in Scotland because of the small size of the country. Initial teacher education is only delivered in seven university faculties of education (and two of them swamp the others); the school inspectorate (HMIE) is a small (national) body, so around only 10 science inspectors move in and out of the schools all the time; local authorities who are school teachers' employers have relatively few science support personnel, but most people who need to know, do know and 'the word is spread' for every new initiative or change. But, to repeat the point made earlier, teachers do teach towards the examination.

On the question of *what* science is taught, there are notable indicators of progress and changes of emphasis, and there is equal measure of tradition elsewhere. A reasonable success was when physics at standard grade (14–16y) swung the subject over from an emphasis on 'principles' to 'applications' (and there is published research evidence recording it – for example, Reid and Skryabiana, 2003). On the other hand, all three subjects are not doing too well at u niversity level, there being detectable drops in applicants in recent years. Some might argue that this has been because science courses at school have maintained their 'science for scientists' appeal, somewhat at the expense of science for everyday life (Aikenhead, 2006). In this regard, one can certainly say that the specification of 'standards' has played its part, the detail of the specification remaining upon the cognitive dimensions of science judged appropriate for 'pipeline' students (to use Aikenhead's term). Scotland, like many other countries, I suspect, has not done enough to make its science courses perceptibly appealing to environmental, personal and social issues. Outcomes or standards in these areas remain inadequately articulated and undervalued. Science educators have themselves to blame.

## Can standards be implemented without centralized assessment?

By describing the Scottish situation, I am hardly in a good position to judge this. I am so immersed in our own circumstances that I see prescription and centralisation as two sides of the one coin (they seem to be inevitable consequences of one another). But, as I hope I have made clear above, much will depend upon *what* is specified and it is vital that intended (scientific and other human) values and attitudes are addressed first.

# References

Aikenhead, G. (2006) *Science Education for Everyday Life: Evidence-Based Practice.* New York, Columbia University: Teachers College Press.

Reid, N. and Skryabiana, E. A.(2003) Gender and Physics. *International Journal of Science Education*, 25(4), 509-536.

Scottish Executive (2006) *A Curriculum for Excellence: Progress and Proposals: A paper from The Curriculum Review Group.* Edinburgh: Scottish Executive. See also original announcement paper (2004) at http://www.scotland.gov.uk/Publications/2004/11/20178/45862#1

## Further reading

Bryce, T. G. K.and Humes, W.M. (Eds) (2003) *Scottish Education. Second edition: Post-devolution.* Edinburgh: Edinburgh University Press. (1088 pages) (See chapter 49, Biology Education by Nicky Souter; chapter 52, Chemistry Education by Douglas Buchanan; chapter 68, Physics Education, by Rothwell Glen; chapter 70, Science Education, by John MacGregor).

# An extract from the Highers Physics National Course Specification: Course details

| CONTENT STATEMENTS | CONTEXTS, APPLICATIONS, ILLUSTRATIONS AND ACTIVITIES |
|---|---|
| **1.3 Newton's Second Law, energy and power** | |
| 1 Define the Newton's law. | Analysis of situations, involving a number of forces acting on an object. |
| 2 Carry out calculations involving the relationship between unbalanced force, mass and acceleration in situations where resolution of forces is not required. | Order of magnitude of forces in rocket motion, jet engine, pile driving, and sport. |
| 3 Use free body diagrams to analyse the forces on an object. | Analysis of skydiving and parachuting, falling raindrops, scuba diving, lift and haulage systems. |
| 4 Carry out calculations involving work done, potential energy, kinetic energy and power. | Discuss energy conservation. |
| **1.4 Momentum and impulse** | |
| 1 State that momentum is the product of mass and velocity. | Experiments involving collisions and explosions of vehicles on a linear air track. |
| 2 State that the law of conservation of linear momentum can be applied to the interaction of two objects moving in one dimension, in the absence of net external forces. | Analysis of interactions between colliding vehicles, snooker balls, motion in space, manned manoeuvring units. |
| 3 State that an elastic collision is one in which both momentum and kinetic energy are conserved. | Discuss rebound and the vector nature of momentum. |
| 4 State that in an inelastic collision momentum is conserved but kinetic energy is not. | |
| 5 Carry out calculations concerned with collisions in which the objects move in only one dimension. | |
| 6 Carry out calculations concerned with explosions in one dimension. | |
| 7 Apply the law of conservation of momentum to the interaction of two objects moving in one dimension to show that: a) the changes in momentum of each object are equal in size and opposite in direction. b) the forces acting on each object are equal in size and opposite in direction. | |
| 8 State that $impulse = force \times time$. | |
| 9 State that $impulse = change\ of\ momentum$. | |
| 10 Carry out calculations involving the relationships between impulse, force, time and momentum. | Sensor and force-time graphs using a computer. Computer simulations for momentum and impulse. Application of momentum and impulse to car safety design, crumple zones, golf, hockey, football and racquet sports. |

# Chapter 15

# On standards in science education in the contemporary Swedish school system

*Helge Strömdahl*

*Linköping University Swedish National Graduate School in Science and Technology Education, FontD, ISV, Holmentorget 10, S-601 74 Norrköping, Sweden*

In the Swedish school context, the 'issue of standards" is discussed in terms of learning goals, manifested as 'goals to aim at' and 'goals to attain'. This paper is partly compiled from national documents on the Swedish school system and partly based on evaluations made by The Swedish National Agency for Education. It focuses on a description of the detailed structure of the mentioned goals via the school sub-ject Chemistry both in the compulsory school 'Grundskolan' and the optional upper secondary school, the 'Gymnasium'. The question of grading is touched upon since this is a central issue in the Swedish debate in alignment to assessment of goals. According to some investigations, the current national tests, mandatory as well as optional, including test banks in physics and biology, seem to have a high level of acceptance among teachers, principals and pupils.

## Introduction

Compulsory schooling in Sweden is from the ages of 7 to 16. If the parents wish, a child can start school at the age of six and municipalities have an obligation to provide a place for all 6-year-olds in a preschool class.

Education is free of charge and parents are not charged for the child's teaching materials, school meals, health services and bus-transport.

The most recent national curriculum for compulsory education (acronym: Lpo 94) entered into effect in 1994 (Skolverket, 1994a). This curriculum was revised in 1998 to include also the preschool class and leisure-time centres for children. The curricu-lum comprises fundamental values and basic objectives and guidelines as well as nationally approved syllabi for the individual subjects. The national syllabi were revised in 2000[1]. Every municipality is obliged to elaborate a local plan which takes into account school organization and development . The national curriculum, national syllabi and the municipality school plan make up the instructions for principals, teachers and students. Since the character of these documents open up for creative

---

1  http://www3.skolverket.se/ki03/front.aspx?sprak=EN

initiatives the content, organization and work methods can be adapted to local conditions, however without contradicting or jeopardizing the national goals, and becomes the 'work plan' for the individual school. The National Agency for Education ('Skolverket' the central administrative authority for the Swedish public school system) is responsible for a national follow-up and evaluation of the school activities in the municipalities.

A similar set of documents have been authorised for the non-compulsory upper secondary school (national curriculum acronym: Lpf 94) (Skolverket, 1994b). Every municipality in Sweden is required by law to offer all pupils, who have completed compulsory school, an upper secondary education. There are 17 national 3-year programs all of which provide eligibility to study at the university or post-secondary level. The guaranteed number of instruction hours (h) varies from program to program. For natural science, social science, and the arts, the total is 2 180 h. The Government determines the specific subjects in a particular program. All of the national programs include eight core subjects: English, the Arts, Physical Education and health, mathematics, general science, social studies, Swedish (or Swedish as a second language) and religion. Together, the core subjects add up to 750 h. Every program gets its character from subjects that are specific to that program. These program-specific subjects comprise a total of 1 450 h. Included in this sum is a project which accounts for 100 h. Thirteen of the programs contain at least 15 weeks at a workplace outside the school, so called 'workplace training'.

Figure 1 briefly describes science-related subjects in the Swedish school system.

| School year | 1 | 2 | 3 | 4 | 5 | 6 | 7 | 8 | 9 | 10 | 11 | 12 |
|---|---|---|---|---|---|---|---|---|---|---|---|---|
| Age | 7(6) | 8 | 9 | 10 | 11 | 12 | 13 | 14 | 15 | 16 | 17 | 18 |
| Level | "Grundskolan" (comprehensive, no sublevels) | | | | | | | | | "Gymnasium" (Upper secondary school ) | | |
| Compulsory/ optional | Compulsory | | | | | | | | | Optional | | |
| Science | biology, chemistry, physics, technology according to the national curriculum and the national syllabi.<br><br>Number of compulsory school teaching hours (= 60 minutes) for science related subjects during school-years 1-9 ( age 7-16) (biology, physics, chemistry, technology) are 800 h out of total guaranteed hours of instruction in all school subjects 6 665 h | | | | | | | | | biology, chemistry, physics, technology in the Natural Science and technology programs. Other programs have an integrated science course. | | |

Figure 1:    Science in the Swedish school system

# How are standards in science education defined?

The basic regulations for the Swedish compulsory school are set out in the Education Act (1985:1100)[1] and the Compulsory School Ordinance (1994:1194)[2]. The national curriculum for the compulsory school, Lpo 94, is determined by the government and parliament and delineates the fundamental values that will permeate the school's activities and the goals and guidelines that are to be applied (Skolverket, 1994a).

Apart from these general regulations, there are also syllabi. These are binding requirements the state imposes on education in different subjects. The introductory text to the syllabi covers *the aim of the subject and its role in education*, and makes clear how the subject contributes to fulfilling the goals of the curriculum, as well as the reasons for studying the subject in order to fulfil different societal and civic needs.

A section on *the structure and nature of the subject* deals with the core of the subject and specific aspects, as well as essential perspectives, which can provide the basis for teaching in the subject.

*Goals to aim for* express the direction the subject should take in terms of developing pupils' knowledge. They clarify the quality of knowledge that is essential in the subject. These goals are the main basis for planning teaching and do not set any limits to the pupils' acquisition of knowledge.

*Goals to attain* define the minimum knowledge to be attained by all pupils in the fifth and ninth year of school. Goals to attain in the ninth year of school are the basis for assessing whether a pupil should receive the Pass grade. The majority of pupils advance further in their learning.

The syllabi are designed to make clear what all pupils should learn, at the same time as they provide great scope for teachers and pupils to organise their work, choose their own materials and working methods. However, demands are put on the qualitative knowledge which teaching should develop among the pupils. At each school and in each class, the teachers are obliged to interpret the national syllabi and together with the pupils plan and evaluate teaching on the basis of the pupil's preconditions, experiences, interests and needs.

Common to all subjects in the compulsory school is that they should impart pleasure in being creative and awaken desire to continue learning. During their education, pupils should develop the ability to draw conclusions and generalise, as well as explain and be able to provide the reasons for their thinking and their conclusions. Fundamental values such as people's inviolability, the freedom and integrity of the

1 http://web2.hsv.se/publikationer/lagar_regler/hogskolelagen.shtml
2 http://web2.hsv.se/publikationer/lagar_regler/hogskoleforordningen/hogskoleforordningen_1.shtml

individual, the equal value of all people, equality between women and men, and solidarity with the weak and vulnerable, should permeate all activities concerning teaching, organisation and working methods.

Biology, physics and chemistry are presented in the curriculum documents under the heading *science studies* and the subjects of geography, history, religion and civics under the heading *social studies*. The division into subjects is a question of tradition, but the aim is not, however, to create boundaries between them. Co-operation across school subjects is seen to be necessary in order to make possible meaningful attainment of knowledge so as to reflect the fundamental values of the national curriculum.

## Common syllabus for biology, physics and chemistry

The common syllabus, designed from a natural science perspective, together with the syllabi for the different school subjects in science, is supposed to make up a meaningful whole.

***Goals to aim at in science studies*** (Excerpt from the common syllabus in science studies)
The school in its teaching of science studies should aim to ensure that pupils

*concerning nature and Man*
• believe in and develop their ability to see patterns and structures which make the world understandable, as well as strengthen this ability through oral, written and investigatory activities.

*concerning scientific activity*
• develop the insight that science is a specific human activity forming part of our cultural heritage

• develop their ability to see how Man's culture influences and transforms nature

• develop the ability to see inter-relationships between their observations and theoretical models

• develop their knowledge of how experiments are performed on the basis of theories, and how this in turn leads to changes in theories.

*concerning use of knowledge*
• develop their concern and responsibility when using nature

• develop the ability to use scientific knowledge and experiences as a basis for examining their views

• develop a critical and constructive attitude to reasoning of their own and others, showing respect and sensitivity to the views of others.

**Goals to attain in science studies** (Excerpt from the common syllabus in science studies)
At the end of the compulsory school (9th year in school, age 16), the following goals should be attained at a general level:

*concerning nature and Man*
• have knowledge of the universe, the earth, life and Man's development

• have an insight into how matter and life is studied at different levels of organisation

• have knowledge of the cycles of nature and the flow of energy through different natural and technical systems on the earth, *concerning scientific activity*

• have a knowledge of scientific ways of working, as well as be able to present their observations, conclusions and knowledge in written and oral form

• have an insight into the interaction between the development of concepts, models and theories on the one hand, and experiences from investigations and experiments on the other

• have an insight into how knowledge of nature has developed and how this has both shaped and been shaped by Man's perceptions of the world

• have an insight into different ways of making nature understandable, through, on the one hand, science with its systematic observations, experiments and theories, as well as, on the other hand, by the approaches used in art, literature, myths and sagas.

*concerning use of knowledge*
• have an insight into the difference between scientific statements and statements based on values

• be able to use their knowledge of nature, Man and his activities as arguments on issues concerning the environment, health and inter-personal relations

• be able to provide examples of how the sciences can be used to create not only better living conditions, but also how science can be abused

• have an insight into the consequences of different aesthetic views on environmental issues.

This is what goals look like at a general level for the three school science subjects. To illustrate what *goals to aim for and goals to attain* mean on the single subject level, the school subject chemistry is chosen as an example.

***Goals to aim for in chemistry*** (Excerpt from the syllabus)

The school in its teaching of chemistry should aim to ensure that pupils

*concerning nature and Man*
• develop their knowledge of elements, chemical compounds and chemico-technical products of importance in daily life

• develop their knowledge of transformation in chemical reactions

• develop their knowledge of the structure of atoms and chemical bonding as explanatory models for chemical processes

• obtain an insight into thinking and knowledge concerning chemistry from earlier times

• develop an understanding of the indestructibility of matter, transformation, recycling and dispersion.

*concerning scientific activity*
• develop their knowledge of how experiments in chemistry are based on concepts and models, and how these can be developed through experiments

• develop their knowledge of how chemistry has influenced our material living conditions and our cultural world view.

*concerning use of knowledge*
• develop their knowledge of how theories and models in chemistry, as well as personal experiences can be used to handle environmental, safety and health issues

• develop their ability to use a knowledge of chemistry, as well as ethical and aesthetic arguments in discussions on the consequences of the application of chemistry in society.

***Goals that pupils should have attained by the end of the fifth year in school***

Pupils should

*concerning nature and Man*
• have some knowledge of the concepts of solids, liquids, gases and boiling, evaporation, condensation and solidification

• be familiar with different kinds of mixtures and solutions

• be familiar with some of the factors that cause substances to be broken down, and be able to give examples of how this can be prevented.

*concerning scientific activity*
• have their own experiences of carrying out experiments with everyday chemical products safely

• be able to make observations about different materials and have an insight into how these can be categorised.

*concerning use of knowledge*
• have an insight into how a knowledge of chemistry can be used in discussions on the use of resources and environmental issues, as well as how a knowledge of chemistry can be used to improve our living conditions

• have an insight into the risks connected with the use of chemicals in the home, how they are labelled and should be handled.


***Goals that pupils should have attained by the end of the ninth year in school***

Pupils should

*concerning nature and Man*
• have some knowledge of some of the elements, chemical compounds and chemico-technical products

• have some knowledge of the most important cycles in nature, and be able to describe some dispersion processes of matter by air, water and the ground

• have some knowledge of the properties of water and be able to describe its role as a solvent, and as a means of transport over the earth and by plants

• have some knowledge of the properties of air and its importance for chemical processes, such as corrosion and combustion.

- be able to make measurements, observations and experiments, as well as have an insight into how these can be designed

- be able to carry out experiments based on a hypothesis and formulate the results

- be able through the use of examples to show how discoveries in chemistry have influenced our culture and view of the world

- have an insight into how experiments are designed and analysed through theories and models.

*concerning use of knowledge*
- be able to use results from measurements and experiments in discussions about environmental issues

- be able to use not only a knowledge of chemistry, but also aesthetic and ethical arguments on issues concerning the use of resources, pollution and recycling

- have some knowledge of industrial applications within the area of chemistry

- be able with the help of examples to show how a knowledge of chemistry has been used to contribute to the improvement of our living conditions, as well as how this has been abused

- be familiar with how Man has been able to handle common chemicals and inflammable substances safely be able to take part in discussions on the use of resources in private life and society.


## Science in the upper secondary school (Gymnasium)

To illustrate *how the goals to aim for* are presented for a specific science subject, chemistry in the natural science program is chosen.

The subject chemistry comprises three courses: **Chemistry A** which builds on the content of the compulsory school's education in chemistry and deals with the structure of electrons, chemical bonding, chemical reactions, simple stoichiometry, simple redox reactions as well as acids and bases. These theoretical issues contribute to a deepening of the knowledge about the occurrence of chemical elements, their properties and areas of use. Apart from being a course in the natural science program, it is also a course in the technology programme.

*Chemistry B*, building on Chemistry A, deals with organic chemistry, biochemistry and analytical methods of chemistry. The course also covers chemical equilibrium, stoichiometric calculations, and some current areas of applications. Chemistry B is a course common to the natural science and environmental branches of the natural science programme.

A third Chemistry extension course provides opportunities for broadening or deepening in one or more sub-areas of chemistry. This course, which is optional, presupposes Chemistry A.

*Goals to aim for* (Excerpt from the upper secondary chemistry syllabus)
The school in its teaching of chemistry should aim to ensure that pupils:
• develop an understanding of the relationship between structure, properties and functions of chemical elements, as well as why chemical reactions take place

• develop their ability to handle chemical laboratory equipment, to choose, plan and carry out experiments, as well as make observations, describe, interpret, and explain chemical processes using natural scientific models

• develop their curiosity and powers of observation, as well as the ability in different ways to search for and use their knowledge in applying chemistry in new contexts

• develop their ability, on the basis of the theories and models of chemistry and their own discoveries, to reflect on observations in their surrounding environment, acquire knowledge of the development of the history of ideas concerning chemistry, and how developments in chemistry have affected Man's world view and the development of society

• develop the ability to analyse and evaluate the role of chemistry in society.

## How can the achievement of science education standards be assessed?

Mandatory national tests in the Swedish compulsory school and gymnasium comprise tests in Swedish, English and mathematics. In the school years K-5, there are two diagnostic tests, in year 5 three optional tests, in years 6–9 three optional diagnostic tests and in year 9 three compulsory tests in Swedish, English and mathematics. Apart from mandatory tests in these three subjects in the gymnasium there are some optional national tests available from 'test banks', among them tests for the science courses physics A and B, biology A and mathematics E. In summary, in each year there are, in total, 14 mandatory tests and 9 tests available in the test banks in the gymnasium. Another 13 tests are under development in the test banks, among them chemistry A.

Hence, there are no mandatory national tests in science subjects in the Swedish school system. The control of pupils' knowledge attainment is placed inthe hands of the individual teachers. Therefore, teacher training and in-service training are important issues to foster teacher professionalism. Collegial cooperation for quality development is supported by the local and national authorities and has been ongoing activity since the introduction of the national curricula Lpo94 and Lpf94 subjects (Skolverket, 1994a; 1994b).

There have been a few special national assessments of pupils' knowledge of school subjects since 1993. Also some areas of school science have been included in these tests, chiefly at secondary level. The results of these assessments have been of importance in guiding teachers' interpretation of the national goals and their ability to assess their own classes. As far as is known, the 'goals to attain' have become a baseline for teachers' work in the classroom, which is also supported by how the current textbooks in the science are written.

The Department of Educational Measurement at Umeå University[4] is responsible for the test banks. The test banks in physics and biology provide items for test construction. The items are constructed in cooperation with especially interested groups of teachers from different parts of the country. Items that show sufficient quality in a certain test are accepted and thoroughly analysed and documented through a multidimensional categorizing system accounting for how the items can be classified as measuring students competences e.g. modelling, reasoning, communication and concept understanding. By the extensive documentation there is not only a firm ground for selection of items but the documentation also makes up a source for teacher development increasing their knowledge and sensitivity for distinctions of learning objectives in alignment with knowledge taxonomies (see, for example, Anderson and Krathwohl, 2001). Their ability to interpret and accomplish the intentions of the curriculum and the syllabi will grow and hopefully be done in a more informed manner. In that vein it would be desirable if test banks also could be available for the compulsory school.

My personal view is that test banks are far better instruments to implement 'national standards' than mandatory national tests, since correctly used they can engage the individual teacher in professional development and thereby increase national quality development in teaching and learning. In that way, the teacher is not just reduced to being a passive administrator to fulfil national goals via mandatory standardized tests. To give responsibility to teachers and have confidence in their ability to make local judgements in implementing standards and to judge attained knowledge is not only an investment in strengthening the teacher profession but also to enhance the overall educational quality.

---

4  http://www.umu.se/edmeas/index_eng.html

# What function does the assessment have?

*Goal- and achievement-related grading*

Traditionally, grading has been of special interest in the discussion of assessment in the Swedish school system. In the international literature about standards, the goals, competences, transparency, responsibility and general assessment are focussed on. This fact is contrary to the interests in Sweden, where questions about goals and assessment are intimately united to research and development in grading the pupils. So, consequently, when the national curricula (Lpo 94 and Lpf 94 ) were introduced, a new grading system also came into effect. The new system awards grades on a 3-point scale, with the possible grades of: Pass (G), Pass with Distinction (VG) and Pass with Special Distinction (MVG) (Skolverket 1994a, 1994b). Criteria for grading in the different subjects are included in the syllabi.

As stated above, the goals are formulated at two levels 'the goals to aim at' and 'goals to attain', the former are guiding the teacher in his teaching and the latter the goals that the pupil shall attain. However, these goals are supposed to be put in concrete form on the local level.

There are some problems connected to grading in relation to the current curriculum. One is the question of the weight that should be put to the goals of societal values stated in the national curriculum and another about equivalence according to the fact that the concrete goals are locally formulated.

To illustrate this, suppose a pupil has done excellently in all tests but advocates non-democratic ideas. Is it possible that he or she can be graded "Pass with special distinction" in the subject 'social sciences'? On the one hand, it is clear that his values are opposed to the fundamental values laid down in the curriculum. On the other hand, it is not 'opposing the goals to attain'. The question is: Should students be graded according to their knowledge or to their own ideas and values? This dilemma was posed and much discussed in the Swedish media in early 2006. No clear consensus was reached among the different parties, the local municipality, the principal at the school and the National Agency for Education.

The national tests have different aims but one often stressed in the Swedish context is the aim to endorse the teachers in their equitable judgement of the pupils' fulfilment of the goals and to make a just grading. Three aspects that address this issue are the individual pupil's fulfilment of the goals, the local group of pupils' fulfilment of the goals and that the test can be prototypical for individual teachers' future actions and collegial professional development.

These categories are overlapping, but they are stressing the fact that it is the teacher who grades the pupils and that the national tests are only making up part of the collected information about the total achievements of a pupil. The national tests are not examination tests as they are designed today.

## What side-effects of testing standards are feared or observed?

Some studies have been carries out on the teachers', principals' and pupils' opinions about the national tests in Swedish schools (Skolverket, 2004). Brief conclusions from these studies are:
• the tests do not have any major impact on the subject content, design of teaching, or selection of text-books

• the school work is not in any crucial sense adjusted to the tests. In the opinion of the more experienced teachers, the tests are not influencing them to deviate from the local goals or criteria, whereas those with less experience feel that the tests are indeed influencing their teaching

• a majority of the teachers state that most of the pupils are motivated for the tests and do their best in the test situation. However, a lot of teachers state that the pupils are stressed and nervous before the tests

• pupils state that they are unsure of the status of the national tests according to grading. They feel that their teachers are ambivalent about the weight of results of national tests compared to local tests. However, the students are positive towards national tests since they just are national, thereby measuring all students in the country in the same way

• the results of the tests are used among teachers and principals to follow-up discussions to promote development at the local school (an opinion often expressed by teachers in school year 5)

• contrary to the latter statement, no or very few contacts for professional development are taken between schools within or without one's own municipality.

To sum up, a general conclusion is that the current tests are accepted among teachers and principals as well as pupils. The opinion among a majority of the teachers and principals is that the tests fulfil their aims. However, the collected opinion among teachers and principals is that the national test system should not be extended to more school subjects or other cohorts of pupils. Additionally, teacher professionalism and experience seem to be an important factor in handling the current national tests in an appropriate way.

## How can standards be implemented without assessment?

In international tests like TIMSS and PISA, Swedish pupils achieve quite well in comparison to other countries' pupils. Evidently, in the Swedish school system, without mandatory national testing in science, goals can be implemented with a satisfying outcome. As said above, continuous development of teacher professionalism and increased responsibility is a necessary presupposition. In the Swedish context national assessment is looked upon as a support to the professional teacher in his/her assignment to implement the intentions of the curricula and syllabi and to evaluate students' learning. Assessment is a necessity to inform the teacher about his/her work and to give feedback to the pupils/students and their parents. On the local level, local tests handled by professional teachers, assisted by national optional diagnostic tests and test banks, there are good possibilities for fortunate implementation of national goals. However, the question of equivalence of grading the students in different schools and municipalities is a perennial question among all parties engaged in the Swedish school system.

## References

Anderson L.W. and Krathwohl, D. R. (2001) *A taxonomy for learning, teaching and assessing. A revision of Bloom's taxonomy of educational objectives*. New York: Addison Wesley Longman, Inc.

Skolverket (2004) *Det nationalla provsystemet i den målstyrda skolan*. Stockholm Skolverket (1994a). The Swedish National Curriculum for Compulsory School, Lpo 94 http://www.skolverket.se/english/index.shtml

Skolverket (1994b). *The Swedish National Curriculum for Upper Secondary School (Gymnasium)*, Lpf 94 http://www.skolverket.se/english/index.shtml

### Further reading

A general entrance and reference to the Swedish school system is the URL www.skolverket.se of the National Agency for Education (Skolverket). The Department of Educational Measurement at Umeå University (http://www.umu.se/edmeas/index_eng.html), commissioned by the Agency, has general responsibility for the national tests.

# Chapter 16

## How to develop, implement and assess standards in science education?

## 12 Challenges from a Swiss perspective

*Peter Labudde*[1]

*PHBern, Institut Sekundarstufe II, 3000 Bern, Switzerland*

Teachers, science educators, policy makers, and many other groups want to improve and set standards in science education[2]. While some countries have already put standards in science education into practice, others are still planning to develop and implement them.

What are the challenges when developing, implementing, and assessing standards? In this article, twelve challenges are described, not only from a theoretical perspective but also from a practical point of view by referring to the situation in Switzerland. These twelve are not the only challenges that are posed. They are, however, particularly demanding and seem to be necessary conditions for the successful development, implementation and assessment of standards in science education.

Switzerland belongs to those countries that have just started to develop standards – an ambitious task in a country with 26 cantons ('states'), each with its own educational system (see Appendix). With 26 different systems for a population of only seven million people, Switzerland may well have the highest density of education systems in the world. As harmonization of all these systems and educational monitoring are urgent, they are the two main goals of the Swiss project, HarmoS (*Harmonisierung obligatorische Schule*: Harmonization of the compulsory school; see box). This kind of output control is new to Switzerland and presents a demanding task for teachers, science educators and policy makers.

---

1 The author is co-director of the 'HarmoS Science' consortium, which is responsible for the development of standards in science education in Switzerland.

2 The term 'science education' given by the symposium committee, is somewhat misleading: A more suitable term would be science teaching or science instruction because the standards discussed at this symposium deal with the instruction at school and not with 'didactics', i.e. the standards refer to the performance of students and not to the performance of science educators.

**The project HarmoS**: The Swiss Conference of Cantonal Ministers of Education (EDK, *Erziehungsdirektorenkonferenz*) initiated the HarmoS project (*Harmonisierung obligatorische Schule*: Harmonization of the compulsory school). The project has the highest priority in Switzerland's educational policy:

"HarmoS intends to establish comprehensive competency levels in specific core areas for compulsory schools in Switzerland. The necessary work in this respect is being accomplished on two levels: The pedagogic-didactic level includes the development of competency models which will make it possible to determine which levels of competency can be expected at a specific time in the compulsory school (grades 2, 6 and 9). The political and legal level relates to the conclusion of an intercantonal agreement on the harmonization of the compulsory school" (EDK, 2004a; EDK, 2004b, Linneweber-Lammerskiten and Wälti, 2005).

HarmoS includes four subjects: mathematics, science, first language, and second language ('foreign language', i.e. one of the other official languages of Switzerland or English). In each of these four subjects, standards will be developed for the end of grades 2, 6 and 9 (for the second language only for grades 6 and 9).

---

**The project is divided into different steps and phases:**
2002–2004 Framing the HarmoS project by the EDK (influenced by Klieme et al., 2004)

2004–2005 Submission of the project, i.e. call for proposals of research consortiums, allocation of the project to four consortiums, each of them responsible for one of the four subjects first language, second language, mathematics or science

**'Scientific phase' under the responsibility of the consortiums, including the following milestones:**
2005–2006 Development of a competency model

2006–2007 Elaboration of hundreds of problems for assessment at grades 2, 6 and 9

2007–2008 Accomplishment of the assessment with a representative nationwide sample

2007–2008 Processing and interpretation of the data

2008 Based on the data, proposal of minimal standards in science education to the policy makers, i.e. to the EDK

> **'Political phase' of the project:**
>
> 2008          Political determination and agreement on the minimal standards by
>                   the EDK
>
> From 2008 Implementation of the standards including:
>                   development of a core curriculum for each of the Swiss language
>                   regions (German, French, Italian, Romansh),
>                   establishment of an educational monitoring system,
>                   establishment of a further support system for schools and teachers

In the following four sections, the twelve challenges will not only be described and analyzed in general, but will also be illustrated by the HarmoS project.

## How are standards in science education defined?

*1      The nature of the standards – depending on the education system and national traditions – needs to be well defined and established*

The educational policy has to fix a frame for the standards to be developed:

• Should there be content standards, performance standards or opportunity-to-learn-standards? (Ravitch, 1995; Klieme et al., 2004; Maag Merki, 2005)

• How do standards differ from curricula and syllabi – if they differ at all?

• Do standards apply to students, teachers or teaching materials – or to anything else? (AAAS, 1993; National Research Council, 1996)

• What are the goals of setting standards? Harmonization between states, schools or teachers; bench marking; control of teachers or development of schools? (Ravitch, 1995; Klieme et al., 2004; Maag Merki, 2005)

• In science: Are the standards intended for the subject science, for the particular subjects biology, chemistry and biology, or for the subject science-technology-society? (Aikenhead, 2005; Labudde et al., 2005; Wey, 2005; Yager, 1996)

• Should the focus be on minimal, regular or maximal standards?

• Do the standards correspond to national traditions, e.g. are teachers familiar with, and acceptant of, the idea of assessment by an unseen written examination or test, based on a given syllabus, marked by a person or persons outside the school (Millar, 2007)?

In 2004, the Swiss Conference of Cantonal Ministers of Education decided to develop performance, i.e. achievement standards for students in science with the option of including domains such as sustainable development, technology, environment, science, and society. This corresponds to the Swiss tradition of teaching science mostly as one subject from K-9, rather than as separate subjects like biology, chemistry and physics.

These standards are minimal or so-called basic standards ("Basisstandards"). The EDK's decision may have been influenced by the idea of mastery learning and by the fact that too many Swiss students reached only the lowest level in the PISA science assessment. This political decision is not uncontested because it could encourage and promote low achievement among students and teachers alike.

The goals of the HarmoS project are to harmonize the 26 cantonal education systems, to establish an educational monitoring and, in doing so, to improve the quality of schools. In a highly federal system, as is the case in Switzerland, a system that does not know any centralized examinations, the first two goals are – although defined as long-term goals – both very ambitious and demanding. (EDK, 2004a)

## 2 The standards must be horizontally and vertically coherent, i.e. coherent from one grade to another and among different subjects

The learning and teaching process is or should be cumulative. Therefore, standards have to be cumulative (Klieme et al., 2004), and consequently coherent from grade to grade (Behrens, 2005). Depending on the national education system, standards should be defined for grades 1-8, K-9 or K-12. Many countries have consistent and compatible curricula:

• Grade 1 to 9: see for example the curriculum "nature – people – environment", i.e. *"Natur – Mensch – Mitwelt"* of the canton of Berne in Switzerland, (Erziehungs-direktion des Kantons Bern, 1995)

• Kindergarten to grade 12: see for example the Canadian 'Common Framework of Science Learning Outcomes' (CMEC, 1997) or the 'National Science Education Standards' of the US (National Research Council, 1996)

A common framework including several grades and different school types, ranging from primary to middle and high school, does not necessarily mean that all school types have the same common subject, for example science. It is possible that science is one subject in primary and middle school, but three subjects (biology, chemistry and physics) at the upper secondary level (high school, *Gymnasium, Lycée*). A consistent common framework, including not only compulsory and post-compulsory school but also universities, would make sense but has – as far as I know – not been realized anywhere yet.

The coherence of standards is not only a question of horizontal coherence, i.e. within a subject from one grade to another, but also of vertical coherence, i.e. among different subjects such as science, mathematics, first language, and second language. This facilitates the integration among subjects (Labudde, 2003; Labudde et al., 2005), the students' learning process, the communication among teachers of different subjects, as well as the implementation of standards.

In Switzerland, standards will be defined for the end of grades 2, 6 and 9. The choice of these grades is due to the education systems in most of the cantons: Primary school includes grades 1–6, lower secondary school (*Realschule, Sekundarschule*) grades 7–9. Compulsory school ends with grade 9 (Appendix). The definition of standards for grades 2, 6 and 9 will ensure horizontal coherence within compulsory school but not between compulsory and post-compulsory schools (Gymnasium and vocational schools). This is definitely a flaw and disadvantage of the HarmoS project.

The horizontal coherence between the four subjects science, mathematics, first and second language is ensured by regular meetings of the so-called strategy group, including members of each of the four consortiums, several experts in international student assessment (members of the Swiss PISA group) and experts of the Swiss Conference of Cantonal Ministers of Education. The strategy group, which meets at least every two months, is standardising the terminology of their competency models, the frame and quality of the problems for the assessment, as well as the sample of the nationwide assessment.

## 3    The competency model includes several dimensions: competencies, contexts, knowledge, affections

The development of a competency model is one of the most demanding challenges mentioned in this article. It needs a lot of expertise in different domains, in particular in science education (didactics of science, *Naturwissenschaftsdidaktik, didactique des sciences expérimentales*), in biology, chemistry and physics, in general education (pedagogy, *Pädagogik, allgemeine Didaktik*), in cognitive psychology, in teacher training, and – last but not least – in daily instruction. Different kinds of competency models are conceivable. They might include main objectives of science education, competency aspects, science contents (concepts, methods and experiments), or levels of performance (see for example Bybee, 1997; Bybee, 2002; Gräber et al., 2002; Marquardt-Mau, 2004). A typical competency model is that of PISA 2003, based on the following concept of scientific literacy (OECD, 2004; p. 286):

> "The emphasis of the PISA 2003 assessment of science is on the application of science knowledge and skills in real-life situations, as opposed to testing particular curricula components. Scientific literacy is defined as the capacity to use scientific knowledge, to identify questions and to draw evidence-based conclusions in order to understand and help make decisions about the natural world and the changes made to it through human activity."

In PISA 2006, the definition of scientific literacy has been slightly broadened and characterized as consisting of four interrelated aspects:

• contexts, i.e. life situations that involve science and technology

• competencies, e.g. identifying scientific questions, using scientific evidence to make and communicate decisions

• knowledge, e.g. about the natural world and about science itself

• affective responses, i.e. how somebody responds to science issues.

These four interrelated aspects make up the framework of the PISA 2006 science assessment, and as such constitute a kind of a model.

The HarmoS science consortium is working on a competency model that includes three dimensions: competencies (*Kompetenzaspekte resp. Kompetenzbereiche, aspects de compétences*), domains of contents (*Themenfelder, Themenbereiche, domaines de contenu*), and levels of understanding (*Niveaus*).

We use the term competencies as defined by Weinert (2001): Competencies are

*"cognitive abilities and skills possessed by or able to be learned by individuals that enable them to solve particular problems, as well as the motivational, volitional and social readiness and capacity to utilise the solutions successfully and responsibly in variable situations".*

The levels of competence have yet to be defined. Schecker and Parchmann (2007) define three categories: reproduction, application, and transfer. Others describe progress maps (Hafner, 2007), a 1 to 8 level model (Millar, 2007), a two level model (Weiglhofer, 2007), or are on the way to develop models of competence development (Langlet, 2007). Our model is very similar to the model described by Schecker and Parchmann (2007) for German standards: a normative structure model with three dimensions called areas of competence, basics concepts, and levels of competence.

The competencies will include skills such as identifying and questioning scientific problems, developing preliminary ideas and plans, carrying out a plan of action, manipulating materials, as well as processing, interpreting and communicating data. The domains of contents are within physical or living systems, e.g. structure and properties of matter, energy and its transformations, the human body/health/well-being, ecosystems, plants and animals. These domains are rather interdisciplinary, more like a STS-approach than driven by the systematics of biology, chemistry, and physics. The domains of contents are strongly influenced by the idea of science for everyday life (Aikenhead, 2005; OECD, 2004; p. 286).

The model can be illustrated in a three-dimensional model as follows:

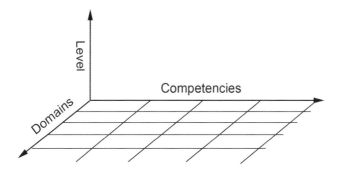

Figure 1:    The competency model includes three dimensions: competencies, domains
of contents, and levels of understanding

The axis of the competencies is the predominant one when developing problems for assessment. In other words, the problems will be competency driven.

## 4    *The competency model is maturely balanced between different claims: it must reflect research results of science education but also a country's traditions and values*

A competency model needs to have different roots:
• new and confirmed empirical results of research in science education: insight into students' preconceptions of science, their conceptual changes, the implementation of science experiments into the learning process, advantages and disadvantages of different teaching methods (see, for example, Boersma et al., 2005; Millar et al., 2000)

• the current valid science curriculum of a country, including the main objectives of science education, the contents typically taught in a country, the preferred teaching methods evaluated by questionnaires or video studies

• general objectives of education of the particular country, such as the value and appreciation of social and communicative skills (Erziehungsdirektion des Kantons Bern, 1995; MAR, 1995)

• the structural frame of science education, i.e. the formal and informal qualification of the science teachers, the possibilities of in-service training, the number of science lessons per week, the equipment and material available in schools

• international tendencies, for example the PISA 2006 concept of scientific literacy, that might have a strong influence on future national standards and curricula. Hence, tendencies that may lead to a kind of globalization in science education.

In this phase, the development of standards is primarily based on normative decisions, although it does not exclude decisions based on empirical research results. It balances tradition and innovation, national and international tendencies, beliefs and empirical research results. The formulation of standards must be understandable and realistic (Klieme et al., 2004; pp. 25-30) to the key players in science education, namely to teachers and students, but also parents, science educators and school administrators.

In Switzerland, a brand-new synopsis and analysis of all 26 cantonal science curricula (Szlovák, 2005a) yields one important basis for the development of the competency model. The analysis enables insight into the main objectives and contents of science education, that are common in most of the cantons. The future competency model must relate to these common objectives and contents in order to accommodate the science teachers of all cantons and accordingly all four linguistic regions of Switzerland with their (Swiss-) German, French, Italian or Romansh mother tongue.

On the other hand, the competency model will be strongly influenced by the research results of science education, by international curricula, frameworks and concepts, such as the PISA notion of scientific literacy, the Canadian Common Framework of Science Learning Outcomes (CMEC, 1997), the US standards (National Research Council, 1996) and the new German standards in science education (KMK, 2005).

As education is strongly related to the particular culture of a country or society, not every idea or insight can be transferred from one country to another. Switzerland is confronted with the particular challenge of developing a common competency model for every one of its four linguistic regions, each of which has its own values and cultures, as only some of them are common in all of Switzerland.

A first 'final' version of the competency model was defined in late 2006.

## 5 The development and definition of standards is a cyclic process, including normative decisions and empirical evaluations

So far the development of a competency model, including different levels of competence, has been a process mainly driven by normative decisions (see challenges 3 and 4). However, setting standards also requires an empirical evaluation of the proposed standards. For example, are the standards ? defined as minimal standards – really minimal or are they too demanding for most of the students? Thus, the standards, as proposed in the competency model, have to be evaluated in a nationwide assessment with a representative sample. The results of this assessment will lead to a revision of the model and the standards, which then again will be subjected to further empirical assessment. As an example hereof, see the development of so-called progress maps in Australia (Hafner, 2007). Moreover, new research results of science education and/or new values of a society emerging from discrepant events or long-term changes of beliefs can influence the cyclic process and the definition of standards.

The competency model of the HarmoS project will be evaluated in a nationwide assessment in 2007/08. Thousands of students, forming representative samples of grades 2, 6 and 9, will solve hundreds of problems. Only the results of this assessment will allow a definition of minimal standards, which will be based both on normative decisions and empirical evidence. By 2008, the HarmoS consortium will propose these standards to the political authorities, i.e. the Swiss conference of Cantonal Ministers of Education (EDK), who will then discuss, approve, and implement the standards by law.

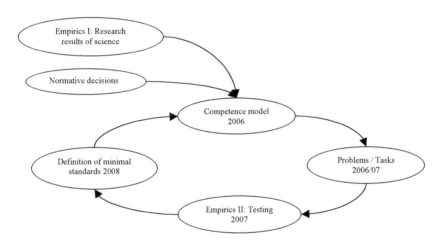

Figure 2: The cyclic process of developing standards (with years of the first cycle)

## 6 *Transparency and involvement of reflective practitioners and key stake holders are necessary conditions to develop and implement standards successfully*

As already described in challenges 3 and 4, the development of a competency model and standards is a very complex task requiring many skills from the people working on the model. In particular, the model must reflect the daily science instruction in a country. This means that teachers – and not only researchers and science educators – necessarily have to be involved in this demanding task. They should have a lot of experience in science teaching, a broad horizon and the capability to reflect on their teaching. The involvement of teachers also ensures the use of comprehensible language in the model and better acceptance by fellow teachers when implementing the standards and later on when monitoring the educational system(s). There is overwhelming empirical evidence of the necessity of involving teachers in the development of new curricular standards and school structures just to name a few (see, for example, Ben-Peretz, 1990; Parke and Coble, 1997; Sabar and Shafiri, 1982).

Apart from reflective practitioners, other key stake holders should also be engaged in the whole process (Behrens, 2005): experts in statistical methods, heads of schools, school administrators, trade unionists, as well as representatives of the ministry of education. The implementation of standards needs a broad basis of legitimation. Therefore, the involvement of all parties concerned is needed in order to ensure the acceptance of reform and its successful implementation.

In the HarmoS project, it was a condition *sine qua non* of the EDK that mostly science educators should be involved in the consortium. Thus, the science consortium includes 12 science educators and two experts in statistics[3], all of whom have different backgrounds with regard to the discipline/school subject (biology, chemistry, physics, environment, health education or pedagogy), the school level (primary or middle school), the linguistic region of Switzerland, as well as the experience in teaching and research. 13 of the consortium members possess a teaching diploma, have taught for many years in different types of schools and are now working as college lecturers, assistant professors or professors in the education of science teachers. The consortium collaborates closely with 21 reflective practitioners, among them teachers working every day at primary or middle schools in different linguistic parts of Switzerland. In addition, a committee of 12 people accompanies the consortium. These people are key stake holders in different domains and institutions such as people from teacher trade unions, universities, teacher colleges, ministry of education, as well as developers of science curricula.

3 This article would not have been possible without the outstanding work of my colleagues in our HarmoS Science consortium. Without their support and without our fruitful discussions about standards in science education, this publication could not have been written. Warm thanks to M. Adamina, L. Bazzigher, B. Bringold, P. Gigon, F. Gingins, B. Jaun-Holderegger, A. Jetzer, B. Knierim, S. Metzger, C. Nidegger, R. Stebler, M. Vetterli, U. Wagner, C. Weber and A. Zeyer.

## How can the achievement of science education standards be assessed and what function does the assessment have?

### 7 Step by step: from standards via a core curriculum to state and/or school curricula

Depending on the chosen definition (see challenge 1, 2nd question), standards mean the same, or not, as core curriculum and/or school curriculum:

In many countries, most of them with one centralized education system (England, France, Japan), standards are synonymous with core curriculum. There is no differentiation between the two and it is commonly claimed that 'the curriculum sets the standards'. Alternatively, instead of standards there are 'goals to aim at' and 'goals to attain' like in Sweden (Strömdahl, 2007) or rather than goals, various terms such as objectives, outcomes, criteria, and competences are used (Bryce, 2007). It may be that in these countries schools still have the possibility to shape the national curriculum to a certain extent in order to give the school a profile – but always within the national curriculum, i.e. within the frame of the national standards (see for example, the chapters in this book devoted to Standards in Finland (Chapter 6) and Sweden (Chapter 15)). Thus Lavonen (2007) explains for Finland:

> "Teachers are valued as experts in curriculum development, teaching and in assessment at all levels. Local curriculum is seen more of a process than a product and it has a central role in school improvement".

In countries with a more federal system such as Australia, Canada, Germany, USA or Switzerland, the situation is completely different (Becker et al., 2005; Criblez et al., 2006): The national standards are only defined as a frame, see, for example, the Common Framework of Science Learning Outcomes in Canada (CMEC, 1997), the National Science Education Standards (National Research Council, 1996) or the *Standards für den mittleren Schulabschluss* (Standards for the outcomes of the medium level of the compulsory school) (KMK, 2005). These standards set a common frame for the development of curricula in the different provinces, states or *Länder*. This means that in many countries with a federal tradition, the terms standards and curricula are not used synonymously. Standards are adopted as a basis for the development of curricula.

Switzerland has a long and strong federal tradition, with cantonal laws, taxes and school systems varying from one canton to another. Federalism is deeply rooted in Swiss history and is constitutive for the self-conception of Switzerland and the Swiss people. Concerning education, each of the 26 cantons has its own curriculum. In an age of increasing mobility, harmonization has proven to be urgent which is why the Swiss Conference of Cantonal Ministers of Education (EDK) initiated the project HarmoS. It will set a common framework of learning outcome in science, mathematics, first and second language (at the end of grades 2, 6 and 9) by the means of standards. The EDK plans to implement the standards in 2008.

These standards will be the basis for the development of common curricula in each of the four language regions, a process that ideally will be finished by 2011 or 2012. This is also completely new in Switzerland because, until now, at least in the two big linguistic regions, the French and the German speaking ones, each of the cantons had its own curriculum. Within the new curriculum, of which there will be one for each language region, and within the frame of the standards, the schools will have the possibility of developing their own profile. This approach is very similar to that of Finland and Sweden (Lavonen, 2007; Strömdahl, 2007).

In conclusion, Switzerland has initiated and started a long process that will lead from national standards to common curricula within one language region.

## 8   A broad spectrum of competencies should be assessed by tests

Upon introducing standards and a curriculum, which might be the same in centralized countries but different in federal countries, they have to be assessed. According to the National Research Council (1996, p. 211)

> "assessment policies and practices should be aligned with the goals, students expectations, and curriculum frameworks. Within the science program, the alignment of assessment with curriculum and teaching is one of the most critical pieces of science education reform".

The assessment can and should be performed on different levels: on the level of the individual learner, the class, the school, the canton (state, province, Land), the nation, and the OECD countries. Teachers, for example, assess the achievement on the level of the individual and, at least indirectly, of the class. Some countries such as France and England have a long tradition of nationwide assessments. PISA is both an international and in a way also a national assessment. Depending on the level, the conditions for all of these assessments are quite different: for a teacher, it is easily possible to let students perform lab-work or a science project in order to assess their competencies. The same is almost impossible to realize in an assessment such as PISA, which must focus on paper-and-pencil tests. Thus, it must always be kept in mind that assessing on an individual and class level are as important if not even more important than national assessments because they alone are directly related to the learning process of the individual.

Another question is whether the assessment should be more content-driven as for example in France (Malléus, 2007) or more competency-driven, or whether it should be driven by both. For example: Should students be tested on whether they know the definition of 'chloroplast' (an organic cell's part responsible for the photosynthesis) or that of the 'de Broglie wave-length' (a question relating to particle and quantum physics)? Or should students be tested on whether they are capable of planning, performing, and evaluating an experiment, e.g. an experiment in which they have to determine whether an effervescent tablet dissolves faster in cold, tepid or warm water. (The three problems given here are taken from the Trends in International Mathematics and Science Study, TIMSS). Researchers and developers of tests will have to settle on what types of problems should be part of a particular assessment.

The political authorities of Switzerland have decided to implement nationwide assessments after the adoption of national standards. Because these will not be adopted until 2008, the first nationwide assessments will be taken in 2011 at the earliest.

The team of HarmoS science has decided to develop problems that are mainly driven by competencies and not by contents. Consequently, the emphasis in the development of standards and curricula will be switched from domain specific knowledge to competencies. The developed problems will be used in the nationwide assessment of 2007-08, the outcome/results of which should become an important basis for the definition of the standards proposed to the policy makers by 2008 (see challenge 5). When developing problems, the HarmoS science consortium will start from the axis of competencies (see figure 1 in challenge 3). For example: How can we assess students' capability to question and identify scientific problems? How can we assess whether students are able to plan, perform, and evaluate an experiment? The HarmoS Science consortium intends to develop problems similar to those of PISA and the TIMSS performance test but dissimilar to the TIMSS paper-and-pencil test.

It is planned that there will be a test in 2007-08 consisting of two parts, a paper-and-pencil test and a performance test containing student experiments as is already common practice in many countries, including Denmark and France (Dolin, 2007; Malléus, 2007). On proposing the standards, the HarmoS consortium will also define opportunity-to-learn standards, e.g. the strong recommendation to let students perform project work, scientific inquiries, technical designs, literature surveys, etc., as in the case of the Netherlands (Driessen, 2007).

## 9    The function of the assessment must be determined and communicated in a transparent manner

As mentioned previously in challenge 1, the goals of setting standards and the functions of the assessment must be clarified. Depending on a country's traditions and values, these may differ from one country to another. In general though, one can distinguish between high-stakes and low-stakes assessment:

The former has severe consequences for students and/or teachers. The assessment is strongly related to a selection process, whereas a student has to pass a nationwide test in order to be admitted to a particular post-compulsory school or university. This is the case in England and France. Furthermore, unsatisfactory results of a school can lead to less funding and those of a class to a reduction of a teacher's salary.

Contrary to high-stakes assessment, low-stakes assessment does not have severe consequences. It serves as a basis for the analysis of the strengths and weaknesses of a system or school and as such promotes the development of a school or of an educational system as a whole.

For the acceptance and the implementation of either assessment, it is absolutely necessary to communicate its intended functions or, even better, to involve and engage teachers and key stake holders in the whole process of defining the goals and functions of the assessment.

Switzerland has absolutely no tradition in centralized assessments, neither on the national nor the cantonal or school level. Teachers have a lot of freedom but also a lot of responsibility. Therefore, it is not surprising that the intended assessment of standards will be a low-stakes one. The assessment, based on a representative sample of an age group, will serve as a monitor, giving the schools, the cantons and the system as a whole a feedback. In other words, the intended function of the tests is to evaluate the efficiency of the educational system ("system monitoring"). The feedback, i.e. the analysis of strengths and weaknesses, should serve as the starting point for different development processes, such as the development of schools, the reflection and revision of standards in science education (see figure 2, the cyclic process in challenge 5), the programs of teacher education, the in-service training of teachers, and the revision of curricula.

Although the EDK has clearly communicated that Switzerland does not intend to use the assessment for selection processes and/or for the control of teachers, some Swiss teachers still fear and oppose the development and assessment of standards. Therefore, the HarmoS Science consortium has decided to organize several public events and invite Swiss science teachers and educators in order to discuss the competency model, the problems for the assessment in 2007, as well as the minimal standards with them.

## What (side-)effects of testing standards are expected or feared?

The following comments hold for countries wanting to introduce standards and assessment. In these countries, teachers, politicians and other key stake holders harbour both expectations and fears towards introducing standards and regional or national assessments.

## 10 Higher competency, more harmonization and better monitoring are mainly expected, but also more school development, intensified collaboration of teachers, better teacher programs

In a survey on the implementation of standards (Behrens, 2005; p. 56) the following is summarized: "In general, standards have more meaning when attached to tests. However, before embarking on a testing strategy, one has to consider a number of key issues: Should the state/federal authority test children every year? Are local, regional and/or national tests to be introduced? What status will the test have? (Auto evaluation, exit exam)". The answers to these and other questions depend on the expectations with regard to the testing (see challenge 9).

In all countries, regardless of whether high-stakes or low-stakes assessments are introduced, it is claimed that testing standards provide more accountability, lead to more students' equality and to higher competencies of the students. Moreover, a harmonization between states, schools and/or teachers is expected. And last, but not least, testing should play a key role in the implementation of a national monitoring system in education. Apart from these expected main effects, there are also a number of side-effects hoped for, among them impulses to school development, more and better co-operation, coordination and collaboration among teachers (which would lead to less teachers with burn-out syndromes), improvement of teacher programs and in-service trainings, students' monitoring of their own learning, as well as improvement of opportunity-to-learn standards, e.g. better and more lab materials in science or new textbooks. There is almost nothing that is not expected from testing standards. Before introducing and testing national standards, it is worthwhile to analyze the experiences of other countries with a longer tradition of national assessments.

From introducing and testing standards, the Swiss Conference of Cantonal Ministers of Education (EDK) expects a higher competency from the students, more harmonization between and within the 26 cantonal systems and the implementation of a monitoring system. Aside from these main goals, the EDK also expects an impetus to school development. This is in accordance with the EDK's efforts to increase the autonomy of schools. (Compared to many other countries, their autonomy is already rather high, e.g. it is the particular school or at least the local authority running the school that chooses and appoints new teachers.)

Ever since the beginning of the HarmoS project in 2002, the EDK has been collaborating with a committee of national and international experts, who work as supervisors for the EDK. The EDK and some of its annex institutions also commissioned several reports in order to analyze the situation in other countries (see Behrens, 2005; Szlovák, 2005b).

## 11  Teaching to the test and control of teachers is feared, but also the disregard of important skills, of certain subjects, of low/high performing students and teachers

In the international literature about standards, one fear seems to be predominant: teaching to the test. This fear is understandable, but one should keep in mind that teaching to the test is in fact intended! Otherwise standards and testing them would not make any sense. For example, if planning, performing and interpreting an experiment in science is a competence to be achieved by the students, and if this competence is tested, then teachers, students, parents, science educators, and politicians expect that planning, performing and interpreting experiments are taught in schools. In other words, they expect teaching to the test.

Teaching to the test is just a cheap slogan and a buzzword. What is meant and feared is that large scale assessments will eventually turn into examinations which focus mainly or only on lower level knowledge, e.g. factual knowledge. Many important competencies cannot be tested in national assessments and there is a danger of them getting lost in the daily business of school when focusing on large scale assessments. For example the competency

• to perform a complex science project
• to show endurance and concentration when working for hours on a scientific problem
• to be curious and eager for science problems
• to be able to cooperate in a research team of peers
• to integrate biology, chemistry and physics within science, but also with other subjects.

The question of how to measure higher order cognitive skills in large scale assessments remains open. But there are also other endangered competencies that are not directly related to science, but are nonetheless very important for the development of both students and science. For example, how can cross-curricular competencies, such as social-communicative skills, creativity, motivation, and interest be tested?

Another fear is that certain school subjects will be neglected or even 'forgotten' (Becker et al., 2005): What about history, sports, music, drama, and arts? They do not get much attention and acknowledgement in the age of TIMSS and PISA. One might argue that this problem is not of any importance for the science community. But do they not belong to the general education of human beings? This question also concerns science teachers and science educators. And to broaden the question: Is it not also an achievement when a child still works well in school, although his or her parents are divorcing? Is it not an accomplishment when a student is engaged in a music band besides school? Performances of this kind cannot be tested in national tests.

A further fear is that the 'good' ('bad') students and teachers will get lost and be forgotten when minimal (maximal) standards are implemented. The type of standard defines the height of the hurdle, which for some of the students (and teachers) will be too high, while for others it will be too low. Frustration can be one of the consequences.

A last, but tremendous fear: one of the most negative side effects, as reported from countries with large scale assessment (Malléus, 2007; Millar, 2007), is that central assessments close down innovation. The originality in teaching suffers because teachers have less freedom to innovate.

Many of these fears also hold for the Swiss HarmoS project. A competency like conducting a complex science project cannot be assessed on a national level. This competence can only be recommended in the competency model, i.e. it partly becomes a kind of 'opportunity-to-learn standard'. The same holds for other competencies in science as well as for most of the cross-curricular competencies.

The HarmoS project only includes four subjects and compulsory school. At the moment, other subjects such as history or music, and other schools such as the *Gymnasium* at the upper secondary level (grades 10–12) are not the focus of the national discussion on standards (Labudde, 2005). Flaws yet to be tackled!

## Can standards be implemented without centralized assessment?

*12    There is a broad range of possibilities that support the implementation of standards without a centralized large scale assessment, in particular the structured learning of teachers with, about and of each other*

In countries without large-scale assessments, the usual and mostly only way of assessment is that teachers carry out an assessment within one class. This allows them to evaluate both the results of the instruction as a whole as well as the learning process and learning result of the individual student. The teacher is able to draw comparisons between the students, between their intended outcome. In addition, a teacher with some years of school experience is able to compare results and the objectives of the official curriculum, and between their results and the results of a class with the results of former classes.

However, there are three aspects missing: firstly, a formal comparison with other classes of other teachers and/or of other schools. Secondly, a structured comparison between the outcomes of a class and the outcome intended by national standards and/or by the curriculum. And thirdly, professional feedback for the teacher.

There are several possibilities to tackle these shortcomings; several of them embedded in inservice-training programs or in school development projects:

- the collaboration of a group of science teachers who exchange their objectives, ideas and methods in science teaching, their science exams and ways of marking them (mark is the same as grade). – i.e. a kind of 'implicit benchmarking' as realized in some countries where schools, school districts or municipalities implement or have to implement 'centralized' tests on a local level (Driessen, 2007; Strömdahl, 2007)

- a so-called item bank with paradigmatic tasks, problems or science projects; an approach already realized or on its way to being realized in several countries (Bryce, 2007; Lavonen, 2007; Schecker and Parchmann, 2007; Strömdahl, 2007; Weiglhofer, 2007)

- a bank with "best-of-practice" examples, maybe leading to official teaching materials or even to a paradigmatic textbook based on models of competence development

- a "soft" kind of centralized assessment, i.e. a voluntary assessment offered by official authorities in order to allow teachers to compare the results of their class with other classes and with the objectives as given in the curriculum; in Switzerland, this kind of test has become popular in the last five years

- complementary standards, such as Science Teaching Standards, Standards for Professional Development or Science Education System Standards in the National Science Education Standards (NRC, 1996)

- a colleague, the principal, the school inspector or a science educator who gives professional feedback which is based on well-defined criteria, intense observations and analyses.

When talking about the implementation of standards and centralized assessment, one should keep in mind that centralized assessment is only one possibility among others to foster the implementation of standards. As sketched above, other options are thinkable and feasible. However, they must be introduced in a formal, official way. For this purpose, suitable structures must be created. Teachers, for example, must be included in the process of development and implementation and they should be convinced to make use of these possibilities (a way which has proved to be very successful in Israel) (Mamlok-Naaman, 2007). This may be a difficult and long way, one that will perhaps prove to be too long, too difficult and too expensive, but it is a way that seems to be worthwhile and successful as the examples of Finland and Sweden show (Lavonen, 2007; Strömdahl, 2007).

As already mentioned, the Swiss authorities have decided to develop a monitoring system which will include centralized tests at the end of grades 2, 6 and 9. It is still an open question whether these assessments will take place every school year (probably not), but it has already been decided that the tests will only be with a representative sample and not with all students of the age group. Furthermore, they will only serve for monitoring the system and not for benchmarking teachers or schools.

These tests will be complementary to the well-established, broad and intensive in-service training programs for teachers and school development projects. These programs, courses, and projects are well accepted, appreciated and attended by the majority of teachers. They lead to exchange, communication and collaboration among teachers allowing them to reflect on their teaching practices and on the performance of their classes.

## Instead of a conclusion

There are other challenges that have not been mentioned or analyzed in this article such as the funding of the development and implementation of standards, the role of trade unions, as well as students with special needs. And there are several open questions, some of which have already been mentioned, others not. Let us keep in mind the following ones:

• How can teachers be supported in their daily business when working hard with their classes to accomplish standards?

• How can teachers get feedback, in particular positive feedback?

• Which possibilities are offered to teachers to learn more about others, from others and with others?

• What are the objectives to be achieved by schools; how much autonomy should or must be given to schools in order to attain them?

• Can we define standards for the implementation of standards?

Maybe some of these and other questions will be answered during the long process of implementing standards. In Switzerland, many institutions and people are currently working on this issue. Their help in HarmoS science is cordially welcome and appreciated. Many thanks to:

• my colleagues of the HarmoS science consortium (cf. footnote 3, p. 286)

- their institutions funding a major part of HarmoS science, i.e. Haute Ecole Péda-gogique BEJUNE, Service de la recherche en éducation Genève, Pädagogische Hochschule der Fachhochschule Nordwestschweiz, Haute Ecole Pédagogique Vaud, Höheres Lehramt Mittelschulen der Universität Zürich, Pädagogische Hochschule Zentralschweiz, Pädagogische Hochschule Zürich

- the PHBern – School of Teacher Education, University of Applied Sciences which is the leading house of the consortium and, apart from the EDK, the main funding institution

- the Swiss Conference of Cantonal Ministers of Education (EDK), in particular Olivier Maradan, Vice-Secretary of the Conference and executive director of HarmoS, and Max Mangold for their formal and non-formal support, their patience and interest in our work.

# Appendix

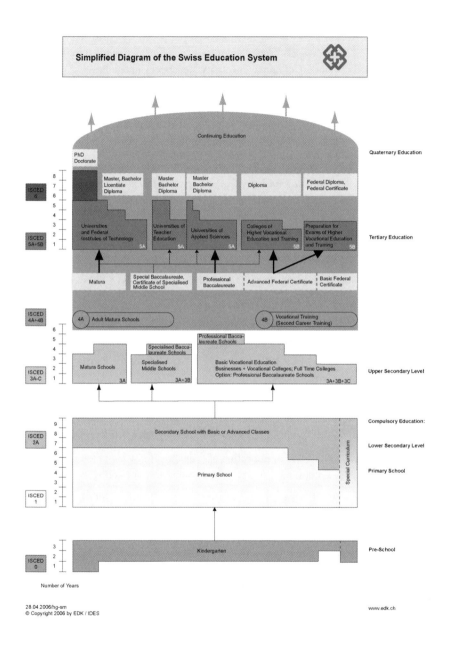

# References

AAAS (American Association for the Advancement of Science) (1993) *Benchmarks for Science Literacy*. New York, Oxford: Oxford University Press.

Aikenhead, G. (2005) *Science Education for Everyday Live: Evidence-Based Practice*. New York, Columbia University: Teachers College Press.

Becker, G., Bremerich-Vos, A., Demmer, M., Maag Merki, K., Priebe, B., Schwippert, K., Stäudel, L. and Tillmann, K.-J (2005). *Standards: Unterrichten zwischen Kompetenzen, zentralen Prüfungen und Vergleichsarbeiten*. Friedrich Jahresheft XXIII 2005. Seelze: Friedrich Verlag.

Behrens, M. (2005) *Analyse de la litterature critique sur le développement, l'usage et l'implémentation de standards dans un système éducatif*. Neuchâtel, Institut de recherche et de documentation pédagogique: 124 pages.

Ben-Peretz, M. (1990) Teachers as curriculum makers. In: T. Husen and N. Postlethwaite (Eds.), *The International Encyclopedia of Education* (2nd ed.). Oxford: Pergamon Press, 6089-6092.

Boersma, K., Goedhart, M., de Jong, O. and Eijkelhof, H. (Eds). (2005), *Research and the Quality of Science Education*. Dordrecht: Springer Publishers. 507 pages.

Bryce, T. (2007) This book, Chapter 14.

Bybee, R. W. (1997) Toward an Understanding of Scientific Literacy. In W. Gräber and C. Bolte (Eds.), *Scientific Literacy.* Kiel: Institut für die Pädagogik der Naturwissenschaften.

Bybee, R. W. (2002) Scientific Literacy – Mythos oder Realität? In W. Gräber, P. Nentwig, T. Koballa and R. Evans (Eds.), *Scientific Literacy. Der Beitrag der Naturwissenschaften zur Allgemeinen Bildung.* Opladen: Leske + Budrich.

CMEC (Council of Ministers of Education of Canada) (1997). Common Framework of Science Outcomes. http://www.cmec.ca/science/framework/

Criblez, L., Gautschi, P., Messner, H. and Hirt Monico, P. (Eds.) (2006). *Lehrpläne und Bildungsstandards: Was Schülerinnen und Schüler lernen sollten.* Bern: hep Verlag.

Dolin, J. (2007) This book, Chapter 4.

Driessen, H. (2007) This book, Chapter 12.

EDK (2004a) *HarmoS – Zielsetzungen und Konzeption.* Bern, Schweizerische Konferenz der kantonalen Erziehungsdirektoren (EDK). http://www.edk.ch/d/EDK/Geschaefte/framesets/mainAktivit_d.html

EDK (2004b) *Projekt HarmoS – Offertenausschreibung für Entwicklung von Kompetenzmodellen.* Bern, Schweizerische Konferenz der kantonalen Erziehungsdirektoren (EDK). http://www.edk.ch/d/EDK/Geschaefte/framesets/mainAktivit_d.html

Erziehungsdirektion des Kantons Bern (1995) *Lehrplan Volksschule: Primarstufe und Sekundarstufe I.* Bern, Berner Lehrmittel- und Medienverlag BLMV. For science see www.nmm.ch

Gräber, W., Nentwig, P., Koballa, T. and Evans, R. (Eds.) (2002) *Scientific Literacy. Der Beitrag der Naturwissenschaften zur Allgemeinen Bildung.* Opladen: Leske + Budrich.

Hafner, R. (2007) This book, Chapter 2.

Klieme, E., Avenarius, A., Blum, W., Döbrich, P., Gruber, H., Prenzel, M., Reiss, K., Riquarts, K., Rost, J., Tenorth, H.-E. and Vollmer, H. J. (Eds.) (2004). *Zur Entwicklung nationaler Bildungsstandards: eine Expertise.* Bonn, Bundesministerium für Bildung und Forschung. German version: http://www.edk.ch/d/EDK/Geschaefte/framesets/mainAktivit_d.html;
French version:
http://www.edk.ch/f/CDIP/Geschaefte/framesets/mainHarmoS_f.html

KMK (2005) *Bildungsstandards im Fach Physik für den Mittleren Schulabschluss.* München: Kluwer Deutschland.

Labudde, P. (2003) Fächer übergreifender Unterricht in und mit Physik: Eine zu wenig genutzte Chance. *Physik und Didaktik in Schule und Hochschule* 1(2), 48-66. www.phydid.de

Labudde, P. (2005) Bildungsstandards für Maturitätsschulen: Herausforderungen und Chancen. *Gymnasium Helveticum* 5, 5-10.

Labudde, P., Heitzmann, A., Heiniger, P. and Widmer, I. (2005) Dimensionen und Facetten des fächerübergreifenden naturwissenschaftlichen Unterrichts: ein Modell. *Zeitschrift für Didaktik der Naturwissenschaften,* 103-115.

Langlet, J. (2007) This book, Chapter 9.

Lavonen, J. (2007) This book, Chapter 6.

Linneweber-Lammerskiten, H. and Wälti, B. (2005) Is the definition of mathematics as used in PISA Assessment Framework applicable to the HarmoS Project? *Zentralblatt für Didaktik der Mathematik* 37(5), 402-407.

Maag Merki, K. (2005) *Wissen, worüber man spricht. Ein Glossar zu Bildungsstandards.* Jahresheft 2005 Friedrichverlag, Standards, 12-13.

MAR (1995) *Verordnung des Bundesrates/Reglement der EDK über die Anerkennung von gymnasialen Maturitätsausweisen.* Bern: Schweizerische Konferenz der kantonalen Erziehungsdirektoren EDK.

Malléus, P. (2007) This book, Chapter 7.

Mamlok-Naaman, R. (2007) This book, Chapter 11

Marquardt-Mau, B. (2004) Ansätze zu Scientific Literacy. Neue Wege für den Sachunterricht. In: A. Kaiser and D. Pech (Hrsg.) *Neuere Konzeptionen und Zielsetzungen im Sachunterricht.* Hohengehren: Schneider, S. 67-83.

Millar, R. (2007) This book, Chapter 5.

Millar, R., Leach, J. and Osborne, J. (Eds.) (2000) *Improving science education: the contribution of research.* Buckingham: Open University Press.

National Research Council (1996) *National Science Education Standards.* Washington D.C.: National Academy Press. http://www.nsta.org/standards

OECD (2004) *Learning for Tomorrow's World – First Results from PISA 2003.* Paris: OECD Publishing.

Parke, H. M. and Coble, C. R. (1997) Teachers designing curriculum as professional development: A model for transformational science teaching. *Journal of Research in Science Teaching*, 34, 773-789.

Ravitch, D. (1995) *National Standards in American Education. A Citizen's Guide.* Washington D.C.: Brookings Institution Press.

Sabar, N. and Shafriri, N. (1982) On the need for teacher training in curriculum development. *Studies in Educational Assessment*, 7, 307-315.

Strömdahl, H. (2007) This book, Chapter 15.

Schecker, H. and Parchmann, I. (2006) This book, Chapter 8.

Szlovak, B. (2005a) *HarmoS – Lehrplanvergleich Naturwissenschaften.* Bern: Schweizerische Konferenz der kantonalen Erziehungsdirektoren (EDK).

Szlovak, B. (2005b) *Bildungsstandards im internationalen Vergleich: Entwicklungen in ausgewählten Ländern.* Bern: Schweizerische Konferenz der kantonalen Erziehungsdirektoren. http://www.wbz-cps.ch/ deutsch/projekte/ folgeseiten/ projekt3_1.html

Weiglhofer, H. (2007) This book, Chapter 3.

Weinert, F. E. (2001) Vergleichende Leistungsmessung in Schulen – eine umstrittene Selbstverständlichkeit. In: F. E. Weinert (Ed.), *Leistungsmessungen in Schulen*. Weinheim: Beltz, 17-31.

Wey, M. T. (2005) The Retrospect and Prospect of Science Education in Taiwan. *Educational Resources and Research*, 64, 1-18.

Yager, R. E. (Ed) (1996) *Science – Technology – Society as reform in science education*. Albany, NY: SUNY Press.

# Chapter 17

## Standards for science education in Taiwan

*Mei-Hung Chiu*

*Graduate Institute of Science Education, National Taiwan Normal University, Taipei, Taiwan*

## Introduction

This paper describes the evolution of standards (recently called 'guidelines') in Taiwan's science curriculum. It also summarizes the strengths and weaknesses, side effects, and implementation of the science curriculum. After reflecting on some results of our students' performance in the Trends in International Mathematics and Science Study (TIMSS) 2003 (Martin et al., 2004), this paper considers the implications for science education per se.

## Background of curriculum reform in Taiwan

Bybee and DeBoer (1994) pointed out that goal statements can be viewed in several different ways. One way is to focus on *what* is to be learned. In this category, the students' outcome goals are to acquire scientific knowledge, learn the processes or methodologies of the sciences, and understand the applications of science, especially the relationships between science and society and science-technology-society. Another way to view the goals of science teaching is to look at the ends to which the knowledge, method, and applications apply.

In general, the basic goals for science curriculum (Bybee and DeBoer, 1994, p. 358) are personal and social development, knowledge of scientific facts and principles, and scientific methods and skills and their application. There goals were embedded in many curriculum designs to cultivate students' scientific literacy.

In general, Taiwan reforms its curriculum every ten years. Since 1993-4, however, changes took place more rapidly than they had in the past. In 1993, the Ministry of Education (MOE) promulgated *Curriculum Standards for Elementary Schools* (with gradual implementation from 1996) and *Curriculum Standards for Junior High Schools* (with gradual implementation from 1997). However, due to rapid societal changes, globalization, promotion of democratic literacy, and an eagerness for education reform, less than two years into the implementation, MOE started to carry out another wave of curriculum reform in 1997 (Chan, 1999).

The current curriculum and instructional reforms in elementary and junior high school education were introduced for two main reasons: to meet national development needs and to meet public expectations. With respect to the first reason, in order to face the 21st century and education reforms taking place in other countries, MOE was actively involved in educational reforms to enable individuals to maximize their potential for enhancing national competitiveness. With respect to the second reason, throughout the past 10 years, the public has been considerably more involved than ever before in educational reform. Parents, intellectuals, and schoolteachers have expressed a need for greater flexibility and involvement in developing, designing, and selecting curricula for education reform. MOE responded to public opinion. The Commission on Educational Reform set up by the Executive Yuan (1996) published *The Consultants' Concluding Report on Education Reform* (also known as the *Action Plan for Educational Reform*, influenced by the earlier proposals of the 410 Union of Educational Reform, a group of academics, industrialists and others). Then, the government organized a mission-oriented project group – the Curriculum Development Special Program Committee, which focused on the nine-year elementary and junior high school education span – to examine and develop a curriculum that supported the claims in 1997. It aimed to

• Emphasize the coherence and integration of the grades 1–9 curriculum
• Use learning areas and integrative teaching as rules
• Construct the core framework with core competencies
• Plan English teaching in elementary schools
• Provide flexible teaching periods for teachers to make good use of school-based curriculum.

In order to accomplish this goal, three stages were proposed (MOE):
Stage 1: Establish the *Special Panel on the development of the elementary and junior high schools curriculum.*

Stage Two: Establish the Panel on *researching and formulating the guidelines of each learning area in the grades 1–9 curriculum.*

Stage Three: Establish the Review Committee on revision and formulation of the elementary and junior high school curriculum.

The General Guidelines were published in 1998 (Ministry of Education, 1998.9.30, see Appendix 1 for the entire framework), followed by the Curriculum Guidelines for Seven Learning Areas for 9-Year Compulsory Education in Elementary and Junior High School (Ministry of Education, 2000). The slogans for educational reform were: "Cultivating students with competences that they can carry with them for a lifetime" and "Throw away the heavy book bags that students cannot carry." The new guidelines for grades 1–9 were then introduced over a four-year period (see table 1 for the implementation agenda and Appendix 2 for the school system. The italic and bold numbers are the grade(s) with new curricula implemented in the school system.) In total, it took four years to have all the grades with new versions of textbooks.

| Academic year | 2001 | 2002 | 2003 | 2004 |
|---|---|---|---|---|
| Grade(s) to be implemented | 1 | 1, 2, 4, 7 | 1, 2, 3, 4, 5, 7, 8 | 1, 2, 3, 4, 5, 6, 7, 8, 9 |

Table 1:     The process of implementation for the grades 1–9 curriculum

Although the curriculum was introduced in the school system, the gap between old and new curriculum content (such as grades 3 and 4 and grades 6 and 7) received limited attention from the government at the beginning of implementation – in particular, students educated with misused constructivism in mathematics. Therefore, several strategies were formulated to solve the problems facing schools. For example, in the successive three years, the government set up consulting teams and workshops to enhance students' arithmetic capability. Also, students took some courses before the schools started to teach for grade 7 (Ministry of Education, 2003a).

The guidelines transferred authority from centralized control to local schools and teachers. As a result, it was the responsibility of the teachers to develop the ability to design teaching materials for their own classes. This policy, which has had both positive and negative effects on our educational system and society, is discussed below. The guidelines specified minimum requirements of knowledge for all students to attain by the end of the second, fourth, sixth, and ninth grades and were designed to specify what each student should accomplish. The guidelines provided qualitative descriptions of content knowledge, but no quantitative descriptions of the content. The development of the guidelines was influenced by the standards or syllabi of other countries, such as the United States' National Science Education Standards (National Research Council, 1996), *Science for All Americans*, (Rutherford and Ahlgren, 1989), which presents a vision and goals for science literacy and *Benchmarks for Science Literacy* (American Association for the Advancement of Science, 1993) which translates the visions into expectations and then *Designs for Scientific Literacy* (American Association for the Advancement of Science, 2001) which proposes ways to choose and configure 13 years (K-12) worth of curriculum materials alignment with specific learning goals, *Scope, Sequence, & Coordination of secondary school science* (National Science Teachers Association, 1993) and Performance Standards (National Center on Education and the Economy, 1995; National Center on Education and the Economy and the University of Pittsburgh (1997a, b, c, 1998a, b, c) (Chiu, 2000). Besides these curriculum reforms (Chiu and Chou, 2005), other academic trends and viewpoints, such as humanism, multiple intelligence theory, constructivism, post-modern, and social constructivism also play important roles in our educational reform.

More specifically, during the reform, the MOE and National Science Council (NSC) initiated a need for a research-based policy for science education. Therefore, the first National Conference of Science Education was held in 2002, opening a new era in science education in Taiwan. Seven issues were addressed and discussed:

Issue 1: Goals, Current Status, and Perspectives in Science Education
Issue 2: Curriculum, Teaching, and Assessment
Issue 3: Science Teacher Education
Issue 4: Promotion of Public Science Education
Issue 5: Humanistic Concern in Science Education
Issue 6: Academic Research in Science Education
Issue 7: Policy for Science Education and Establishing an Environment for Science Education

(Ministry of Education and National Research Council, 2003).

Some problems discussed during the conference included the pressure of the entrance exam, students' lack of creativity, attitudes toward science, and the opportunity to learn science. After the conference, MOE issued a White Paper for Science Education, which identified missions for science education for the short term and long term (table 2).

The White Paper outlined several disadvantages of our science education (Ministry of Education and National Research Council, 2003):

• Entrance examination guiding teaching: In order to help students with their entrance test, teachers used rote learning. However, this did not stimulate student interest in learning.

• Societal and parental expectations: Entering high school is embedded in our culture. Therefore, over-learning became a typical phenomenon in schools.

• The depth of learning content: Although less is more in developing the guidelines, having different versions of teaching materials was still overwhelming for students.

• The gap between students from suburban and rural areas: Many students attend cram school (after-school programs) to enrich their knowledge of learning materials. This happens more in rural areas than suburban ones.

Both MOE and NSC took action in response to this document by initiating several science education programs (i.e., development of teaching, learning, and assessment modules for the grades 1–9 curriculum guidelines projects and deep-rooted projects for each learning area in schools). Appendix 3 lists the projects involved developing materials and providing professional development for teachers related to grades 1–9 science education by the NSC. With NSC's promotion, most projects relevant to grades 1–9 were in 2001 and 2003. Some projects published their findings in journals (for example, Chang and Chiu, 2005).

| Time Frame | Missions for Science Education |
|---|---|
| Short Term | 1. Related groups should be coordinated when implementing plans and using the budget.<br>2. Goals of science education should be evaluated on a regular basis to meet the requirements of education, society, and global trends.<br>3. All practices related to science education should be integrated and correspond to educational goals.<br>4. Evaluations for science education practices should be carried out to serve as review and reference guidelines for future policy amendment. |
| Long Term | 1. Related regulations should be drawn up for organizations, personnel, procedures, and budgets under this policy.<br>2. Related academic research and evaluation of information should serve as a basis for policy amendment and plan implementation.<br>3. The training of policy makers and administrators for science education should be enhanced. |

Table 1: *Missions for Science Education* (Ministry of Education and National Research Council, 2003, p. 34)

## Definitions of guidelines in science education

Although many countries use standards to express the contents of their curricula, it is not always clear what is to be covered. Also, the way researchers used standards might not mean standards for the entire country to follow (such as National Science Education Standards in the United States, (National Research Council, 1996)). The first use of guidelines instead of standards demonstrated the merits of the new curriculum in Taiwan. The guidelines were in five parts: rationale, goals, core competencies, learning areas, and implementation.

The changes that took place from this educational reform were moving from a national need to societal and personal needs; from standards to guidelines; from a national version of textbooks to multiple versions of textbooks; from elite education to general disciplines; from a content orientation to cultivating competences; from centralization to de-centralization; and from an academic rationalism approach to a personal relevance and social relevance approach.

Table 3 shows the placement and curriculum design for science disciplines for the school system years 1–12. The system contained five levels for the science curriculum: grades 1–2 for Level 1 (life curriculum, including social studies and science), grades 3–4 for Level 2 (integrated science), grades 5–6 for Level 3 (integrated science), grades 7–9 for Level 4 (integrative science, though most schools taught individually), and grades 10–12 for Level 5 (individual subjects).

Note: Compulsory school ends with grade 9. At the time, the guidelines were mainly for grades 1–9, but the committee members for the senior high school curriculum standards took the guidelines into account when they developed and modified the standards for high school.

| School Year | 1 | 2 | 3 | 4 | 5 | 6 | 7 | 8 | 9 | 10 | 11 | 12 |
|---|---|---|---|---|---|---|---|---|---|---|---|---|
| Age | 7 | 8 | 9 | 10 | 11 | 12 | 13 | 14 | 15 | 16 | 17 | 18 |
| Level | | | I ←——— Elementary school ———→ I | | | | I ← Junior high → I | | | I ← Senior high → I | | |
| | | | Lower level | Medium level | | High level | | | | | | |
| Compulsory/Options | | | I ←——————————— Compulsory ——————————→ I | | | | | | | I ←Option/Selected→ I | | |
| Title of Science Subjects | I ←Life Curriculum→ I | | | I ←——————— Science and Technology ———————→ I | | | | | | Physics, Chemistry, I ← Biology, and →I Earth Science | | |
| Content | | | I ←Integrated with Physics, Chemistry, Biology, Earth Science, and Technology→ I | | | | | | | Individual I ← science subject →I | | |
| Criteria | | | I ←——————————— Based on national guidelines ——————————→ I | | | | | | | | | |

Note: Compulsory school ends with grade 9. At the time, the guidelines were mainly for grades 1–9, but the committee members for the senior high school curriculum standards took the guidelines into account when they developed and modified the standards for high school.

Table 3: A Summary for School Years, Ages, and Curriculum Design

## Curriculum Goals – Scientific and Technological Literacy for All Students

The rationale for the science and technology learning areas centered on the use of scientific knowledge for daily life, matching students' mental and physical development and individual cognitive development, eliciting personal potential, respecting multicultural values, living in a modern society, stimulating personal potential, cultivating democratic literacy, valuing multi-cultures, and nurturing scientific intelligence.

Based on the general goals for the reform, the main goals of the new guidelines of the science and technology learning area at grades 3–9 can be organized as follows:

- To cultivate an interest in and a passion for science inquiry and habits of active learning

- To acquire methods of inquiry and a basic competence in learning science and technology and to be able to apply one's learning to daily life

- To cultivate a loving environment, to treasure resources, and to respect life

- To cultivate competence in communication, teamwork, and getting along harmoniously

- To cultivate independent thinking and problem solving and stimulate their potential

- To be aware of and explore the interactive relation between humans and technology.

For the science and technology learning area, the committee identified eight major components of scientific and technological literacy as core competences and then provided more detailed indicators for each component (see figure 2). Each component contained competence indicators to be reached at the end of second, fourth, sixth, and ninth grades – in contrast to the past, when standards for science education mainly covered cognition, process skills, and scientific attitudes. The grades 1–9 curriculum general guidelines for science included these three components and nature of science, intelligence of thinking, and other perspectives. The latter three components were included for the first time in the curriculum. Not only did the content of the guidelines change, but the guidelines focused on curriculum coherence and on a design that integrates biology, physics, chemistry, earth science, and technology into one learning area – science and technology – for the science curriculum.

The eight components of scientific literacy are detailed below (also see figure 1).

1. *Process skills:* Observation, comparison, and categorization organization and relation; induction and influence; and communication.

2. ***Cognition of science and technology***: Understanding of animals and plants, observation of phenomenon and changes of phenomenon, and understanding of relationships of concepts (e.g., electricity, refraction, gravity).

3. ***Nature of science***: Observation, hypothesis testing, drawing inferences, understanding the inquiry process and development of scientific theories, and awareness of the rules governing the universe.

4. ***Development of technology***: Understanding the process of generation and development by technology.

5. ***Scientific attitudes***: Love for inquiry and discovery and careful investigation.

6. ***Intelligence of thinking*** (habit of thinking): Making inferences, problem solving, and critical and synthetic thinking.

7. ***Applications of science***: Ability to apply science and technology in daily life, knowledge of the relation between scientific knowledge and equipment, and the ability to judge and make decisions about societal issues.

8. ***Design and production***: Cultivation of hands-on skills, making good use of the Internet and working tools to develop products, and the ability to modify products for different functions.

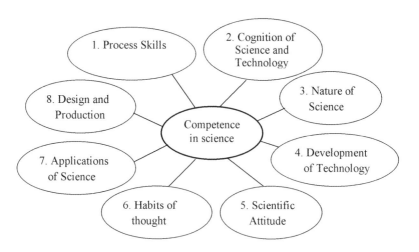

Figure 1:     The Components of the Science and Technology Learning Area

The guidelines of science content area include five topics, 13 titles, and several sub-titles. The five major topics that formed the entire structure are: *Composition and properties of nature, Effect of nature, Evolution and continuity, Life and environment, and Sustainable development*. In addition, science content should focus on the knowledge and skills of science, research and the development of such attitudes as: respect for all forms of life, a love of the environment, and the ability to utilize information as well as apply such knowledge and skills to daily life (Ministry of Education, 2003b). Besides, six issues (information, human rights, environmental, lifetime learning, gender equity, and craft education) should be fused into the STLA curriculum design. The contents required for grades 7–9 appear in table 4. Table 4 revealed that contents in the earth science have been placed at grade 7 which was different from traditional curriculum design to teach earth science at grade 9.

| Topic | Title | Codes and Sub-Title | | Grade* |
|---|---|---|---|---|
| Composition and properties of nature | Environment of the Earth | 110 | Composition of the Earth (rock, water, and air) | 7th |
| | | 111 | The Earth and the cosmos | 7th |
| | Creatures on the Earth | 120 | Biosimilarity | 7th |
| | | 121 | Biodiversity | 7th |
| | Composition and properties of matter | 130 | Structure and function of matter | 7th – 8th |
| | | 131 | Pattern and characteristics of matter | 8th |
| Effect of Nature | Change and equilibrium | 210 | Variations of the Earth's surface and crust | 7th |
| | | 211 | Variations of the weather | 9th |
| | | 212 | Day and night and seasons | 7th |
| | | 213 | Homeostasis and regulation of animals | 7th |
| | | 214 | Temperature and heat | 8th |
| | | 215 | Movement and force | 9th |
| | | 216 | Sound, light, and waves | 8th |
| | | 217 | Patterns and changes of energy | 9th |
| | | 218 | Chemical reaction | 8th |
| | | 219 | Chemical equilibrium | 8th |

Figure 2:     A simplified overview of the change process (Fullan and Stiegelbauer, 1991)

| | | 219 | Chemical equilibrium | 8th |
|---|---|---|---|---|
| Effect of Nature | Interaction | 220 | Variations on the Earth | 9th |
| | | 221 | Creatures' responses to environmental stimulus and animals' behavior | 7th |
| | | 222 | Electromagnetic interaction | 9th |
| | | 223 | Gravitational interaction | 9th |
| | | 224 | Water and solution | 8th |
| | | 225 | Oxidation and reduction | 8th |
| | | 226 | Acids, bases, and salts | 8th |
| | | 227 | Organic compounds | 8th |
| | Structure and function | 230 | Structure and function of plants | 7th |
| | | 231 | Structure and function of animals | 7th |
| Evolution and continuity | Continuity of life | 310 | Reproduction, heredity, and evolution | 7th |
| | History of the Earth | 320 | Stratum and fossil | 7th |
| Life and environment | Life science and technology | 410 | Food | 8th |
| | Protection of environment | 411 | Materials | 8th |
| | | 412 | Application of machines | 9th |
| | | 413 | Electricity and its application | 9th |
| | | 414 | Information and communication | 8th |
| | | 415 | Residence | 9th |
| | | 416 | Transformation | 9th |
| | | 420 | Natural disaster and prevention | 9th |
| | | 421 | Environmental pollution and prevention | 9th |
| | | 510 | Creatures and environment | 9th |

| | | | | |
|---|---|---|---|---|
| Sustainable development | Preservation of ecosystem | 511 | Relationship between humans and nature | 9th |
| | | 512 | Maintenance and use of resources | 9th |
| | | 513 | Development and use of energy | 9th |
| | Science and humanity | 520 | Development of science | ** |
| | | 521 | Arts of science | ** |
| | | 522 | Ethics of science | ** |
| | Invention and civilization | 530 | Creativity and production | 9th |
| | | 531 | Civilization and science/ technology | 9th |

* Optional (Grades 3–9 should cover these topics at each specific level but not in a rigid manner (in terms of the grade). This table is as an example for grades 7–9.)

** These topics belong to affection or philosophical parts. They should be embedded into teaching activities, not taught didactically. They should be infused into activities in different topics.

Table 4:     Contents of the science and technology learning area for grades 1–9

Each title and sub-title in the table has an indicator showing what is expected at each level (for more information, see Appendix 4, the numerical number gives the level in our educational system, level 2 for grades 3–4, level 3 for grades 5–6, level 4 for grades 7–9). From grades 3–9, pupils need to understand different degrees of depth of chemical reaction. For example, pupils at grades 7–9 have to understand chemical reaction (218, a topic code) as stated in 4a, 4b, 4c, and 4d below. The nationwide assessment will follow these indicators to search for appropriate test items for the entrance examination to the university. The following are indicators for chemical reactions for pupils to achieve at each level.

Sample example (218 Chemical reaction)

*The changes of matter in daily life*
2a. Notice some changes in daily life and the characteristics of matter that change.

*The influence of light, temperature, and air on the changes of matter*
3a. Recognize some illustrations of chemical change in daily life (the milk soured or fermented, for example) and find through experiment that the possible causes are light, air, or temperature.

*The meanings of reaction*
4a. Can explain the meaning of the formula in an equation.
4b. Can explain the chemical change in simple chemical symbols.

*The change of chemical reaction*
4c. Understand the diversity of changes in an experiment (three states, precipitate, and the changes of color and temperature).

*Reaction rate and catalyst*
4d. Can indicate what influences the chemical reaction rate and understand the function of a catalyst in the chemical reaction.

Examples of indicators for the concept of *acids, bases, and salts*

*226 Acids, Bases, and Salts*
*The acid-base properties of common food*
2a. Can use the scent, touch, and taste to discriminate the acid-base properties of common food.

*The pH of matter*
3a. Understand the acid-base property of a solution when salts are dissolved and the operational definitions of acid, base, and salt through an experiment; know the characteristics of solutions of an acid and a base; and realize how to apply and discriminate between them in daily life.

*Acid-base indicator*
3b. Can use indicators to differentiate the acidity, basicity, or neutrality of a solution and use simple materials to make the indicator.

*Neutralization*
3c. Can use an indicator to observe the acid-base property change of the acid-base mixed solution.

*Electrolyte and non-electrolyte*
4a. Know the characteristics of ions and understand that the electrolyte solution conducts electricity with the ions.
4b. Use the experiment to discriminate between electrolytes and non-electrolytes and explain that the solutions of acids, bases, and salts are electrolytes.

*The definition and reaction of acid, base, and salt*
4c. Can explain the definitions and characteristics of an acid, base and salt, and the relationship between the hydrogen ions and hydroxide ions in the solution. Understand the reaction of an acid solution with a metal and with marble through an experiment.

*The acid-base properties of matters*

4d. Discuss the acid-base properties of a metal and nonmetal oxide solutions through an experiment.

*Acid-base indicators*

4e. Know the common indicators in the laboratory (litmus, phenolphthalein and phenol red, for example) and the colors in the different acid-base environments and use the color changes of the universal indicator to obtain the pH value of a solution.

*Neutralization*

4f. Observe the change that put the acid (base) solution into the base (acid) solution through an experiment (exothermic process and producing the salt). Discuss the purposes (flavoring, salting, washing, and sterilizing, for example) and the dangers of the salts in daily life according to the general properties of the salts.

*The brief introduction of pH value*

4g. Understand the definition of pH value, and the relationship between the pH value, the concentration of hydrogen ions (without calculation), and the acid-base property.

In summary, there are many ways to categorize a curriculum. For example, Fogarty (1991) delineated 10 ways to integrate curriculum, the fragmented, connected, nested, sequenced, shared, webbed, threaded, integrated, immersed, and networked models. The first three models are for within single disciplines, the models 4 to 8 are for across several disciplines, and the last two for within and across learners. By adopting Fogarty's models into our design, we have models 1 and 2 for each of the science disciplines. As for across science disciplines, the threaded model was the central theme for the curriculum and the others (sequenced, shared, webbed, and integrated) were more or less used in the developing process. The curriculum team made strenuous efforts to provide the opportunities for students to connect their knowledge into a systematic and meaningful network. These categories aim to help designers to differentiate or pinpoint what the goals of curricula intend to achieve. Several main characteristics of our science curriculum are discussed below.

## Characteristics of the science curriculum

### (i) From standards to guidelines

The major reform for the science education curriculum was to encourage interconnection between different science disciplines by setting up the guidelines by topics (e.g., composition and properties of nature) and not by subjects (e.g., physics, chemistry). Although the guidelines allow some flexibility in ordering the contents, the topics listed in the guidelines must be taught during each level. Therefore, to some extent, the guidelines also act as standards even though they are not called standards.

## (ii) Change intended goals for each grade to each level

In the past, standards to accomplish were specified for a particular grade. The guidelines no longer act in this way; they are for a level instead of a grade. The intention was to release the authority of organization of the textbooks from the Ministry and provide more opportunities for creative work in developing curriculum by public.

## (iii) Integration of subjects

Throughout the past few decades, science courses were separated or integrated. It was clear that Taiwan was heading toward integrated curriculum changes. However, despite our integrated curriculum design, teachers are not trained to teach different science subjects. Therefore, the majority of teachers continue to teach the natural sciences separately using the skills and knowledge with which they feel more comfortable.

## (iv) Less is more

Over the years, several topics (such as reversible reactions, electrolysis, and reaction rates) have been eliminated from the curriculum, leaving a more reasonable amount of content to be covered within the limited time allowed in the school curriculum.

## (v) Link science to daily life and technology

Apart from introducing scientific concepts, the design of textbooks and laboratory activities were directed toward applications of scientific knowledge for solving problems in daily life.

To summarize, our curriculum guidelines focus mainly on one perspective of student learning: the content of science. They do not delineate a design for matching professional development for science teachers to teach the curriculum changes, standards for assessing student performance, standards for evaluating school systems in implementing the new science program or curriculum, or standards for the whole national science education system. For successful implementation of the radical changes in science education, a holistic framework for standards must be considered seriously and logically. The author considered this partial approach from curriculum perspective only was the major/potential flaw of this curriculum movement.

# Side effects of the curriculum change in science

The side effects of the curriculum and educational system are complicated. To understand them better, it is instructive to examine the effects from two perspectives: a positive perspective and a negative one.

## (i) The positive side

As the Ministry of Education (2003a) aimed for, the curriculum for Grades 1-9 has the following characteristics: (1) to integrate science disciplines, (2) to adjust the structure of learning areas, (3) to fuse contextual problems and societal issues into the curriculum design, (4) to promote school-based curriculum development, (5) to empower a dialogue mechanism for team teaching, (6) to address the need for core competences, (7) to enhance localization as well as globalization, (8) to encourage more lab activity, (9) to allow a diversity of teaching strategies and assessments development, and (10) to make the use of different versions of textbooks available (as opposed to the past national version of textbook). The following discussion elaborates on these curriculum characteristics:

### Integration of science disciplines

As stated earlier, in order to narrow the learning gap between different science subjects, the guidelines emphasize on the linkage between topics and broader dispositions, attitudes, and beliefs about the nature of scientific knowledge and about scientific thinking. It de-emphasizes the view that knowledge consists of distinct parts that should be treated separately. Rather, it provides students with the opportunity to experience and build a rich connection among various kinds of knowledge via integrated curriculum design activities.

### School-based Curriculum Development (SBCD)

One of the challenges for the grades 1–9 curriculum was the implementation of School-based Curriculum Development (SBCD). SBCD took into account the unique characteristics of students and made good use of local school learning environments and, yet, still provided the full scope and sequence of scientific knowledge and skills required by the curriculum guidelines. One advantage of SBCD is that it gives science teachers the opportunity to provide different versions of science learning materials to their students. Further, teachers in different learning areas are encouraged to form a team to design cross-disciplinary modules for specific topics. It provides opportunities for making teacher networking connections. At present, many teachers have received master degrees in science or educational teaching to increase their power of teaching. And action speaks louder than words. Teachers learn more from being involved in the design of teaching materials and assessment items. Such involvement gives them a better understanding of the spirit of the curriculum guidelines.

*Multiple teaching strategies and assessment in schools*

One of the side effects of SBCD is that teachers take into account local characteristics of the science environment (such as the ecosystem in a sub-urban community) and then develop new strategies to teach science. Therefore, the assessment was changed to reflect the teaching modules, from summative assessment to formative assessment and even dynamic assessment as well as portfolio assessment. Assessment directs teachers' and students' attention to particular topics and skills as well as responding to questions or testing in instruction.

*In-service professional development*

For the past few years, several cities have required teachers to put in 90 hours of professional development over five years. Many teachers attend workshops and conferences to fulfill the requirements, thereby stimulating their teaching and enriching their background knowledge about teaching. However, there were no restrictions on what courses they could take. Obviously, by taking courses irrelevant to their teaching, teachers will not improve their teaching. However, this was still not sufficient to equip teachers satisfactorily for the changes incurred in the curriculum reform.

For the grades 1–9 curriculum, the government provided various channels for teachers to become acquainted with the curriculum. Workshops were held, seed schools were formed, consulting teams (members from the Guidelines Committee) were provided, and websites were established which had information about the curriculum, including learning materials and teaching modules.

*Development of science education textbooks*

After the release of the grades 1–9 curriculum guidelines in 2000, the government no longer played the role of developing textbooks (until 2003). All book publishers were allowed to distribute their textbooks, as long as they passed an evaluation. Luckily, following the long history of development of national, MOE-sponsored version of textbooks, there were experts and teachers, experienced in textbook writing who were recruited to write textbooks, after the market had been opened up. However, this number was insufficient for the book publishers, and some less experienced scientists and teachers were recruited who learned to write through the process. The quality control of the writers became a challenge for the curriculum developers.

## (ii) The negative side

*Lacking required competence and knowledge to develop school-based curriculum*

Along with the positive effects of SBCD, there were also disadvantages of the program. For example, in order to design the modules, teachers needed background knowledge and the ability to transform goals and guidelines into instructions. In addition, science educators were concerned about the validation and reliability of teaching modules and continuity of materials. In particular, the meaning of 'integrated curriculum' might not be the same to all teachers, parents, or even to all science educators.

Was 'integrated curriculum' the same 'interdisciplinary teaching', 'thematic teaching', ' synergistic teaching'? If not, how they were different from each other? How do our teachers perceive them?

Also, as it is, teachers have to prepare teaching materials, lab activities, and assessment items as well as grade homework. They could hardly find yet more time to develop their own curricula. Liao (2005) points out that SBCD is centered around the following concepts: school-based, teacher-centred, and student approach – that is, it is based on science teachers in each school district, their direct knowledge of district resources, as well as their students' abilities and backgrounds. Liao points to several disadvantages of SBCD: an insufficient amount of time to develop or prepare a new curriculum; a gap between teachers' ability and the content they were set to teach; the disharmony of the integrated teaching materials; a lack of school resources; and parents' concerns regarding the course design for entrance examinations. Although some workshops were sponsored by the MOE to help teachers get acquainted with the rationality behind the new guidelines, teachers still lacked the ability and time to develop well-structured courses.

*Insufficient time of preparation for launching the textbooks*

Because the policy was announced late and the schools were about to use the textbooks, none of the textbooks (except the recently published national version) was piloted on the market for students to use. In addition, due to time limitations, the evaluation process failed to check for complete fulfillment of guideline requirements, and unevaluated textbooks were published. Several problems surfaced after these textbooks were being used. For example, in these books, there were errors in content, continuity problems, difficulty in judging learning outcomes and poor coverage for the university entrance exam. Further, they were more expensive than the previously used national versions.

Although publishers offered different versions of textbooks and supplies for schools, parents and teachers were not satisfied with the quality and prices of the textbooks. MOE decided, again, to launch an official national textbook in 2003. This policy change was consistent with parent and teacher expectations. Unfortunately, the textbooks for science and technology sponsored by the government were also found lacking – teachers wanted teaching materials, reference books, and test items for use with the textbooks, none of which was provided. As Shen (2005) pointed out, Grade 1–9 Curriculum reform was not a well organized nor a long-term planned project and the revisions suffered because of severe time constraints. The reform was too rushed.

*Teaching for the entrance examination*

In recent years, the most influential policies in our educational system were the implementation of the grades 1–9 curriculum and changes in the entrance examination system. The latter consisted of moving from a national annual examination to Fundamental Academic Attainment Testing, held twice a year for entering senior high schools. The newly developed system, which began in 2001, aimed to assess students' fundamental knowledge and ability learned in the three junior high school years. Because the test items assess students' comprehensive, analytical, and problem-solving abilities stated in the national guidelines, the test tries not to include items related to rote memory. The format of test items is mainly multiple choices. Natural science is considered one test area and includes physics, chemistry, biology, earth science, and health education. Technology is not assessed.

It was said that the test assessed only the concepts that all textbooks on the market covered. Theoretically, any test items not covered by all textbooks were to be eliminated from the test. Although the government made such assurances, teachers still tried to cover all the concepts in each version of the textbooks to make parents and students comfortable with exam preparations.

Lyu (2002) shows that over half (52,9%) the teachers in the science and technology learning area did not agree that implementation of Fundamental Academic Attainment Testing would lead to the level of student development required by the end of ninth grade.

It is not news that most teachers teach to the test. If so, we could make good use of this attitude by replacing or including creative problem-solving items into the entrance examination. However, the difficulty of testing performance ability is not easy to solve nationwide.

Although curriculum guidelines provide minimum requirements for each student to attain, publishers offered many types of learning materials for mastering skills (practice-oriented). The teachers tried to cover all the materials in the most popular textbooks and required students to buy many learning materials for mastering test items at the 9th grade. Not only did the cost for school learning materials became a financial burden for parents, but the extra expenditure of after school programs also increased the financial burden for the parents and increased the discrepancy of students' learning outcome between the rural and suburban areas.

## SWOT analysis model [1]

The following table uses a SWOT (strengths, weaknesses, opportunities, threats) analysis model to summarize the reform in science education. This analysis framework uses two perspectives to analyze an environment: internal analysis and external analysis. The internal analysis covers strengths and weaknesses. The external analysis covers opportunities and threats.

Table 5 reveals the SWOT analysis for our system and curriculum. The author intends to use this table to pinpoint several major factors in our system. As the table shows, our educational reform has some advantages that change the atmosphere in the schools and society, but also creates problems or so-called challenges for us to face and solve.

1 This idea was proposed by a discussant at the symposium and then discussed in groups during it.

|  | Strengths<br>(Helpful in achieving the objects) | Weaknesses<br>(Harmful in achieving the objects) |
|---|---|---|
| Internal Attributes | 1. Compulsory education from grades 1-9<br><br>2. Parents' high respect for education<br><br>3. The need for curriculum reform for more interaction between top-down and bottom up approaches<br><br>4. Involvement of scientists, science educators, and teachers as a team<br><br>5. Increased interaction between different disciplines in science and between science and technology<br><br>6. More versions of textbooks from which teachers can choose<br><br>7. Offering opportunity for teachers to develop uniqueness teaching modules in science | 1. Lack of textbook piloting before market launch<br><br>2. Less experienced textbook writers<br><br>3. Competence guidelines that are too vague to follow<br><br>4. Overemphasis on application and lack of focus on basic skills and concepts<br><br>5. More focus on cognition of the content than on developing attitudes toward science<br><br>6. Unbalanced distribution of resources<br><br>7. Too little time for implementation<br><br>8. Guidelines developers different from item developers<br><br>9. Lack of concern for students who were changing from the old to the new curriculum<br><br>10. Lack of coherence of content knowledge structure<br><br>11. Failure of the pre-service teacher program to change early enough so that new teachers were prepared for the new curriculum<br><br>12. Lack of a holistic framework and supporting system for the reform |

| | *Opportunities* | *Threats* |
|---|---|---|
| *External attributes* | 1. Teachers involved in more professional development activities<br>2. Creation of diverse courses and activities<br>3. Healthy competition among book publishers<br>4. More flexible teaching styles<br>5. Integration of more disciplines<br>6. More opportunities to interact with other teachers to explore productive teamwork | 1. Increase in students' learning burden by teachers' attempts to cover all the content in the textbooks<br>2. Student preparation for tests and not for developing creativity<br>3. Increased nationwide competition<br>4. Increased financial burden and anxiety for students' families<br>5. Failure to field-test textbooks before release<br>6. Too many non-professional people involved in the reform<br>7. In-service teachers' failure to understand the new curriculum and novice teachers' or intern teachers' failure to realize the changes of the new curriculum<br>8. Time pressure |

Table 5:    SWOT analysis for our system and curriculum

## How are achievements in science education assessed?

We can examine this question at three levels: local, national, and international.

### (i) Assessment at local level

A paper-and-pencil test is the major method used in schools to evaluate students' school performance. It is still a challenge to persuade teachers to adopt hands-on (performance) assessments. Most schools do not have lab assistants to support teachers in running experiments. Therefore, most teachers are reluctant to conduct laboratory activities regularly in schools. However, all students are encouraged to undertake activities outside the regular classroom work, for example, by designing experiments for science fairs, writing reports after visiting science museums, and making good use of website information.

Traditionally, we graded students on a 100-point scale and assessments focused on calculations more than conceptual understanding. Nowadays, grading is on a five-point scale, A to E. Numerical scores can be provided by the school administration, if a parent requests it.

Other issues dealing with school performance include:

• Students' school performance is sometimes considered when applying for high schools

• Most assessments are summative, not formative or dynamic

• In-class quizzes are conducted periodically.

Portfolio assessments were also introduced to science teachers a few years ago. Teachers requested that students collect their learning documents, products, and notes throughout the school year and then teachers provided feedback about their portfolios. On one hand, it allowed students to keep track of their learning and to develop self-reflective abilities. On the other hand, this kind of science teaching port-folio requires teachers to be able to evaluate students' work and, further, to provide suggestions for improvement. Without a well-prepared background knowledge of portfolio teaching and enough time for this activity, teachers were not willing to take greater responsibility for their own teaching by conducting portfolio reviews. There-fore, the constructive approach of assessing students' performance did not survive long.

### (ii) Assessment at national level

Appendix 5 shows the total number of test items for each science subject in the National Basic Competence Test (NBCT) for junior high school students and how they were scored in terms of correct items for the past five years. Appendix 6 shows how to calculate the gain scores for NBCT. Not all the items were weighted the same. Appendices 7 (from 2005) and 8 (from 2006) present some examples from the NBCT to show how the test items were designed to match the indicators shown in the guidelines. In Appendix 5, it reveals that there was an increasing number of test items for earth science while a decreasing trend for health education. This showed that the importance of science literacy has shifted from health education to earth science.

In addition to the national entrance examinations for high schools and colleges/universities, there is a newly developed nationwide trend study, Taiwan Assessment of Students Achievement (TASA), launched in 2005 (National Education Research Institute, 2005; 2006). The purpose of the TASA study is to collect students' results to create a longitudinal databank of our students. It aims to provide information on changes in students' abilities at different levels so that policies can be made with a long-term perspective. Theoretically and practically, the databank with output-oriented records from students can help us understand how adoption of the grades 1–9 curriculum changed their learning as well as the strengths and weaknesses of the curriculum in cultivating students' scientific literacy.

The target students for TASA were fourth, sixth, eighth, and eleventh graders to be tested on language (Chinese and English), mathematics, science, and social studies. The preparation work to develop test items started in 2004, and 464 schools were chosen to be tested randomly. About 15 000 sixth graders were stratified by locations and sizes of schools and randomly selected to assess whether their performance reached the level stated in the guidelines learning areas in English and Mandarin. Mathematics, science and technology, and social studies were not tested. This year, about 80 000 students from fourth, sixth, eight, and eleventh grades will be tested for all the fields, except fourth graders will not be assessed for science. About 200 students will have performance assessments. The results will be released in December, 2006.

In addition, the Taiwan Education Panel Survey (TEPS), sponsored by Academic Sinica, MOE, and NSC, is carried out by the Academic Sinica, Institute of Social Studies, and Institute of European and American Studies, which cooperate in designing and executing this national longitudinal study. The purpose of this project is to collect student, parent, teacher, and school data. It started in 2001.

Also, six years ago, the NSC sponsored an integrated research project (about 30 projects in physics, chemistry, and biology) to develop sets of two-tier test items (adopted from Treagust 1988; 1995) to diagnose students' misconceptions (or so-called alternative conceptions) (Chiu, in press). A special issue of *International Journal of Science Education* will publish the results of this integrative project. At present, we have collected and analyzed national data that might help us understand how well students have learned science as well as how difficult it is to learn science.

### (iii) Assessment at international level

How did our students perform in science compared to students from other countries? This discussion is based on the international report dealing with TIMSS 2003 data (Martin et al., 2004). Table 6 reveals that our students outperformed internationally in the TIMSS 1999 (ranking the first) and 2003 (ranking the second). However, our

325

students did not show as high an interest in science as that found in many other countries and was considerably lower than the international average. Only 18% in 1999 and 16% in 2003 agreed a lot with the statement, "I enjoy learning science." The proportion that agreed a little with the statement dropped from 53% to 34% in the two surveys, whereas the proportion that disagreed increased from 29% to 49%. In other words, about half our students did not like science at all. How will we, as science educators, face this challenge? What kind of alarm does it set off?

| Year | *TIMSS 1999* | *TIMSS 2003* |
|---|---|---|
| Number of countries participated | **(n=38)** | **(n=46)** |
| | | (+4 benchmarking participants) |
| Number of students from Taiwan | 5889 | 5379 |
| Average scale score for science | 569 (4.4) [1]* | 571 (3.5) [2] |
| International average | 488 (0.7) | 474 (0.6) |
| Physics | 552 (3.9) [2] | 569 (3.3) [3] |
| Chemistry | 563 (4.3) [1] | 584 (4.0) [1] |
| Life Science | 550 (3.3) [1] | 563 (3.1) [2] |
| Environmental Science | 567 (4.0) [2] | 560 (3.1) [2] |
| Earth Science | 538 (3.0) [3] | 548 (3.1) [4] |
| Scientific Inquiry and Nature of Science | 540 (4.9) [4] | |
| I enjoy learning science—Disagree | 29% | 49% |
| Self-Confidence in Learning Science (SCS) | High SCS (617): 14%<br>Medium SCS (572): 61%<br>Low SCS (538): 25% | High SCS (616): 28%<br>Medium SCS (560): 38%<br>Low SCS (548): 34% |
| Students' Valuing Science (SVS) | | High SVS (600): 26%<br>Medium SVS (571): 49%<br>Low SVS (544): 25% |

*Note: (): means standard deviation
      []: means ranking among participating countries

Table 6: Students' performance in the TIMSS 1999 and 2003

The results in table 6 reveal that although we ranked first in achievement for the high school level, only 28% of students felt self-confident (third from the bottom), 38% for the intermediate level, and 34% for the low level. Apparently, most students did not recognize their effort in science in school. Therefore, their self-confidence was not as high as one would expect. This was not only true for Taiwan, but for Hong

Kong, Korea, and Japan as well. Due to the great pressure associated with the entrance examination and imposed by parents, Asian students do not have a high degree of self-confidence regardless of their performance.

As for gender differences, the average international scale scores were 471 points for girls and 477 points for boys in overall performance. Compared to other countries, there was no significant difference between genders for Taiwan (girls: 571, s.d.=3.8, boys: 572, s.d.=3.8) in 2003. We also noticed that among those Asian countries/areas, only Singapore and Taiwan did not show gender differences, whereas Hong Kong, Japan, and Korea showed that males significantly outperformed females, the same as for the United States and England (Martin et al., 2004; Chiu, 2006). Unfortunately, the input from the results of TIMSS 2003 did not have any impact on policy making in science education in Taiwan. The Programme for International Student Assessment (PISA) was being carried out again in 2006 for grade 10 students. It has yet to be proven, if these data will have an effect.

## Implementation

### (i) Changing teachers' beliefs

Teachers tend to hold stereotypes about education or traditional beliefs about teaching, for example, that teaching centers on testing. However, the new curriculum aims to teach students competences for lifetime learning and to gain self-motivation to live better in the future. To address this change, MOE provided several opportunities for teachers to get acquainted with the curriculum. For example, the designers of the guidelines held many discussions, teacher training programs, study groups, and action research projects in schools for the grades 1–9 curriculum. They also organized many conferences, workshops, and lectures in schools to convey the merits of the curriculum and set up consulting teams for science in every city. Such teams helped teachers to improve their teaching and conveyed the ideas of grades 1–9 curriculum guidelines to other teachers. The idea was that these teams would help other teachers in the same district change their traditional beliefs about instruction and, accordingly, contribute better to helping towards students' understanding of science and their appreciation of it.

The curriculum carried new expectations for teachers, who were now expected to be more active in the classroom. One impact of the guidelines and other in-service training programs was that teachers realized their potential for generating effective and creative teaching materials – but some teachers were still redundant to accept the challenge.

## (ii) Professional development

As stated earlier, teachers need to complete 90 hours of courses over a five-year period. Although it did not specify which courses should be taken, teachers were encouraged to play an active role in their own professional development. Several in-service masters programs were offered to create a larger pool of teachers with higher degrees. These initiatives influenced their teaching and the policies for recruiting teachers in schools.

In order to generate more test items for entrance examinations, the Committee of the Basic Competence Test for Junior High School students invited teachers to submit test items for the item bank. Following the screening and revising process of the items, teachers could receive an honorarium for their contributions. Such contributions allow teachers to improve their understanding of the creation of test items that match curriculum goals and guidelines.

Currently, we do not have teacher status ranking in the elementary and secondary schools. The process or mechanism for professional evaluation of teachers is still a sensitive issue among teachers and scholars.

## (iii) Use of textbooks

Most teachers rely on textbooks in their teaching. Because the current textbook market is competitive, book publishers generally provide schoolteachers with CDs, Power-Point files, teaching materials, and samples of test items to encourage selection of their textbooks. Not only do book publishers see a profit being derived from their textbooks, but also from selling their test booklets and reference books.

## (iv) Link between universities and schools

It has been widely recognized that scientific literacy is desirable and developmental in the compulsory years in order to prepare students for involving science in their adult lives (Fensham, 2000). Similarly, for teachers, being lifetime learners is not simply to teach what they learned as a university student, but also to expand and update their knowledge of science throughout their lives. Accordingly, researchers in science or science education should have the societal responsibility to help schoolteachers to empower their teaching in schools.

*(v) Put research into practice*

In addition, MOE and the NSC supported some projects financially to develop tools to evaluate students' cognition, attitudes toward science, and hands-on skills as well as the nature of science, the application of science, and other perspectives in scientific literacy. This initiative generated several evaluation tools and teaching modules for helping researchers and teachers to understand the nature of the guidelines and provided resources to science teachers for their teaching.

*(vi) Establish and empower a national research centre*

As stated in the beginning of this article, educational reform is a continuous and evolutionary process. In order to monitor the process and enhance its power, an institute with professional experts to develop, implement, and evaluate the curriculum is quite important and necessary. Besides, teacher professional development should be given extraordinary attention. A temporary national research institute has been established and currently functions as a curriculum developing and professional development centre sponsored by the government. However, it still does not show its visions and mission for long term perspective.

*(vii) Evaluation system*

Evaluation can serve policy in two ways (Madaus and Kellaghan, 1992). First, information can inform policymakers about the state of education or about the performance or achievements of certain groups of children. Second, evaluation information serves policy when it is used as an administrative device to implement policy. However, the evaluation has not gained sufficient attention so far. The author considers that the Ministry of Education should set up the evaluation standards for school administrators, teachers, parents, and society at large, understand what to expect from our education and how to empower our system to make our students more competitive internationally.

*Making good use of outcomes of international comparative studies*

It is not a unique phenomenon to take the results of both national and international assessments into account. The results from nationwide and international comparisons could reflect some educational problems. Concerned about students' literacy in science, some countries used such information to make educational system changes. For example, in Germany, both educators and parents were disappointed with its performance in PISA, and action was taken to solve the problem by the German Ministry of Education (BMBF). Danish Ministry of Education faced the falling performance results from PISA 2000 also had OECD Secretariat undertake a pilot review of the quality and equity of schooling outcomes in Denmark (OECD, 2004). Similarly, in the United States, the National Standards of Science Education challenge all educational systems to make dramatic changes in teaching and learning in science (Anderson and Helms, 2001). Also, the Bush government reacted to the underrepresented performance on science scores in the SATs by setting goals for improving students' scores (U.S. Department of Education, 1991) and instituting the No Child Left Behind (NCLB) Program (U.S. Department of Education , 2002, January 8). Twenty one states decided to require high school students to take science courses at least three years before they graduate. In 2005, the Department of Education announced the New Path for No Child Left Behind Program and indicated that explicit improvement and effectiveness had been made by NCLB (U.S. Department of Education, 2005.4.18). Taiwan has participated in several international studies, however, the policy makers did not seriously take the outcome into account when they faced the educational reform or made decisions for science education programs. From the perspective of policy making, cases from other countries could be examplars as references.

## Concluding Remarks

Scientific and technological literacy is now a major goal of elementary and secondary schools in Taiwan and we are moving from teaching knowledge per se to an integrated curriculum of major scientific concepts, basic abilities, and technology for all students.

In response to this challenge, Taiwan has changed its national standards to guidelines in which the government no longer requires publishers and teachers to follow strict rules in preparing textbooks and in teaching the curriculum. This is not 'new wine in old bottles'. It has its vision and ideal to pursue and to accomplish. At present, there are no data available to evaluate the impact of this change. However, there are several ongoing studies, for instance, PISA 2006, TIMSS 2007, and TASA, which might shed some light on the effectiveness of this reform compared to that experienced by other countries.

Why should we have standards and assessment in science education? Ravitch (1993) while pointing out, that the US was one of the few countries that did not have national standards, noted two reasons for adopting national standards. First, they encouraged equal opportunities for learning and high learning achievement. Secondly, without standards, there is no way to enhance expectations from educational system.

The reform of science education must be viewed as part of a general education reform (Bybee and DeBoer, 1994). It is an evolutionary process that reflects the needs of society, parents, schoolteachers, economic status, and international development. As van den Akker (1998) points out, although many pressures for curriculum change come from outside schools, it is naïve to expect much from top-down strategies of curriculum reform. Not only did the curriculum need more comprehensive and systematic approaches that took the many perspectives of a system into account, but we also needed to start with a realistic time frame. Reform is not something that happens overnight; a thoughtful and profound change has to be well planned beforehand. As the White Paper indicates, we need a system of science education that includes evaluations of our science education programs so that we better understand how our students learn, how our teachers teach, and how school systems provide support for the successful cultivation of scientific literacy.

Finally, I will relate a story told in Howard Gardner's *To Open Minds* (1989) to help us think about how and what we do to educate our children for their future place in the world.

> *"... My wife Ellen, our year-and-a-half-old son, Benjamin, and I [Gardner] lived there [in the heart of Nanjing, China]... Benjamin loved to carry the key around, shaking it vigorously. He also liked to try to place it into the slot. ... Because of his tender age, lack of the manual dexterity, and incomplete understanding of the need to orient the key "just so," he would usually fail. Benjamin was not bothered in the least. He loved to bang the key on the slot and probably got as much pleasure out of the sounds it made, and the kinesthetic sensations he felt, as he did those few times when the key actually found its way into the slot.*
>
> *Both Ellen and I were perfectly happy to allow Benjamin to bang the key near the key slot ... But I soon observed an intriguing phenomenon. Any Chinese attendant nearby... would come over to watch Benjamin. As soon as the observer saw what our child was doing ... she attempted to intervene. In general, she would hold onto his hand and, gently but firmly, guide it directly toward the slot, reorient it as necessary, and help Benjamin to insert the key." (pp. 3-4)*

While reading this, Benjamin's smile of enjoyment with the key seemed to disappear right in front of me. When we make plans for our children's learning, do we really teach them something – or do we take away the opportunity for exploration?

# References

American Association for the Advancement of Science (1993) *Benchmarks for science literacy*. New York: Oxford University Press.

American Association for the Advancement of Science (2001) *Designs for science literacy. Project 2061*. New York: Oxford University Press.

Anderson, K. D. and Helms, J. V. (2001) The ideal of standards and the reality of schools: Needed research. *Journal of Research in Science Teaching*, 38, 3-16.

Bybee, R. W. and DeBoer, G. E. (1994) Research on goals for the science curriculum. In D. L. Gabel (Ed.), *Handbook of research on science teaching and learning* (pp357-387). New York: Macmillan Publishing Co.

Chan, P. C. (1999) The background and nature of revising grade 1–9 curriculum guidelines. *Educational Research Information (in Chinese)*, 7(1), 1-13.

Chang, S. N. and Chiu, M. H. (2005) The development of authentic assessments to investigate ninth graders' scientific literacy: In the case of scientific cognition concerning the concepts of chemistry and physics. *International Journal of Science and Mathematics Education*, 117-140.

Chiu, M. H. (2000) An introduction and comment on New Standards for Science. *Science Education Monthly (in Chinese)*, 228, 2-15.

Chiu, M. H. (2006) Science performance and some related factors of Taiwan eight-graders found in TIMSS 2003. In C. N. Chang (Ed.), *Report of Taiwan TIMSS 2003 – Based on the trends in international mathematics and science study 2003* (pp. 5-44). Taipei, Taiwan: Science Education Center, National Taiwan Normal University.

Chiu, M. H. (in press) A national survey of students' conceptions of chemistry in Taiwan. *International Journal of Science Education*.

Chiu, M. H. and Chou, C. C. (2005) The development of science education for the past 100 years in the U.S. (in Chinese). *Educational Resources and Research*, 64, 19-40.

Department of Statistics, Ministry of Education, R.O.C. (2004) *Education in the Republic of China*. Taipei, Taiwan, R.O.C.

Executive Yuan (1996) *The consultants' concluding report on educational reform by the Committee on Educational Reform*.

Fensham, P. J. (2000) Issues for schooling in science. In R. T. Cross and P. J. Fensham (Eds.), *Science and the citizen for educators and the public* (pp. 73-77). Melbourne: Arena Publications.

Fogarty, R. (1991) Ten ways to integrate curriculum. *Educational Leadership*, 49 (2), 61-65.

Gardner, H. (1989) *To open minds: Chinese clues to the dilemma of contemporary education*. New York: Basic Books, Inc.

Liao, Y. C. (2005) Problems and perspectives of school-based curriculum development (in Chinese). *Study Information*, 6, 66-71.

Lyu, P. L. (2002) *A study of science and technology learning area teachers' cognition and attitude toward grade 1–9 curriculum guidelines*. Unpublished masters thesis. Taipei: National Taiwan Normal University.

Martin, M. O., Mullis, I. V. S., Gonzalez, E. J. and Chrostowski, S. J. (2004) *TIMSS 2003 international science report: Findings from IEA's trends in international mathematics and science study at the fourth and eighth grades*. Chestnut Hill, MA: International Association for the Evaluation of Educational Achievement (IEA), TIMSS and PIRLS International Study Center, Boston College.

Madaus, G. F. and Kellaghan, T. (1992) Curriculum evaluation and assessment. In P. W. Jackson (Ed.), *Handbook of Research on Curriculum* (pp. 119-154). New York: Simon & Schuster and Prentice Hall International.

Ministry of Education (1998) *Grade 1-9 curriculum guidelines*. Taipei: MOE.

Ministry of Education (2000) *Curriculum Guidelines for Seven Learning Areas for 9-Year Compulsory Education in Elementary and Junior High School*. Taipei: MOE.

Ministry of Education (2003a) *Grade 1–9 curriculum guidelines: Science and technology learning area*. Taipei: MOE.

Ministry of Education (2003b) *Educational reform: Why & how*. Taipei: MOE.

Ministry of Education and National Science Council (2003) *The white paper for science education*. Taipei: MOE.

National Center on Education and the Economy (1995) *Performance standards* (consultation draft). Pittsburgh, PA: Learning Research and Development of Center.

National Center on Education and the Economy and the University of Pittsburgh (1997a, 1998a) *New Standards: Performance Standards: Volume 1: Elementary School*. National Center on Education and the Economy and the University of Pittsburgh.

National Center on Education and the Economy and the University of Pittsburgh (1997b, 1998b) *New Standards: Performance Standards: Volume 2: Middle School*. National Center on Education and the Economy and the University of Pittsburgh.

National Center on Education and the Economy and the University of Pittsburgh (1997c, 1998c) *New Standards: Performance Standards: Volume 3: High School*. National Center on Education and the Economy and the University of Pittsburgh.

National Education Research Institute (2005) *Taiwan assessment of students' achievement working paper report for the year of 2005*. Taipei: National Education Research Institute.

National Education Research Institute (2006) *Description of a pilot study for Taiwan assessment of student' achievement http://tasa.naer.edu.tw/explanation.html*

National Research Council (1996) *National science education standards.* Washington, D.C.: National Academic Press.

National Science Teachers Association (1993) *Scope, sequence, and coordination of secondary school science (Vol 1: The content core)*. Washington D.C.: NSTA.

OECD (Organisation for Economic Co-operation and Development) (2004) OECD Programme for International Student Assessment. *PISA Newsletter*, 10, 1-3.

Ravitch, D. (1993) Launching a revolution in standards and assessments. *Phi Delta Kappan,* 74, 10, 767-772.

Rutherford, F. J. and Ahlgren, A. (1989) *Science for all Americans*. New York: Oxford University Press.

Shen, S. S. (2005) The study on nine-year integrated curriculum of Taiwan: From the perspective of social context and international development (in Chinese). *Educational Resources and Research*, 18-34.

Treagust, D. (1988) Development and use of diagnostic tests to evaluate students' misconceptions in science. *International Journal of Science Education,* 10(2), 159-169.

Treagust, D. F. (1995) Diagnostic assessment of students' science knowledge. In S. M. Glynn and R. Duit (Eds.), *Learning science in the schools: Research reforming practice* (pp. 327-346). Mahwah, NJ: Erlbaum.

U.S. Department of Education (1991) *America 2000: An Education Strategy.* Washington DC: U.S. Department of Education.

U.S. Department of Education (2002) *No Child Left Behind Act of 2001*. Washington, DC: Department of Education. (Data was retrieved from http://www.ed.gov/nclb/overview/intro/guide/guide_pg12.html#history or http://www.whitehouse.gov/news/reports/no-child-left-behind.html)

U. S. Department of Education (2005.4.18.) *Spellings discusses "New Path for No Child Left Behind" Policy with elementary school principals.* Retrieved from http://www.ed.gov/news/pressreleases/2005/04/ 04182005.html

van den Akker, J. (1998) The science curriculum: Between ideals and outcomes. In B. Fraser and K. G. Tobin (Eds.), *International handbook of science education*, (pp. 421-447). Dordrecht: Kluwer Academic Publishers.

# The Content of the General Guidelines

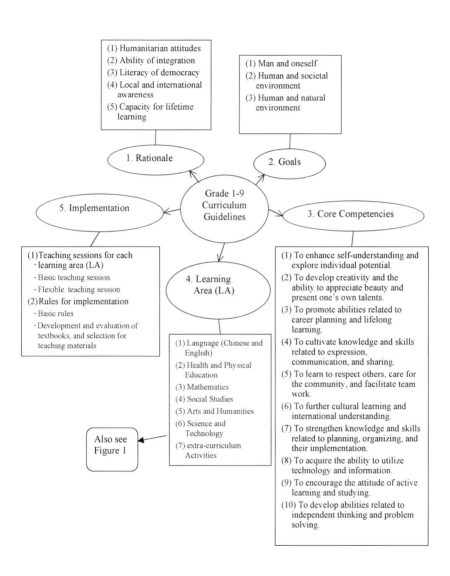

(1) Humanitarian attitudes
(2) Ability of integration
(3) Literacy of democracy
(4) Local and international awareness
(5) Capacity for lifetime learning

(1) Man and oneself
(2) Human and societal environment
(3) Human and natural environment

1. Rationale

2. Goals

Grade 1-9 Curriculum Guidelines

5. Implementation

3. Core Competencies

(1) Teaching sessions for each · learning area (LA)
· Basic teaching session
· Flexible teaching session
(2) Rules for implementation
· Basic rules
· Development and evaluation of textbooks, and selection for teaching materials

4. Learning Area (LA)

(1) Language (Chinese and English)
(2) Health and Physical Education
(3) Mathematics
(4) Social Studies
(5) Arts and Humanities
(6) Science and Technology
(7) extra-curriculum Activities

Also see Figure 1

(1) To enhance self-understanding and explore individual potential.
(2) To develop creativity and the ability to appreciate beauty and present one's own talents.
(3) To promote abilities related to career planning and lifelong learning.
(4) To cultivate knowledge and skills related to expression, communication, and sharing.
(5) To learn to respect others, care for the community, and facilitate team work.
(6) To further cultural learning and international understanding.
(7) To strengthen knowledge and skills related to planning, organizing, and their implementation.
(8) To acquire the ability to utilize technology and information.
(9) To encourage the attitude of active learning and studying.
(10) To develop abilities related to independent thinking and problem solving.

# The current school system of Taiwan
## (Department of Statistics, Ministry of Education, R.O.C., 2004)

| School Age | Normal Age | | | | | | | | | | | | | | | |
|---|---|---|---|---|---|---|---|---|---|---|---|---|---|---|---|---|

School Age / Normal Age

| 25 | 30 |
| 24 | 29 |
| 23 | 28 |
| 22 | 27 |
| 21 | 26 |
| 20 | 25 |
| 19 | 24 |
| 18 | 23 |
| 17 | 22 |
| 16 | 21 |
| 15 | 20 |
| 14 | 19 |
| 13 | 18 |
| 12 | 17 |
| 11 | 16 |
| 10 | 15 |
| 9 | 14 |
| 8 | 13 |
| 7 | 12 |
| 6 | 11 |
| 5 | 10 |
| 4 | 9 |
| 3 | 8 |
| 2 | 7 |
| 1 | 6 |
|  | 5 |
|  | 4 |

Higher Education

Doctoral Program

Working Experience

Working Experience

Dep. Of Medicine After Bachelor

Dept. of Medicine

Dept. of Dentistry

Master Program

University & College

Sr. Sec. Education

Nine-Year Compulsory Education

Pre-School Education

Combined High School

Senior High School

Senior Vocational School

Technical College (4 YRS.)

Technical College (2 YRS.)

Junior College (2 YRS.)

Working Experience

Jr. College (5 YRS.)

Tech. & Jr. College Education

Junior High School

Primary School

Kindergarten

Nine-Year Compulsory Education

Pre-School Education

Special Education

Senior High (Vocational)

Junior High

Primary

Kinder-garten

Supplementary And Continuing Education

Open Uni., Cont. College & Cont. Uni.

Cont. Jr. College

Cont. Sr. Sec. School

Supp. Jr. High School

Supp. Primary School

336

## Projects sponsored by NSC for grades 1–9

## Nature and Technology learning area

|  | 1999 | 2000 | 2001 | 2002 | 2003 | 2004 | 2005 | 2006 |
|---|---|---|---|---|---|---|---|---|
| Theory in science education | 1 | | | | | | | |
| Coordinating projects or workshop/conference | | | 2 | 1 | 2 | 1 | | |
| Mathematics education | | 1 | 5 | 6 | 32 | 4 | 1 | 1 |
| Science education | 1 | 9 | 26 | 17 | 30 | 12 | 6 | 3 |
| Informational education | | 1 | | | | | | |
| Applied science | | | | | | 1 | 1 | |
| Public science | | | | | 1 | 1 | | |

2001–2003: Workshop or conference related to grades 1–9 curriculum reform.

2003: Two coordinating projects for maths and science projects in 2003.

2004 annual report for project on grades 1–9 curriculum reform.

Data were retrieved from http://www.nsc.gov.tw on 25 August 2005.

Appendix 4

# Some examples of indicators for science curriculum for grades 1–9

*110 Composition of the Earth (rocks, water, and air)*

### Water, air, and land
1a. Notice the existence of water, air and land in the environment.
1b. Notice the stones, sand, and soils, which have their own features and can be differentiated, on the surface of the Earth.

### The characteristics of water, air, and land
2a. Notice and describe the three states of water because of temperature. Notice that many substances can dissolve in water and air is combustion supporting.

### Water in the Earth
3a. Be aware that there is water vapor in the atmosphere, and it sometimes rains when water vapor is condensed into cloud.
3b. Be aware that seawater is salty and freshwater exists in rivers, lakes, and soils only.

### The important composition of air and their characters
3c. Can produce oxygen and carbon dioxide with a simple experiment and inspect their characteristics to be aware that oxygen and carbon dioxide are in the air.

### The composition and characteristics of rocks
3d. Observe and know that rock consists of a variety of minerals.
3e. Be aware that different minerals have their own obvious properties.
3f. Be aware that different rocks have different uses (such as architecture materials, smelting materials, and so on).

### Lithosphere, atmosphere, and hydrosphere
4a. Know the distribution of land and sea on Earth.
4b. Use models to understand the internal construction of the Earth.
4c. Be aware that the atmosphere surrounds the Earth, and the temperature of the atmosphere changes with the height.
4d. Know the hydrosphere of the Earth: the groundwater, rivers, lakes, and sea.
4e. Recognize the difference between the freshwater and the seawater and that we cannot drink the seawater directly.

### The biosphere
4f. Realize the distribution domain of the creatures, the environmental factors that maintain the creatures living on Earth, and the importance of humans cherishing and protecting the Earth's environment.

## The composition of the atmosphere
4g. Understand the important composition and characteristics of the atmosphere (oxygen, hydrogen, water vapour, carbon dioxide).

*225 Oxidation and Reduction*

### The way to avoid oxidation
2a. Can realize with daily illustrations that combustion needs air and instantiate how to separate air to prevent spoiling (sop the peeled apple in the salt water, for example).

### Combustion and fire fighting
3a. Know the three factors of combustion (flashpoint, combustible, and combustion supporter, usually oxygen), and the three factors to introduce the common principles of fire extinguishing as well as the emergency measures in a fire accident.

## The environment that catalyzes the oxidation reaction
3b. Reason out the possible causes of rust and the methods to prevent rust through experiment.

### The activity of elements and the compounds
4a. Understand the activity of the common metal and nonmetal elements and their compounds through experiment.

### Combustion and metal smelting
4b. Can explain that oxidation is matter combined with oxygen, for example, matter burning to an oxide oxidation, and that the reduction is the oxide losing oxygen, through an experiment.
Can understand the oxidation and reduction of the metal smelting process through collecting data.

### Chemical battery and electrolysis
4c. Realise the general definition of oxidation and reduction and the use of the method in a chemical battery, through experiments with a zinc-copper battery and electrolyzing a solution of copper sulphate.

### Respiration
4d. Understand that respiration is an example of oxidation and reduction.

### The application of oxidation and reduction
4e. Know the application of oxidation and reduction in daily life (for example, use a strong oxidant to bleach clothes).

### The stories of scientists and inventors
2a. Introduce scientists' investigations at the appropriate time.
2b. Indicate stories of famous science inventors in Taiwan and China.

### The developmental process of science
2c. Introduce the research process of science at the appropriate time to understand that the development of science needs the effort of science researchers with strong willpower and the courage to innovate.
2d. Introduce the evolutional history that humans use science to improve their lives.

### Stories of scientists
3a. Introduce scientists' research activities in China and the West.

### The discovery process of science
3b. Introduce the discovery process of science with the appropriate teaching materials to understand the relationship between the experiment and theory of science.

### Stories of scientists (Again for different levels of students)
4a. Understand the important findings and its process of science through reading and collecting references.

### The discovery process of science *(Again for different level of students)*
4b. In the appropriate science activity, describe scientists' critical thought, explorative thought, and creative thought in the discovery process of science.

Appendix 5

## Total number of test items for each science subject in the national basic Competence Test for junior high school students

|  | Physics | Chemistry | Biology | Earth Science | Health Education |
|---|---|---|---|---|---|
| 2002-$1^{st}$ | 16 | 17 | 10 | 5 | 10 |
| 2002-$2^{nd}$ | 19 | 10 | 13 | 7 | 9 |
| 2003-$1^{st}$ | 17 | 10 | 13 | 9 | 9 |
| 2003-$2^{nd}$ | 15 | 17 | 14 | 5 | 7 |
| 2004-$1^{st}$ | 17 | 11 | 11 | 8 | 11 |
| 2004-$2^{nd}$ | 16 | 11 | 12 | 7 | 12 |
| 2005-$1^{st}$ | 19 | 10 | 9 | 15 | 5 |
| 2005-$2^{nd}$ | 18 | 13 | 8 | 15 | 4 |
| 2006-$1^{st}$ | 16 | 14 | 10 | 13 | 5 |
| 2006-$2^{nd}$ | 16 | 13 | 12 | 14 | 3 |

# Number of correct answers and scale scores for the national basic Competence Test for junior high school students (twice a year: in May and July)

| # of correct answer | 2002 -1 | 02 -2 | 03 -1 | 03 -2 | 04 -1 | 04 -2 | 05 -1 | 05 -2 | 06 -1 | 06 -2 |
|---|---|---|---|---|---|---|---|---|---|---|
| 0 | 1 | 1 | 1 | 1 | 1 | 1 | 1 | 1 | 1 | 1 |
| 1 | 1 | 1 | 1 | 1 | 1 | 1 | 1 | 1 | 1 | 1 |
| 2 | 1 | 1 | 1 | 1 | 1 | 1 | 1 | 1 | 1 | 1 |
| 3 | 1 | 1 | 1 | 1 | 1 | 1 | 1 | 1 | 1 | 1 |
| 4 | 1 | 1 | 1 | 1 | 1 | 1 | 1 | 1 | 1 | 1 |
| 5 | 1 | 1 | 1 | 1 | 1 | 1 | 1 | 1 | 1 | 1 |
| 6 | 3 | 2 | 1 | 1 | 1 | 1 | 1 | 3 | 1 | 1 |
| 7 | 4 | 3 | 2 | 1 | 1 | 1 | 2 | 4 | 1 | 1 |
| 8 | 5 | 4 | 4 | 2 | 1 | 1 | 3 | 5 | 3 | 2 |
| 9 | 7 | 5 | 5 | 3 | 2 | 2 | 4 | 7 | 4 | 4 |
| 10 | 8 | 6 | 6 | 4 | 3 | 3 | 6 | 8 | 5 | 5 |
| 11 | 9 | 7 | 7 | 5 | 4 | 4 | 7 | 9 | 6 | 6 |
| 12 | 10 | 8 | 8 | 6 | 5 | 5 | 8 | 10 | 7 | 7 |
| 13 | 11 | 9 | 9 | 7 | 7 | 6 | 9 | 11 | 8 | 8 |
| 14 | 12 | 10 | 10 | 8 | 8 | 7 | 10 | 12 | 9 | 9 |
| 15 | 13 | 11 | 11 | 9 | 9 | 8 | 11 | 13 | 10 | 10 |
| 16 | 14 | 12 | 12 | 10 | 10 | 10 | 12 | 14 | 11 | 11 |
| 17 | 15 | 13 | 13 | 11 | 11 | 10 | 13 | 15 | 12 | 12 |
| 18 | 16 | 14 | 14 | 12 | 12 | 11 | 14 | 16 | 13 | 13 |
| 19 | 17 | 15 | 15 | 13 | 13 | 12 | 15 | 17 | 14 | 14 |
| 20 | 18 | 16 | 16 | 14 | 14 | 13 | 16 | 18 | 15 | 14 |
| 21 | 18 | 17 | 17 | 15 | 15 | 14 | 17 | 19 | 16 | 15 |
| 22 | 19 | 17 | 18 | 16 | 16 | 15 | 17 | 20 | 17 | 16 |
| 23 | 20 | 18 | 19 | 17 | 17 | 16 | 18 | 21 | 18 | 17 |
| 24 | 21 | 19 | 20 | 18 | 18 | 17 | 19 | 22 | 19 | 18 |
| 25 | 22 | 20 | 21 | 19 | 18 | 18 | 20 | 22 | 20 | 19 |
| 26 | 23 | 21 | 22 | 20 | 19 | 19 | 21 | 23 | 21 | 20 |
| 27 | 24 | 22 | 22 | 20 | 20 | 20 | 22 | 24 | 21 | 21 |
| 28 | 25 | 23 | 23 | 21 | 21 | 21 | 23 | 25 | 22 | 21 |
| 29 | 25 | 23 | 24 | 22 | 22 | 22 | 24 | 26 | 23 | 22 |

| # of correct answer | 2002 -1 | 02 -2 | 03 -1 | 03 -2 | 04 -1 | 04 -2 | 05 -1 | 05 -2 | 06 -1 | 06 -2 |
|---|---|---|---|---|---|---|---|---|---|---|
| 30 | 26 | 24 | 25 | 23 | 23 | 23 | 24 | 27 | 24 | 23 |
| 31 | 27 | 25 | 26 | 24 | 24 | 24 | 25 | 28 | 25 | 24 |
| 32 | 28 | 26 | 27 | 25 | 25 | 25 | 26 | 28 | 26 | 25 |
| 33 | 29 | 27 | 28 | 26 | 26 | 26 | 27 | 29 | 27 | 26 |
| 34 | 30 | 28 | 29 | 27 | 27 | 27 | 28 | 30 | 28 | 26 |
| 35 | 31 | 29 | 29 | 28 | 28 | 27 | 29 | 31 | 29 | 27 |
| 36 | 31 | 30 | 30 | 28 | 29 | 28 | 30 | 32 | 29 | 28 |
| 37 | 32 | 30 | 31 | 29 | 30 | 29 | 31 | 33 | 30 | 29 |
| 38 | 33 | 31 | 32 | 30 | 31 | 30 | 32 | 34 | 31 | 30 |
| 39 | 34 | 32 | 33 | 31 | 32 | 31 | 32 | 34 | 32 | 31 |
| 40 | 35 | 33 | 34 | 32 | 33 | 32 | 33 | 35 | 33 | 32 |
| 41 | 36 | 34 | 35 | 33 | 34 | 33 | 34 | 36 | 34 | 33 |
| 42 | 37 | 35 | 36 | 34 | 35 | 34 | 35 | 37 | 35 | 34 |
| 43 | 38 | 36 | 37 | 35 | 36 | 36 | 36 | 38 | 36 | 35 |
| 44 | 39 | 37 | 38 | 36 | 37 | 37 | 37 | 39 | 37 | 36 |
| 45 | 40 | 38 | 39 | 37 | 38 | 38 | 38 | 40 | 38 | 37 |
| 46 | 41 | 39 | 40 | 39 | 39 | 39 | 39 | 41 | 39 | 38 |
| 47 | 42 | 40 | 41 | 40 | 40 | 40 | 40 | 42 | 40 | 39 |
| 48 | 43 | 41 | 42 | 41 | 41 | 41 | 41 | 43 | 41 | 40 |
| 49 | 44 | 43 | 44 | 42 | 43 | 43 | 43 | 44 | 43 | 41 |
| 50 | 45 | 44 | 45 | 43 | 44 | 44 | 44 | 45 | 44 | 42 |
| 51 | 47 | 45 | 46 | 45 | 45 | 45 | 45 | 46 | 45 | 44 |
| 52 | 48 | 47 | 47 | 46 | 47 | 47 | 46 | 48 | 46 | 45 |
| 53 | 49 | 48 | 49 | 48 | 48 | 48 | 48 | 49 | 48 | 47 |
| 54 | 51 | 50 | 50 | 49 | 50 | 50 | 49 | 50 | 49 | 48 |
| 55 | 53 | 52 | 52 | 51 | 52 | 52 | 51 | 52 | 51 | 50 |
| 56 | 55 | 54 | 54 | 54 | 54 | 54 | 53 | 54 | 53 | 52 |
| 57 | 57 | 56 | 57 | 56 | 56 | 57 | 56 | 56 | 56 | 55 |
| 58 | 60 | 60 | 60 | 60 | 60 | 60 | 60 | 60 | 60 | 60 |

Note: There were 58 items tested in each time of the national examination. The total scores are 60 points in all. Each item was weighted the same. It depended upon how many students answered correctly for that specific item. For instance, if a student had 57 test items answered correctly, he might be scored differently in different year (56 points for 2002-2, 55 points for 2006-2).

Appendix 7

# Examples of assessment items in the basic Competence Test in 2005

The following items were tested at the second test in 2005.(2005/ 7/09-10) and was retrieved from http://www.bctest.ntnu.edu.tw/ on August 15, 2006 (announced by The Committee of The Basic Competence Test for Junior High School Students)

Please read the following statements, and then answer questions 54–56.

There are four unlabelled glass bottles with white solids. The teacher says they are NaOH, $CaCl_2$, $CaCO_3$, and $Na_2CO_3$. Students have to identify these chemicals by experiments and label them. Mary, John, Alan, and Susan number these glasses A, B, C, and D, and using the procedures below, recorded the results in the table below.

|  | Result | | | |
|---|---|---|---|---|
|  | A | B | C | D |
| Put 1 gram of the solid and 10ml water in the test tube, and shake the mixture | Not dissolved | Dissolved | Dissolved | Dissolved |
| Add 1–2 drops of phenolphthalein in the solution | ---- | Red | Red | Transparent |
| Put 1 gram of the solid in the test tube, and add a few drops of dilute hydrochloric acid | Bubbled | Bubbled | No bubble | No bubble |

Note: Because A does not dissolve, they do not add the phenolphthalein solution.

54. A and B bubble when adding in dilute hydrochloric acid. So, which of the following is the common particle of A and B?
   (A) $Ca^{2+}$   (B) $Na^+$   (C) $OH^-$   (D) $CO_3^{2-}$

**Competence** Indicator: (code: 1-4-5-2)
Read the data in the table and the report, and understand the inner content (what does this mean?) of the data.

The content of the test item: 130-4g Is this the paragraph in the syllabus?
Through the knowledge of the atom model (the electron, proton, and neutron), understand the chemical quality, element, and compound of the atom.

55. Concerning the four students' experiment results, which of the following is true?

(A) Add the dilute hydrochloric acid in A, and produce hydrogen.
(B) Add the dilute hydrochloric acid in B, and produce oxygen.
(C) The C solution is acidic.
(D) The D solution is alkaline.

**Competence Indicator: (code: 1-4-5-2)**
**(Pupils can) Read the data in the table and the report, and understand the inner content of the data.**

**The content of the test item; (code: 218-4c)**
**Know the different changes in the experiments (the three states, precipitate, and the changes of color and temperature).**

56. Mary, John, Alan, and Susan each labels the four glass bottles A, B, C, and D as indicated in the table below. According to the results of the experiments, whose labels are correct?

| | A | B | C | D |
|---|---|---|---|---|
| Mary | $CaCO_3$ | $Na_2CO_3$ | NaOH | $CaCl_2$ |
| John | $CaCO_3$ | NaOH | $CaCl_2$ | $Na_2CO_3$ |
| Alan | $Na_2CO_3$ | $CaCO_3$ | $CaCl_2$ | NaOH |
| Susan | $Na_2CO_3$ | $CaCl_2$ | NaOH | $CaCO_3$ |

(1) Mary    (2) John    (3) Alan    (4) Susan    Confusing as you are using A B C D for the chemicals and the students.

**Competence Indicator: (code: 1-4-4-4)**
**(Pupils can) Can experiment, and according to the results, criticize or understand the concept, the theory, and the appropriateness of the models.**

**The content of the test item: (code: 226-4f)**
**Observe the changes of adding an acidic (basic) solution to a basic (acidic) solution through an experiment (exothermic process and produce the salt). According to the properties of a salt, discuss the uses (flavoring, salting, washing, and sterilizing) and dangers from in daily life.**

**Examples of assessment items from the first basic Competence Test in 2006**

25. Using Figure 11 below, which of the following statements about an athlete at the time of the sport and the parts of brain is correct?

(A) A can increase the heartbeat and accelerate the blood circulation.

(B) B can keep the body balanced to prevent the athlete from falling.

(C) C can reduce the depth of breath and slow down the consumption of oxygen.

(D) D can cause the reflex to make the athlete run with greater speed.

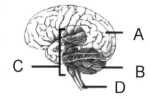

**Competence indicator: (code: 2-4-2-1)**
**(Pupils can) Inquire into the physiological functions of the parts of plants and animals, and know how these parts coordinate to become a life organism.**

**Test content: (code: 213-4d)**
**Understand the types and functions of the neuron cell, and understand the human nervous system as well as the situation of their coordinating operation.**

42. Mr. Guo illustrates the idea of elements gaining and losing electrons while explaining the chemical formula. He utilizes the models of the re-entrant angle and salient angle as the teaching aid. As figure 20 illustrates, Model A shows the combination that the sodium ion loses an electron and chlorine ion gets an electron, whereas Model B shows the combination that magnesium ion loses two electrons and chlorine ion gets one electron. Accordingly, which of the following chemical formulas most likely stands for Model C?

(A) $Co_2$
(B) $Mg_3N_2$
(C) $Al_2O_3$
(D) $CaCO_3$

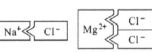

A

Figure 20

**Competence indicator: (code: 2-4-4-5)**
**(Pupils can) Know the composition and structure of the matter, and the relation between the element and a chemical compound, and understand the chemical reaction and re-arrangement of the atoms.**

**Test content: (code: 130-4j)**
**Symbol of an element and chemical formula – Pupils show their understanding of element symbols and name principle and method of the simple chemical compound.**

49. Xiao Ming rode the Ferris wheel at an amusement park,. The gondola on the Ferris wheel performed uniform circular motion slowly. As figure 24 shows, if during the process of riding the Ferris wheel, A and C were at the same horizontal height, B was at the highest point, and D was at the lowest point. Which of the following statements is true? (If you ask this question, you should get full marks by just saying yes or no)

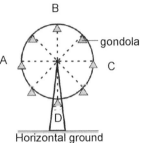

(A) His potential energy was largest in position D. Figure 24.

(B) Whatever his position on the gondola, his speed was always the same.

(C) His kinetic energy was the same in positions A and C.

(D) In any position, the sum of potential energy and kinetic energy was the same.

**Competence indicator: (code: 1-4-3-2)**
**(Pupils can) Based on the data to infer the attribute and causality.**

**Test content: Energy has many kinds of types – Know kinetic energy, potential energy, heat energy, nuclear energy, etc., the different kinds of energy.**

# Chapter 18

## Standards for science education in the United States: Necessary Evil?

*Norman G. Lederman and Judith S. Lederman*

*Department of Mathematics and Science Education Illinois Institute of Technology, Chicago, Illinois 60616-3793, USA*

### National reforms and Standards in U.S. Science Education: History and background

Quietly, in 1985, the American Association for the Advancement of Science (AAAS) began a long-term initiative to reform K-12 education in natural and social science, mathematics, and technology. The initial product of this effort was *Science for All Americans* (Rutherford and Ahlgren, 1989), a vision statement of a reform effort more popularly known as *Project 2061*. One year later, the National Council of Teachers in Mathematics (NCTM) began its effort to delineate national standards in mathematics curricula, teaching, and assessment for K-12 levels. The culmination of this effort was the publication of NCTM's *Curriculum and Evaluation Standards* (NCTM, 1989). Although the work on *Project 2061* actually preceded that of the mathematics community, the NCTM Standards are often credited with beginning the flurry of standards development projects currently seen at the national, state, and local levels.

Although the various reforms have much in common, they are different in some areas, resulting in significant implications. However, before one can truly understand the proposed reforms and their potential implications it is important to understand the context of science curriculum and instruction in the U.S. Figure 1 illustrates how science instruction and science coursework is typically distributed across grades K-12.

It is important to note that the distribution of science instruction and coursework presented in figure 1 is highly variable across states and school districts. Currently, at the high school level, there is much debate about the 'proper' sequence of biology, chemistry, and physics. The 'physics first' movement advocates that a physics course should precede courses in biology and chemistry instead of following such courses. Perhaps the widest variation in science instruction exists at the K-5 levels. There is more stress on basic skills (e.g., reading, writing, and mathematics) in these grades and some students get virtually no science instruction during their elementary school years. The reform documents in science education have improved the situation somewhat.

| Grade | K | 1 | 2 | 3 | 4 | 5 | 6 | 7 | 8 | 9 | 10 | 11 | 12 |
|---|---|---|---|---|---|---|---|---|---|---|---|---|---|
| Pupils' age | 5 | 6 | 7 | 8 | 9 | 10 | 11 | 12 | 13 | 14 | 15 | 16 | 17 |
| Level | Elementary School | | | | | | Middle School | | | Secondary/High School | | | |
| Science subjects | Broad integrated attention to life, physical, earth, and space science is distributed across all grade levels. The exact sequence and depth of instruction varies considerably by state and school district. | | | | | | Separate courses sequentially offered in earth/space science, life science, and physical science typically span these grades. All students take the sequence of courses. | | | Separate courses in the sequence of earth/space science, biology, chemistry, and physics is typical, but variation in this sequence is common. Also, advanced courses in biology chemistry, and physics are common. Students are required to take 2-3 science courses for graduation. | | | |

Figure 1:     Science in the U.S. School System

The discussion of the national reform documents in science education is presented in chronological sequence and does not represent a rank ordering by impact or preference. At the same time as these reform efforts were taking place in the field of science, similar efforts were taking place in other subject matter disciplines. As one reads about the vision of the various reform documents in science education it is also useful to keep in mind the forces driving the development of these reforms and the stakeholders involved. In the U.S., the two primary driving forces in science education were the dismal U.S. standing in international academic comparisons at the K-12 levels and the continually decreasing pipeline of scientists, engineers, and individuals in related technical fields. As with previous reform efforts in the U.S., situations that are perceived to have implications for national defense and/or competitiveness in the international marketplace are rarely ignored. In terms of the development of the following reform efforts, numerous stakeholders have been involved. However, the scientific, business, and educational communities have been responsible for the majority of the concrete work of translating general vision statements into concrete reform documents and standards for student learning.

### *Science curriculum reforms: Project 2061 and SS&C*

After three years of planning, Project 2061 was launched in 1985 under the direction of F. James Rutherford (AAAS, 1993; Rutherford and Ahlgren, 1989). Project 2061 is based on the belief that the K-12 education system should be reformed so that all American high school graduates are science literate (i.e., students will possess the knowledge and skills to lead interesting, responsible, and productive lives in a culture and society increasingly influenced by science and technology).

There are six assertions that guide Project 2061:

348

1. Reform must be comprehensive and center on all children, grades, subjects, and represent a long term commitment

2. Curriculum reform should be dictated by our collective vision of the lasting knowledge and skills needed by our students and future citizens

3. The common core of learning in science, mathematics, and technology should focus on science literacy as opposed to preparation of students for careers in science. The core curriculum should emphasize connections among the natural and social sciences, mathematics, and technology. The connections with these areas and the arts, humanities, and vocational subjects should be clear as well

4. Schools should teach less and teach it better. Superficial coverage of specialized terms and algorithms should be eliminated. This is the source of the often quoted phrase, 'less is more'

5. Reform should promote equity in science, mathematics, and technology education, serving all students equally well

6. Reform should allow more flexibility for organizing instruction than is currently common

The initial, and most influential documents produced by Project 2061 were *Science for All Americans* (Rutherford and Ahlgren, 1989), which presents a vision and goals for science literacy, and *Benchmarks for Science Literacy* (AAAS, 1993), which translates the vision of *Science for All Americans* into expectations (i.e., benchmarks) for core content by the end of grades 2, 5, 8, and 12. More recently, *Designs for Science Literacy, Curriculum Materials Resource, Resources for Science Literacy: Professional Development, Blueprints for Reform*, and the *Atlas of Science Literacy* have been published. These resources are designed to assist teacher educators in the preparation of teachers in a manner consistent with the goals of Project 2061 and to assist practicing teachers in the implementation of project goals in their classrooms.

The Scope, Sequence, and Coordination of Secondary School Science (SS&C) reform initiative advocated coherent, carefully-sequenced science curriculum which is thematic and interdisciplinary. SS&C had four publications, with the most significant being the Content Core (NSTA, 1992; Pearsall, 1993). The publication of A *High School Framework for National Science Education Standards* (NSTA, 1995), although an SS&C publication, was the first in a series that lead to NSTA's shift toward the adoption of the National Science Education Standards. Full support for the NSES is now published in both an NSTA position statement (NSTA, 1998) and the publication of the series of *Pathways to the Science Education Standards* (Texley and Wild, 2004).

Similar actions have been taken by many state science teachers associations (e.g., Oregon, Illinois and New York). Overall, SS&C advocates science programs that help students answer questions such as, "How do we know?," "Why do we believe?," and "What does it mean?"

### *National Science Education Standards (NSES)*

In January 1996 the National Research Council of the National Academy of Sciences (NRC) published the *National Science Education Standards* (NRC, 1996).

The project is a more comprehensive endeavour than either Project 2061 or SS&C, as it not only provides a vision for scientific literacy but also a framework for how the vision is to be realized. It is important to note that the primary overlap of purpose between the *NSES* and *Benchmarks for Science Literacy* is with respect to the subject matter standards/benchmarks. The *NSES, however,* advocate that all citizens be able to develop and conduct a scientific investigation while *Project 2061* simply advocates that our citizens be able to understand the various aspects of a scientific investigation. As such, the *NSES* can be viewed as the more ambitious document. However, it can also be argued that, relative to the goal of scientific literacy, an understanding *about* scientific inquiry is far more valuable and realistic that the ability to conceive, design, and carry out a scientific investigation. Nevertheless, most educators would certainly agree that the best way to teach *about* inquiry is to have students *do* inquiry and then reflect on what they have done. Much confusion continues to exist about the differences between *doing* inquiry and knowledge *about* inquiry. Consequently, the NRC published an addendum to the NSES specifically about inquiry (NRC, 2000).

The goals for school science specified in the *NSES* are to educate students that are able to:
(i)   use scientific principles and processes appropriately in making personal decisions
(ii)  experience the richness and excitement of knowing about and understanding the natural world
(iii) increase their economic productivity, and
(iv)  engage intelligently in public discourse and debate about matters of scientific and technological concern.

The *NSES* is based on four basic principles (decreased from seven in the 1994 draft) (table 1).

1. Science is for all students.
2. Learning science is an active process.
3. School science reflects the intellectual and cultural traditions that characterize the practice of contemporary science.
4. Improving science education is part of systemic education reform.

Table 1:    Four principles of the National Science Education Standards (1996)

Six sets of standards are delineated in the *NSES* and comprise the majority of the published document: Science Teaching standards, Standards for Professional Development, Assessment in Science Education, Science Content Standards, Science Education Program Standards, and Science Education System Standards.

School systems across the nation, as well as professional organizations, have recently focused more on the *NSES* as a reference point rather than the others. Consequently, subsequent discussion on the implications of reform for teaching and learning will use the *NSES* as a reference point.

The *standards for the teaching* of science clearly outline how instruction should be revised so that it models scientific inquiry. In particular, these standards elaborate on how teachers should design their lessons so that students are placed in situations that require them to collect or analyze data and arrive at inferences or conclusions concerning the meaning of the data. There is a strong emphasis on student-centered instruction with the ideal being situations in which students develop questions of interest, designs to answer the questions and then carry out the investigation.

Interestingly, the *standards for professional development* parallel the standards for teaching. That is, the teacher is also viewed as a learner who enters every learning situation (in this case professional development) with background knowledge and predispositions. As a consequence, the professional development standards move away from a "one size fits all" mentality as well as the artificial distinction between pre-service and in-service teachers.

The *standards for assessment* clearly recognize that students represent what they have learned in as diverse ways as they are known to have learned. The standards also recognize that the types of in-depth knowledge stressed in the content standards are not easily assessed, in general, by traditional paper and pencil tests. Consequently, these standards stress the use of a variety of assessment techniques such as performance tasks, portfolios, and samples of thought in addition to the traditional methods.

The *content standards* really do not differ much from other lists of traditional content, except that an effort to focus more on overarching themes is evident. Perhaps the most noticeable feature of the content standards is the emphasis on nature of science and inquiry (doing as well as knowing). The doing of inquiry is not new to science teachers. We have had students collect data, make measurements, draw inferences, etc. for many years. However, the standards also stress that students know *about* inquiry. This involves learning outcomes such as: there is no single scientific method, all science does not necessarily involve an experiment, and that different scientists may come to different conclusions even though they completed the same procedures.

Although all the NSES standards are used in various aspects of science education and teaching, classroom teachers rely on the Science Content Standards section on a daily basis for instruction.

The content standards consist of seven topical areas that are organized into K-4, 5-8, and 9–12 grade levels. These seven areas (which are not listed in any order of importance) are presented in table 2.

- Science as Inquiry
- Physical Science
- Life Science
- Earth and Space Science
- Science and Technology
- Science in Personal and Social Perspectives
- History and Nature of Science

Table 2: *NSES* Content Science Standards Strands

The specific outcomes related to each topical area are organized into a logical and developmentally appropriate sequence with increasing complexity as one moves to higher grade levels. For example, within Life Science, the scope and sequence of topics appears as follows:

**K-4**
- Characteristics of Organisms
- Life Cycles of Organisms
- Organisms and Environment

**5–8**
- Structure and Function in Living Systems
- Reproduction and Heredity
- Regulation and Behavior
- Populations and Ecosystems
- Diversity and Adaptation of Organisms

## 9–12 The Cell

• Molecular Basis of Heredity
• Biological Evolution
• Interdependence of Organisms
• Matter, Energy, and Organization in Living Systems
• Behavior of Organisms

The specific standards for Life Science in grades 9–12 are provided here as an example of how the topics listed in the scope and sequence are eventually manifest into outcomes for students:

*Life Science*

### CONTENT STANDARD C: As a result of their activities in grades 9–12, all students should develop understanding of

• The cell
• Molecular basis of heredity
• Biological evolution
• Interdependence of organisms
• Matter, energy, and organization in living systems
• Behavior of organisms

### GUIDE TO THE CONTENT STANDARD
Fundamental concepts and principles that underlie this standard include

### *THE CELL*

• Cells have particular structures that underlie their functions. Every cell is surrounded by a membrane that separates it from the outside world. Inside the cell is a concentrated mixture of thousands of different molecules which form a variety of specialized structures that carry out such cell functions as energy production, transport of molecules, waste disposal, synthesis of new molecules, and the storage of genetic material.

• Most cell functions involve chemical reactions. Food molecules taken into cells react to provide the chemical constituents needed to synthesize other molecules. Both breakdown and synthesis are made possible by a large set of protein catalysts, called enzymes. The breakdown of some of the food molecules enables the cell to store energy in specific chemicals that are used to carry out the many functions of the cell.

• Cells store and use information to guide their functions. The genetic information stored in DNA is used to direct the synthesis of the thousands of proteins that each cell requires.

• Cell functions are regulated. Regulation occurs both through changes in the activity of the functions performed by proteins and through the selective expression of individual genes. This regulation allows cells to respond to their environment and to control and coordinate cell growth and division.

• Plant cells contain chloroplasts, the site of photosynthesis. Plants and many microorganisms use solar energy to combine molecules of carbon dioxide and water into complex, energy rich organic compounds and release oxygen to the environment. This process of photosynthesis provides a vital connection between the sun and the energy needs of living systems.

• Cells can differentiate, and complex multicellular organisms are formed as a highly organized arrangement of differentiated cells. In the development of these multicellular organisms, the progeny from a single cell form an embryo in which the cells multiply and differentiate to form the many specialized cells, tissues and organs that comprise the final organism. This differentiation is regulated through the expression of different genes.

### THE MOLECULAR BASIS OF HEREDITY

• In all organisms, the instructions for specifying the characteristics of the organism are carried in DNA, a large polymer formed from subunits of four kinds (A, G, C, and T). The chemical and structural properties of DNA explain how the genetic information that underlies heredity is both encoded in genes (as a string of molecular "letters") and replicated (by a templating mechanism). Each DNA molecule in a cell forms a single chromosome.

• Most of the cells in a human contain two copies of each of 22 different chromosomes. In addition, there is a pair of chromosomes that determines sex: a female contains two X chromosomes and a male contains one X and one Y chromosome. Transmission of genetic information to offspring occurs through egg and sperm cells that contain only one representative from each chromosome pair. An egg and a sperm unite to form a new individual. The fact that the human body is formed from cells that contain two copies of each chromosome – and therefore two copies of each gene – explains many features of human heredity, such as how variations that are hidden in one generation can be expressed in the next.

• Changes in DNA (mutations) occur spontaneously at low rates. Some of these changes make no difference to the organism, whereas others can change cells and organisms. Only mutations in germ cells can create the variation that changes an organism's offspring.

## BIOLOGICAL EVOLUTION

• Species evolve over time. Evolution is the consequence of the interactions of (1) the potential for a species to increase its numbers, (2) the genetic variability of offspring due to mutation and recombination of genes, (3) a finite supply of the resources required for life, and (4) the ensuing selection by the environment of those offspring better able to survive and leave offspring.

• The great diversity of organisms is the result of more than 3.5 billion years of evolution that has filled every available niche with life forms.

• Natural selection and its evolutionary consequences provide a scientific explanation for the fossil record of ancient life forms, as well as for the striking molecular similarities observed among the diverse species of living organisms.

• The millions of different species of plants, animals, and microorganisms that live on earth today are related by descent from common ancestors.

• Biological classifications are based on how organisms are related. Organisms are classified into a hierarchy of groups and subgroups based on similarities which reflect their evolutionary relationships. Species is the most fundamental unit of classification.

## THE INTERDEPENDENCE OF ORGANISMS

• The atoms and molecules on the earth cycle among the living and nonliving components of the biosphere.

• Energy flows through ecosystems in one direction, from photosynthetic organisms to herbivores to carnivores and decomposers.

• Organisms both cooperate and compete in ecosystems. The interrelationships and interdependencies of these organisms may generate ecosystems that are stable for hundreds or thousands of years.

• Living organisms have the capacity to produce populations of infinite size, but environments and resources are finite. This fundamental tension has profound effects on the interactions between organisms.

• Human beings live within the world's ecosystems. Increasingly, humans modify ecosystems as a result of population growth, technology, and consumption. Human destruction of habitats through direct harvesting, pollution, atmospheric changes, and other factors is threatening current global stability, and if not addressed, ecosystems will be irreversibly affected.

## MATTER, ENERGY, AND ORGANIZATION IN LIVING SYSTEMS

• All matter tends toward more disorganized states. Living systems require a continuous input of energy to maintain their chemical and physical organizations. With death, and the cessation of energy input, living systems rapidly disintegrate.

• The energy for life primarily derives from the sun. Plants capture energy by absorbing light and using it to form strong (covalent) chemical bonds between the atoms of carbon-containing (organic) molecules. These molecules can be used to assemble larger molecules with biological activity (including proteins, DNA, sugars, and fats). In addition, the energy stored in bonds between the atoms (chemical energy) can be used as sources of energy for life processes.

• The chemical bonds of food molecules contain energy. Energy is released when the bonds of food molecules are broken and new compounds with lower energy bonds are formed. Cells usually store this energy temporarily in phosphate bonds of a small high-energy compound called ATP.

• The complexity and organization of organisms accommodates the need for obtaining, transforming, transporting, releasing, and eliminating the matter and energy used to sustain the organism.

• The distribution and abundance of organisms and populations in ecosystems are limited by the availability of matter and energy and the ability of the ecosystem to recycle materials.

• As matter and energy flows through different levels of organization of living systems – cells, organs, organisms, communities – and between living systems and the physical environment, chemical elements are recombined in different ways. Each recombination results in storage and dissipation of energy into the environment as heat. Matter and energy are conserved in each change.

## THE BEHAVIOR OF ORGANISMS

• Multicellular animals have nervous systems that generate behavior. Nervous systems are formed from specialized cells that conduct signals rapidly through the long cell extensions that make up nerves. The nerve cells communicate with each other by secreting specific excitatory and inhibitory molecules. In sense organs, specialized cells detect light, sound, and specific chemicals and enable animals to monitor what is going on in the world around them.

• Organisms have behavioral responses to internal changes and to external stimuli. Responses to external stimuli can result from interactions with the organism's own species and others, as well as environmental changes; these responses either can be innate or learned. The broad patterns of behavior exhibited by animals have evolved to ensure reproductive success. Animals often live in unpredictable environments, and so their behavior must be flexible enough to deal with uncertainty and change. Plants also respond to stimuli.

• Like other aspects of an organism's biology, behaviors have evolved through natural selection. Behaviors often have an adaptive logic when viewed in terms of evolutionary principles.

• Behavioral biology has implications for humans, as it provides links to psychology, sociology, and anthropology.

Although most individuals focus on subject matter when considering *NSES*, it is important to remember that subject matter outcomes represent only one portion of the *NSES*. More detailed information about the National Science Education Standards can be found at the National Research Council (NRC) website.[1]

The *NSES* is very clear in stating that the standards (especially the content standards) are *not* meant to be a curriculum. Different states and school systems reserve the right to define their own curriculum inclusions so that school offerings can be customized to local needs and interests. So, for example, states like Illinois have chosen to place less emphasis on marine environments than Oregon, whereas Oregon places more emphasis on volcanoes than Illinois. In Nevada, there is a stress in state standards on mining that is not evident in the standards of Illinois or Oregon. The message is clear, the NSES content standards are a framework from which to design curriculum, but also allows flexibility in the specific content emphasized from one state to another.

The *standards on science programs and systems* are designed to equip teachers and administrators with the rationale for reform and the system and program needs to accomplish the visions of the NSES. The overall message is that science education reform is not the responsibility of one group of individuals, but rather the result of a joint effort by numerous constituencies in the school and community. In order to accomplish reform, there needs to be a common vision from teacher, to administrator, to community, and the necessary resources must be provided. If we want teaching and learning to be inquiry-oriented, the *NSES* states, then teachers have to value inquiry, appropriate professional development must be provided, assessment must be reorganized, and administrators must value inquiry and help provide the support teachers need to make the shift to inquiry instruction.

For better or worse, the United States does not have a centralized educational system. The goals, curriculum, and focus of educational systems are left to the discretion of individual states (analogous to provinces and counties in other countries). In addition, individual cities and local school districts maintain some freedom in placing variations on what is specified at state level. Consequently, with respect to standards, there are no

---

1  http://www.nap.edu/readingroom/books/nses/html/

national standards in science or any other discipline. This context has a significant impact on how standards are viewed and assessed in the U.S. Although none of the reform documents can claim to be mandated national standards, most states and school districts follow some subset of what is portrayed in the aforementioned documents.

As a consequence of the local control that characterizes the U.S. educational system, the two primary reform documents (i.e., *Benchmarks* and *NSES*) are adamant in their claim that the 'standards' each provides should not be construed as a national curriculum, just a set of goals and guidelines. AAAS and the NSES both clearly state that they provide no direction on how standards are to be reached. Hence, they each claim not to be a curriculum. However, it is just as clear that many of the standards presented (e.g., those related to inquiry) have significant implications for instruction. In the end, to what degree the two reform documents constitute an advocated curriculum is based on how one views the intimacy of the relationship between curriculum and instruction.

Finally, it is important to note that there are slight differences between *Benchmarks* and *NSES* for both subject matter and grade level categories that are not important to this discussion. Probably of most importance is that scientific inquiry is viewed as subject matter by both reform documents and both reform documents emphasize students' understandings ABOUT inquiry in addition to the *NSES* more extensive emphasis than *Benchmarks'* on the more traditional DOING of inquiry. Overall, one distinguishing characteristic of standards in the U.S. is that emphasis is placed on performance as well as knowledge. It is not assumed that if a student can do something, he/she has an understanding of what he/she has done. Again, although the standards statements are quite specific most of the time, neither carries any national mandate. This situation has a significant impact on how they are perceived by states, school administrators, and teachers and how they are assessed.

## How can science standards be assessed and what is the purpose of assessment?

There is nothing magical about the assessment of science standards, if the standards are well-stated. In short, functional standards are those that are quite clear about what is expected in terms of student knowledge and abilities. In the U.S., the *Benchmarks* are more consistently written in a form that has clear indications for assessment than the *NSES*. Regardless, the primary problem that exists with the assessment of science standards is that they typically focus on higher level thinking skills and abilities in addition to the more common lower level knowledge. The problem here is not with the assessment of standards, per se, but the observation that assessment approaches in science have not kept pace with the currently stated goals of science education. That is, most large-scale assessments still focus on lower level knowledge. On the one hand, those who develop assessments are not as skilled in developing assessments for higher level thinking. On the other, there is often a concern that variability in resources may give some schools and districts an advantage in terms of meeting the outcomes stated in current standards. This concern inevitably leads to an assessment that focuses on the lowest common denominator, an assessment that does not adequately get at the intent of current standards in science.

That said, the science standards in the U.S. could be validly assessed using a variety of traditional tests, divergent assessments and performance tasks. In reality, what is stated in science standards present nothing unique in terms of assessment, just a challenge to the way we typically assess student learning. Still, the reason for developing standards does have a clear impact on the development and approach to assessment tools. Although the U.S. does not have a national curriculum or national testing, the development of standards was meant to serve as a guide for the improvement of science teaching and learning across all grade levels. Consequently, there is always some concern that assessments be fairly consistent (standardization is an ideal, but not a necessity) from one location to another. This consistency is not much of a problem (save the concern about variability of resources) with respect to "traditional" subject matter, but is a significant concern in areas related to higher level thinking and performance skills such as those related to scientific inquiry. Assessment of higher level thinking and scientific inquiry involves approaches that are divergent and difficult to score. Scoring rubrics need to be agreed upon and then those doing the scoring must be "trained" to a level of acceptable consistency. For example, the following is a scoring rubric developed in the state of Oregon to assess fifth grade students' ability to do scientific inquiry:

| | 5<sup>TH</sup> Grade<br>**Framing the Investigation (F)**<br>Use observations/concepts to formulate and express scientific questions/ hypotheses to frame investigations. |
|---|---|
| 6 | a) Explains the origin of the question and/or hypothesis based on background, which is relevant to the investigation.<br>b) Expresses a clear question and/or hypothesis with advanced support for thinking.<br>c) Formulates or reframes a question and/or hypothesis which can be answered or tested using data and provides focus for a scientific investigation. |
| 5 | a) Links background to the question and/or hypothesis.<br>b) Expresses a clear question and/or hypothesis with detailed support for thinking.<br>c) Formulates or reframes a question and/or hypothesis which can be answers or tested using data gathered in a scientific investigation. |
| 4 | d) Provides some support or background (prior knowledge, preliminary observations, or personal interest and experience), which is relevant to the investigation.<br>e) Expresses a question and/or hypothesis with some support for thinking.<br>f) Formulates or reframes a question and/or hypothesis which can be explored using data in a simple scientific investigation. |
| 3 | d) Provides a background, which is either irrelevant or missing.<br>e) Expresses a question and/or hypothesis, which is not supported.<br>f) Formulates or reframes a question and/or hypothesis which provides limited opportunity for data collection. |
| 2 | g) Not applicable.<br>h) Expresses a question and/or hypothesis, which is not understandable.<br>i) Formulates or reframes a question and/or hypothesis which cannot be explored through a simple scientific investigation. |
| 1 | g) Not applicable.<br>h) Does not express the purpose of the investigation as either a question or a hypothesis.<br>i) Not applicable (see q). |

Once developed, extensive professional development was provided by the state to 'train' teachers in the use of the scoring rubric. That is, teachers were "trained" by having them score similar pieces of students' work so that different teachers would give the same score using the scoring rubric independently. The goal, of course, was to insure that teachers throughout the state would be scoring students work on scientific inquiry consistently regardless of school, district, or location. Consistency in scoring

| | **5ᵀᴴ Grade**<br>**Designing the Investigation (D)**<br>Describes designs for scientific investigations to provide data which address/explain questions/hypotheses. |
|---|---|
| 6 | j) Records logical procedures with an obvious connection to the student's scientific knowledge. (Teacher guidance in safety and ethics is acceptable.)<br>k) Communicates an organized design and detailed procedures.<br>l) Presents a practical design appropriate for answering the question or testing the hypothesis with evidence of recognition of some important variables. |
| 5 | j) Records logical procedures, which imply a connection to student's scientific knowledge. (Teacher guidance in safety and ethics is acceptable.)<br>k) Communicates a general plan including some detailed procedures.<br>l) Presents a practical design for an investigation, which addresses the question or hypothesis and attempts to provide a fair test. |
| 4 | m) Records logical procedures with only minor flaws. (Teacher guidance in safety and ethics is acceptable.)<br>n) Communicates a summary of a plan and some procedures, but generally lacks detail.<br>o) Presents a practical plan for an investigation, which substantially addresses the question or hypothesis. |
| 3 | m) Records generally logical procedures having flaws. (Teacher guidance in safety and ethics is acceptable.)<br>n) Communicates an incomplete summary of a plan, with few procedures.<br>o) Presents a practical plan related to the topic, which minimally addresses the question or hypothesis. |
| 2 | p) Records, which are significantly flawed. (Teacher guidance in safety and ethics is acceptable.)<br>q) Communicates an incomplete summary of a plan, which is difficult to follow.<br>r) Presents a plan somewhat related to the topic which may not address the question or hypothesis. |
| 1 | p) Records procedures, which are wholly inappropriate.<br>q) Communicates a plan or procedure, which cannot be followed.<br>r) Presents a plan which is impractical or unrelated to the topic. |

was considered essential within schools, school districts, states, or nationally. This consistency in scoring is also considered essential regardless of the level of assessment scope. Several states in the U.S. (similar to Oregon) have taken on this task with respect to scientific inquiry (mostly the doing of inquiry as opposed to knowledge about inquiry) with only moderate success. In addition, during the process of developing consistency standards were typically revised to assist the process, resulting in student

| | **5ᵀᴴ Grade**<br>**Collecting and Presenting Data (C)**<br>Conduct procedures to collect, organize, and display data. |
|---|---|
| **6** | s) Records accurate data and/or observations consistent with complex procedures.<br>t) Designs a data table (or other format) for observation and/or measurements, which is efficient, organized, and uses appropriate units.<br>u) Transforms data into a student-selected format(s) which is most appropriate to clarify results. |
| **5** | s) Records accurate data and/or observations completely consistent with the planned procedure.<br>t) Designs a data table (or other format) for observations and/or measurements, which is organized and uses appropriate units.<br>u) Transforms data into a student-selected format(s) which is complete and useful. |
| **4** | v) Records reasonable and sufficient data and/or observations generally consistent with the planned procedure.<br>w) Designs a data table (or other format) useful for recording measurements or observations.<br>x) Transforms data (e.g., graphs, averages, percentages, diagrams, tables) with teacher support and with minimal errors. |
| **3** | v) Records reasonable data and/or observations consistent with the planned procedure, with some obvious errors.<br>w) Designs a data table (or other format), which is inadequate for recording measurements of observations.<br>x) Does not transform data into a teacher-recommended format. |
| **2** | y) Records insufficient data and/or observations inconsistent with the planned procedure.<br>z) Uses a teacher supplied data table with minimal errors.<br>aa) Not applicable. |
| **1** | y) Records data and/or observations unrelated to the planned procedure.<br>z) Does not correctly use a teacher supplied data table.<br>aa) Not applicable. |

outcomes that are at a lower level than initially intended. Quite simply, lower level knowledge and abilities are more easily assessed and agreed upon than the more ambitious outcomes specified in most science standards.

The desired goal of assessment of standards in the U.S. is to provide feedback on how well schools and the nation are doing with respect to higher expectations of its students. The goal of assessment is not to be punitive or to serve as a measure of teacher

| | 5TH Grade<br>Analyzing and Interpreting Results (A)<br>Analyze results to develop conclusions. |
|---|---|
| 6 | bb) Reports results and identifies simple relationships (e.g., connecting one variable to another).<br>cc) Explicitly uses results to address the question or hypothesis and illustrates simple relationships.<br>dd) Not applicable. |
| 5 | bb) Reports results accurately and identifies obvious patterns (e.g., noting a pattern of change for one variable).<br>cc) Explicitly uses results to address the question or hypothesis.<br>dd) Not applicable. |
| 4 | ee) Summarizes results accurately.<br>ff) Responds to the question or hypothesis with some support form results.<br>gg) Not applicable. |
| 3 | ee) Summarizes results incompletely or in a misleading way.<br>ff) Responds to the question or hypothesis without support from results.<br>gg) Not applicable. |
| 2 | hh) Summarizes results inaccurately.<br>ii) Provides a response(s) to the question or hypothesis, which is unrelated to the investigation.<br>jj) Not applicable. |
| 1 | hh) Omits results in summary.<br>ii) Does not respond to the question or hypothesis.<br>jj) Not applicable. |

and school success, but more formative in providing feedback for further revision of curriculum and instruction. Nevertheless, assessment in the U.S. inevitably is used to compare teachers and schools with each other to determine who is 'best.' Hence, there is a consistent concern for making assessments fair across different locations with different needs and resources. So, in the U.S. we are a bit schizophrenic in terms of our stated role for assessment and how assessments are typically used and viewed. Again, the problem here is not really with our ability to assess the current set of science standards as much as it is with how assessments are viewed and used.

Regardless of whether assessments of standards are used for formative or summative purposes, there is another problem when it comes to fairly assessing how schools or larger constituencies are doing with respect to meeting standards. Standards in science are written for specific grade levels and the standards for one grade level (or grade level category) assume that those standards for previous levels have been addressed and achieved. This has significant implications for assessment of the current science standards in the U.S. We have had numerous reforms and reform documents over the past century and few have accomplished what they have intended. The public and education community has become skeptical of educational reform and they have grown impatient in terms of finding out if the current innovation has had its desired impact. As expected we are now in the process of developing assessments of various types that will be used for students at various grade levels for both knowledge and performance outcomes. However, it seems that assessments used in high school (grades 9–12) will be inappropriate because there is an inherent assumption that students in grades 9–12 have had reform-based instruction in grades K-8. It may be that we need to have assessment approaches gradually integrated in a staggered manner so that students are not inappropriately held accountable for knowledge and abilities that have not been addressed in schools over a long and consistent manner through several years. Not considering the foundational knowledge and skills provided by schooling in previous grades may doom any large scale assessment into concluding that the reforms, as specified in standards, have not been successful.

## Standards and their side-effects

The side-effects of the standards and their assessment has been a perennial problem in the U.S. Prior to the onset of the standards era, several states (e.g., New York, California) have had state-wide examinations in certain subject matter areas (e.g., science, mathematics, English, social studies). In such cases, teachers have been directly or indirectly evaluated based on their students' scores on such tests. Consequently, teachers have made a concerted effort to teach to the test. Indeed, several publishers in the U.S. put out review books that contain subject matter tutorials and old state exams for students' review. Unfortunately, teachers use these books to tutor students for the test several months in advance, at the expense of time that should be spent on the actual curriculum. As a former student in the New York City school system, I am aware that many teachers begin reviewing for the June statewide examinations (i.e., Regents Examination) shortly after the first of the year. There is a fear in most states that assessments of standards in science education will give rise to the same practice of teaching to the test.

In response to teachers expending too much instructional time on the Regents Examinations, the examination was revised to include several sections with optional sections. That is, students could choose an area within a subject matter (e.g., ecology or biochemistry on the biology exam) and answer those questions instead of all students answering all of the same questions. Unfortunately, the result of this change simply caused teachers to focus on their reviews on certain areas at the expense of others. In short, you could determine what teachers groups of students had by the optional area they chose on the examination.

Oregon has attempted to alleviate fears of teaching directly to the test by taking the position that the statewide examinations will only include a subset of the official standards. Thus, teachers are now left guessing what will actually be assessed relative to the official standards. Still, this really does not solve the problem. Most teachers continue to teach to the full set of standards hoping to capture whatever subset is chosen. There is, of course, an alternative way to view the fear of "teaching to the test." There is more than a significant number of individuals that would argue that what we should be doing IS teaching to the test as long as what is being tested is important knowledge and skills and that the teaching consists of more than just having students practice examination questions. In short, there is the view that the standards comprise the learning objectives for students and these objectives should guide instruction and assessment.

What is easily assessable remains a problem, as discussed in the previous section. Large scale, mass administered, assessments eventually turn into examinations that focus on lower level knowledge as opposed to higher level knowledge and skills. Quite simply, lower level skills and knowledge are more easily assessed, as they involve less debate and ambiguity. The fear, of course, is that the movement to assess standards will result in assessments that focus on lower level knowledge as opposed to the more highly desired higher level thinking skills and abilities. A good example in the U.S. comes from portfolio assessments. About a decade ago many states decided that portfolio assessment provided more valid measures of what students have learned than the more traditional paper and pencil test. The logic involved the idea that since students learn in diverse ways, they also exhibit what they have learned in diverse ways. The portfolio was supposed to provide students with the freedom to document what they have learned in whatever way they preferred. Unfortunately, there was an immediate need in states to somehow standardize across locations what was included in a portfolio and how it should be organized. There is always an automatic reflex when it comes to assessment to standardize. Otherwise, how could we possibly compare student performance from one location to another? The result of attempts to standardize has resulted in rather inflexible guidelines for the scoring of portfolios. Hence, the reason why portfolio assessment was adopted was undermined by our views on what makes a valid large-scale assessment.

It seems that there will always be a tension between the desire to have large-scale assessments (especially with respect to national standards) and the desire to have assessments that are authentic and relevant to students in particular locations. This tension has not been solved in the U.S. and the dominant tendency is to move toward standardized assessments that inevitably become assessments of lower level knowledge.

# Standards implementation and centralized assessment

As discussed earlier, the U.S. does not have a nationally centralized educational system. The curriculum and the assessment of the curriculum goals/objectives are left up to the prerogative of individual states and local school districts. Because there is no national curriculum there can also be no nationally centralized assessment of standards. Indeed, the standards are not "national standards" as they may be in other countries (e.g., Taiwan). However, this situation does not prevent school districts and states from having their own "centralized" assessments. So, centralization can and does exist in the U.S., but at a lower level than what we might find in other countries.

Under the Bush administration, the U.S. has passed the legislation known as 'No Child Left Behind'. This legislation is a comprehensive attempt to improve the quality of education and it focuses on teacher qualifications and student learning. One aspect of this legislation significantly emphasizes educational accountability and attention to standards. As a consequence, the legislation requires that all states have statewide assessments in various subject areas, so the number of statewide assessments is increasing significantly according to specified timelines. Again, these assessments are at the state level as opposed to the national level. New York and California have had statewide assessments for many years and are, therefore, the most prominent when it comes to discussions of 'centralized' state level assessments. If instructional goals/objectives are not assessed, students quickly learn/assume that they are not important. There is much research to show that this is commonly true at the classroom level. Teachers have determined this on their own over the years as well. With respect to standardized assessments, the evidence in the U.S. indicates that teachers will spend more instructional time on those topics and ideas that are assessed as opposed to those that are not. This situation is typically derived from teachers' knowledge or assumptions that they will be evaluated by administrators, based on their students' performance. Teachers really cannot be blamed for this occurrence, as it makes perfect sense to focus your attention on student learning in the areas that will comprise your teaching evaluation. There is little doubt that such would be the case for any "centralized" assessment of science standards.

The current approach in the U.S. to dealing with the assessment of standards follows two distinct tracks. Various states are developing assessments to comply with federal legislation. Unless assessments are developed, states will lose their federal educational funding. The assessments that are being developed are keyed to state level subject matter standards, and these are usually a subset of the standards delineated in *Benchmarks* or *NSES*. There is also diversity in whether the assessments are totally 'traditional' paper and pencil or combinations of 'traditional' test items and divergent assessment items. This approach can be considered 'softer' than rigidly centralized assessments of standards as they allow for attention to localized needs and resources instead of taking a 'one size fits all' approach.

At the national level, the National Academy of Science (as well as several other organizations) is developing *Systems for State Science Assessment* (NRC, 2006) in support of student learning. These systems provide guidelines for the characteristics of assessment systems. So, although there will be no national test in the U.S., it is hoped that the state level assessments that are developed will possess some common characteristics related to what we have learned about effective and valid assessment of student learning. Again, there can be no specified content for assessments at the national level, but there are attempts to guide the development of local assessments by national organizations. This approach to assessment is, of course, quite similar to the guidance that the *NSES* and Benchmarks are trying to provide for curriculum and instruction.

Overall, having a version of 'centralized' assessment that is more localized than the national level, may be a good alternative to the more familiar national test and national curriculum. The more localized approach allows for the accommodation of some specific local concerns and interests that national approaches cannot accommodate. It is not clear if the difference in approaches is substantive or just psychologically more accepted. And, of course, I am speaking from a U.S. culture that has never accepted the idea of a national curriculum or national assessment.

It appears that the assessment of standards will have unavoidable problems. There will always be concerns with 'teaching to the test' or the concern that an standardized or national assessment will reduce the standards from higher level innovation to 'lower level' student outcomes out of necessity. In some sense, there is a problem of global perception. As long as the standards, regardless of country, are viewed as a comprehensive set of student outcomes to be assessed, problems will persist. Perhaps a perspective taken from other professions could provide some guidance.

Medical doctors, lawyers, engineers, and teachers typically must be certified or licensed by some authoritative organization, whether it be a professional society or a branch of government. In each case, there are certain core knowledge, abilities, and beliefs that an individual must possess to be 'officially' licensed/certified. However, it is also well known that the education provided during one's education in a professional field is not equal across educational institutions. There are some medical schools that everyone knows are better than other schools, and yet they both produce licensed doctors. The same is true of law schools and schools of teacher education. My brother-in-law graduated from a very prestigious law school in the U.S. All lawyers in the U.S. need to pass a standardized exam to become licensed. I asked him what made his school better than other schools with similar pass rates on the certifying exam. His response was that some schools teach you how to pass the exam while others teach you how to be a lawyer. Clearly this view assumes there is some discrepancy between what one needs to know to pass the examination and what there is to know to be an effective lawyer. Is there something to be learned here?

At present, standards are viewed as a comprehensive set of knowledge and abilities. Hence, the outcomes specified are viewed as equivalent to what is tested on national tests. We have already seen the problems with this perception. What if nations considered national tests that assessed the standards, but also assessed knowledge beyond the standards? In short, the standards would be viewed as minimal core knowledge (not in a negative sense) for all students, but assessments would recognize that there are knowledge and skills that go beyond the standards. In short, the national or state examinations would assess more than the national standards. Such a system would help ameliorate some of the unavoidable problems associated with assessment, but would still allow the existence of standards, and their assessment, to provide valuable educational guidance. Of course, this 'solution' is untenable without additional changes in perception. The public, policy makers, and education community would have to adopt the view that meeting minimal/core standards is acceptable, as opposed to being a weakness. This would allow schools and school systems to feel good about what their students achieved, while it would allow those going beyond the standards to document what their students know and are able to do. How to accomplish this change in perception is difficult and I do not claim to have an answer. However, this modest proposal seems to be a potential solution to the problems that we all experience when standards are viewed and assessed as a comprehensive set of knowledge and abilities.

## Lessons learned, lessons lost

Of course, hindsight is always 20/20. Nevertheless, it is useful to imagine how things could have been done differently, for better or for worse. Such reflections can serve to inform others deciding to pursue the standards approach to improving science teaching and learning. In the U.S., the stated standards have always had to straddle the fence in terms of specificity. On the one hand, the U.S. does not have any mandated national standards and so only reform documents that afford some flexibility would be received in a positive way. All states would want to reserve their mandated right to implement curriculum and instructional approaches that seem most appropriate for their local needs. On the other hand, in an effort to maintain flexibility, many argue that the U.S. standards are stated so vaguely that they provide little guidance and are relatively useless in providing guidance to individual localities or any potential for promoting any common progress in the areas of teaching and learning of science. After all, districts and states can interpret the current standards in ways that justify most of the status quo. If the U.S. is truly concerned with promoting some level of unified change, in a climate with no national curriculum, standards with more specificity are needed. Certainly, localities have the legal right to choose or not to follow the stated standards, but the standards should have been written more specifically to targeted student outcomes.

Although the *NSES* have attempted to provide a pathway for the improvement of science teaching and learning that was derived from the perspective of policy makers as well as classroom teachers (i.e., there was extensive involvement of classroom teachers in the development of the standards), a more concerted effort was needed to 'sell' the idea of standards to the educational community. That is, most classroom teachers viewed the *NSES* as another set of prescriptions dictated from 'above.' This is probably an unavoidable situation because all classroom teachers can never be involved in the development of any reform. However, more effort was needed, in advance, to provide the rationale for needing standards and the value they would serve. The U.S. has a history of failed educational reforms and this history should have been used to inform the latest vision of educational reform. Teachers needed to be convinced, in advance, that standards were needed and that these standards represented something different than the past. The powers that be needed to convince teachers that their students' learning would be improved as a result of the *NSES* before the document was officially published.

Related to this last issue is the issue of professional development. Widespread instructional and educational change is difficult at best, but hopeless without extensive and continuous professional development. Again, history tells us that teachers are resistant to change and change requires extensive professional development that is continuous over a significant amount of time. Nevertheless, the *NSES* was introduced without the finances to provide the support teachers need to develop awareness of the standards, valuing of the standards, and action based on the standards. More than a trivial number of teachers in the U.S. do not know the *NSES* and *Project 2061* are different reform documents and a significant number have the perspective that the standards, whichever ones, will disappear in the same fashion as other reforms in the history of U.S. science education. Extensive professional development is needed if teachers are expected to value visions of educational change and make the effort needed to achieve change. In addition, teachers need extensive support in changing their instructional practices. Simply knowing what changes are expected is not enough. Teachers need support in making changes and they need to be provided with concrete examples of what instructional change looks like in their own classrooms. Support needs to consist of more than a multiple week workshop with minimal follow-up. Support should provide teachers with monthly face-to-face contact with professional developers and such support should continue throughout the academic year. Naturally, such professional development is expensive, but extensive educational change is expensive. In retrospect, the implementation of standards-based change was compromised by the lack of attention to professional development.

## A few final comments

It should be clear from the preceding pages that the development and assessment of standards is no simple matter. In the U.S. the lack of any centralized educational system makes the development and use of standards even more complicated. Many validly question the value of standards because of the many problems they can create. However, as the title of my paper conjectures, standards are probably a necessary evil.

The word "evil" is probably too strong, but it is meant to convey the negatives that standards development and assessment may bring. However, in my opinion, standards are necessary because they help to provide guidance to any educational system, whether centralized or not, in terms of both instruction and assessment. There is old adage that states, "If you don't know where you are going, how will you know when you get there?" Although it is used when speaking about instructional goals and objectives, the statement has some relevance to the consideration of standards. Whether one is considering a nation or a more localized school system, goals are needed to provide direction and to serve as "benchmarks" by which the system can determine how well it is moving toward the accomplishments of its goals. Standards can serve this same purpose, while also allowing for the flexibility needed within a dynamic educational system. Of course, standards are not a perfect solution to all of our educational problems, but it seems that the alternative of having no standards is far less desirable. Yes, they are a necessary evil. Still, the jury is still out in terms of whether the use of standards has had a positive impact on teaching and learning of science in the U.S. Certainly, the nature of discourse about teaching and learning has changed. However, changes in classroom practice and in student learning are entirely different matter.

## References

AAAS (American Association for the Advancement of Science) (1993) *Benchmarks for science literacy*. New York: Oxford University Press.

NCTM (National Council of Teachers of Mathematics) (1989) *Curriculum standards for school mathematics*. Reston, VA: NCTM.

NRC (National Research Council) (1996) *National science education standards*. Washington, DC: National Academy Press.

NRC (National Research Council) (2000) Inquiry and the *national science education standards*. Washington, DC: National Academy Press.

NRC (National Research Council) (2006) *Systems for state science assessment*. Washington, DC: National Academy Press.

NSTA (National Science Teachers Association) (1992) *Scope, sequence, and coordination of secondary school science: Relevant research*. Washington, DC: Author.

NSTA (National Science Teachers Association) (1995) *A high school framework for national science education standards*. Washington, DC: Author.

NSTA (National Science Teachers Association) (1998) (http://www.nsta.org/positionstatement&psid=24

Pearsall, M. (Ed.) (1993) *Scope, sequence, and coordination of secondary school science: The Content Core.* Washington, DC: National Science Teachers Association.

Rutherford, F. J. and Ahlgren, A. (1989) *Science for all Americans.* New York: Oxford University Press.

Texley, J. and Wild, A. (2004) *NSTA Pathways to the science standards. 2nd Ed.,* Arlington, VA.: NSTA Press.

## Notes on selected references

American Association for the Advancement of Science (1993) *Benchmarks for science literacy.* New York: Oxford University Press.

A comprehensive listing of what students should know and be able to do covering grades K-12. This document is derived from *Science for all Americans* and it presents outcomes in a concrete form that is easily understood by educators.

National Research Council (1996) *National science education standards.* Washington, DC: National Academy Press.

Specifies what students should know and be able to do spanning grades K-12. The document is also more comprehensive than most as it also presents standards for teaching, assessment, school systems, and school programs.

Rutherford, F. J., and Ahlgren, A. (1989) *Science for all Americans.* New York: Oxford University Press.

This text presents the original vision for reform in science education that lead to the development of specifications for student learning outcomes. An excellent source for the underlying rationale of current learning standards.

**Part C**

# A coda

# Chapter 19

# Standards: an international comparison

*Peter Nentwig* and *David Waddington*[*][#]

*Leibniz-Institut für die Pädagogik der Naturwissenschaften (IPN),
Olshausenstraße 62, 24098 Kiel, Germany*

[#]*Department of Chemistry, University of York, York YO10 5DD, UK*

This international symposium held in Germany in February 2006 had as its primary aim to make international experience with standards in science education available to the German public, since such standards had just recently been introduced to this country's school system. The symposium was generously funded by the German Research Foundation (DFG).

The work of the symposium, however, will be of interest to an international audience as it compares how standards in science education are dealt with in other countries – novices in the field as well as countries with a longer history of educational standards. In this chapter, the information that was given both in the chapters of this book and during discussions at the symposium is summarised, taking the questions that were used to structure the symposium as a guide.

## 1    Why set standards?

Standards have been and are being introduced into education systems of many countries for a variety of reasons. The major driving force where standards are just now being implemented seem to be the disappointing results these countries have obtained in international comparative studies. Politicians are alarmed when their nation's educational system appears to be less effective than was believed. National competitiveness is seen at risk in general, and in the area of science and technology in particular, when more and more students leave compulsory schooling with, as judged by the international comparisons, mediocre results and when fewer students are choosing a further education in these fields.

Other purposes of standards and the subsequent evaluation of how well they are attained are often stated to be: *To provide a mechanism for accountability* – teachers and schools are increasingly held responsible for the results of their work by students, parents and educational authorities. *To provide feedback* – students and even more so parents have a vital interest in knowing where they stand in comparison with potential competitors for a good start into a successful working life. Teachers and schools need to know if what they provide for students is sufficient, and educational authorities want to know how well the resources that are invested into the educational system are used. *To promote educational equality* – the setting of compulsory standards and the evaluation of their attainment are widely seen as a means to improve the outcome of the societal investment into the educational system. In some countries with either a federal state system (such as the US) or a highly differentiated school system (such as Germany), or both (such as Switzerland), the harmonization of education is a strong motivation to set standards in order to abolish disparities among states or systems. The success of students is often hampered by the social injustice from unequal chances, and common standards are meant to at least unify the core of the educational intentions *To improve teaching* – the enhancement of science teaching is seen as a necessity in many countries, and standards are introduced to provide teachers with a scope to improve their teaching.

Perhaps a simple overarching reason for their introduction is to set "explicit and defensible standards to guide improvements in student achievement and to measure and evaluate the effectiveness, efficiency and equity of schooling" (Hafner, 28).[1]

## 2    How are standards in science education defined?

### Terms used

Terms such as standards, curriculum, competencies and goals appear to be used differently in different countries. Indeed, some of the terms do not even appear in some languages. Thus in this section, their use during the symposium will be discussed in order to obtain a common ground for further discussion.

It may be easier first to go back to dictionary definitions, where a standard is defined as *an accepted or approved example of something against which others are judged or measured*, a curriculum as *a course of study*, a competence as the *ability to perform a task* and a goal as *the purpose towards which an endeavour is directed* (Collins English Dictionary, 2007).

These definitions fit in with the hierarchy outlined by Dubs in the subsequent chapter in which he develops the theme that standards must be seen as a consequence of defining the core curriculum followed by the competencies required. Thus only when the curriculum has been defined does one seek to define standards that in turn leads one to seek ways of assessing whether the standards have been reached. Indeed one might add that all this must be preceded by the delineation of the major national educational goals.

1  In this chapter, these references indicate the source of quotations in this book.

Now let us look in more depth at the ways the terms are used in the various accounts. Indeed, in most English speaking countries the term 'standards' is used to describe what is expected to be the result of teaching and learning efforts at school, or, in more precise words, "what students should know and be able to do in specified areas of learning at regular intervals throughout their schooling" (Hafner, 23). The word has also been adopted in many other countries even where it is not genuinely part of the native language.

Other terms are used as well for that same notion. Bryce clearly admits the semantic confusion in Scotland: "We have played about with various terms; objectives, outcomes, criteria (as in grade-related criteria), competences, standards (though that term is not usually equated to the others), endeavouring to get clarity; always falling short of complete behavioural specification" (Bryce, 257). In other countries, addressing the same concept, other terms are used. In Australia, 'frameworks' have been developed, while in Taiwan 'guidelines' "act as standards even though they are not called standards" (Chiu, 315).

In the Swedish national syllabi, the issue of standards is discussed in terms of 'learning goals', manifested as 'goals to aim at' and 'goals to attain', which equates to the definition of a goal as the *purpose towards which an endeavour is directed*, and Malléus writes, in turn, that in France, it is the 'programme officiel' that is, in effect, the arbiter of standards.

How, "what a pupil should know, understand, and be able to do in science" (Lavonen, 109) is defined, however, varies from country to country.

## *Standards or Curriculum*

Hafner agrees with Dubs when she writes that "Standards may be defined through the curriculum and/or through descriptions of student performance. … Ideally standards should be defined through both curriculum and descriptions of performance and there should be a high correlation between the defined standards in each of these areas" (Hafner, 26).

It is commonly claimed that 'the curriculum sets the standards' (Labudde, 287), again agreeing with the Dubs model. A distinction between them can, perhaps, best be made by looking at the locus of control. The dictionary definition for a curriculum which is given above, *a course of study*, defines what the learners are supposed to be confronted with in the teaching process, to a varying extent enriched by considerations as to why this confrontation should take place and how it might best be organized. "It is the program used by the school as a means of accomplishing its purposes" (Oliver, 1969). This describes the input into the teaching/learning process, and its control through a curriculum can be called 'input-control'. England defines a

National Curriculum, and statements therein are prefaced 'pupils should be taught'. Following Millar's distinction, this is the *intended* curriculum, and he describes mechanisms to safeguard its similarity with the *implemented* curriculum. Other countries follow comparable routes by prescribing in more or less detail what should be taught – the input is controlled by the curriculum, the 'guidelines', the 'Lehrplan'. The outcome of the teaching effort, however, is uncertain without the next stage of development, the use of standards.

Therefore, in spite of all the best intentions, the intended and even the implemented curriculum are not necessarily identical with its *attained* version. The latter is the output of the process, and in order to control this, several countries have resorted to a definition of standards, which constitutes a certain result of the teaching/learning process that has to be produced by the teacher, the school or the system. The means, by which this result can be attained, is then left open – and will most likely be described in a curriculum. Germany, among others, has followed this approach by defining standards in the sense of hurdles that learners have to take, leaving it to its federal states to provide a (core-)curriculum. This is, of course, counter to the model described above.

In some cases, as in some states of the US, a mixture of the two paradigms – input-control and output-control – can be observed, when a curriculum describes what is to be taught in school, but at the same time an established system of examinations implicitly defines what the outcome has to be. In England and Wales, the National Curriculum not only defines what is to be taught but there are explicit standards which are used to check the level which the student has reached.

## *Standards or Goals*

Goals are often used to describe rather general principles of education that schools are supposed to follow. In Denmark, for example, they are called 'common goals', which describe "national binding goals for the subject, written in general phrases" (Dolin, 75). "The *general aims* for biology, for example, are (in brief): 'Students must acquire knowledge about living organisms and the surrounding nature, the environment and health, and applications of biology – with emphasis on the understanding of connections'" (Dolin, 75).

In the US National Science Education Standards, goals for school science are outlined in rather broad terms such as "use scientific principles and processes appropriately in making personal decisions" (Lederman, 350). In Finland "the general and subject specific goals described in the national curricula are, from the point of view of legislation, standards (compared to law) and they are the guidelines municipalities and teachers have to follow. These goals describe what pupils are expected to learn in general and in each subject during their studies at comprehensive school" (Lavonen,

105). For the subject matter such a goal might be: "In grades 7 – 9 the pupils will learn in chemistry the physical and chemical concepts that describe the properties of substances and learn to apply those concepts" (Lavonen, 107).

## *General goals or specific goals*

In most cases there is a level below such general demands and expectations. The distinction is most explicitly made in Sweden, where two types of goals are defined:

"*Goals to aim for* express the direction the subject should take in terms of developing pupils' knowledge. They clarify the quality of knowledge that is essential in the subject. These goals are the main basis for planning teaching and do not set any limits to the pupils' acquisition of knowledge. Goals to attain define the minimum knowledge to be attained by all pupils in the fifth and ninth year of school. Goals to attain in the ninth year of school are the basis for assessing whether a pupil should receive the Pass grade" (Stroemdahl, 265).

Finland also states that "there are actually two kinds of standards in the Finnish curriculum", (Lavonen, 105) the above mentioned general aims and '*final-assessment criteria*', describing "outcomes, what pupils should understand and be able to do" (Lavonen, 106). These 'final-assessment criteria' and the Swedish 'goals to attain' can be seen as standards in the narrower, output-oriented sense of the term.

## *Content standards or performance standards*

Content standards are a widely spread way of describing what should be taught in school, most often assigning contents to age- or grade-levels. They are not necessarily but usually input-oriented, and they often are closely related to a curricular understanding of standards. "As regards the *intended* curriculum, 'standards' relate to the content and emphasis of the science programme" (Millar, 83). In Scotland, "at the heart of the arrangements document [in Physics] are 16 pages of content statements" (Bryce, 256).

Very explicit statements of content standards can be found in the US National Science Education Standards (NSES). Despite the uniform phrase for the content standards that "as a result of their activities … all students should develop …" (Lederman, 353), which suggests an output-orientation, they tend to "not differ much from other lists of traditional content, except that an effort to focus more on overarching themes is evident. Perhaps the most noticeable feature of the content standards is the emphasis on nature of science and inquiry (doing as well as knowing)" (Lederman, 351).

Performance standards, on the other hand, relate to the outcome of teaching and learning processes. They define, what students are expected to know or be able to do at a certain stage of their school career. Austria and Switzerland, influenced by the development in Germany, have decided to introduce performance – or attainment – standards. Performance standards only make sense, when their attainment is empirically assessed, or, as Lavonen puts it, "the need for real standards which would guide assessment … was recognised" (Lavonen, 106). The curriculum in Finland therefore describes final-assessment criteria (as performance standards). In New South Wales of Australia, "the descriptions of levels of achievement of learning are derived from the curriculum outcomes which are used to develop explicit statements of student performance or performance standards. … Performance standards are made more explicit by including performance descriptions" (Hafner, 37). In England and Wales, similarly, 'level descriptions' define what kind of performance is expected (Millar, 89).

Curricula often state what students are expected to know or be able to do. Without the assessment, these statements remain unproven expectations. Linked with an evaluation of the process outcomes, these expectations might be considered performance standards. The National Curriculum in England and Wales might be seen as an example: the attainment targets define in detail what the expected learning outcomes are. They are accompanied by a well-established assessment system that makes them true performance standards.

## *Standards as competences*

Bryce (in defining standards) suggests that the Scottish system is "always falling short of complete behavioural specification" (Bryce, 257) and this is echoed implicitly in the accounts concerned with other countries. Several countries have therefore resorted to breaking down expected student performance to competences. The term is used in slightly different ways. In Taiwan, for example, "the committee identified eight major components of scientific and technological literacy as core competences and then provided more detailed indicators for each component. … Each component contained competence indicators" (Chiu, 309). The competence indicators presented in the Taiwanese contribution show a strong emphasis on cognitive abilities of knowing and understanding.

In Portugal, using a concept of competence of French origin, there is "a National Curriculum (NC) whose standards are defined in the form of general and specific competences. … These competences include *knowledge* (substantive, procedural or methodological, epistemological), *reasoning, communication and attitudes*" (Galvao *et al.*, 240).

Another variation is used in Denmark, where "the traditional content demands (such as knowing the laws of Newton) and the traditional *bildung* aspect have been supplemented with a set of *competence* goals, recommending the formulation of goals for the science subjects in terms of competences. ... Four science competences are described:

• An empirical competence: The ability to observe, describe, experiment, measure, etc.

• A representation competence: The ability to represent the phenomenon in different ways (graphs, figures, pictures, etc.) and to shift between the representations.

• A modelling competence: The ability to reduce complexity, determine causalities, build and use different kinds of models, etc.

• A perspective competence: The ability to put the science into perspective, to reflect on the role of science in society, to assess scientific knowledge in relation to other knowledge, etc. (very much a competence formulation of the *bildung aspect*)" (Dolin, 77).

In the German speaking countries the term goes back to Weinert (2001), who defines 'specialized cognitive competences' as "clusters of cognitive prerequisites that must be available for an individual to perform well in a particular content area" (p.47). Specialized cognitive competences require long-term learning, a broad experience, a deep understanding of the topic, and automatic action routines that must be controlled at a high level of awareness. According to Weinert, competences do not only include cognitive abilities but also the motivation and willingness to apply knowledge in different situations.

For German science education, following a framework for the development of national education standards (Klieme, 2003), four areas of competence have been determined: subject knowledge, epistemological/methodological, communicative and evaluative competence. As Austria and Switzerland are basing their standards on the same framework, their development is very similar.

In Scotland, the objectives/standards/criteria are stated under three broad headings (referred to as 'Outcomes'), which might also be seen as competences:

1. Demonstrate knowledge and understanding related to the content of the unit.

2. Solve problems related to the content of the unit.

3. Collect and analyse information related to [Higher Physics] obtained by experiment.

Where competences constitute the standards, they are more or less explicitly organized in two- or three-dimensional structures. In France, for example, "what is expected from the students is listed in three paragraphs, namely knowledge, abilities and attitudes" (Malléus, 130). The implicit dimensions are these three areas of competence and the subject domain. Similarly in Portugal, "these competences include *knowledge* (substantive, procedural or methodological, epistemological), *reasoning, communication and attitudes*" (Galvao *et al.*, 240), and again the specific subject domain would form the second dimension.

The English National Curriculum implicitly represents a three-dimensional concept: "A set of 'level descriptions' was added, providing thumbnail sketches of the **sort of performance** that might be expected of a student who was working at **each level** in a given **attainment target**" (Millar, 89). Next to 'sort of performance' (competence) and 'attainment target' (content domain), 'levels of attainment' form the third dimension.

The German standards for the science subjects explicitly use a *structure model* of competence, which is built of three structural elements:

1. *Areas of competence*: Expected abilities are structured by four categories: subject knowledge, application of epistemological and methodological knowledge, communication, and judgement.

2. *Basic concepts*: The content domain is organized by the description of basic concepts of a subject, e.g. the connection between matter and particle models, or the energy concept.

3. *Levels of competence*: Three levels are used as guidelines: reproduction, application, and transfer.

In the contribution of Schecker and Parchmann in this book, this model is visualized as a three-dimensional matrix.

In either case, these are static structural models. *Developmental models* describe assumptions about the growth of competences and about stages in the process of learning science. Such models might "relate to either:

• a 'continuum of learning' construct which focuses on what students can demonstrate they know and can do as they progress conceptually and is independent of the age of the student or

• a 'years of schooling' construct which focuses on what students should know and should be able to do as they progress chronologically and is dependent on the age of the student" (Hafner, 25).

The concept of 'key stages' in England and Wales might be seen as an example of the former type, the content-standards of the NSES in the US as an example of the latter.

As of now, competence-models for the definition of standards are normative constructs. Germany and Switzerland both currently attempt to test their models empirically with preparatory studies. In Germany, for example, it is among the tasks of the Institute for Educational Progress (Institut zur Qualitätsentwicklung im Bildungswesen, IQB) to develop national proficiency scales and associated norms of student achievement (Rupp and Vock, 2007).

## Minimal or regular standards

Minimal standards set the lowest possible hurdle. Teaching efforts have to ensure that, except for students with severe learning disabilities, everyone can meet these standards, i.e. learn enough to master the hurdle. Such standards are reported from New South Wales of Australia. Sweden also defines minimal standards:

> *"Goals to attain define the minimum knowledge to be attained by all pupils in the fifth and ninth year of school. Goals to attain in the ninth year of school are the basis for assessing whether a pupil should receive the Pass grade. The majority of pupils advance further in their learning" (Stroemdahl, 265).*

Where minimal standards are set, there is a tendency to hold teachers and schools responsible for the "result of effective teaching and learning" (Hafner, 36).

Regular standards, on the other hand, as they are reported from Austria, Germany, and Switzerland, define what the average learner is expected to achieve. They "describe the main features of a typical student's performance measured against the outcomes for the course" (Hafner, 38). In Finland, for example, "the final-assessment criteria define the level of knowledge and skill needed for a grade of eight (8), on a scale 4 … 10" (Lavonen, 109). Some students will exceed, others will fail. As a tendency, the responsibility for success is left with the individual student.

## Standards where and when

Countries with a centrally governed educational system tend to set standards in a central way. In France, for instance, "the knowledge and competencies are specified by a decree" (Malleus, 130) of the Minister of Education, while in the UK the National Curriculum is published by the Department of Education and Science. However, a centrally structured state does not necessarily lead to centrally set standards, as the Swedish and the Finnish examples indicate. While global goals of education determine the general direction, "the local education providers … have to plan the local curriculum with teachers based on the *National Core Curriculum for Basic Education* … The local education providers are also responsible for organising general assessment of the schools and use the data for evaluating how well the goals have been achieved" (Lavonen, 102).

In countries with a more federal system such as Australia, Germany, Switzerland and US, the national standards are defined as a frame, which provides the setting for the development of specific standards and curricula in the different provinces, states or Länder. The link between the national framework and the actual realization in the states can be tighter, as seems to be the development in Germany, or looser as in the US where "none of the reform documents can claim to be mandated national standards, (but) most states and school districts follow some subset of what is portrayed in the aforementioned documents" (Lederman, 358).

Finally, a definition must clarify for which point in time the standards are set. Some countries, such as France, Germany or Portugal formulate their standards of science education for and place the assessment of their attainment at just one point in time, the end of compulsory education at school, usually grade 9 or 10. In Austria, "a start was made in 2005, by the Ministry of Education, to produce standards for science for upper secondary schools (grade 12). ... Assessment of standards will be carried out at the end of grade 12" (Weiglhofer, 62).

Other countries have chosen to define standards for several grade levels – fifth and ninth year of school in Sweden, fourth, sixth, and ninth in Finland. Switzerland (Grades 2, 6, and 9) and Taiwan (Grades 2, 4, 6, and 9), for example, even include primary education into their system of science education standards. In New South Wales, "the performance standards are typically written for two years of schooling and set expectations of the quality of learning to be achieved by the end of Years 2, 4, 6, 8, 10 and 12" (Hafner, 37), and in some states of the US, standards are even set for every single year of school (K-12).

## 3    How can the achievement of science education standards be assessed?

It depends. Most of all it depends on the intended function of the assessment, which will be addressed in the following section.

"In general, standards have more meaning when attached to tests", is a statement from the Swiss contribution (Labudde, 291). This is a mild understatement. In general, standards are meaningless, unless their attainment is assessed one way or another. Standards will have little credibility with teachers, children or parents, unless it can be shown how individual students, classes or school systems perform relative to the expected measure. In fact, in a situation where the setting of educational standards is not a customary concept to the teaching profession, "the successful implementation of standards will depend crucially on the development of suitable assessment tasks" (Schecker and Parchmann, 160).

'Intended curricula' may be full of desirable goals, but it is the 'attained curriculum' that counts, and its assessment must be integral part of any effort to set educational standards. "The basic and the secondary education curricula require that the evaluation activities should be considered part and parcel of educational processes" (Galvao et al., 244). If, indeed, standards, teaching process and assessment are an inseparable triad, *"assessment policies and practices should be aligned with the goals, student expectations, and curriculum frameworks. Within the science program, the alignment of assessment with curriculum and teaching is one of the most critical pieces of science education reform"* (Mamlok, 288).

## *General considerations*

This *alignment of assessment with curriculum and teaching* is obviously difficult, particularly when the concept of standards is newly introduced to a country and a culture of assessment has not yet been established. Dolin describes an experience that probably many countries have made in the beginning of the development towards the assessment of standards in education: "The guiding examples have so far been awful – simple computer based multiple choice questions which only test (more or less) rote learning" (Dolin, 79). The process of matching standards, teaching and evaluation requires efforts of its participants on all levels. *"It is rigorous, extensive and costly. The process includes* (for Australia):

• appointing an examination committee for each course

• developing a writing brief and exam specifications

• assessing the exam paper against the content and outcomes of the syllabus and against the exam specifications and brief

• developing marking guidelines

• appointing markers – the total number of markers involved in marking all the Higher School Certificate examinations across all course examinations is several thousand

• check the appropriateness of the marking guidelines through piloting

• marking the scripts and ensuring accuracy and consistency of markers throughout marking

• aligning student performance with performance bands through a judging process

• reviewing the outcomes of the judging process by expert committees" (Hafner, 41).

Validity of assessment is the issue in question. If there is not "a strong connection between the learning situations created by the teacher and the assessment of the students involved in these situations" (Galvao et al., 244), the outcomes of the assessment are of little value for either participant in the education process.

The assessment of standards-attainment can be undertaken on different levels with different perspectives. The individual student can be in the focus, a class, a school, a region or a country. Organization and methodology of the assessment will have to be adjusted accordingly. Individual students or even a class might be assessed for their practical performance in a laboratory situation, which would be unlikely, if not impossible, for a sample that goes beyond the size of a school. It is claimed that "in science, in particular, the internal assessment provides a more valid assessment of students' practical skills than can be achieved by the external pen and paper examination instrument" (Hafner, 41). Others, however, state that "it is still a challenge to persuade teachers to adopt hands-on (performance) assessments" (Chiu, 323).

Ideally, the assessment should be "multidimensional, drawing information from various sources and based on a variety of teaching and learning techniques" (Mamlok, 206). However, for assessments on a larger scale, paper-and-pencil questionnaires are the most common instruments. Even then, though, a variety of formats is possible for assessment tasks. Effort should be spent "to make it appropriate to the cognitive demand (multiple-choice and short structured questions for more factual recall; extended, more open-ended tasks with novel features for problem-solving and application, etc…)" (Bryce, 258).

Some countries simply use data from already existing large scale studies, like Australia using TIMSS data for Year 8 and data from the OECD PISA studies for 15 year olds, most of whom would be in 9th grade. Other countries create assessment tasks following the philosophy of PISA with "information that may be given in the form of texts (newspaper articles, scientific texts, description of experiences, interviews), figures, tables, graphs and so on. The items of each set may be closed (for instance, true/false, association or multiple choice) or open (a short composition or a long composition with instructions), according to the competences being evaluated. For example, a set of items can be based on the description of a situation/experience related to the process of science construction, to daily life, to the environment or to technology" (Galvao et al., 246).

Test-banks are often provided, which typically contain high quality tests with high content validity and large variation in items (item type and cognitive load). "Teachers eagerly use these tests in their course assessment because they are geared to the goals in the curriculum" (Lavonen, 112). For the national monitoring of standards-attainment Germany has even founded a new agency for the production of large itembanks in the context of the recent implementation of standards (cf. Rupp and Vock, 2007).

Beyond such rather general considerations the question how the achievement of science education standards can be assessed largely depends on two further conditions. It seems of importance whether the assessment is organized locally or centrally and whether tests are administered internally by the school or by external authorities.

## *Centrally or locally organized assessment*

There seems to be a growing tendency to organize the assessment of standards attainment centrally, either by existing administrative structures or by agencies created for this purpose. Some countries have a long history of central examinations as a means of surveying schools' results with respect to the previously set standards. A characteristic of the English education system, for example, is its long-established reliance on external examinations. "Historically, examinations in the UK have their origin in assessment procedures for entry to the universities and the civil service in the 19th century, designed to avoid favouritism and the effects of patronage, and to replace these with a more meritocratic selection procedure" (Millar, 84).

Many of the states within the US execute state-wide tests to evaluate the outcomes of their schools' teaching (with a prosperous industry of test providers), and "during the last five years more and more federal states in Germany have shifted from exams developed by a school or an individual teacher to central exams. ... Large sets of items for nation-wide large-scale assessments in theses domains are being developed by the newly founded Institute for Quality Development in the Educational System (Institut zur Qualitätsentwicklung im Bildungswesen, IQB). The development of a science item database starts in 2007" (Schecker and Parchmann, 156). Denmark is following the same route, when since very recently students are tested "by centrally designed problems for the first time in year 2 (Danish reading skills), year 3 (mathematics) etc. (but the first prescribed test in natural science is interestingly enough at year 8)" (Dolin, 79). In Taiwan, also, "there is a newly developed nationwide trend study, Taiwan Assessment of Students Achievement (TASA), launched in 2005" (Chiu, 325).

The current trend clearly seems to be directed towards centralized assessment of standard attainment. Finland, however, is going the other direction, with one of their general education policy principles being "devolution of decision power and responsibility to the local level" (Lavonen, 102). "There are no national final examinations at the end of comprehensive schooling. Legislation ensures that at the local level (municipalities) school administration people with teachers have a duty to evaluate their education provision (self-evaluation) and to take part in external evaluations which are organised for example by the National Board of Education based on samples" (Lavonen, 111). It will be interesting to observe how the Finnish example, considering their excellent PISA results, might become a new role-model in future.

## *External or internal assessment*

Closely related to the central-local issue the question rises, whether the assessment should be conducted with an external or an internal perspective. The UK, for example, has a long and well established history of external examinations, i.e. "examinations set and marked by someone other than the student's teacher and not seen by the student or teacher in advance" (Millar, 84). Teachers and students seem to accept the fact that a written examination from the outside, based on a clearly defined National Curriculum, evaluated by unseen people in an external institution, is the measure by which their teaching and learning results are judged. Other countries use similar models of centralized external examinations like the French 'baccalaureat', to name just one further example

External assessment certainly bears the weakness that particularities of schools or individuals, their resources and working conditions, can be taken into account only in very limited ways. Internal assessment is therefore favoured by others because of its alleged higher degree of validity. "Schools are required to use a variety of tasks in internal assessment to give students the opportunity to demonstrate outcomes in different ways. ... In science, in particular, the internal assessment provides a more valid assessment of students' practical skills than can be achieved by the external pen and paper examination instrument" (Hafner, 41).

Internal assessment, of course, raises the issue of reliability. Measures taken in a class or a school are difficult to compare with data from other environments. This is discussed in the English contribution:

> *"For example, teachers assemble portfolios of examples of student work that they think indicate that the student is at National Curriculum levels 4, 5, 6 and 7 – and then meet with others to review and discuss these. ... The intention is to 'calibrate' the teacher as a measuring instrument – and then rely on his or her judgment in other cases"* (Millar, 97).

Another way of safeguarding reliability of measurement is proposed in Finland, where assessment criteria are defined nationally, which are then used in internal examination procedures to assess students' performance. "In the national curriculum, the description of good performance at the end of fourth and sixth grade and the *final assessment (evaluation's) criteria* at the end of ninth grade specify, on a national basis, the knowledge and skill levels that constitute the basis of pupil assessment" (Lavonen, 109).

In order to guarantee both validity and reliability, a mix of external and internal assessment instruments is used in some countries. For example, in Australia, the use of both internal assessment and external examinations of student achievement "allows measures and observations to be made at several points and in different ways throughout each course. Taken together, it is believed that the external examinations and internal assessment marks should provide a more valid and reliable assessment of the achievement of the knowledge, understanding and skills described for each course than either would by itself" (Hafner, 40). Another example comes from the Netherlands, where this mix is regulated in a 1:1 ratio when it comes to assessing the attainment of standards set in the national curriculum for biology, chemistry and physics: "The student's result is determined by the national exam (50%) and the average result of the school examination portfolio (50%)" (Driessen, 231). This school examination portfolio covers a wide range of activities, allowing students to demonstrate a variety of competences.

## *Content or competence*

An important question is raised in the Swiss contribution: should the assessment be more content-driven or more competence-driven (or should it be driven by both)? "For example: Should students be tested on whether they know the definition of 'chloroplast' (an organic cell's part responsible for the photosynthesis) or that of the 'de Broglie wavelength' (a question relating to particle and quantum physics)? Or should students be tested on whether they are capable of planning, performing, and evaluating an experiment, e.g. an experiment in which they have to determine whether an effervescent tablet dissolves faster in cold, tepid or warm water" (Labudde, 289). Others may see that both are important to assess.

Paper-and-pencil procedures, which are easily administered and evaluated, are favoured by administrators for large-scale assessment. This drives the assessment towards content-based questions whereas, as has been discussed, there is a growing tendency world wide towards more competence-driven ways of defining standards, and ways have to be found to assess them. For example, "in the Portuguese educational system, it is now considered essential that students' assessment focus on several competences besides content" (Galvao *et al.*, 244).

However, as the discussion about the quality of PISA-items has already shown, "it is a fundamental problem that the more you orientate the aims of science towards competencies, the more difficult it is to assess these competencies within the school system" (Dolin, 81). Many countries are currently struggling with this problem, as they are trying to develop valid, reliable, and feasible instruments to assess more of students' science competences beyond their content knowledge.

# 4    What function does the assessment have?

Methodology, organization and execution of the assessment are strongly influenced by its intended function. Depending on who or what is in its focus – the individual student, the teacher, the school, parts or the whole of the educational system, parts or the whole of a country's student population – the assessing authority may have different intentions.

Generally speaking, one might distinguish between high-stakes and low-stakes assessment. With low-stakes assessment, 'feedback' is the major key word. The assessment serves as a basis for the analysis of the strengths and weaknesses of individuals, a school or a system and thus promotes their respective development and improvement. The low performing student might receive remedial classes, a teacher whose students perform lower than the norm might be offered counselling, or dissatisfied policy makers might decide to change a malfunctioning system. High-stakes assessment, on the other hand, leads to severe consequences for the assessed. It is often linked with a process of appraisal or selection. Only students with sufficient marks might be admitted to the next step on the educational ladder, the school whose classes demonstrate unsatisfactory results in comparison with others might be put under the authority's tutelage, or the underperforming teachers might ultimately lose their jobs. 'Accountability' is a strong issue in this context, where those in the focus of the assessment are held accountable for their performance.

A similar distinction is suggested in the Australian contribution: Assessment "is used substantially to inform teaching and learning rather than for reporting purposes and can be referred to as **assessment for learning**. On the other hand, assessment that is used substantially to report on achievement of standards to parents or to the system is referred to **as assessment of learning**" (Hafner, 27).

In either case, if the assessment is to play a constructive role in the context of standards, "it is absolutely necessary to communicate its intended functions or, even better, to involve and engage teachers and key stake holders in the whole process of defining the goals and functions of the assessment" (Labudde, 290).

## *Assessment as feedback for improvement*

"National and State Ministers have openly stated that the aim of assessing and reporting progress against the National Goals through the Assessment Program is to drive school improvement and enhance outcomes for students" (Hafner, 33). This statement from the Australian contribution is probably true in most countries. Authorities want the assessment to be seen as challenge, not as a threat. Official documents most often emphasize the formative character of the assessment. "The official purpose of the formative assessment is to improve instruction and learning" (Dolin, 79).

Assessment programs are designed to monitor the state of an education system and to develop it further by providing information to stakeholders at different levels of the system. "They provide the government with information to monitor standards over time, to monitor the impact of particular programs and to make decisions about resource allocation. They provide schools and teachers with information about whole school, class and individual pupil performance that they can use to make decisions about resource allocation and to support learning in the classroom" (Hafner, 43).

Ideally, within this concept of assessment as constructive feedback for improvement, "the goal of assessment is not to be punitive or to serve as a measure of teacher and school success, but more formative in providing feedback for further revision of curriculum and instruction" (Lederman, 362). Of course, it is almost inevitable that, where data exist, they invite comparison and competition. It is thus important to make and keep assessment programs fair across different learning opportunities. "Should the learning culture be raised by standards – which is emphasized by the school administration – it is necessary to introduce 'opportunity-to-learn'-standards (class size, scale of foreign pupils, conditions of classroom work, location of the school, intensity of selection etc.)" (Weiglhofer, 67).

Such assessment as feedback for improvement can be located at every level of the system, in a classroom at the hands of an individual teacher or nationwide, driven by an assessment agency. In the Swedish context, for example, these levels cooperate: "national assessment is looked upon as a support to the professional teacher in his or her assignment to implement the intentions of the curricula and syllabi and to evaluate students' learning. … On the local level, local tests handled by professional teachers, assisted by national optional diagnostic tests and 'test banks', there are good possibilities for fortunate implementation of national goals" (Stroemdahl, 275).

The attitude towards assessment is similar in Finland: "With the help of this information the schools performing below the average have had the opportunity to take the steps needed to rectify the situation on a local as well as regional level. Evaluation findings are not used to brand and punish poorly performing schools" (Lavonen, 111).

## Assessment for system monitoring

National assessment was, however, also used by the Finnish National Board of Education to monitor students' science skills nationally and also in different parts of the country. This function of assessment can be found in almost every country, particularly with large scale, centralized external tests. Germany, for example, has, together with the implementation of educational standards for the science subjects, set up an institution (*Institut zur Qualitätsentwicklung im Bildungswesen, IQB*) for primarily this purpose (Rupp and Vock, 2007). Among its main tasks is to find out whether the educational system is able to reach the goals set by the national standards. As in other cases, one of the initial motivations for the introduction of standards and the assessment of their attainment was to perform better in international comparison, when the results in studies like TIMSS and PISA came as an unpleasant surprise.

Whether a whole cohort of students at a given level – usually the end of compulsory education at grade 9 or 10 – should be tested, or whether a representative sample of an age group would be enough for the purpose of system monitoring, is reported diversely. The French contribution offers a reasonable compromise: "If the goal is to know to what extent individuals or a school performs, all the students should be tested. If the objective is to inform the national educational system, then samples of the overall population will suffice" (Malléus, 140).

## *Assessment for harmonization*

In countries with a federal structure, national assessment helps to harmonize standard related performance between states or regions of a country. For Switzerland, for example, the urgent need for harmonization among 26 cantons ('states'), each with its own educational system, was the driving force in implementing national standards and monitoring them through national tests. Not incidentally the Swiss project is named HarmoS (*Harmonisierung obligatorische Schule: Harmonization of the compulsory school*). In similar ways, Germany with its strong federal tradition is planning to use national assessment procedures to moderate diverging developments.

While Switzerland is a small country with a high density of educational systems, the coherence of educational achievement might be threatened by mere distance on the Australian continent. There "public reporting against national targets may ultimately influence the state/territory curriculum to align their curriculum more closely with the assessed standards" (Hafner, 33).

## *Assessment to observe adherence to curriculum*

Finally, among assessment strategies of a more formative character in the sense that they provide feedback to stakeholders on whichever level, there are those that are meant to safeguard the coherence between the intended and the attained curriculum. This is especially the case where there is a binding national curriculum. The English contribution states it clearly that in their view for this purpose the most powerful mechanism is "the use of unseen externally set and marked examinations and tests to measure student attainment at different points. ... This assessment model strongly encourages teachers to cover all of the curriculum content, as they do not know which parts will be examined in any given year" (Millar, 91).

## *Assessment as basis for benchmarking*

Whereas assessment for feedback purposes usually is of rather low-stake character, high-stakes assessment can be found where the consequences for students, teachers or school can be severe in the case of dissatisfying achievement. This function is not always as directly stated as in the Danish contribution to this book: "An obvious – and official – function of final grades in the Gymnasium is as a mechanism of selection" (Dolin, 79).

Normally, national or regional external testing of standards attainment is not used directly for judging students' performance, although this does occasionally occur, as is reported from some of the states in the US. In these cases, "the assessment is strongly related to a selection process, whereas a student has to pass a nationwide test in order to be admitted to a particular post-compulsory school or university" (Labudde, 289). In Germany, for example, the 'Einheitliche Prüfungsanforderungen für das Abitur (EPA)' (Unified examination requirement for the Abitur) are setting such a standard for the end of high school education, which is tested nationwide, with variations between the federal states. The results of this test set the switches into higher education. At lower secondary level, the national tests that are about to be implemented, are not supposed to be used for individual appraisal, but "concurrently to the IQB-assessments, the federal states have developed or are still preparing their own standard-related performance tests which are used as part of the grading process for the final exams in upper and lower secondary schools" (Schecker and Parchmann, 156).

Similarly in the Netherlands, "all assessment in junior secondary education determines the promotion of pupils to the next class and the determination of what is considered to be the most appropriate type and level of secondary education commensurate with their capabilities" (Driessen, 232), and in New South Wales of Australia "the government has clearly stated that it strongly believes that external examinations are necessary for the rigorous, independent and equitable evaluation of secondary school students' performance" (Hafner, 43).

Where assessment data from external tests are not directly used to judge student performance, they serve as benchmarks for internal assessment in other cases. In Sweden, for example, where there is a strong emphasis on the teacher to judge student performance, the national tests are only part of the collected information about the total achievement. And yet these national tests provide the benchmark "to endorse the teachers in their equitable judgement of the pupils' fulfilment of the goals and to make a just grading" (Stroemdahl, 273). In Scotland, the grade-related criteria (GRC) "are certainly used by teachers and by the assessment system to articulate various levels and qualifications. (eg. a pupil must achieve a Standard Grade at level 1 or 2 (of 7) to enter a Higher course)" (Bryce, 258).

Obviously teachers can be in the focus of assessment as well as their students. Several contributions indicate that students' performance can be used as an indicator for their teachers' quality. Examination results of students as indicator for the teacher's competence is not the case everywhere, but one can see "tendencies opening up for a closer link between student performance and individual teacher evaluation" (Dolin, 80). In the Netherlands, for example, one of the functions of national tests at the end of the last school year is the "benchmarking of teacher quality" (Driessen, 232). In some cases consequences can be severe from denied promotion to a reduction of salary.

In a low-stakes situation, evaluation findings will not be used "to brand and punish poorly performing schools" (Lavonen, 111). In several countries, however, the external assessment of student performance can be of high-stakes character not only for the students or their teachers but for a whole school. There seems to be a growing tendency to make students' test results public by 'league tables' in the media. These data on the performance of students are widely used to judge the quality of schools, which, in effect, "may influence, inter alia, parents' decisions about which school their child should attend" (Millar, 91). In a softer and not so public version, schools are obliged "to publish their results in information leaflets for parents of their (future) students" (Driessen, 232).

While educators warn of superficial judgement on the basis of just "conventional academic achievement terms" (Bryce, 258) without taking into account statistical indicators of the socio-economic factors pertaining to the context in which a school operates, political authorities seem to be attracted by the possibilities of benchmarking between schools. "Some policymakers plan to use benchmarks as an instrument to increase competition among schools" (Schecker and Parchmann, 156).

In the optimistic scenario, weak results of a school will lead to support for improvement, as is the case in Sweden or Finland. In the Netherlands, for schools with extremely poor results a program may follow, "designed to improve the results from the school, supervised by the national school inspectorate" (Driessen, 232). In the worst case, as is reported, for example, from some of the states in the US, a school with repeatedly dissatisfying results may be put under custody of the authorities or ultimately face closure.

# 5      What side-effects of testing standards are feared or observed?

The discussion about science education standards and their assessment is controversial in many countries. While their proponents see them as a means to enhance the quality of instruction, sceptics either see or fear a number of drawbacks. While many of the good intentions, as stated in the goals of implementing standards, seem to be realized, some negative effects are reported in most of the contributions to this book – and a few unintended positive side-effects as well.

## Standards lead to teaching-to-the-test

Of course, say some. "Teaching-to-the-test is in fact intended! Otherwise standards and testing them would not make any sense. For example, if planning, performing and interpreting an experiment in science is a competence to be achieved by the students, and if this competence is tested, then teachers, students, parents, science educators, and politicians expect that planning, performing and interpreting experiments ARE taught in schools. In other words, they expect teaching-to-the-test" (Labudde, 292). Once standards are set, teachers are supposed to conform to them, and if the test, indeed, measures what is meant by the standards, "in a positive sense, standard-based assessments can 'force' teachers to change their classroom-activities in a more preferable direction from a science education perspective" (Schecker and Parchmann, 158).

But, of course, as a slogan, teaching-to-the-test looks at the other side of the coin. What is meant and feared is that the centralized assessment of standards, as it is applied in many countries, will eventually turn into thumb-screws for students, teachers, schools … the whole system, which finally stares at nothing but test-scores and percentages. If, indeed, test-scores are the main, if not only, criteria for success, responsible teachers must teach to the test for their students' their schools' and, not least, to their own benefit. "The most important side effect of the national test is that teachers emphasize the teaching for the national test. In the construction of written tests for the school examination, most teachers copy questions from former national exams instead of developing questions, which are congruent to the learning, classroom activities and teaching" (Driessen, 233). Teaching-to-the-test may not be an inborn defect of assessing the attainment of standards, but the pitfalls are many, and they seem not to be avoided in many cases. Some of these traps will be delineated in the following passages.

## External assessment tends to emphasize lower-level skills

As was elaborated in the section on the definition of standards in this chapter, "the systems of education tend to lay stress more and more upon competencies, often defined in broad and general terms" (Malléus, 141). But the more complex the requirements that the learners are expected to meet, the more difficult the proof seems to be, if the goals are truly attained. "With a socio-cultural approach to teaching and learning, you aim to teach students to be able to deal with everyday situations involving science. But it is very difficult to assess such competences in a (de-contextualised) oral or written test" (Dolin, 81). Many states in the US, besides the UK, perhaps have the most widely implemented system of standards in science education including large-scale, external assessment. The problem of assessing complex learning outcomes is summarized in the US contribution to this book as follows: "The problem here is not with the assessment of standards, *per se*, but the observation that assessment approaches in science have not kept pace with the currently stated goals of science education" (Lederman, 359).

What applies to the assessment of skills within the immediate science domain, is probably even more true for competences that are not directly related to science but are nonetheless important in science education, such as creativity, ability to work in a team, problem solving ability, etc. "Many important competencies cannot be tested in national assessments and there is a danger of them getting lost in the daily business of school when focusing on large scale assessments" (Labudde, 292).

Because of this frequently reported difficulty in measuring complex competences, a "tilting of competency-based assessment towards a content-based assessment" (Malleus, 141) is observed, in consequence shifting the focus of teachers' efforts towards "facts and the measurable. An increased focus on assessment of learning leads teachers to *teach for the exams* instead of *teaching and assessing for learning*" (Dolin, 80). The English contribution, on the basis of a well established tradition of external examinations of common standards, states that "assessment by external (mainly written) examinations has the significant negative characteristic of giving greater weight to attainments that can be assessed in this way – often resulting in an undue emphasis on the ability to recall information under examination conditions. This in turn can encourage forms of teaching that focus on these, rather limited, aspects of science learning" (Millar, 96). From the US, the same experience is reported. "Large scale, mass administered, assessments eventually turn into examinations that focus on lower level knowledge as opposed to higher level knowledge and skills. Quite simply, lower level skills and knowledge are more easily assessed, as they involve less debate and ambiguity" (Lederman, 365).

Together with the degeneration of assessment approaches, a lack of skill "in developing assessments for higher level thinking" (Lederman, 359) is reported. Teachers certainly "have not been trained to identify and/or measure competencies" (Malléus, 141), but there is perhaps not much more expertise in test development for the evaluation of complex competences. "Recapitulating the situation, there is a strong need for good assessment tools" (Schecker and Parchmann, 156).

Related to the fear that teaching and assessment in science might be constricted to the easily measurable is the risk that the curriculum as such might be "narrowed down to those subjects which are assessed – and within subjects to the teaching of those topics which are most likely to feature on examinations and tests and the development of the kinds of knowledge that are most frequently tested" (Millar, 96). Several other contributors express their worry that 'minority subjects' might be neglected, if they do not appear on the assessment agenda.

## Standards can stifle innovation

One desired effect of the introduction of standards to science education is a certain unification and standardisation of classroom teaching with the aim to raise the overall quality. This is probably the case in many countries, although there seems to be little hard evidence. On the other hand, it is observed, "that some originality in teachers/teaching has been a casualty" (Bryce, 258). The constructivist approach has had a strong influence on science education. Many teachers have developed teaching strategies beyond the traditional provision of subject knowledge, employing alternative methods such as role play, use of portfolios, project work, etc. "But there is a danger that more emphasis on summative assessment could be at the expense of some of the present good and productive sides of science education" (Dolin, 80). Concern about students' learning outcomes in terms of test scores may have raised the competition among schools for altogether better results, but one observed side effect "has been to stifle innovation; schools are reluctant to risk departing from the known, lest their results become worse" (Millar, 96).

Lab work in science classes is certainly not a fancy innovation, but even this seems to be threatened, when the emphasis is on the "teaching and testing of subject knowledge at the expense of skills such as experimental chemistry laboratory studies, seen by many students as one of the most appealing aspects of their chemistry course" (Driessen, 234). Since the evaluation of students' laboratory skills is not easily done with large scale assessment approaches, it is mostly left to their teachers' judgement. "However, the criteria used in marking this have led to similar, rather dull, investigations being carried out in many schools, chosen to provide opportunities for students to display specific features, or mention specific points, that gain marks. In schools, a great deal of shaping and coaching goes on, to help students maximise their marks – and there is little sense that the outcomes tell you anything useful about the student's ability to engage thoughtfully in a practical scientific investigation" (Millar, 97).

## Nationwide assessment invites questionable use of data

Large bodies of data are assembled in national or state-wide external assessments. Depending on the stated goals of the standards/assessment combination, they are used for a variety of purposes from student diagnosis to system monitoring. In France, for example, "the goal is to help the teachers to identify which competencies … are attained by individual pupils and which are not. Parents are informed of the results of their child. … Unfortunately, the local authorities are more prone to misuse this information in the form of league tables than the teachers are to adapt their teaching and assessments to the needs of their pupils" (Malléus, 139).

League tables, although official practice in some countries, seem to be an unintended deterioration of assessing standards attainment in most of the others. It is feared by many that "school benchmarking will become more important than the use of careful empirical investigations for a general quality development process and for changes in educational policy based on system monitoring data" (Schecker and Parchmann, 156). According to the Scottish experience "the effect is to define 'good schools' in conventional academic achievement terms" (Bryce, 258). This is below established pedagogical knowledge. "A large and sustained body of research evidence, coming from work on school effectiveness, indicates that over 70% of the variation in student attainment at age 16 can be accounted for by the variation in student attainment on entry at age 11 – which in turn is strongly correlated with measures of the social and economic background of students" (Millar, 95). The comparison and ranking of schools on the basis of assessment scores alone, not taking into account their background variables – possibly even with negative consequences for the low achieving – seems unfair.

This understanding has led to the concept of measuring added-value with the central idea that a school's assessment results can be predicted by background variables such as socio-economic factors or students' entrance achievement. "If a school's actual outcomes are better than this prediction, the school has 'added value' over the period; their students have done better than could have been predicted on the basis of their prior attainment alone. Conversely, a school may produce outcomes that are less good than their input would have predicted. This can be useful for internal planning – and may offer a fairer basis of comparison between schools" (Millar, 95).

Another fear, particularly among teachers, is that of potential misuse of assessment data as an "instrument of control and discipline of teachers" (Weiglhofer, 67). This fear was expressed in a study, commissioned by the Austrian Ministry of Education with 1000 secondary schoolteachers. Experiences in the US show that this worry is not without cause. "Teachers have been directly or indirectly evaluated based on their students' scores on such tests. Consequently, teachers have made a concerted effort to teach to the test" (Lederman, 364).

## Large-scale assessment costs time and money

"The cost of external statewide testing and marking is significant with major security issues to be considered at all stages of the tests and examinations – setting, distribution, sitting the exam and marking" (Hafner, 45). But it is not the money alone that needs to be spent on large-scale assessment. Of perhaps even greater concern is the time that is occupied, not just by the testing event as such but more so by the preparation for it. External assessment is most likely to affect the teaching. Responsible teachers will do their best to prepare their students for the test, especially when severe consequences are at stake for either the students, the teacher or the school.

"Many teachers begin reviewing for the June statewide examinations ... shortly after the first of the year" (Lederman, 364). It is argued that this time should rather be spent on teaching to the curriculum than on rehearsing last year's test items.

## Some unintended assets

While there is fear that the setting of standards, combined with large-scale external assessment might produce some unwanted side-effects, the reports in this book indicate a few unexpected virtues.

It has already been argued that teaching-to-the-test can be seen as a challenge rather than a threat. "With good standards and well chosen problems teaching to the test is a chance rather than a risk" (Schecker and Parchmann, 158).

Another positive aspect is seen in the separation of roles between teacher and examiner when it comes to high-stakes assessment. If test scores strongly influence students' opportunities for future learning, many teachers seem to be happy to delegate the testing to an "invisible" external agency. Not only is an external test perceived as more objective and consistent over a range of schools, but it also relieves the teachers of some of their responsibility.

Finally a special effect is expected particularly in the German speaking countries, where standards are just being implemented. Because these countries have long relied on the input-orientation of their educational systems through "Lehrpläne" (which are more than syllabi), there is hardly any established experience with output-oriented teaching. Science education departments at universities and elsewhere certainly will provide frameworks, textbooks and other resources, but time is pressing, and there fore "teachers will have to come up with and produce a lot of ideas themselves for quite some time. This might be a burden but also a chance to foster co-operation among the concerned teachers and a better culture of in-service training" (Schecker and Parchmann, 159).

## 6    Can standards be implemented without centralized assessment?

It seems widely accepted that some kind of standards, common goals or national curriculum should make it clear to teachers, students and everybody else involved, what knowledge and competence students are expected to have attained in science at certain age levels. It seems equally accepted that it somehow needs to be evaluated, if the standards are met, if the teaching and learning was successful with regards to the standards. The question is, whether this evaluation has to be centralized and external. This question is particularly crucial in countries, where the notion of standards is rather new and needs to be implemented.

The Austrian contribution to this book makes a strong statement: "If (the) focus is put on comparability, centralized assessment will be inevitable. If the aspect of support is in the centre of attention, diagnostic quality, support of the weaker pupils, pupil-centred achievement examinations will become more important" (Weiglhofer, 68). Other reports indicate that there may be other possibilities of evaluating whether standards have been met without necessarily resorting to large-scale external assessment programs.

The most consequent alternative would be assessment by teachers within the school setting. While this allows the teacher to include both the actual test performance and the learning process and the individual development of the students, this approach certainly bears certain shortcomings: teacher evaluation lacks comparability between other classes or schools and is prone to even unintended bias, coherence with the outcomes expected by the standards is not necessarily safeguarded, and the teachers have to do without feedback from a more general position.

Several means are suggested to deal with these concerns. Teacher cooperation within a school and beyond can help to overcome subjectivity and to align teachers' judgements. It would be "a kind of 'implicit benchmarking" (Labudde, 294) to achieve higher objectivity, when groups of teachers in school districts got together to coordinate their ways of assessing their students' learning outcomes.

They could be supported with item-banks of well tested tasks that could either be used directly or serve as models for the development of their own examination tasks. Such item-banks exist or are under construction in several countries, usually provided by central agencies of a kind. Ideally the items would come along with reference values from samples representative for the class(es) in question. Their own students' performance in relation to the standard sample would then give the teachers feedback on the results of their teaching.

Rather than tasks from an item-bank to choose from, complete tests might be offered to schools, again with representative reference, on an optional basis. These tests might be centrally developed, administered and marked by official authorities, but with voluntary participation they would avoid a number of the aforementioned potential side-effects. They would "allow teachers to compare the results of their class with other classes and with the objectives as given in the curriculum; in Switzerland, this kind of test has become popular in the last five years" (Labudde, 294). Such optional tests are offered in several countries. "Overall, having a version of 'centralized' assessment that is more localized than the national level, may be a good alternative to the more familiar national test and national curriculum" (Lederman, 367). If, on the other hand, there is a political need to monitor the whole system, "this might be more economically and effectively done by assessing samples of students in a sample of schools in any given school year – rather than making all sit an external test" (Millar, 98).

Either way, with individual evaluation, cooperating teacher groups, or item-banks to choose from, *"standards without centralised assessment"* is not easy for teachers and local authorities. Therefore, this decision is taken seriously in teacher education programmes, and student teachers are trained for organising assessments. Moreover, the National Board of Education is organising in-service training for teachers ..." (Lavonen, 112). If non-centralized (local) assessment is to be an option, the training of teachers (and everybody else involved at local level) seems to be a crucial prerequisite.

Altogether, "assessment is a necessity to inform the teacher about his/her work and to give feed-back to the pupils/students and their parents. On the local level, local tests handled by professional teachers, assisted by national optional diagnostic tests and 'test banks' there are good possibilities for fortunate implementation of national goals" (Stroemdahl, 275).

## 7    Some other issues that might be worth noting

Standards are usually meant to raise the quality of schooling, which almost goes hand in hand with educational reform, where standards are newly introduced. Reform, however, cannot be the responsibility of just one group of agents; it needs the joint effort of all stakeholders in the field. "In order to accomplish reform, there needs to be a common vision from teacher, to administrator, to community, and the necessary resources must be provided" (Lederman, 357). One group, however, that seems absolutely indispensable in the process of developing, implementing and assessing standards, is the teachers themselves. Not only are they the ones who are most familiar with the daily science instruction in a country, the involvement of teachers also ensures the use of comprehensible language and better acceptance by fellow teachers. "There is overwhelming empirical evidence of the necessity of involving teachers in the development of new curricular standards ..." (Labudde, 286).

But, of course, the development of new curricular standards is not normally the primary focus of teachers. "History tells us that teachers are resistant to change" (Lederman, 369), and even if it is not active resistance, it is certainly not easy for teachers to break with well tried methods, sometimes having to change teaching habits of a lifetime. Change therefore requires "extensive professional development that is continuous over a significant amount of time" (Lederman, 369). If teachers are to play an active role in the development, implementation and assessment of standards, they need every possible support to qualify themselves for this demanding task. If this support is denied, if teachers cannot develop professionally, any reform towards standards is likely to share the fate of many of their predecessors – teachers will sit it out and wait for the next.

Such abiding attitude will prevail ever more, if teachers have the feeling that they are not valued as partners in the process, but mere recipients of yet another directive from above. An alternative concept is indicated in the Finnish contribution: "*The culture of trust* means that education authorities and national level education policymakers believe that teachers, together with principals, headmasters and parents, know how to provide the best possible education for children and youth at a certain region" (Lavonen, 102). Trust through professionalism requires responsible teachers and responsible authorities, who together, it seems in Finland, can move, if not mountains, at least standards in science education.

## Summary

Standards are set in education for a variety of reasons, the most common ones being: to monitor the educational system, to provide a mechanism for accountability, to promote educational equality, and to provide feedback for schools and teachers for them to improve their teaching.

Standards and curricula are inseparably linked. Their 'order of appearance', however, is discussed controversially. In Australia and in many other countries, 'the curriculum sets the standards', which means that first the curriculum is defined, sometimes preceded by a declaration of more general goals of education, and the standards are derived from there. Germany and some other countries are taking the opposite route. First standards are set and then curricula are developed by which students are enabled to reach the standards.

While some standards are content-driven, there seems to be a trend towards competence-driven standards. Competences are defined in a variety of ways, and various competence models are suggested.

Standards are usually set at the end of certain levels of education, but some countries define standards for shorter intervals in biannual or even yearly sequence.

It seems widely agreed that the attainment of standards needs to be assessed, and that for this assessment to be meaningful, standards, curriculum and assessment must be well aligned. Paper-and-pencil tests, whose limitations are commonly seen, are nonetheless prevalent practice. These limitations become particularly apparent, where competence-based standards are defined. More practice-oriented measures are often avoided for feasibility reasons.

Large differences are observed between countries concerning the question whether the assessment should be organized centrally or locally and administered by external or internal agents. There seems to be a tendency, however, towards state wide external examinations.

This kind of assessment also seems to produce the most side-effects, 'teaching-to-the-test' being the most prominent keyword in most reports. Others fear that standards with centralized external assessment might favour lower-level skills and stifle innovation or are worried that the collected data might be used for questionable purposes.

Altogether there seems no doubt that the control of the output of educational efforts is necessary and that setting standards and assessing their attainment is a reasonable means to that end.

## References

Collins English Dictionary (2007) Glasgow: HarperCollins.

Klieme, E., Avenarius, H., Blum, W., Döbrich, P., Gruber, H., Prenzel, M., Reiss, K., Riquarts, K., Rost, J., Tenorth, H.-E. and Vollmer, H. J. (2003) *Zur Entwicklung nationaler Bildungsstandards. Eine Expertise*. Bonn: Bundesministerium für Bildung und Forschung.

Oliver, A. (1969) *Curriculum improvement*. New York: Dodd, Mead & Comp.

Rupp, A. and Vock, M. (2007) This book, Chapter 10.

Weinert, F. (2001) Concept of Competence: A Conceptual Clarification. In: D. Rychen & L. Salganik (Hrsg.) *Defining and Selecting Key Competencies* (pp 45-65). Göttingen: Hogrefe & Huber.

# Chapter 20

# Education Standards: attempting a critical judgement of development – a reflection of the symposium

*Rolf Dubs*

*Institute of Economic Education, University of St. Gallen, Dufourstrasse 40a, CH 9000 St. Gallen, Switzerland*

## 1 Critical questions and definition of objectives

The debate about standards of education began in 1976 in Great Britain. Callaghan, then Prime Minister, made a speech in Oxford, now known as the Ruskin Speech, calling for a 'National Debate' on four issues: the curriculum, the assessment of standards, the education and training of teachers and the relationship of education and working life. A series of conferences and papers ensued over the next few years leading to the National Curriculum amongst other things. It was in 1983 that *Nation at Risk* appeared in the United States and in 1991, for example, the committee on Science Education and Standards and Assessment began its work.

In the German speaking countries, however, they were scarcely mentioned at that time, because during the last decade the European pedagogical discussion has been mainly concerned with changes in school input (adaptation of structural and pro-grammatic settings, guidance for schools with increasing autonomy, adaptation of curricula and timetables, allocation of finances). The necessity to rescue schools from flying blind and to place output orientation in the foreground, was only recognised by the public at large and by politicians when the TIMSS and PISA results, which were not ubiquitously satisfactory, became better known. As a result of this, suggestions were made by educationalists for output-oriented measures (quality management in schools, comparative studies, etc). At the same time attention was drawn to the discussion on education standards in the United States which, towards the end of the last century, brought more and more confusion, and also led to increasingly critical judgements (cf. Shavelson et al., 1992). Political institutions in Europe began to concern themselves with education standards in a way that was in part uncritical. Sometimes this led to the introduction of activities which had not been properly thought through, in the belief that urgent problems in education, such as increasing imbalances in the school development of children and adolescents, more students leaving school who had underachieved, straitened finances, etc. could be solved simply by introducing education standards.

However, it was not until Klieme, Prenzel and their colleagues (2003) produced a comprehensive and critical report, bringing together the threads of the various arguments that education standards could be seen to be a sensible concept for the improvement of schools and of teaching in German-speaking countries. Once they had convincingly demonstrated the wisdom and practical use of education standards, ministries and school practitioners began hastily to draw up and introduce education standards. As these plans were often put into practice without theoretical foundation or careful reflection about the proposed curriculum, much confusion regarding concepts and terms then ensued. This is a phenomenon that had been observed in the US and in other countries that had introduced standards. As the theme is both interesting and promising, more and more academics have been working on education standards, leading to an almost unmanageable flood of literature on the subject. This continues to confuse even more because it mostly remains rooted in general terms and is unable to show in an established theoretical manner, how education standards can be put into use in everyday school life, so that teaching in the classroom can indeed be altered and improved.

One is almost tempted to fall back on the Slogan Theory (Komisar and McCellan, 1961) and their application by Apple (1992) in connection with education standards in the teaching of mathematics. According to this idea, education standards merely present a slogan with which followers of specific ideas are recruited in order to organise a movement with definitions which are as unfocused as possible, and which, thanks to the slogan, will gain as many supporters as possible. With these supporters, specific aims concerning schools and educational policy are supposed to be reached. For mathematics, Apple has discovered three aims behind the standard suggestions of the National Council of Teachers of Mathematics: a non-elite curriculum for mathematics which is not dependent on either talent or ability, but is suitable for all students; a curriculum aiming at mathematical learning, which begins with realistic problems in real life; and a curriculum which strives to connect the assessment of achievement with both the curriculum and local resources.

If standards are pre-determined from above and the normative basics have not been reflected and made transparent, and education goals are pursued which are not generally accepted, they will remain ineffective in school practice, whatever slogan is used. This aspect alone makes it necessary to examine critically the normative basics and the aims of curricula and of the education standards that are built on these.

As there are so many education standards, few of which are convincing, teachers, most of all, raise the question as to what is actually new in them. At first the answer is simple: until now the steering has been input-oriented. In order to assess the effectiveness of the school objectively, the achievement of students and of schools must be measured in an output-orientated process. Thus, the school as a whole can be directed (improved) based on data, and the learning results of the students can be accurately recorded, with the aim of improving the quality of the school continuously.

Useful as this innovation is, it can only be of use when there are meaningful, substantial and unambiguous education standards. In this respect, the conditions are not good. At the one extreme they are nothing but a new edition of traditional operational objectives (cf., for example, the education standards in the German federal state of North Rhine Westphalia), and at the other extreme people are satisfied with general, imprecise statements regarding ability and contents (see, for example, the project 'Understanding University Success' for American High Schools, 2003). In this symposium too, no consensus was reached as to how education standards should be formulated. It would, however, be presumptuous to believe that one form of presentation and formulation of education standards could be agreed upon. Indeed, it is crucial that the presentation and means of implementation are suitable for each region and which are in sympathy with their political and school cultures. Success in the development and implementation of education standards will depend significantly on their local form and the interaction between authorities and the schools or, more precisely, their teaching staff. This factor will make the effective implementation of education standards in federal states, with distinctive cultural characteristics, even more difficult. Therefore the unification of education standards (particularly with the aim of inter-state comparison) needs very careful study.

One question that has remained largely unanswered is the preparation and training of teachers for **standard-based teaching**. Unfortunately it is already evident that the mistakes made in the 1970s, with operational learning objectives and curriculum research, are being repeated. Concepts and plans are developed and eventually decisions are made from above, but teachers are not prepared for such teaching. There are three reasons for this. First of all in many places there is a lack of money, which could be used to offer a systematic teacher training and development programme. Secondly, many school authorities, unable to understand sufficiently the increasing pressure being put on teachers, still believe that innovations can be mastered by self-study. In the face of such complex projects as education standards this feeling that self-study is enough simply remains an illusion. Thirdly, few academics are making the effort to describe and illustrate in detail what standard-based teaching in the classroom might look like. If further in-service training for teachers is not put into place soon, then the slogan 'education standards' may well be doomed.

We must therefore ask ourselves whether the symposium has suggested solutions to these problems. The answer is yes and no. Yes, because the discussion has provided insight into the events happening in many countries, while at the same time providing a stimulus and contributing greatly to critical reflection. No, because in fact no concrete results could be 'signed and sealed'. In this chapter, the discussion will be not about concepts and academic opinions, as presented in the individual papers, but rather an attempt will be made to pose once again the questions where there were differences of opinion, or where matters were left unclear. A model may provide a structural aid, containing the separate steps that are of significance in the process of development and implementation of education standards.

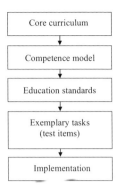

```
┌─────────────────────┐
│   Core curriculum   │
└─────────────────────┘
          ↓
┌─────────────────────┐
│  Competence model   │
└─────────────────────┘
          ↓
┌─────────────────────┐
│ Education standards │
└─────────────────────┘
          ↓
┌─────────────────────┐
│  Exemplary tasks    │
│   (test items)      │
└─────────────────────┘
          ↓
┌─────────────────────┐
│  Implementation     │
└─────────────────────┘
```

Figure 1:     Steps for the development and implementation of education standards

## 2    The separate steps

### 2.1    The core curriculum

It is noticeable that, in most states and projects regarding standard development, little attention is paid to the pedagogical creative idea. (What general goals will the curriculum serve?). Also, little heed is given to the normative basic concept (Which values form the foundation of the teaching plan?). The work of curriculum development is often limited to the adaptation of contents. A fundamental reflection rarely takes place – probably fearing lengthy controversies (e.g. fundamental questions about the significance of science in the curriculum) as the result of the experience in curriculum research in the 1970s. Although relevant curricular literature is available (cf. for sciences, Bybee, 1993; Gräber and Bolte, 1997; Millar et al., 2000; Gräber et al., 2002), the work on standards usually starts over-hastily with competence models. The fact is then overlooked that competence models are strongly defined by the creative ideas for a subject. Depending on the direction and aim of the subject and the basic values it is placed upon, different competence models can be generated. From the point of view of this author, who is not a natural scientist, three creative ideas may be feasible for science teaching.

Firstly it is possible to imagine **propaedeutic, exemplary teaching**, in terms of Wagenschein (1973), where the principle is to introduce the learners to the paradigms and nature of sciences by means of selected problems. Secondly it might be possible to put a '**Scientific Literacy**' in the foreground which will convey an 'active listening competence' to the students in the sense of imparting a general education for everyone, so that they will be able to judge and differentiate in the fields of nature and technology. This approach can be put into practice in various degrees, as presented by Bybee (2002) (nominal Scientific Literacy, functional Scientific Literacy, also conceptional and procedural Scientific Literacy). Thirdly, the focus of science teaching could be placed on the **necessities in life**, **requirements for work and leisure time needs**, aiming at the daily use of technology and its theoretical background. These three possible curricular creative ideas show without further explanation that they call for different fields of competence. For a scientific propaedeutic approach other attitudes, motivations and abilities are needed than for a curriculum that is directed towards daily necessities and leisure time needs.

This leads to a first important realisation: the paradigm of education standards will only be able to change teaching significantly if fundamental curricular considerations are placed ahead of all theoretical and formal deliberations regarding implementation and assessment of standards. These fundamental considerations have to build on a precise understanding of the desired creative idea, and be limited in a consistent way to a curricular core knowledge of the subject which serves not only as the foundation for a practicable **conceptional understanding** but also as a means of access to new **knowledge**, i.e. the foundation for necessary self-regulated learning later in life. In other words: only fundamental curricular considerations can create the conditions needed for convincing long-term effective education standards.

## 2.2    Competence models

This symposium too shows that there is still fairly widespread uncertainty concerning competence models. Although there are many programmatic competence models available, which were mainly developed pragmatically, based on experience, they are neither grounded in theory nor anchored in a clearly defined creative idea. Further, they have not been empirically tested (an exception is the work by Hammann [2004] in which competencies are shown for natural experimentation in science).

This author has presented a draft for the subject of economics in grammar schools and vocational training schools (Dubs 2004a). With the creative idea of economics in mind as 'Civic information in Business and Economics' (qualification of the learners to evaluate economic-political events), he has analysed economic texts and official statements in the media in which competencies are required to understand and evaluate them. Not surprisingly a competence model emerged which was very close to the cognitive taxonomy of Bloom *et al.* (1956).

The discussion about the concept of competence was influenced mainly by the competence definition of Weinert (2001), which comes from a cognitive competence that does not concentrate on abstract intellectual knowledge, but rather on domain-specific knowledge with its related abilities and holistic problem-solving ability. This concept also questions the simplifying classification of competences in subject, method, social and self-competence. Competences are thus seen to be acquired abilities, which develop as a result of a structured teaching-learning process and which, by ensuing learning, may be altered and augmented and become self-regulated. The final aim is to advance a process of cumulative competence-building. Therefore competences can be described as follows: they are the personally acquired and reliably available ability to solve domain-specific problems as holistically as possible in the various fields of learning and knowledge and, with limited generalisation, to deal with new demands.

If this concept of competence is to provide the basis for competence models, then the following specifications are necessary:

(1) It is essential that the competences are not randomly connected with the contents of the teaching plan. It is necessary to determine in which contexts, in which age groups and under which influences partial competences are necessary and built up accordingly. This will give students the ability, by cumulative learning, to employ advanced competences when problems arise. Only when it is possible to overcome the prevalent additive compilation of partial competences by cumulative learning will the development of applicable and enduring competences be guaranteed. Therefore the aggregation of competence dimensions (partial competences) in a competence model remains a fundamental requirement for competence-oriented teaching. This process of cumulative competence development has, however, not yet been systematically researched.

(2) The attainment of competences presupposes subject knowledge and well-formed subject-related competence, which are determined by the creativity of the curriculum. Further, well-formed subject-related competences are an unconditional premise for the development of multidisciplinary competences. Nevertheless the transfer effect of multidisciplinary competences must not be overestimated.

(3) However, neither the subject knowledge nor pedagogical and psychological knowledge by itself is sufficient for the development of competence models and education standards. Competences should be formulated in such a way that action potential (performance) is discernible, i.e. that the learners can demonstrate in specific tasks that they can make use of the required competences successfully in real situations (cf. Oser o.J). Therefore the reconstruction of learning processes within the subject system and the subject-specific logic of knowledge acquisition must not be neglected.

An appealing competence model is presented by Deutscher Verein zur Förderung des mathematischen und naturwissenschaftlichen Unterrichts, MNU (2006, see also Langlet, 2007) (figure 2).

Beginning with one competence area (subject knowledge, epistemological competence, evaluation competence), separate competences are dissected, dimensioned and placed in different levels, and exemplary tasks are allocated to these levels. The desired competence development is defined as follows: starting from the everyday

410

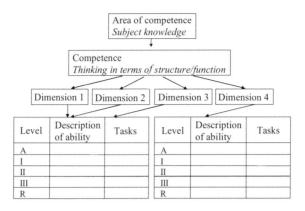

Figure 2:    Competence model for biology

preconceptions of the pupils (competence level A), the intended alterations in the direction of scientific concepts will be differentiated over several years and competence levels (level I to III). The final form (R) is a level of reflection and evaluation. Competence level II is regarded as the normal level, which must be reached in every school by the majority of students. Higher levels of competence are to be regarded as an option that can be attempted at different learning paces and with different learning methods. Competence descriptions beyond level II can serve therefore as an encouragement for further, differentiated learning options. Table 1 shows the competence model for Biology produced by MMU (2006, see also Langlet, 2007).

However, this example poses a list of questions, which need to be discussed with every competence model.

First of all, good teachers will ask what actually is new in this competence model. They will maintain that they have always promoted these competences. In specific cases this may be so. For many in the teaching profession, who may perhaps have succumbed to routine, the model may indicate ways to develop further the current and dominant additive teaching design towards cumulative and competence-oriented teaching by means of teaching procedures which are systematically focused on separate partial competences.

Secondly we have to discuss how these competences are formulated in education standards together with subject contents (recorded as basic concepts in the sense of structured knowledge). If we consider the implementation of this project, then the education standards are merely presented in the form of traditional operational learning goals. They are formulated in a relatively taut form and thus make the problem of adequate freedom of teaching relevant again. Particular attention is to be paid to the danger of 'teaching-to-the-test'.

411

| Level | Subject knowledge | Epistemological competence | Evaluation |
|---|---|---|---|
| **A Preconceptions**<br>• Description of biological (scientific) phenomena with everyday concepts | • Use of everyday concepts to describe biological phenomena | • Use of intuitive problem-solving strategies and forms of logic | • No knowledge, awareness or application |
| **I Nominal scientific literacy**<br>• Knowledge and definition of biological (scientific) terms and facts | • Reproduction of (basic) knowledge | • Reproduction of scientific problem-solving procedures and other skills | • Knowledge, awareness, unreflected application |
| **II Functional Scientific Literacy**<br>• Application of acquired knowledge | • Use of knowledge on unknown phenomena | • Application of scientific problem-solving procedures and other skills | • Simple (elementary) reasoning and application |
| **III Conceptual and procedural scientific literacy**<br>• Comprehension of basic biological and scientific terms and processes | • Comprehension of subject-specific basic concepts and appropriate use | • Comprehension of specific biological modes of understanding the world in comparison with other sciences | • More complex reasoning<br>• Comprehension of the application<br>  ➤ reasons for the reasoning<br>  ➤ expansion of the context |
| **R Multidimensional scientific literacy**<br>• Comprehension of multidisciplinary biological and scientific terms and processes (meta-reflection) in social and scientific contexts | • Comprehension of multidisciplinary basic concepts in a social and scientific context | • Theoretical comprehension of scientific models of understanding the world in comparison with other academic fields | • Comprehension of the meaning of a partial competence<br>• Meta-reflection |
| **Criteria** | **Increasing complexity of reasoning, reflection and comprehension** | | |

Table 1:    Competence model for biology

Thirdly we have to consider seriously how teachers are made familiar with the competence model and the education standards. The processing of the proposed model, from comprehension to transfer into the actual teaching, is both demanding and time-consuming. Once again there is the danger that specialists and particularly enthusiastic teachers will conceive models which, for teaching staff without further training and without the investment of a great deal of personal work, cannot be implemented – a phenomenon which has caused many pedagogical innovations to fail.

To summarise, the following points need to be considered: without convincing competence models, education standards cannot lead to effective innovations in teaching situations. These, and not comparative output checks or system-monitoring data, must be the primary aim of the new paradigm. Therefore rash political activities in which the education standards are introduced as quickly as possible, should be slowed down and priority placed for the time being on well-founded competence models. The many existing, but insufficiently verified, competence models show that a great deal of research work must be done.

## 2.3    Education Standards

### 2.3.1    On the concept of standards

In the meantime many different descriptions of education standards are available. One of the first attempts at clarification was undertaken by Ravitch (1995). By standards she understands the establishing of contents, benchmarks and resources by which the learning processes of the pupils are influenced. They have a double significance in that they are to be understood on the one hand as a target (what is to be done?) and on the other hand as a measure (how well has this to be done?). She differentiates specifically between three interconnected types of standards.

(1) **Content standards** (content or curriculum standards): These describe what teachers are to teach and pupils are to learn. They provide a clear, specific description of the abilities and knowledge that are to be taught.

(2) **Performance standards:** These serve to determine the level of achievement and answer the question, what is good enough? They describe which level of achievement is unsatisfactory, acceptable and particularly good.

(3) **Opportunity-to-learn standards** (expectations in the learning opportunities): These define the accessibility of learning programmes, teachers and further resources which are available to schools so that the content and performance standards may be reached.

It is essential for the formulation of the standards to be based on the idea of these three interconnected kinds of standards. So far, the aspect of opportunity-to-learn standards has scarcely been taken into account. The connection between the achievements to be attained by the students and the necessary resources are not being systematically addressed.

If we observe the newer developments in different European countries, we see that three other dimensions may be distinguished (Klieme et al., 2003):

(1) **Education aims** (normative understanding of education standards): At this level the social claim on the school, the educationally desired, is expressed. The education aims are the foundation for teaching, and it is their task in the formation of performance standards to steer the course and to introduce innovations.

**(2) Competences and tasks** (subject-specific standards): Here the competences are decided upon which the pupils must have in order to reach the important aims of the school. Education standards specify the general aims in the form of competence requirements.

**(3) Assessment by means of tests** (evaluative understanding of education standards). The assessment of the level of competence reached in schools, classes and of the individual learner is an indispensable part of the concept of education standards. Only test results can provide information about the attainment of the education aims and permit systematic and continuous quality development.

This division into three parts presents a definite advantage over the original US conception of 'achievement standards' which has concentrated for a long time on cognitive achievements. Reflected education aims which imply an extended understanding of achievement (cognitive, affective, psycho-motor and volitional) and integrate competences (abstaining from the questionable division into subject-related, social, methodological and self-competence) lead to multifaceted and not just to easy-to-assess standards.

From this an important conclusion is reached: if education standards are formulated without comprehensive curricular considerations, then the approach can scarcely provide a significant contribution to the renewal of schools. Therefore all attempts to implement education standards in the shortest possible time – as may be observed at present in Swiss grammar schools – remain questionable because existing forms are merely transferred into new forms of presentation. If, for example, we consider the teaching of science in many Swiss grammar schools, we can observe that more and more frequently, university-level subject matter is being introduced. There is no recognisable reflection of the creative idea of teaching behind this (phrased more traditionally: there are no systematic considerations about common education aims or education contents).

An exciting factor in the symposium discussion was the variety in the conceptions of education standards. Each country has its own conception, in which however, the influence of terms introduced by Ravitch and by Klieme et al. was repeatedly recognisable. As every country starts with different educational policies, theoretical assumptions and educational goals of education standards, there will never be **one** best system of standards. Therefore the system of one country can never be transferred unaltered to another country. It would however also be wrong if each country wanted to discover everything anew. Given the complexity of educational standards, system comparisons, as carried out in the symposium, are extremely valuable. It is nevertheless essential for every country to establish a secure theoretical basis for its own individual needs and for the responsible authorities to ensure good project management, so that education standards can be introduced in a viable and well ordered manner. Poor framework requirements (unrealistic time schemes, insufficient resources, lack of a convincing theoretical concept, unclear terminology, no implementation plan with practical examples) jeopardise the sustained implementation of education standards.

If we consider the findings from the symposium we can recognise the following areas in which significant differences of opinion remain, even among academic experts: the relationship between curricula and education standards, the formal presentation of the standards and the expected level to be reached.

## 2.3.2  The relationship of curricula and education standards

The relationship of syllabus, core curriculum and education standards is still largely unresolved. Based on an analysis, the following observations can be made for science education.

(1) The standards are divided up into large blocks with fundamental standards (general foundation skills), standards for social aspects (science and society), and subject-specific standards for subjects such as biology, chemistry, physics and environmental studies. The standards are written as conventional learning goals e.g. *Understanding University Success* (Association of American Universities, 2003). The fundamental standards are partly ability-oriented and partly ability- and content-oriented. The subject-specific standards are ability- and content-oriented. In this case, freedom for teachers is limited to methodology.

(2) Based on the content-area and with basic concepts for the description of biological processes, precise catalogues of learning-aims can be put together which are directed towards the competence model. (MNU, 2006; see also Langlet, 2007). As above, teaching freedom is limited to methodology.

(3) It is also conceivable to present the competences and basic concepts, separate from each other, in tabular form, so that the teachers retain their didactic and methodological freedom to decide with which content they choose to develop single partial competences and to build these into full competences. (As no science example is available to the author, reference is made to the subject of Economic Studies in Dubs, 2004a.)

If we consider these three possibilities, a dilemma in education standards becomes apparent. The construction of valid and comparable tests for precisely formulated standards is indispensable. This limits teaching freedom, leads to formulations that are not very different from existing learning objectives and can, once again, provoke 'teaching-to-the-test'. If less precise formulations are chosen, the construction of valid and comparable tests becomes more difficult. However, it does increase the freedom of teaching. For education standards to fulfill their function, even more research is called for, because the closer they come to existing learning objectives, the less they will prevail in the classroom. Unless there is compulsory testing of standards, teachers will not take them seriously and they will become as ineffective as the learning objectives movement of the past.

There is no agreement on whether a syllabus is necessary as well as standards. The argument is often presented that syllabuses continue to be necessary so that the constructive context of the contents of a subject or group of subjects is not lost. It is argued that a fundamental orientation, based on a syllabus, is important for the teachers, and that standards alone would not be sufficient. In its absolute form this statement is not correct. The more precisely the standards are formulated, the less necessary a syllabus becomes. Consequently, the question of the necessity of a syllabus can only be answered when the formulation of the education standards is decided.

It is agreed however, that the curricula, on which the standards are based, must be **core curricula**. They contain an obligatory texture of subjects for which the education standards are being developed, they present the structure of general education, and they initiate the modes of understanding the real world needed in life. And so school as an institution becomes 'the social form, in which cultures, increasingly similar throughout the world, define the contents and norms of life and at the same time it becomes the pedagogical form in which our culture can be explained and taught, thereby making its core of knowledge and orientation binding' (Klieme et al., 2003, 79). Core curricula do not describe all the possible learning contents, they narrow things down to the essential minimum of themes and content relevant to schools. They concentrate on basic structures (concepts) and serve as a key to learning, i.e. they produce conditions for self-regulated learning later in life. Apart from this aspect of content, the core curriculum poses the old learning-theoretical question regarding cognitive structures, as Bruner attempted to solve decades earlier (Bruner, 1966). What do such subject-specific structures look like, and how are they constructed?

Interestingly, the problems concerning the construction of the core curriculum still remain largely unheeded. The following method was attempted in the Swiss federal school system in the HarmoS project (see Labudde, 2007). Educationalists in specific subjects analysed all the curricula of the 25 cantons in order to ascertain the common factors. This was done on the assumption that the content common to all curricula would result in the core content, because if 25 groups of curriculum planners reflect on the subject content and arrive at contents which are in part the same, then these must provide the core content. This work has to a large extent been completed for mathematics and for the first language (EDK, 2004). Although the curricula in the individual cantons differ greatly in concept and structure, both subjects as far as the end of the 8th school year show great congruence in contents (75% - 80% of the content matched). This procedure can however lead to a fossilisation of the existing, which becomes all the more hazardous when it is a matter not only of fundamental competences but also of specific competences for demanding learning tasks. This is why, with particular regard to the changes in society, new core curricula should be developed and legitimised, so that in fact it is necessary to come back to the results of the **curriculum theory**.

Further in connection with the core curricula, there is the question of whether the education standards are to be minimal, regular or maximal. In this instance also, the symposium revealed greatly varying opinions. Here the view is advanced that a decision depends on various criteria (purpose of standards, pedagogical feasibility, teaching autonomy of schools). If, by means of the standards, the achievement level in schools is to be raised, then **maximal standards** are justifiable (*cf.* for example McLaughlin and Shepard, 1995 for the US). However then the question of feasibility arises: What happens to the weaker students? In addition there is the risk for the schools that they will lose their autonomy. **Regular standards** are intended to establish a level of average expectation. This definition can be found in the specifications for the science subjects set by the Federal Republic of Germany (Deutscher Verein zur Förderung des mathematischen und naturwissenschaftlichen Unterrichts, 2005). Here competence level II is equivalent to regular standards. The competence levels that reach beyond this can be regarded as options, which can be aimed for with different learning speeds and methods. With these definitions the same education status for all learners can be aimed for, with the chance for 'good' classes to advance. However, curricular autonomy remains limited. **Minimal standards** aim at minimum requirements that are to be attained by all pupils. Many teachers are opposed to this simple definition, arguing that such demands will lead to a further decline in achievement. This opinion will remain correct as long as the minimal standards are not defined in a wider context. Using the three aforementioned criteria the minimal standards are characterised as follows: The aim of the education standards must be to establish for a specific quota of the total available number of teaching hours (e.g. 70%) which goals are to be reached by as many pupils as possible. (An old US rule says that 80% of the learners must reach 80% of the standards). This minimum is to ensure, taking into account the mobility of the parents, that all learners will have the same foundation for schools of further education, and that a basis will be created for a comparable evaluation and for monitoring. The schools should be allowed to use the remaining teaching time (e.g. 30%) as they think fit, whether as an attempt to reach higher standards or to work on additional optional content. With this definition, individual schools will retain a partial autonomy in their own curriculum, thus accommodating the paradigm of the 'partially autonomous school'. This solution also makes pedagogical sense: compulsory requirements and free spaces guarantee that on the one hand minimal demands will be met, and on the other hand the teaching staff will not lose every form of teaching freedom and have the possibility to reach much more than the bare minimum with academically more capable pupils. With this description the objection regarding decline of achievement becomes invalid. It also has the advantage that it takes into account the wish of schools to have as much autonomy as possible (Dubs, 2005a).

### 2.3.3 Characteristics and formulation of education standards

The model in figure 3 for the structuring of education standards found general acclaim at the symposium (see Schecker and Parchmann, 2007).

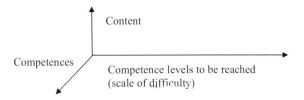

Figure 3:     Model for the structure of education standards

The characteristics of good education standards as explained by Klieme et al. (2003) were also seen to be broadly acceptable:

**(1) Subject specificity:** Education standards refer to one particular learning field. They present the core ideas of this field: fundamental structures, basic principles of the discipline, ways of thinking and procedures. The connection to subject knowledge must be maintained. Standards free of subject content which reflect 'key qualifications', such as methods for problem-solving, creative thinking, etc., remain largely transfer-ineffective. It is equally pointless to have separate subject-, social, methodological and self-competences. They must be integrated.

**(2) Focusing:** The standards concentrate on the essential aspects of a learning field (core fields) and do not attempt to be a complete description of the field.

**(3) Cumulativity:** They refer to competences which can be reached by a certain point in time: partial competences develop into competences, producing cumulative, systematic and cross-linked learning.

**(4) Obligation for everyone:** As minimum standards they provide a set of requirements which are expected from all learners, and in all schools.

**(5) Differentiation:** Education standards differentiate between competence levels which make learning development understandable and provide diagnosis possibilities for countries and schools (but not, however, for individual students).

**(6) Comprehensibility:** The standards are brief, comprehensible and clearly formulated, so that the expectations are unambiguous and tasks can be formulated consistent to the standards.

(7) **Practicability:** Education standards are in essence challenging, but they are realistic for everyday school and do not place excessive demands on teachers.

It is interesting to note that there is still no uncontested form of presentation of education standards. Wherever they have been introduced quickly, they are, as has already been suggested, largely similar to existing learning objectives. This fact even led a high ministerial official in Switzerland to state 'that there is no better form of presentation than operational learning objectives, and therefore something could repeat itself once more: euphoria – disillusionment – differentiated renewal'. Education standards will probably remain operational learning objectives in one form or another, which might not even be a problem under certain conditions: they must not fall back into behaviourism, but rather express structure and procedures of the learning fields, i.e. they are recognisably of a cognitive nature. They are oriented towards problem areas and strive cumulatively for a cross-linked view. They must be seen to be clearly connected to the core curriculum and its normative goals and to the competence model.

Unfortunately these conditions have not been fulfilled in many of the education standards that have already been implemented. And so it is necessary that research takes on the question of how to formulate consistent education standards. Otherwise criticisms could be seen as confirmed when asking in what way education standards are different from learning objectives in the daily life of a school.

*Exemplary tasks (test items)*

Whether education standards are significant can only be shown when they can be made concrete by means of tasks and tests which must be developed and given to the learners before the standards become compulsory. Only an analysis of the task solutions and test results can ascertain whether the desired competences have been covered and indeed whether it is possible to assess them, and ensure that they do show if progress has been made over time by the learners. In consequence, the successful introduction of competence models and education standards relies upon one first important phase of **verification**, using tasks. The standards will only be useful, if consistent tasks and tests can be produced from them. This verification presupposes that teachers are prepared for teaching to standards that can here be described as competence-oriented. In the symposium, this aspect was merely discussed on the side, although it makes little sense to work out standards and to record their significance by means of tests while allowing the teaching to continue in a traditional way. We will come back to this in section 2.5.

Only when there is proof that significant tests can be developed from the standards can the next assignment, **system monitoring**, be started. This will allow to control on the level of the education system of a country whether the learners have acquired the competences and can make use of them, together with their knowledge, so that the goals on which the standards are based, have indeed been reached. **System monitoring** should become the most important project in the implementation of education standards. The results can of course also be used for the **evaluation of individual schools**, but not for ranking them against each other (which in view of the ever-increasing differences in school input, such as social background of the learners, different resources, etc., has little significance). Such evaluation should rather serve the reflection on one's own teaching practice within the internal concept of quality management and school development in every single school. Education standards are totally unsuitable for **the diagnosis of individual students**. For this, education standards would be too comprehensive, inasmuch as they are not presented in the form of simplistic learning objectives. Diagnosis and fostering make it necessary to examine and control smaller learning areas in which partial competences are built up. Today successful procedures are available. The Swiss 'class cockpit' is worth mentioning here (Moser, 2003). It is a test system to ensure quality in the teaching and learning of the German language and in mathematics. The participating teachers find test items on a site (www.klassencockpit.ch) based on the curriculum, which they can download three times a year to give to their students. In addition to the results of their own class, teachers also get reference values, based on a representative sample of 600 students, which, in the sense of a self-evaluation, allow a survey both for their class and for individual learners.

There was hardly any dissent about the general relevance of tasks and tests at the symposium, but certainly so about particular questions. The problem of 'teaching-to-the-test' was an obvious one. The general statement, education standards might lead teachers to 'teach-to-the-test', is certainly too undifferentiated. It is certainly true that teachers and learners orient themselves both motivationally and cognitively by what and how will be tested (O'Neil et al., 2004). But tests are not just measuring achievement. Learning for a test is in itself a learning process which is the more influenced the more transparent and meaningful the test items are. Testing is only meaningless when it is done without clear direction towards the learning goals and without diagnostic evaluation.

It is also true that poor test programs increase social inequality and heighten the already existing discrimination of certain social groups (Orfield and Kornhaber, 2001). However, tests which reflect strictly the standards, should enhance test quality. With the definition of competence levels, they should also better take into account the background and circumstances of the school and the individual pupil, particularly for diagnostic purposes. It is also obvious that many tests only assess additively acquired factual knowledge and cognitive routines in rather meaningless ways. The systematic assessment of basic skills and routines that might promote 'teaching-to-the-test' need not always be without sense. More and more often pupils fail because such routines are not assessed anymore, and are therefore not learned anymore.

Finally, a common misunderstanding needs to be considered. Education standards do not cover all learning fields and they do not measure the attainment of all goals of education. Especially regarding minimal standards in a partially autonomous school, as indicated above, other subjects can be assessed by the teachers themselves with other evaluation procedures.

Thus 'teaching-to-the-test' is not necessarily a consequence of education standards, but depends on the quality of the tasks and on their distribution in items for reproduction and transfer. The latter is an aspect, which has not yet been emphasized sufficiently. Good test exercises should satisfy the following conditions (cf. Baker, 2004):

(1) Education standards must be clear and in accordance with the competence models so that valid tasks can be constructed.

(2) Tests are to be put together in such a way that they will be suitable for different pupil subgroups (framework of tasks, language, levels of competence).

(3) Tests must reflect teaching as it is experienced, i.e. the test items must be formulated in such a way that good teaching is evident in the results (awareness of the teaching given).

(4) Tasks must follow long-term considerations, e.g. the tasks have to be oriented in the direction of long-term cumulative learning.

(5) Good technical test quality must be guaranteed.

The difference between reproduction and transfer tasks must be considered with much more care than hitherto (*cf.* Metzger and Nüesch, 2004). In reproduction tasks, learners can show that they master what they have learned. In transfer tasks, it is a matter of transferring what has been learned to new situations. If the test items place too much emphasis on transfer, they will more and more measure general intelligence, which will lessen their value for monitoring and self-reflection. Therefore more attention must be paid to the division of tasks into reproduction and transfer when constructing tests.

During the symposium there was little discussion about the question of task and test construction. A great deal of effort is called for in order to find a work mode for task construction. This mode must make clear the way in which the tasks and tests are consistently derived from the educational goals through the core curriculum and the competences relating to the competence model and education standards. This should, however, not be a simple deduction, but rather an iterative process with reasonable (and not objective) decisions. For this the exercises must be inventive, because inventive exercises impede 'teaching-to-the-test' much more than the many routine tasks that are already available. This is why, particularly with regard to task conception, the cooperation between psychometricians, science educators and active teaching staff is important. It would be wrong to leave this field exclusively to the psychometricians.

## 2.5    The implementation of education standards

This symposium too showed something which is becoming more and more typical in the implementation of innovations in education: only successful implementations are reported, without a focus on the implementation procedure. However, we are very rarely shown how teachers are prepared for a new paradigm, for example, what form of in-service training is offered, which materials are supplied, how the problem of being overworked is coped with by the teachers, etc.

Therefore the following theory is put forward: If we cannot show quickly and in a practical way which changes will be brought about by education standards in the classroom itself, so that they produce better learning results, then education standards will not become established in school practice, and they will suffer the same fate as the operational learning goals in the 1970s.

It is argued here that the teachers should to be prepared for **competence-oriented teaching**, because competence-oriented education standards must lead to teaching that demonstrably develops and promotes the competences of the students. What such teaching might look like is a matter for discussion. We are attempting an approach which does not purport to be something completely new, but which will provide impulses for a deliberate change in teaching (figure 4).

The final aim of all teaching must be to impart to students those competences and that knowledge (to strive for education standards), which will enable them to enjoy lifelong, self-initiated and self-directed learning. Behind this objective, there is a structured basic knowledge (declarative knowledge) and also procedural knowledge, which comprises work techniques, learning strategies, thought strategies, social and communicative strategies and also meta-cognition. Together with motivation and the will to learn something, many partial competences can be built up, which when put together, will lead to the competences that are addressed by education standards. In order to develop and concentrate the partial competences, active learning with practical tasks and problems is necessary, which is problem- or action-oriented (the thought-provoking usage of learning objects suggested by Achtenhagen (1992). Teaching-learning arrangements are therefore the starting point for individual learning sections. This teaching-learning process demands a many-facetted attitude on the part of the teacher. At the beginning the students are to be guided firmly towards the building of partial competences and the concentration of these to form competences. As the learning proceeds, the teacher should act more indirectly (less guidance), and finally move to counselling (Dubs, 2005b).

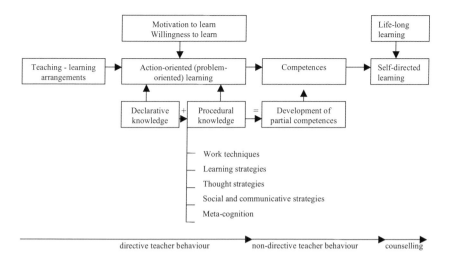

Figure 4:    Model for the structure of education standards

The implementation of this model proves to be difficult because teachers, particularly those who are not aware of their own thinking and learning processes (weakly developed meta-cognition), have difficulties in guiding the development of partial competences (acquisition of partial competences in connection with declarative knowledge). They declare repeatedly that they facilitate procedural knowledge in a dialogue with the learners and that they serve as a model for learning. But in reality they teach as before without paying attention to the procedural learning. If there is no success in breaking down this barrier, then the standard movement will quickly reach its limits.

# 3    Framework conditions

## 3.1    Implementation of education standards

Education standards present an essential innovation. As with every new improvement, therefore, the question of how to implement successfully is significant. In the symposium the question was discussed on whether education standards should be implemented by the authorities 'from the top down' or whether co-operative or co-determined procedures are more advantageous.

In the US, above all, an evolution can be traced in the field of curriculum development. It was originally believed that extensive intervention programmes with central strategies, implemented from the top down, would be effective in embedding the innovation. However, they were not really successful because the reactions to innovative measures from the different levels of politics, administration and schools varied greatly. In many cases the innovation was asking too much of local school authorities and schools and resources were diverted from their original purpose; the need for control was enormous, and so the intended goals could not be reached. It could also be shown, however, that centrally innovated projects need not necessarily fail, if the various levels in a school system with their particular characteristics, as also the local given factors, are taken into consideration (Peterson et al., 1986). In today's perception, reforms are only effective when the central prescriptions allow for changes to meet local conditions. The relation between micro and macro levels of management must be carefully tuned; and the foundation for what is new must be properly prepared, so that teachers are sufficiently motivated to have the interest and appreciation of the project aims. Great political visions at the centre are not enough. Further, teaching materials must be available that provide the basis for the work in school development. Networks of teaching staff, interested in the innovation, are of more significance than mere directives from above (for example, contributions in Odden, 1991). Networks are formed most readily when a practice-oriented introduction and in-service training for teachers are begun in good time. This training should, however, not take place sporadically, but rather regularly and it must, above all, lead to cooperation between colleagues. It must be consistent (agreement between the general ideas and the possibilities of the school) and sufficiently stable (the project must not be constantly diluted with new goals and conditions) (for example, Desimone, 2002). Even when these conditions have been fulfilled, a standard-based reform remains a protracted process, and O'Shea (2003) has shown that, even after intensive in-service training, many teachers had difficulty in planning lessons and in evaluating the learning results diagnostically.

Clearly, top-down processes alone are not enough for the successful introduction of education standards. Certainly the impulse must come from above. It must, however, be much more intensively linked with an 'interpretation process' (Spillane et al., 2002). A thorough introduction to education standards, that makes their significance comprehensible. The process must be well planned, sufficiently continuous and teacher-oriented. The school development processes in the schools must be used to prepare teachers for education standards well before they are implemented.

Above all in the German-speaking countries, education standards have in many cases been decreed as administrative acts. Many authorities, unaware of the complexity of the approach, believed that the generally accepted change of paradigm from input to output orientation would take effect immediately on introduction, and most importantly, believed that the weaknesses revealed by PISA could be quickly remedied. In reality this procedure led to a great deal of resistance (often resulting from a lack of knowledge). As in addition many important questions are still poorly clarified, there is a lack of consistency and continuity in many processes of implementation. This in turn leads to uncertainty and further opposition or indifference in many teachers. Therefore it is necessary to warn not to over-hastily declare the standards mandatory.

There are many unanswered research questions that must be answered first. At the same time the 'interpretation process' should be started and the in-service training be continued and only as a final step, the education standards be declared binding. Their introduction and implementation are extraordinarily time-consuming. The 'top-down process', seen in many countries, will fail, and the total attempt will become yet another historical reminiscence if the political and academic hyperactivity is not better controlled.

## 3.2 Application variations of education standards

The original idea of education standards was to obtain output-oriented data about the competences of children and adolescents of one whole country or several countries (as in TIMSS and PISA), in order to compare the students' performance between countries and/or schools, and/or to improve the quality of the schools by means of data-based monitoring systems. It soon became apparent that the effort to implement a broad testing scheme is very great, and so the original idea of extensive, nation-wide tests was increasingly abandoned and many application variations were devised (table 2).

---

1. **Tests based on education standards for education monitoring and for school comparison (obligatory)**
   1.1 The tests are carried out throughout the whole country (e.g. individual US member states, England)
   1.2 The tests are carried out using random samples of all the students of one country (e.g. Austria, Switzerland [planned])
   1.3 The tests are carried out on a local level (e.g. Sweden, France, some US member states)

2. **Tests carried out voluntarily using education standards**
   2.1 The tests are according to education standards and can be retrieved optionally (desired conception of teaching communities)

3. **Test banks without direct connection to education standards**
   3.1 Curriculum-oriented tests are available, which can be used optionally (e.g. Cockpit in Switzerland)

4. **Tasks from TIMSS and PISA are used**
   4.1 Continuation of the TIMMS and PISA activities for education monitoring and for school comparisons (e.g. Australia, Taiwan)

---

Table 2:    Application variations of education standards

The more a country attempts to improve its education system systematically and comprehensively, and turns away from its hitherto 'blind flight' approach, the more important compulsory education monitoring on the basis of commonly accepted standards becomes.

It is also indispensable when new curricula are introduced that their effectiveness must be monitored to demonstrate the value added in comparison with the old curriculum. Therefore it is to be expected that standard-based monitoring will accelerate the implementation process of a new curriculum. However, because of time, effort and expense , the procedure will only be feasible with random samples. Whether voluntary tests will be effective in the long run, remains to be seen. Although the starting success of Cockpit in its early stages is very good, it is uncertain whether fatigue as a result of an overload for the teachers will reduce the effect. Wherever quality management is firmly anchored in the schools (Dubs, 2004b), it is easily imaginable that the voluntary form can be sufficient.

### 3.3    The significance of education standards in the school system

In many places education standards are only dealt with selectively and with little regard to the total development of the school system. The following questions are still largely unanswered:

How binding are the education standards? This question has to be considered from the perspective of curriculum autonomy, as also the definition of the standards as regular or minimal standards (Section 2.3.2).

How do the tasks and competences of school administration change with education standards, and how does the coordination between internal and external quality management function? In order to avoid even more uncertainty, a comprehensive solution must be sought which will regulate the responsibilities and organisation. With reference to school autonomy and quality management problems are already arising in many countries between internal and external supervision, and these are becoming more acute with the introduction of education standards.

How will the feedback system be implemented? It is important to avoid data being collected and merely put into files. Quality improvement will only become apparent when systematic feedback leads to school development work in every school.

Should the results of the attainment of standards in individual schools influence the allocation of financial means? Should schools with good results be rewarded financially, as defenders of a competition-oriented school maintain, or should weaker schools receive additional financial support, as is demanded by those who are intent on equality? This question too has not been fully discussed. Should education standards only be introduced for native language, first foreign language, mathematics and science, or for all subjects? There is a great danger that through the restriction to a few specified subjects by education standards the questionable splitting into 'important' and 'less important' subjects will be intensified, and that the one-sidedness of many traditional educational concepts concerning the importance of subject matter will become again pronounced.

These questions are meant to indicate the holistic nature of the education standards and caution against seeing them in isolation. Stability and consistency in pedagogical measures demand a holistic approach. If this is not maintained, new problems and pressure will follow for individual schools and for teaching staff, and this will further impede readiness for reform.

# 4    Closing remarks

If education standards are indeed to contribute to improvement in the quality of teaching in schools, then they must be more than a mere slogan. Whether this claim can be maintained is still in the balance. Too many questions still need answering. The actual conditions needed to ensure lasting improvements have not yet materialised:

• What are the content structures of the core subjects?

• Will it be possible to create convincing competence models that do not simply cast well-known and well-worn material into a new form?

• How will education standards be formulated so that they are competence-oriented and unambiguous, without relapsing into the area of simple, restricting behavioural objectives?

• What is being done to guide the teachers so that they can recognise the significance and usefulness of education standards, and will be able to provide competence-oriented teaching that is substantially better than what good teachers have always provided?

And finally one can come back to the convincing and critical thoughts by Heid (2006, 20-21): 'Standards define or operationalise what is desired or prescribed as the result of organised learning. They leave open what this is dependent on – on which highly complex construction of conditions or causes. However, for a positive, standard-conform, as well as for a negative effect of individual learning, ('chance') factors (constellations) may be responsible, which may not be dependent on, or influenced by, competent, professional activities – both practical and political – in a controlled manner.' If one pursues this thought, then the character of education standards becomes an issue once more: Do they present a slogan which is to re-think the important, unsolved tasks, such as strengthening political support for children, adolescents and families, improving the reliability of political measures to strengthen teachers professionally and socially, and providing holism, a sustainability and consistency of the innovations in schools and in classrooms? Or will they be supported and implemented in such a way that, despite unfavourable factor constellations, they will become a true instrument for quality improvement in schools?

# References

Achtenhagen, F. (1992) Lernen, Denken, Handeln in komplexen ökonomischen Situationen. In F. Achtenhagen and E. G. John (Hrsg.), *Mehrdimensionale Lehr-Lern-Arrangements*. Wiesbaden: Gabler, 39-42.

Apple, M. (1992) Do the Standards Go Far Enough? Power, Policy, and Practice in Mathematics Education. *Journal of Research in Mathematic Education*, 23 (5), 412–431.

Association of American Universities (2003) *Understanding University Success*. Eugene: University of Oregon, Center for Educational Policy Research.

Baker, E. L. (2004) Reforming Education through Policy Metaphors. In Th. Fitzner (Hrsg.), *Bildungsstandards. Internationale Erfahrungen – Schulentwicklung – Bildungsreform*. Bad Boll: Evangelische Akademie, 150-163.

Bloom, B., Englehart, M., Furst, E., Hill, W. and Krathwohl, D. (1956) *Taxonomy of Educational Objectives. The Classification of Educational Gools. Handbook I: Cognitive Domain*. New York: Longman Green.

Bruner, J. S. (1966) *Toward a theory of instruction*. Cambridge: Harvard University Press.

Bybee, R. W. (1993) *Reforming Science Education: Social Perspective and Personal Reflections*. New York: Teachers College Press.

Bybee, R. W. (2002) Scientific Literacy – Mythos oder Realität? In W. Gräber, P. Nentwig, Th. Koballa and R. Evans (Hrsg.), *Scientific Literacy. Der Beitrag der Naturwissenschaften zur Allgemeinen Bildung*. Opladen: Leske + Budrich, 21-43.

Desimone, L. M. (2002) How Can Comprehensive School Reform Models be Successfully Implemented? *Review of Educational Research*, 72(3), 433-479.

Dubs, R. (2004a) Bildungsstandards – ein erfolgsversprechender Paradigmawechsel? Ein Umsetzungsversuch als Diskussionsgrundlage im Fach Volkswirtschaftslehre. In M. Wosnitza, A. Frey and R. S. Jäger (Hrsg.), *Lernprozess, Lernumgebung und Lerndiagnostik. Wissenschaftliche Beiträge zum Lernen im 21. Jahrhundert*. Landau: Verlag Empirische Pädagogik, 38-55.

Dubs, R. (2004b) *Qualitätsmanagement in Schulen*. Bönen: Kettler.

Dubs, R. (2005a) *Die Führung einer Schule. Leadership und Management*. Zürich: Verlag SKV.

Dubs, R. (2005b) Bildungsstandards: Das Problem der schulpraktischen Umsetzung. *SEMINAR Lehrerbildung und Schule*, 11(4), 15-33.

EDK (Schweizerische Konferenz der kantonalen Erziehungsdirektoren) (2004) *HarmoS: Lehrplanvergleich – Erstsprache*. Bern: EDK.

Gräber, W. and Bolte, C. (Eds.) (1997) *Scientific Literacy*. Kiel: Institut für die Pädagogik der Naturwissenschaften.

Gräber, W., Nentwig, P., Koballa, Th. and Evans, R. (Hrsg.) (2002) *Scientific Literacy. Der Beitrag der Naturwissenschaften zur Allgemeinen Bildung*. Opladen: Leske + Budrich.

Hammann, M. (2004) Kompetenzentwicklungsmodelle. Merkmale und ihre Bedeutung – dargestellt anhand von Kompetenzen beim Experimentieren. *Mathematisch-naturwissenschaftlicher Unterricht*, 57(4), 196-203.

Heid, H. (2006) Ist die Standardisierung wünschenswerten Lernoutputs geeignet, zur Qualitätsverbesserung des Bildungswesens beizutragen? *Gymnasium Helveticum*, 60(2), 19-22.

Klieme, E., Avenarius, H., Blum, W., Döbrich, P., Gruber, H., Prenzel, M., Reiss, K., Riquarts, K., Rost, J., Tenorth, H.-E. and Vollmer, H. J. (2003) *Zur Entwicklung nationaler Bildungsstandards. Eine Expertise*. Frankfurt a.M.: Deutsches Institut für internationale pädagogische Forschung.

Komisar, B. P. and McCellan, J. E. (1991) The Logic of Slogans. In B. O. Smith & R. M. Ennis (Eds.), *Language and Concepts in Education*. Chicago: Rand McNally 1968, 194-214.

Labudde, P. (2007) This book, Chapter 16.

Langlet, J. (2007) This book, Chapter 9.

McLaughlin, M. and Shepard, L. A. (1995) *Improving Education through Standard-Based Reform: A Report by the National Academy of Education Panel on Standards-Based Education Reform*. Stanford, CA: National Academy of Education.

Metzger, C. and Nüesch, C. (2004) *Fair prüfen. Ein Qualitätsleitfaden für Prüfende an Hochschulen*. St. Gallen: Institut für Wirtschaftspädagogik.

Moser, U. (2003) *Klassencockpit im Kanton Zürich. Ergebnisse einer Befragung von Lehrerinnen und Lehrern der 6. Klassen über ihre Erfahrungen im Rahmen der Erprobung von Klassencockpit im Schuljahr 2002/2003*. Zürich: Kompetenzzentrum für Bildungsevaluation und Leistungsmessung an der Universität Zürich.

O'Neil, H. F., Abedi, J., Lee, Ch., Miyoshi, J. and Mastergeorge, A. (2004) Monetary Incentives for Low-Stakes Tests. In Th. Fitzner (Hrsg.), *Bildungsstandards. Internationale Erfahrungen – Schulentwicklung – Bildungsreform*. Bad Boll: Evangelische Akademie.

O'Shea, M. R. (2003) *Implementing State Academic Standards in the Classroom. Paper presented at the Annual Meeting of the American Association of Colleges for Teacher Education*. New Orleans, LA, January, 24-27.

Odden, A. R. (Ed.) (1991) *Education Policy Implementation.* Albany, NY: The State of University of New York Press.

Orfield, G. and Kornhaber, M. L. (Eds.) (2001) *Raising Standards or Raising Barriers? Inequality and High-Stakes Testing in Public Education.* New York: The Century Foundation Press.

Oser, F. (o. J.) *Standards: Kompetenzen von Lehrpersonen.* Fribourg: Universität Fribourg, Pädagogisches Institut.

Peterson, P., Rabe, B. and Wong, K. (1986) *When Federalism Works.* Washington: Brookings Institution Press.

Ravitch, D. (1995) *National Standards in American Education.* Washington: Brookings Institution Press.

Schecker, H. and Parchmann, I. (2007) This book, Chapter 8.

Shavelson, R., Baxter, G. and Pine, J. (1992) Performance Assessment. Political Rhetoric and Measurement Reality. *Educational Researcher*, 21(4), 22-27.

Spillane, J. P., Reiser, B. J. and Reimer, T. (2002) Policy Implementation and Cognition: Reframing and Refocusing Implementation Research. *Review of Educational Research*, 72(3), 387-431.

Wagenschein, M. (1973) *Verstehen Lehren. Genetisch – Sokratisch – Exemplarisch* (4. Aufl.). Weinheim: Beltz.

Weinert, F. E. (2001) Concepts of Competence: A Conceptual Clarification. In D. S. Rychen and H. L. Salganik (Eds.), *Defining and Selecting Key Competencies.* Göttingen: Hofgrefe, 45–65.

# Biographies of the authors

## Tom Bryce

Tom Bryce is Professor of Education in the Faculty of Education at the University of Strathclyde. He holds degrees in Physics and Educational Psychology and taught Physics in secondary schools before moving into pre-service teacher education.

His research interests have centred on practical assessment, national monitoring (in both areas directing/co-directing national projects), conceptual difficulties in learning, and developmental trends. Recent publications in *the International Journal of Science Education* include articles on the teaching of controversial issues in science; misconceptions and the use of bridging analogies; and children's cosmologies.

He has interests in wider issues in education, particularly in secondary school learning and assessment, and is co-editor of the major, award-winning text *Scottish Education*. He is currently working on the third edition.

At Strathclyde he was Faculty Vice Dean for Research between 1997 and 2002.

## Mei-Hung Chiu

Mei-Hung Chiu is Professor of Science Education at the Graduate Institute of Science Education (GISE) at the National Taiwan Normal University (NTNU). She has a BS degree in chemistry from NTNU, and a Masters and PhD degrees from the Harvard Graduate School of Education. She has been a research associate and visiting scholar in the Learning Research and Development Center at the University of Pittsburgh, USA. Since 1991, she has been a member of the GISE, chairperson of the Institute, and national representative for the Committee of Chemical Education of IUPAC. She has also served as curriculum development and evaluation expert for science education at different age levels. Her research interests and publications are mainly in the areas of students' conceptions, mental models, and conceptual change in science learning.

Her recent work was to complete a 6-year project of national survey of students' conceptions in learning science sponsored by the National Science Council in Taiwan.

## Jens Dolin

Jens Dolin is associate professor and director of research at the Institute for Philosophy, Education and the Studies of Religion of the University of Southern Denmark. He has a MSc degree in geography and physics and a PhD in physics education.

He was an upper secondary teacher for many years, gradually moving into pre- and in-service teacher education and educational research. He has done research in teaching and learning science (with focus on dialogical processes, forms of representations and the development of competencies), general pedagogical problems (bildung, competencies, evaluation) and organizational change (reform processes, teacher conceptions). He is engaged in the development, implementation and evaluation of new science curricula and international comparative studies.


## Heleen Driessen

Heleen Driessen is a curriculum development expert for natural sciences in secondary education at the Netherlands Institute for Curriculum Development (SLO) and teaches science for public understanding and chemistry. She has a Masters degree in chemistry and teacher qualifications in chemistry, physics and science for public understanding from the University of Nijmegen together with other qualifications in psychiatry and special needs.

From 1990, she has been concerned with school curriculum development and research and national curriculum development and has published educational resources in chemistry, physics, science for public understanding and technical design and curriculum documents. Since 2002, she has been secretary of several national committees for curriculum renewal in chemistry and project director of *Nieuwe Scheikunde* (New Chemistry). Her major task is the integrated development and implementation trajectory of a new national curriculum for chemistry involving learning communities of teachers and science experts. Major interests are in the professional development of teachers and renewal of assessment.


## Rolf Dubs

Rolf Dubs was Professor of Economic Education at the University of St. Gallen. He was also President of this University, Director of the Institute for Economic Education and Director of the MBA-Programmes.

He has a doctoral degree in Business Administration from the University of St. Gallen and a Doctor Honoris causa from the Universities of Economics of Vienna and Budapest and from the Technical University of Dresden. He was a Member of Parliament and Brigadier General.

He worked at Harvard, Stanford, the University of Texas at Austin and Michigan State University. His research interests are in School Management, Curriculum Theory and Learning Theory. His publications include School Management, Teacher Behaviour and Curriculum Theory for Economics and Business Administration.


## Ana Freire

Ana Freire taught Physics and Chemistry in secondary schools before moving to the Department of Education of the Faculty of Sciences, Lisbon University. She obtained a PhD degree in Education with the specialization in Science Education and now she is a professor of Science Education and initial and in-service trainer of science teachers.

She is also a member of the Research Centre on Education at the Faculty of Sciences in the University of Lisbon.

She has been involved in research about teachers' conceptions and practices; teachers' professional knowledge and development; STS activities and has published and supervises master and doctoral projects in these areas.


## Cecília Galvão

Cecília Galvão is professor of pedagogy and science education at the Faculty of Sciences of Lisbon University (FCUL).

After graduating in Biology (1980), she was a secondary school Biology teacher for about ten years. During this period she worked on several curricular developments. Projects. In 1989 she started working as an assistant in the Department of Education at the FCUL and concluded a Master in Education degree with a thesis in the area of Methodology of Science Education (1991).

She completed her PhD degree in Education with a thesis on the *Beginning of a Science Teaching Career* (1998) and co-ordinated several projects in the areas of professional development of teachers and science education, some of them international.

At the invitation of the Ministry of Education, she co-ordinated the team responsible for the document of Specific Competences in Physical (Physics and Chemistry) and Natural (Biology and Geology) Sciences, which integrates the National Curriculum. She was the co-ordinator, as well, of the group responsible for the document with the *Curricular Guidelines for Physical and Natural Sciences for the 3rd cycle of Basic Education* (12 to 15 years old) that began to be implemented in Portugal in 2002/2003.

Her research interests are in teachers' professional development, health education and narratives in education, having published in these different fields.

Presently she belongs to the co-ordination team of the Centre of Research of Education of the Faculty of Sciences and is a mmber of the executive Committee of the Department of Education (FCUL).


## Rosemary Hafner

Rosemary Hafner is President of the New South Wales Science Teachers' Association (STANSW), a member of the Australian Science Teachers' Association (ASTA) Federal Council and former editor of ASTA's journal. As NSW Board of Studies Inspector, Science she undertook the development of the Years 7–10 Science syllabus and the syllabuses for Biology, Chemistry, Earth and Environmental Science, Physics and Senior Science for the post-compulsory years of schooling. She was co-writer of 23 books published by the Board of Studies to support the implementation of the K – Year 6 Science and Technology Syllabus and is currently the Co-ordinating Supervisor of Marking for the Higher School Certificate and Year 10 examinations. She has completed curriculum development projects for Abu Dhabi and Papua New Guinea and is currently researching the correlation between the intended and implemented curriculum.

## Peter Labudde

Peter Labudde is Professor at the PHBern (School of Teacher Education – University of Applied Sciences, Bern) where he runs the Department of Teacher Education for the upper secondary level. After his PhD in Physics and a Teacher Diploma for Upper Secondary Schools he worked for seven years as a teacher of physics, chemistry and maths. A post-doc year led him to the School of Education at the University of California, Berkeley.

From 1988, he has been engaged in teacher education. His habilitation (1998) dealt with constructivism in physics education. In addition to this topic he has researched on learning and teaching processes in science education, video studies in physics instruction, gender issues, integrated science and teacher education.

Since 2005 he has been the co-director of the consortium that is responsible for the development of standards in science education in Switzerland.

## Jürgen Langlet

Jürgen Langlet is Governmental Inspector of Lower Saxony Schools. After his States Examination (equivalent to MA) in Biology, Chemistry and Philosophy, he worked as a teacher in Bremervörde and at the German school of Genova, Italy. Following this, he worked at Lüneburg in pre-service teacher training for over 10 years and for the last 7 years, he has been a staff-member of MNU (German association for the promotion of mathematics and science teaching), responsible for Biology, and simultaneously vice-president for school biology in vdbiol (Association of German biologists).

He is also working at the University of Hamburg, with in-service courses for biology teachers in behavioural sciences, philosophy of science, bioethics, competences and standards in science education.

## Jari Lavonen

Jari Lavonen is Professor of Physics and Chemistry Education and Director of the Subject Teacher Education Section at the Department of Applied Sciences of Education, University of Helsinki. Previously he was a Senior Lecturer in Science Education (1992–2003) and Lecturer in Physics and Chemistry (1985–1992).

He is a President of the Finnish Association for Research on Teaching of Mathematics and Sciences and a director of the Finnish Graduate School for Research in Science and Mathematics education.

His main research interests are connected to science and technology teaching and learning, science teacher education and the use of ICT in science and technology education. He has participated in writing of several National Science Curricula since 1992.

## Judith Lederman

Judith Sweeney Lederman is the Director of Teacher Education in the Department of Mathematics and Science Education at Illinois Institute of Technology. Prior to her appointment at IIT, Dr. Lederman was a science teacher educator at Oregon State University and Providence College. Her experience with informal education includes her work as Curator of Education at the Museum of Natural History and Planetarium in Providence, RI. She presents and publishes nationally and internationally on the teaching and learning of science in both formal and informal settings and has co-authored an elementary science teaching methods text. She has served on the Board of Directors of the National Science Teachers Association and is currently President of the Council for Elementary Science International.

## Norman Lederman

Norman G. Lederman is Chair and Professor of Mathematics and Science Education at the Illinois Institute of Technology. He received his PhD degree in Science Education and possesses MS degrees in both Biology and Secondary Education. Prior to his 20 + years in science teacher education, he was a high school teacher of biology and chemistry for 10 years.

His research includes work on the development of students' and teachers' conceptions of the nature of science and scientific inquiry.

He is a former President of the National Association for Research in Science Teaching (NARST) and the Association for the Education of Teachers in Science (AETS). He has also served as Director of Teacher Education for the National Science Teachers Association (NSTA).

## Pierre Malléus

After graduating from the University of Paris, Pierre Malléus taught physics and chemistry in high schools. In 1976, he became a regional inspector in physics and chemistry for secondary schools in the Eastern region of France. He was awarded his PhD degree in electrical engineering from the *Institut National Polytechnique de Lorraine* (Nancy) in 1994.

From 1995, he has been general inspector at the French Ministry of National Education. He has been a member of the working group D of the European Commission on the Objective 1.4 'Increasing recruitment to scientific and technical studies" (2002–2004). He worked as a member of the steering committee of the OECD concerned with the "Declining interest in Science studies among young people' (2005). He is a member of the international expert group for PISA-OECD 2006.

**Rachel Mamlok-Naaman**

Rachel Mamlok-Naaman has PhD and MSc degrees in science education, and a BSc degree in chemistry.

Since 1989, she has been a member of the Chemistry Group in the Science Teaching Department of the Weizmann Institute of Science, Head of the National Centre for Chemistry Teachers at the Institute, and a senior member of the Chemistry Group and of the Science and Technology-for-All Group. She is engaged in the development, implementation and evaluation of new curricular materials and research on students' perceptions of chemistry concepts. Her publications are principally in the areas of scientific and technological literacy, teachers' professional development, assessment and curriculum development.

**Robin Millar**

Robin Millar is Salters Professor of Science Education at the University of York. He studied theoretical physics at university and then obtained a PhD in medical physics, before deciding to train as a teacher. After teaching for eight years in secondary schools in Edinburgh, he moved to York in 1982 as a lecturer in education.

His research and writings are mainly concerned with the development of students' understanding of science concepts, the role of practical work, the development of scientific reasoning, and the curriculum implications of an emphasis on scientific literacy. He has directed several large research projects, most recently as co-ordinator of the Evidence-based Practice in Science Education (EPSE) Research Network funded through the UK Economic and Social Research Council's Teaching and Learning Research Programme (TLRP). He was a member of the management and writing teams for Salters' GCSE Science and of the Advisory Committee for Salters Horners Advanced Physics. He played a central role in the development of the innovative AS-level syllabus Science for Public Understanding. He currently co-directs the Twenty First Century Science project, which has developed teaching materials to implement a new science curriculum model for 15 – 16 year olds in England, consisting of a core course for all students with an explicit scientific literacy emphasis, augmented by additional optional courses in pure and applied science for those students who may wish to study science at more advanced levels.

**Peter Nentwig**

Peter Nentwig has been a researcher at the Leibniz-Institute for Science Education (IPN) at the University of Kiel since 1976. He has a diploma in chemistry and taught for several years in various schools before joining the IPN. He has also been engaged in teacher education at the Educational Faculty of the University in Kiel. For several years he was active in in-service education for teachers, both giving courses and doing research in that field. Additionally he was involved in national as well as international associations of teacher educators. More recently his work has been concerned with issues of Scientific Literacy, which has led to several international symposia. He is currently involved in the PISA study and in the development and evaluation of the chemistry curriculum, *Chemie im Kontext.*


### Teresa Oliveira

Teresa Oliveira graduated from the University of Lisbon in Biology and obtained a Masters degree in Education from Boston University and a PhD degree in Education – from the Faculty of Science and Technology, University of Lisbon.

She is, at present, Professor at the Faculty of Science and Technology, University of Lisbon, and a member of the Research Centre in Education at the Faculty. Her main interests are in-service and continuous teacher education. She is a Coordinator of several national and European research projects and of several European projects. Her publications are related to Education, Multiculturalism and Vocational Studies.

She is a member of the editorial committee of European Journal of Vocational Training.


### Ilka Parchmann

Ilka Parchmann is a Professor of Education in Chemistry at the University of Oldenburg. After her PhD, she spent three months with the University of York Science Education Group, before she started her teacher training for chemistry and biology for secondary schools. From 1999 until 2004, she worked at the Leibniz Institute for Science Education (IPN) in Kiel. Her main research areas are the development and evaluation of context-based teaching and learning and the implementation of new approaches, supported by inservice-training courses. She is one of the project leaders of the Chemie im Kontext programme.


### Pedro Reis

Pedro Reis taught biology in secondary schools before moving to the Superior School of Education at Santarém, where he is currently Head of the Sciences and Mathematics Department and Professor of Science Education and is concerned with both initial and in-service training of science teachers. He is also a member of the Research Centre on Education at the Faculty of Sciences in Lisbon University. He has published and been involved in research about: teachers' conceptions and practices; teachers' professional knowledge and development; students' conceptions on the nature, teaching and learning of science; the discussion of socioscientific issues in science education; and the use of ICT in science education.

## André A. Rupp

André Rupp is currently a visiting Professor at the associate level at the Institute for Educational Progress (Institut zur Qualitätsentwicklung im Bildungswesen, IQB) at the Humboldt University in Berlin, Germany. After three years of teacher education training in Germany he moved to the US where he received an MA degree in Applied Linguistics in 1999 and an M.S. degree in Statistics in 2001, which inspired him to continue his education with a PhD degree in Measurement, Evaluation and Research Methodology which he received in 2001 from the University of British Columbia. After two years as an Assistant Professor at the University of Ottawa, he returned to Germany in 2005 to work at the IQB where he pursues his psychometric, methodological, and language-related research interests. He is specifically interested in theoretical foundations and practical applications of multiple classification models for cognitive diagnosis, both for the calibration of standards-based assessments and for the development of innovative formative assessment systems in schools.


## Sascha Schanze

Sascha Schanze is Professor of Chemistry Education at the Institute for Science Education at the University of Hannover. After his state examination in Chemistry and Mathematics for secondary schools, he was awarded a PhD in chemistry education at the IPN in Kiel in 2001. From 2001 until 2003 he was performing the evaluation in the project med:u - eLearning in medical education. His emphasis in this project was on ensuring quality of the implemented system. As a member of the EU-projects Co-Lab and ReCoIL that are bringing computer-based inquiry learning into classroom and of the Scientific Network NetCoIL, his main focus was on collaborating using computer-based learning environments.

Since February 2006 he is head of the Department of Chemistry Education in Hannover. His major research interest continues to be concerned with inquiry learning and using and integrating new media in chemistry teaching. In the debate of implementing science standards into practice in Germany, he is emphasising the epistemological competencies.


## Horst Schecker

Horst P. Schecker has been Professor of Physics Education at the University of Bremen since 2002. After graduating as a high school teacher, he wrote his doctoral thesis on students' alternative frameworks in Newtonian mechanics. His habilitation (1995) was based on research and development on System Dynamics approaches in physics teaching. From 2001 to 2003, he led an R&D project of five German universities on multimedia in university physics courses.

Since 2005 he has been President of the German Gesellschaft für Didaktik der Chemie und Physik (GDCP).

Current projects focus on modelling students' competence structures and on implementing new ways of working with problems in physics classes.

**Helge Strömdahl**

Helge Strömdahl is Professor in Science Education at Linköping University and Director of the Swedish National Graduate School in Science and Technology Education Research. He has a Masters degree in chemistry and mathematics and a PhD in education, especially chemistry education. He taught chemistry and mathematics in upper secondary school before moving into the Swedish national educational administration as Director at the National Agency for Education working with curriculum development. For some years he worked in teacher education and staff development at The Royal Institute of Technology in Stockholm.

He has published research articles on the teaching and learning of physical quantities especially 'amount of substance' and conceptual change. His present research interest focuses on the development of a semantic/semiotic model of attaining scientific terms in coherent structures.


**Miriam Vock**

Miriam Vock is a research scientist at the Institute for Educational Progress (Institut zur Qualitätsentwicklung im Bildungswesen, IQB) at the Humboldt University in Berlin. She received her Masters degree in Psychology from the University of Münster, Germany, in 2000, where she worked in several scientific projects concerning the development of intelligence tests, program evaluation and research on giftedness and talent. In 2004, she obtained her PhD degree in Psychology from the University of Münster. In her dissertation, she developed IRT-based working memory scales for the assessment of cognitive abilities in gifted children. At the IQB, her research interests focus on the development and validation of standards-based tasks, the psychological and motivational factors which influence the academic development of students, and specific developmental trajectories of gifted students.


**David Waddington**

David Waddington was Professor and Head of the Department of Chemistry at the University of York. He founded and was the first Director of the University of York Science Education Group (UYSEG) and the Chemical Industry Education Centre. During this period, UYSEG, with the help of educators and teachers across the UK, established the suite of Salters courses.

He was Chairman of the teaching commissions of both the International Unions of Pure and Applied Chemistry and the International Council of Scientific Unions.

He has been awarded the Royal Society of Chemistry's Nyholm Medal, the first Brasted Award of the American Chemical Society for his international work and is holder of the Grand Cross of the Order of Scientific Merit in Brazil.

He has written and edited 20 books in chemical education and about 70 papers on his Chemistry research. At present, he holds an Emeritus Chair at York an Honorary Professorship at the Mendeleev University, Moscow and is currently a visitor at IPN.

**Hubert Weiglhofer**

Hubert Weiglhofer is an Associate Professor at the Department of Science Education and Teacher Training, University of Salzburg.

After graduating from the University of Graz in Biology he moved to Salzburg, where he first worked as a biology, chemistry and physics teacher at a vocational school and then as an Assistant Professor at the Department of Science Education, where he completed his doctoral thesis on drug prevention in 1985 and his habilitation on health education in 2001.

His present research interests focus on health education, teacher training, and assessment and curriculum development.